SOLA SCRIPTURA
TOPICAL BIBLE™

TM

SEVEN SYMBOLS
OF HEALING

SOLA SCRIPTURA
TOPICAL BIBLE™

TM

SEVEN SYMBOLS
OF HEALING

Featuring the text of the **New American Standard Bible (NASB)**

Compiled by:

Daniel John

Smart Publishing Ltd.

solascriptura.ca

Sola Scriptura Topical Bible:
Seven Symbols of Healing

Paperback Edition
ISBN 978-1-77885-033-2
Copyright © 2009, 2017, 2022
Smart Publishing Ltd.
Surrey, British Columbia   Canada
solascriptura.ca

Compiled by: Daniel John

Cover by: Daniel John

*   *   *   *   *

Other editions of this publication,

Sola Scriptura Topical Bible: *Seven Symbols of Healing*

Kindle: ISBN 978-1-77885-035-6   ePub: ISBN 978-1-77885-031-8
PDF: ISBN 978-1-77885-032-5   Hard Cover: ISBN 978-1-77885-034-9

Sola Scriptura Topical Bible: *Seven Symbols of Jesus*

Kindle: ISBN 978-1-77885-021-9   ePub: ISBN 978-1-77885-022-6
PDF: ISBN 978-1-77885-023-3
Paperback: ISBN 978-1-988271-19-6   Hard Cover: ISBN 978-1-77885-020-2

Editions of: **Sola Scriptura Topical Bible**: *Top 20 Spiritual Symbols*

Kindle: ISBN 978-1-988271-14-9   ePub: ISBN 978-1-988271-13-2
PDF: ISBN 978-1-988271-12-5
Paperback: ISBN 978-1-988271-86-6   Hard Cover: ISBN 978-1-988271-87-3

are available at: solascriptura.ca

TABLE OF CONTENTS

*The fear of the Lord is the beginning of **wisdom**,*

*and the **knowledge** of the Holy One*

*is **understanding**.*   *Proverb 9:10*

All Scripture is given by inspiration of God,

and is profitable for doctrine, for reproof, for correction,

for instruction in righteousness;

that the man of God may be complete,

thoroughly equipped for every good work.

2 Timothy 3:16-17

Dedicated To All Who Love The Word of God.

FOREWORD

Welcome, to a powerful, new way to understand the spiritual message and meaning of *The Holy Bible*.

As God has used the words of the Old and New Testaments to teach a message of wisdom and salvation to humanity, the **Sola Scriptura Topical Bible** is an expanded Concordance that lists all of the verses that mention some of the most important spiritual symbols and topical themes that are used in *The Bible* to tell that story.

To show the full context of how a spiritual keyword is being used, and to better understand its meaning within a verse of Scripture, additional verses have been provided before and after the verse that contains the **keyword**, which is highlighted in **bold** font.

As reading all of the verses that relate to a spiritual topic is the only way to know everything that *The Bible* itself says about it, reading all of the related verses in order provides a unique understanding of how the meaning of the topical symbol changes, and sometimes becomes even more spiritual, as the story progresses from the books of the Old Testament to its conclusion in the New Testament.

This book in the **Sola Scriptura Topical Bible** series contains the Biblical verses of seven important related spiritual topics, which were chosen as being among the most valuable for gaining a basic knowledge and understanding about Jesus Christ.

This work was created so that every person can more easily read the important words of *The Bible* for themselves, and be able to more fully contemplate the meaning of the spiritual message of God's Holy Word.

As **Sola Scriptura** means *"the Scriptures alone"*, because *"each person must be fully convinced in his own mind"* (*Romans 14:5*), a verse by verse Commentary on the meaning of the spiritual themes and topical keywords of the Chapters of this book is not included in this text, and is left for a future work. Until then, other resources can be consulted for additional information and meanings, such as a *Bible Dictionary*, *Bible Commentary*, or a *Concordance*.

INTRODUCTION

Since our beginning, humanity has searched for the meaning of this physical, earthly life. Many people believe that God has created mankind on the earth to know Him, and to worship Him. God is Spirit (*John 4:24*), and as an educator of humanity, He has communicated a spiritual message to us, using the physical things of this world as symbols, that our human minds can understand. Many people also believe that God's guidance to us, can be found within the Scriptures of the Holy *Bible*.

"You search the Scriptures, for in them you think you have eternal life…"

~ *Jesus Christ (John 5:39)*

Understanding *The Bible* (Latin: *biblios* - meaning "little books") can be challenging because *The Bible* is actually two different covenants, in two sets of books, that have been bound together as a single volume, for almost two millennia.

The Latin word *testament* means *covenant*, and these two covenants are known as the Hebrew **Tanakh**, or the **Old Testament**, and the **New Testament**, or the Christian covenant. In most modern translations of *The Bible*, there are 39 little books in the Old Testament, and 27 books in the New, for a total of 66 books in a standard Protestant *Bible*.

Together, the 66 *little books* of *The Bible* were written by some forty men, over a period of more than 1,600 years, in three different languages (Hebrew, Aramaic & Greek). So what do the one thousand plus pages of *The Bible* say? How can the meaning of its message be understood?

One way to understand something about the message that is contained within the words of *The Bible* is to study the topics and themes that it uses. To see what *The Bible* says about something, it is necessary to read all of the Scriptures that mention the topic. For this purpose, a Concordance is useful to show the location (Chapter & Verse) of all of the occurrences of a topical theme word, such as *angel* or *gospel*.

However, a Concordance only lists the chapter and verse of where the topic word is found, and the reader must then flip through *The Bible* to find and read the exact verse that contains the topical keyword. In order to understand the context of how the topical keyword is used in the verse, and therefore what it might mean, it is usually necessary to also read the verses that appear immediately before and after the verse that contains the keyword itself; and this process can be time-consuming and confusing to find the beginning and end of the meaningful context.

So that one can quickly and easily read for themselves all of the related words of God on a given topic, this book attempts to display all of the verses mentioning various important spiritual themes in full their context, so that reading a topical Chapter would show everything that *The Bible* itself says about the subject. *The Bible* does not say anything more or less about a topic or theme than everything that it says about it;

from both the Old and the New Testaments.

To quickly see all of the verses that relate to a given topic, this book presents the power of a contextually expanded Concordance, in the easy-to-read format of a novel. The verses provided in each topical Chapter are comprehensive, and include every relevant reference from both the Old and the New Testaments. Reading all of the Scriptures that relate to a topic in sequence allows the mind to be able to quickly see all of the related information, and to arrive at a point of personal truth and understanding, about the underlying spiritual message that is contained within of the word of God.

> *"...line upon line, line upon line, here a little, there a little."*
>
> ~ *Isaiah 28:10 & 13*

As each topical theme becomes understood, it can be seen how their spiritual symbols are interwoven to provide a storyline, which is the meaning, purpose, and message of *The Bible*. In many of these topical Chapters, the meaning of a symbol can be seen to become less physical, and more spiritual, or even purely symbolic, as the storyline progresses from the Old Testament, to its fulfillment in the New Testament.

Reading the Old Testament is necessary to understand how the symbols of the topical themes are later presented and used by Jesus Christ, and the writers of the New Testament.

While not all of the Scriptures provided within each Chapter of this book may be necessary to understand the meaning of a topical theme, they are all included, so that the references for each topic is complete. As a study tool, the reader can mark or highlight for future reference, those passages that are of most importance and interest.

As for the title of this work, *Sola Scriptura* is a Latin term that means "the Scriptures alone" or, "only the Scriptures". *Sola Scriptura* was one of the *solae*, or *solas*, which were among the primary foundational doctrines of the reformers of the medieval Catholic Church, and were popularized by the German priest, Martin Luther, in the early 16th century.

The other important *solas* of the Reformation are *Sola Fide* - Faith alone (that salvation is through faith in Jesus Christ alone), and *Sola Gratia* - Grace alone (that salvation is by the grace of God alone). The later additions of *Solus Christus* - Christ alone (Jesus Christ alone is our Lord, Savior, and King) and *Soli Deo Gloria* - to the Glory of God alone (that we live for the glory of God alone), brought the number of fundamental *Solas* to five.

Sola Scriptura means that the Scripture of *The Bible* alone is the highest and final authority on all matters that deal with salvation. For the reformers, this meant that each person should read the words of God for themselves, and in their own language (and not in Latin, by either necessity or force) to see what *The Bible* itself says, and to be inspired by God for the meaning of those words, and not unduly influenced or completely controlled by the theological doctrines and traditions of men, or of any particular church, denomination or group.

As *Sola Scriptura* means by *the Scriptures alone,* the Scriptures included within the Chapters of this book are presented without comment, and in the same order as they appear within a standard *Bible*.

As this work is intended as a reference, and contains only the verses and words of the Scriptures, other resources should be consulted to gain a deeper understanding of what each topical symbol means. This search should begin with an examination of the origins of the keyword in the original language(s), through the use of an original language *Lexicon*, *Interlinear* and *Dictionary*, although some basic meanings and definitions have been provided for the topical keywords.

Other resources that help to give a fuller knowledge and understanding of the symbolic keywords of the spiritual symbols include a topical *Bible Concordance* (as *Strong's* or *Young's*), a *Bible Commentary,* and an *Encyclopedia*.

As for the meaning of the spiritual message of *The Bible*, the more that the topical Chapters of this book are read, the greater your understanding of the Word of God will grow to be.

May the Holy Spirit of God guide us to understand His Holy Word.

Daniel John

2009

NOTES ON READING THIS BOOK

This book contains seven topical Chapters, each of which focuses on a different important spiritual topic or theme.

All quoted verses are from the **New American Standard Bible (NASB)** version of the Scriptures. For more information, visit the Lockman Foundation at *lockman.org*.

This section of notes provides the methodology that was used to define the topical theme of each Chapter, and provides information on how the selection of included verses was made.

In these notes the following terms are used:

Keyword	A word that identifies a topical theme. *(see page ix)*
Keyword Phrase	A **keyword** that consists of two or more words.

Verse	A verse from *The Bible*; a line of Scripture.
Concordant Text	A verse, or series of consecutive verses, from a book of *The Bible*, that usually includes a topical **keyword** or **keyword phrase**. "Concordant" is used in the sense that all of the provided texts are discussing the same topical symbol or spiritual theme.
	Most **Concordant Texts** include additional lines of Scripture, before and/or after the verse that includes a **keyword**. These additional verses help to provide sufficient context to understand the use and meaning of the topical keyword within the Scriptures.

For more information about the features of this book,
please see the following sections of Notes:

1. READING THE CONCORDANT TEXTS

A *Concordant Text* is a verse, or a series of consecutive verses, from a book of *The Holy Bible*, that usually contains a topical **keyword** or **keyword phrase**. The Concordant Texts provided in each Chapter of this book are all related to the same spiritual topic or theme.

Where possible, every scriptural occurrence of a topical keyword has been included within the Concordant Texts of each Chapter. Also included are any other keywords that have the same meaning, along with any related keywords, which may include derivatives of a keyword's English root, such as nouns, verbs, adjectives, and adverbs, etc. For example, the Chapter titled **Believe** includes the tertiary keywords *believes*, *believing*, and *believed*. For more information on the types of keywords (main, secondary, tertiary) see page *ix*.

In a few topical Chapters, some scriptural occurrences of a listed keyword were not included within the provided set of Concordant Texts. For more information on the two types of "Inclusion Exceptions" see page *xi*.

In a few Chapters, verses from *The Bible* were included as a Concordant Text even though they do not contain one of the Chapter's listed keywords. While not always directly mentioning a topical keyword, any additional included verses contribute to understanding the spiritual theme of the Chapter.

The seven spiritual topics are presented as Chapters in alphabetical order, and the verses that they contain are presented in the order in which they appear in a standard or NASB edition of *The Bible*.

1. The Concordant Texts of each topical Chapter appear in the same order as most *Bibles*, beginning with the *Book of Genesis* in the Old Testament, and ending with the *Book of Revelation* in the New Testament.

2. *The Bible* chapter and verse reference for each set of Concordant Texts is listed at the end of the set of included verses. Use this reference to locate the full story in a standard *Bible*.

3. For easy identification, the keywords that appear within the Concordant Texts of each topical Chapter are highlighted in **bold** font.

4. The length of the included Scriptures in each set of Concordant Texts has been edited to provide sufficient context to understand the use and the meaning of the topical keyword or keyword phrase. For additional context, use the Scripture reference at the end of each set of concordant verses to find the original verse(s) in a standard *Bible*.

5. Quotation marks are used to attribute words to a specific speaker only if a speaker is identified within the provided set of Concordant Texts.

6. "Selah" and other Hebrew liturgical terms and musical expressions (as found in the books of *Psalms* and *Habakkuk)* have been omitted.

SYMBOLS USED within The CONCORDANT TEXTS:

~   Indicates that the end of a long *Bible* verse has been omitted because it does not contribute to the spiritual understanding of the symbolic theme of the topical Chapter. The omitted portion of a verse is cut off after either a comma, a colon, a semi-colon, a dash, or a period.

He ordered them to be **baptized** in the name of Jesus Christ. ~   *Acts 10:48~*

...   Indicates that the middle part of a long series of verses has been omitted from the provided Concordant Texts because the verses do not directly contribute to the spiritual understanding of the topical theme of the Chapter.

      The missing verses are indicated by ...   ... within the Concordant Texts, and by ... within the scriptural reference which is located at the end of the Concordant Set. Use this reference to locate the omitted verses in a *Bible*.

They cast lots, and the lot fell on Jonah. ...

... So they picked up Jonah and threw him into the sea, and the sea ceased from its raging.   *Jonah 1:7...15*

<list>   Indicates that the middle of a series of verses that form a long list has been omitted from the provided Concordant Texts.

      The missing verses are indicated by ..<list>.. and the miss-

>   ing part of the list is indicated by > within the scriptural reference for the Concordant Set. Use this reference to locate the omitted verses in a standard *Bible*.

The book of the genealogy of Jesus **Christ**, the son of David, the son of Abraham: Abraham begot Isaac, Isaac begot Jacob, and Jacob begot Judah and his brothers.

     Judah begot Perez and Zerah by Tamar, Perez begot Hezron, and Hezron begot Ram.   *..<list>..*   Eliud begot Eleazar, Eleazar begot Matthan, and Matthan begot Jacob.   *Matthew 1:1-3 > 15-16*

[ ]   Square brackets indicate that the verse(s) does not appear in all translations of *The Bible*, but is included in the NASB edition.

As they went along the road they came to some water; and the eunuch said, "Look! Water! What prevents me from being **baptized**?" [And Philip said, "If you believe with all your heart, you may." And he answered and said, "I believe that Jesus Christ is the Son of God."]   *Acts 8:36-38*

2. CHAPTER HEADER

Each Chapter in this book begins with a header that details some basic information about the topical theme of the Chapter.

The header of each Chapter has three parts:

Title Block

TITHE
/ TITHES / TITHING + TENTH*

Definitions

Definitions

Tithe
1. The tenth part of goods or income, usually a voluntary contribution, paid as a tax for the support of the temple or church etc.
2. To give or pay a tithe of goods or money.
3. To give tithes to, or to pay tithes on, as income.
4. To levy or impose a tithe on, as money.
5. Any tax, levy or tribute, especially of one-tenth.
6. To exact or collect a tithe.
7. A tenth part (or small part) of something.

1. **Title Block**

   The Title Block identifies the spiritual or topical theme of the Chapter. It lists all of the keywords and keyword phrases that have been included within the provided Concordant Texts of the Chapter. For more information on the Chapter Title Block, and the different types of keywords, see the following page.

2. **Definitions**

   The definition section provides basic word definitions and meanings for some of the spiritual and symbolic keywords that are included within the topical Chapter. Generally, only those definitions of a keyword that are relevant and applicable to the topical theme of the Chapter have been included. While several definitions are provided, even including some modern or secular meanings, additional meanings and definitions can be found in a standard dictionary, *Bible Dictionary*, *Concordance* (as *Strong's* or *Young's* etc.) or *Bible Commentary*.

3. TITLE BLOCK

The first part of each **Chapter Header** features a **Title Block** that identifies the topical **keywords** and **keyword phrases** that have been included within the Concordant Texts of the current Chapter, along with any omissions (see *Inclusion Exception* on the following page) and/or any *Keyword Phrase Variations (see page xi)*.

KEYWORD TYPES:

1. **Main Keyword**   (*Chapter Title*)

   This **keyword** or **keyword phrase** is the title of the Chapter, and it defines the starting point for the list of topically related keywords.

2. **Secondary Keyword**   *Symbol:* **+**

   This keyword or keyword phrase is closely related or similar in meaning to the **main keyword**, but it does not share its root in English.

3. **Tertiary Keyword**   *Symbol:* **/**

   A **tertiary keyword** shares the same English root as the keyword that proceeds it in the list of keywords in the Title Block. **Tertiary keywords** are other forms of the **main** or **secondary** keyword that proceeds it in the list, and can include nouns, verbs, adjectives, adverbs, etc.

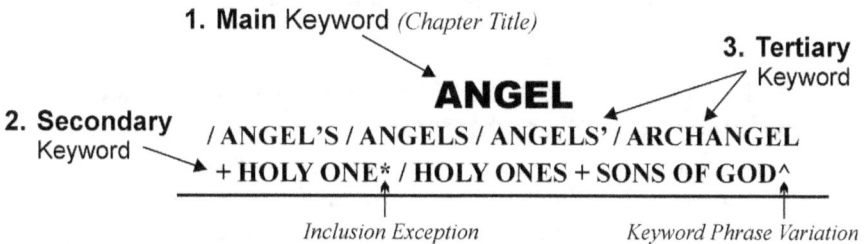

---

1. Main Keyword *(Chapter Title)*

3. Tertiary Keyword

ANGEL

2. Secondary Keyword

/ ANGEL'S / ANGELS / ANGELS' / ARCHANGEL
+ HOLY ONE* / HOLY ONES + SONS OF GOD^

Inclusion Exception   *Keyword Phrase Variation*

Inclusion Exception   *Symbol:* *****

Indicates that not all occurrences of the keyword or keyword phrase have been included. See section *3 A.* on the following page.

Keyword Phrase Variation   *Symbol:* **^**

The words that make up a keyword phrase may appear in a variety of arrangements, and/or may include additional words. See section *3 B.*

3 A. INCLUSION EXCEPTION   Symbol: *

An **inclusion exception** is a term that identifies a topical keyword or keyword phrase in the Title Block for which every scriptural occurrence has not been included within the Concordant Texts of the current Chapter. If the keyword or keyword phrase does not have an asterisk * to the right of it, then all of the related Scriptures containing the keyword, as found within the NASB version of the Old and New Testaments of *The Bible*, have been included in the Concordant Texts of the Chapter.

In some Chapters an explanation for the inclusion exception may be noted as the last line of the Title Block (and sometimes specified by a reference number [1.] to the right of the keyword).

There are two types of inclusion exceptions:

1. The keyword has two (or more) different meanings

Some topical keywords and keyword phrases have more than one distinct meaning. In such cases, only those occurrences of the keyword as found in the Scriptures that are topically related to the symbolic theme of the current Chapter have been included within the Concordant Texts of the Chapter. An example is in the Chapter titled **Fasting** (not included in this book) which includes the keyword "fast". The word "fast" can refer to quickness and speed, or to hold something firmly (*to hold fast*), as well as the abstinence from eating food, as in *to fast* or *fasting*. For the purposes of this book, only those Scriptural occurrences of the word "fast", as in fasting - to abstain from food - have been included in the Concordant Texts of the Chapter titled **Fasting** (which includes **Fast***).

2. The keyword has both a physical meaning and also a spiritually symbolic connotation

Some keywords have both a literal, physical, earthly or secular meaning, and also a distinctly different spiritual or symbolic meaning and use, where the word refers to something of God, either in the spiritual realm or as a metaphor for God or Heaven.

Generally, where a keyword can represent something that is both physical and also something purely symbolic or spiritual, only those occurrences of the keyword that are of spiritual significance to the symbolic theme have been included within the Chapter.

An example is the Chapter titled **Kingdom***. The word "kingdom" is used in *The Bible* with reference to both the physical kingdoms that are the countries, nations and empires of the earth (as Israel, Judah, Assyria etc.), and also to the spiritual "Kingdom" that represents God, Heaven, or even the Church. For the purposes of this book, references to the physical nations of the earth, such as the kingdoms of Israel, Judah, Babylon, and Assyria, etc. were not included within the provided Concordant Texts of the topical Chapter titled **Kingdom***.

3B. KEYWORD PHRASE VARIATION   Symbol: ^

Sometimes in Scripture the group of words that form a keyword phrase can include additional words that provide further descriptive meaning, context or content. An example is the Chapter titled **Son of God^**, which includes other variations of the keyword phrase, such as the "**Son of** the living **God**", "**Son of** the Most High **God**", "His only begotten **Son**", etc.

In a few cases, the sequence of the individual words that comprise a keyword phrase can also appear in a rearranged or different order, such as "**God's Son**".

Where a keyword phrase has a variety of possible word additions and/or arrangements, all combinations and forms of the keyword phrase, as found in the NASB translation of the Scriptures, have generally been included within the Concordant Texts of the topical Chapter, although not all of the additional derivatives and combinations of the keyword ^ phrase have been specifically listed in the Title Block of the Chapter.

The presence of multiple word combinations and variations of a keyword phrase in the Concordant Texts of a Chapter is indicated by a ^ to the right of the listing of the keyword phrase in the Title Block, as in **Son of God^**.

~ End of Notes ~

THE BOOKS OF THE BIBLE

OLD TESTAMENT

The HEBREW COVENANT / TANAKH

1 Genesis	14 II Chronicles	27 Daniel
2 Exodus	15 Ezra	28 Hosea
3 Leviticus	16 Nehemiah	29 Joel
4 Numbers	17 Esther	30 Amos
5 Deuteronomy	18 Job	31 Obadiah
6 Joshua	19 Psalms	32 Jonah
7 Judges	20 Proverbs	33 Micah
8 Ruth	21 Ecclesiastes	34 Nahum
9 I Samuel	22 Song of Solomon	35 Habakkuk
10 II Samuel	23 Isaiah	36 Zephaniah
11 I Kings	24 Jeremiah	37 Haggai
12 II Kings	25 Lamentations	38 Zechariah
13 I Chronicles	26 Ezekiel	39 Malachi

NEW TESTAMENT

The CHRISTIAN COVENANT

1	Matthew	10	Ephesians	19	Hebrews
2	Mark	11	Philippians	20	James
3	Luke	12	Colossians	21	I Peter
4	John	13	I Thessalonians	22	II Peter
5	Acts	14	II Thessalonians	23	I John
6	Romans	15	I Timothy	24	II John
7	I Corinthians	16	II Timothy	25	III John
8	II Corinthians	17	Titus	26	Jude
9	Galatians	18	Philemon	27	Revelation

The

CONCORDANT

TEXTS

of SEVEN IMPORTANT
SPIRITUAL SYMBOLS
about HEALING

HEAL

**/ HEALING(S) / HEALS / HEALER / HEALED / HEALTH
/ HEALTHY + CURE(S) / CURING / CURED
/ CLEANSE* / CLEANSING* / CLEANSED* + RECOVER*
/ RECOVERY* / RECOVERED* + RESTORE*
/ RESTORED* + GET WELL^ + MADE WELL*^**

Definitions

Heal
1. To make healthy, whole, or sound; to restore to health; to free from ailment, illness, disease or injury.
2. To cure from illness, disease, injury or affliction.
3. To make a wound or broken bones, etc. to become whole or sound; to patch up; to mend.
4. To free from evil; to cleanse, to purify.

Health
1. The condition where the body or any of its parts are functioning normally and properly; freedom from disease or ailment.
2. The general condition of the body or mind with reference to soundness, vigor, vitality etc.

Healthy
1. Indicating or suggestive of health; free from disease or malfunction; functioning normally or properly.
2. Possessing or enjoying good health or a sound and vigorous mentality.
3. Pertaining to or characterized by good health; of a sound and vigorous mind.
4. Conducive to good health; healthful.
5. Prosperous or whole; sound.

Cure
1. To restore to health.
2. To relieve or rid of illness or ailment.
3. A successful remedial treatment; restoration to health.
4. A means, method or course of healing or restoring to health; a remedy.

Cleanse
To be made clean, sound, well, or whole after injury, illness or disease; healed; restored.

Recover
To get back or regain one's health or strength, especially after illness.

Restore
To bring back to a state of health, soundness or vigor.

OLD TESTAMENT

Abraham prayed to God, and God **healed** Abimelech and his wife and his maids, so that they bore children. For the Lord had closed fast all the wombs of the household of Abimelech because of Sarah, Abraham's wife.   *Genesis 20:17-18*

Moses said, "What if they will not believe me or listen to what I say? For they may say, 'The Lord has not appeared to you.' "

The Lord said to him, "What is that in your hand?"

And he said, "A staff."

Then He said, "Throw it on the ground."

So he threw it on the ground, and it became a serpent; and Moses fled from it.

But the Lord said to Moses, "Stretch out your hand and grasp it by its tail" - so he stretched out his hand and caught it, and it became a staff in his hand - "that they may believe that the Lord, the God of their fathers, the God of Abraham, the God of Isaac, and the God of Jacob, has appeared to you."

The Lord furthermore said to him, "Now put your hand into your bosom." So he put his hand into his bosom, and when he took it out, behold, his hand was leprous like snow.

Then He said, "Put your hand into your bosom again."

So he put his hand into his bosom again, and when he took it out of his bosom, behold, it was **restored** like the rest of his flesh.

"If they will not believe you or heed the witness of the first sign, they may believe the witness of the last sign."
                    Exodus 4:1-8

Moses led Israel from the Red Sea, and they went out into the wilderness of Shur; and they went three days in the wilderness and found no water.

When they came to Marah, they could not drink the waters of Marah, for they were bitter; therefore it was named Marah.

So the people grumbled at Moses, saying, "What shall we drink?"

Then he cried out to the Lord, and the Lord showed him a tree; and he threw it into the waters, and the waters became sweet.

There He made for them a statute and regulation, and there He tested them.

And He said, "If you will give earnest heed to the voice of the Lord your God, and do what is right in His sight, and give ear to His commandments, and keep all His statutes, I will put none of the diseases on you which I have put on the Egyptians; for I, the Lord, am your **healer**."

Then they came to Elim where there were twelve springs of water and seventy date palms, and they camped there beside the waters.   *Exodus 15:22-27*

If men have a quarrel and one strikes the other with a stone or with his fist, and he does not die but remains in bed, if he gets up and walks around outside on his staff, then he who struck him shall go unpunished; he shall only pay for his loss of time, and shall take care of him until he is completely **healed**.   *Exodus 21:18-19*

The Lord spoke to Moses, saying, "Speak to the sons of Israel, saying: 'When a woman gives birth and bears a male child, then she shall be unclean for seven days, as in the days of her menstruation she shall be unclean.

'On the eighth day the flesh of his foreskin shall be circumcised.

'Then she shall remain in the blood of her purification for thirty-three days; she shall not touch any consecrated thing, nor enter the sanctuary until the days of her purification are completed.

'But if she bears a female child, then she shall be unclean for two weeks, as in her menstruation; and she shall remain in the blood of her purification for sixty-six days.

'When the days of her purification are completed, for a son or for a daughter, she shall bring to the priest at the doorway of the tent of meeting a one year old lamb for a burnt offering and a young pigeon or a turtledove for a sin offering.

'Then he shall offer it before the Lord and make atonement for her, and she shall be **cleansed** from the flow of her blood. This is the law for her who bears a child, whether a male or a female.

'But if she cannot afford a lamb, then she shall take two turtledoves or two young pigeons, the one for a burnt offering and the other for a sin offering; and the priest shall make atonement for her, and she will be **clean**.' "   *Leviticus 12:1-8*

The Lord spoke to Moses and to Aaron, saying, "When a man has on the skin of his body a swelling or a scab or a bright spot, and it becomes an infection of leprosy on the skin of his body, then he shall be brought to Aaron the priest or to one of his sons the priests.

"The priest shall look at the mark on the skin of the body, and if the hair in the infection has turned white and the infection appears to be deeper than the skin of his body, it is an infection of leprosy; when the priest has looked at him, he shall pronounce him unclean.

"But if the bright spot is white on the skin of his body, and it does not appear to be deeper than the skin, and the hair on it has not turned white, then the priest shall isolate him who has the infection for seven days. The priest shall look at him on the seventh day, and if in his eyes the infection has not changed and the infection has not spread on the skin, then the priest shall isolate him for seven more days.

"The priest shall look at him again on the seventh day, and if the infection has faded and the mark has not spread on the skin, then the priest shall pronounce him **clean**; it is only a scab. And he shall wash his clothes and be **clean**.

"But if the scab spreads farther on the skin after he has shown himself to the priest for his **cleansing**, he shall appear again to the priest. The priest shall look, and if the scab has spread on the skin, then the priest shall pronounce him unclean; it is leprosy. When the infection of leprosy is on a man, then he shall be brought to the priest.

"The priest shall then look, and if there is a white swelling in the skin, and it has turned the hair white, and there is quick raw flesh in the swelling, it is a chronic leprosy on the skin of his body, and the priest shall pronounce him unclean; he shall not isolate him, for he is unclean.

"If the leprosy breaks out farther on the skin, and the leprosy covers all the skin of him who has the infection from his head even to his feet, as far as the priest can see, then the priest shall look, and behold, if the leprosy has covered all his body, he shall pronounce **clean** him who has the infection; it has all turned white and he is **clean**.

"But whenever raw flesh appears on him, he shall be unclean. The priest shall look at the raw flesh, and he shall pronounce him unclean; the raw flesh is unclean, it is leprosy. Or if the raw flesh turns again and is changed to white, then he shall come to the priest, and the priest shall look at him, and behold, if the infection has turned to white, then the priest shall pronounce **clean** him who has the infection; he is **clean**.

"When the body has a boil on its skin and it is **healed**, and in the place of the boil there is a white swelling or a reddish-white, bright spot, then it shall be shown to the priest; and the priest shall look, and behold, if it appears to be lower than the skin, and the hair on it has turned white, then the priest shall pronounce him unclean; it is the infection of leprosy, it has broken out in the boil.

"But if the priest looks at it, and behold, there are no white hairs in it and it is not lower than the skin and is faded, then the priest shall isolate him for seven days; and if it spreads farther on the skin, then the priest shall pronounce him unclean; it is an infection. But if the bright spot remains in its place and does not spread, it is only the scar of the boil; and the priest shall pronounce him **clean**."

Leviticus 13:18-23

If a man or woman has an infection on the head or on the beard, then the priest shall look at the infection, and if it appears to be deeper than the skin and there is thin yellowish hair in it, then the priest shall pronounce him unclean; it is a scale, it is leprosy of the head or of the beard.

But if the priest looks at the infection of the scale, and indeed, it appears to be no deeper than the skin and there is no black hair in it, then the priest shall isolate the person with the scaly infection for seven days.

On the seventh day the priest shall look at the infection, and if the scale has not spread and no yellowish hair has grown in it, and the appearance of the scale is no deeper than the skin, then he shall shave himself, but he shall not shave the scale; and the priest shall isolate the person with the scale seven more days.

Then on the seventh day the priest shall look at the scale, and if the scale has not spread in the skin and it appears to be no deeper than the skin, the priest shall pronounce him **clean**; and he shall wash his clothes and be **clean**.

But if the scale spreads farther in the skin after his **cleansing**, then the priest shall look at him, and if the scale has spread in the skin, the priest need not seek for the yellowish hair; he is unclean. If in his sight the scale has remained, however, and black hair has grown in it, the scale has **healed**, he is **clean**; and the priest shall pronounce him **clean**.

When a man or a woman has bright spots on the skin of the body, even white bright spots, then the priest shall look, and if the bright spots on the skin of their bodies are a faint white, it is eczema that has broken out on the skin; he is **clean**.

Leviticus 13:29-37

The Lord spoke to Moses, saying, "This shall be the law of the leper in the day of his **cleansing**. Now he shall be brought to the priest, and the priest shall go out to the outside of the camp.

"Thus the priest shall look, and if the infection of leprosy has been **healed** in the leper, then the priest shall give orders to take two live clean birds and cedar wood and a scarlet string and hyssop for the one who is to be **cleansed**.

"The priest shall also give orders to slay the one bird in an earthenware vessel over running water. As for the live bird, he shall take it together with the cedar wood and the scarlet string and the hyssop, and shall dip them and the live bird in the blood of the bird that was slain over the running water. He shall then sprinkle seven times the one who is to be **cleansed** from the leprosy and shall pronounce him **clean**, and shall let the live bird go free over the open field.

"The one to be **cleansed** shall then wash his clothes and shave off all his hair and bathe in water and be **clean**.

"Now afterward, he may enter the camp, but he shall stay outside his tent for seven days. It will be on the seventh day that he shall shave off all his hair: he shall shave his head and his beard and his eyebrows, even all his hair. He shall then wash his clothes and bathe his body in water and be **clean**."

"Now on the eighth day he is to take two male lambs without defect, and a yearling ewe lamb without defect, and three-tenths of an ephah of fine flour mixed with oil for a grain offering, and one log of oil; and the priest who pronounces him **clean** shall present the man to be **cleansed** and the aforesaid before the Lord at the doorway of the tent of meeting.

"Then the priest shall take the one male lamb and bring it for a guilt offering, with the log of oil, and present them as a wave offering before the Lord. Next he shall slaughter the male lamb in the place where they slaughter the sin offering and the burnt offering, at the place of the sanctuary - for the guilt offering, like the sin offering, belongs to the priest; it is most holy.

"The priest shall then take some of the blood of the guilt offering, and the priest shall put it on the lobe of the right ear of the one to be **cleansed**, and on the thumb of his right hand and on the big toe of his right foot.

"The priest shall also take some of the log of oil, and pour it into his left palm; the priest shall then dip his right-hand finger into the oil that is in his left palm, and with his finger sprinkle some of the oil seven times before the Lord.

"Of the remaining oil which is in his palm, the priest shall put some on the right ear lobe of the one to be **cleansed**, and on the thumb of his right hand, and on the big toe of his right foot, on the blood of the guilt offering; while the rest of the oil that is in the priest's palm, he shall put on the head of the one to be **cleansed**. So the priest shall make atonement on his behalf before the Lord.

"The priest shall next offer the sin offering and make atonement for the one to be **cleansed** from his uncleanness. Then afterward, he shall slaughter the burnt offering. The priest shall offer up the burnt offering and the grain offering on the altar. Thus the priest shall make atonement for him, and he will be **clean**.

"But if he is poor and his means are insufficient, then he is to take one male lamb for a guilt offering as a wave offering to make atonement for him, and one-tenth of an ephah of fine flour mixed with oil for a grain offering, and a log of oil, and two turtledoves or two young pigeons which are within his means, the one shall be a sin offering and the other a burnt offering.

"Then the eighth day he shall bring them for his **cleansing** to the priest, at the doorway of the tent of meeting, before the Lord. The priest shall take the lamb of the guilt offering and the log of oil, and the priest shall offer them for a wave of-fering before the Lord.

"Next he shall slaughter the lamb of the guilt offering; and the priest is to take some of the blood of the guilt offering and put it on the lobe of the right ear of the one to be **cleansed** and on the thumb of his right hand and on the big toe of his right foot.

"The priest shall also pour some of the oil into his left palm; and with his right-hand finger the priest shall sprinkle some of the oil that is in his left palm seven times before the Lord. The priest shall then put some of the oil that is in his palm on the lobe of the right ear of the one to be **cleansed**, and on the thumb of his right hand and on the big toe of his right foot, on the place of the blood of the guilt offering.

"Moreover, the rest of the oil that is in the priest's palm he shall put on the head of the one to be **cleansed**, to make atonement on his behalf before the Lord. He shall then offer one of the turtledoves or young pigeons, which are within his means. He shall offer what he can afford, the one for a sin offering and the other for a burnt offering, together with the grain offering. So the priest shall make atone-ment before the Lord on behalf of the one to be **cleansed**.

"This is the law for him in whom there is an infection of leprosy, whose means are limited for his **cleansing**."

Leviticus 14:1-32

When the man with the discharge becom-es **cleansed** from his discharge, then he shall count off for himself seven days for his **cleansing**; he shall then wash his clothes and bathe his body in running water and will become **clean**.

Then on the eighth day he shall take for himself two turtledoves or two young pigeons, and come before the Lord to the doorway of the tent of meeting and give them to the priest; and the priest shall offer them, one for a sin offering and the other for a burnt offering.

So the priest shall make atonement on his behalf before the Lord because of his discharge.   *Leviticus 15:13-15*

Miriam and Aaron spoke against Moses because of the Cushite woman whom he had married (for he had married a Cushite woman); and they said, "Has the Lord indeed spoken only through Moses? Has He not spoken through us as well?"

And the Lord heard it. (Now the man Moses was very humble, more than any man who was on the face of the earth.)

Suddenly the Lord said to Moses and Aaron and to Miriam, "You three come out to the tent of meeting." So the three of them came out.

Then the Lord came down in a pillar of cloud and stood at the doorway of the tent, and He called Aaron and Miriam.

When they had both come forward, He said, "Hear now My words: If there is a prophet among you, I, the Lord, shall make Myself known to him in a vision. I shall speak with him in a dream.

"Not so, with My servant Moses, he is faithful in all My household; with him I speak mouth to mouth, even openly, and not in dark sayings, and he beholds the form of the Lord. Why then were you not afraid to speak against My servant, against Moses?"

So the anger of the Lord burned against them and He departed. But when the cloud had withdrawn from over the tent, behold, Miriam was leprous, as white as snow. As Aaron turned toward Miriam, behold, she was leprous.

Then Aaron said to Moses, "Oh, my lord, I beg you, do not account this sin to us, in which we have acted foolishly and in which we have sinned. Oh, do not let her be like one dead, whose flesh is half eaten away when he comes from his mother's womb!"

Moses cried out to the Lord, saying, "O God, **heal** her, I pray!"

But the Lord said to Moses, "If her father had but spit in her face, would she not bear her shame for seven days? Let her be shut up for seven days outside the camp, and afterward she may be received again."

So Miriam was shut up outside the camp for seven days, and the people did not move on until Miriam was received again.   *Numbers 12:1-15*

The Lord shall cause you to be defeated before your enemies; you will go out one way against them, but you will flee seven ways before them, and you will be an example of terror to all the kingdoms of the earth.

Your carcasses will be food to all birds of the sky and to the beasts of the earth, and there will be no one to frighten them away.

The Lord will smite you with the boils of Egypt and with tumors and with the scab and with the itch, from which you cannot be **healed**.

The Lord will smite you with madness and with blindness and with bewilderment of heart; and you will grope at noon, as the blind man gropes in darkness, and you will not prosper in your ways; but you shall only be oppressed and robbed continually, with none to save you.   *Deuteronomy 28:25-29*

A people whom you do not know shall eat up the produce of your ground and all your labors, and you will never be anything but oppressed and crushed continually. You shall be driven mad by the sight of what you see.

The Lord will strike you on the knees and legs with sore boils, from which you cannot be **healed**, from the sole of your foot to the crown of your head.

The Lord will bring you and your king, whom you set over you, to a nation which neither you nor your fathers have known, and there you shall serve other gods, wood and stone.

You shall become a horror, a proverb, and a taunt among all the people where the Lord drives you.   *Deuteronomy 28:33-37*

See now that I, I am He, and there is no god besides Me; it is I who put to death and give life.

I have wounded and it is I who **heal**, and there is no one who can deliver from My hand.   *Deuteronomy 32:39*

It came about when all the kings of the Amorites who were beyond the Jordan to the west, and all the kings of the Canaanites who were by the sea, heard how the Lord had dried up the waters of the Jordan before the sons of Israel until they had crossed, that their hearts melted, and there was no spirit in them any longer because of the sons of Israel.

At that time the Lord said to Joshua, "Make for yourself flint knives and circumcise again the sons of Israel the second time."

So Joshua made himself flint knives and circumcised the sons of Israel at Gibeath-haaraloth.

This is the reason why Joshua circumcised them: all the people who came out of Egypt who were males, all the men of war, died in the wilderness along the way after they came out of Egypt. For all the people who came out were circumcised, but all the people who were born in the wilderness along the way as they came out of Egypt had not been circumcised.

For the sons of Israel walked forty years in the wilderness, until all the nation, that is, the men of war who came out of Egypt, perished because they did not listen to the voice of the Lord, to whom the Lord had sworn that He would not let them see the land which the Lord had sworn to their fathers to give us, a land flowing with milk and honey. Their children whom He raised up in their place, Joshua circumcised; for they were uncircumcised, because they had not circumcised them along the way.

Now when they had finished circumcising all the nation, they remained in their places in the camp until they were **healed**.

Then the Lord said to Joshua, "Today I have rolled away the reproach of Egypt from you." So the name of that place is called Gilgal to this day.   *Joshua 5:1-9*

They sent and gathered all the lords of the Philistines to them and said, "What shall we do with the ark of the God of Israel?"

And they said, "Let the ark of the God of Israel be brought around to Gath." And they brought the ark of the God of Israel around.

After they had brought it around, the hand of the Lord was against the city with very great confusion; and He smote the men of the city, both young and old, so that tumors broke out on them. So they sent the ark of God to Ekron.

And as the ark of God came to Ekron the Ekronites cried out, saying, "They have brought the ark of the God of Israel around to us, to kill us and our people."

They sent therefore and gathered all the lords of the Philistines and said, "Send away the ark of the God of Israel, and let it return to its own place, so that it will not kill us and our people." For there was a deadly confusion throughout the city; the hand of God was very heavy there. And the men who did not die were smitten with tumors and the cry of the city went up to heaven.

Now the ark of the Lord had been in the country of the Philistines seven months. And the Philistines called for the priests and the diviners, saying, "What shall we do with the ark of the Lord? Tell us how we shall send it to its place."

They said, "If you send away the ark of the God of Israel, do not send it empty; but you shall surely return to Him a guilt offering. Then you will be **healed** and it will be known to you why His hand is not removed from you."

Then they said, "What shall be the guilt offering which we shall return to Him?"

And they said, "Five golden tumors and five golden mice according to the number of the lords of the Philistines, for one plague was on all of you and on your lords. So you shall make likenesses of your tumors and likenesses of your mice that ravage the land, and you shall give glory to the God of Israel; perhaps He will ease His hand from you, your gods, and your land."   *1 Samuel 5:8 - 6:5*

Behold, there came a man of God from Judah to Bethel by the word of the Lord, while Jeroboam was standing by the altar to burn incense.

He cried against the altar by the word of the Lord, and said, "O altar, altar, thus says the Lord, 'Behold, a son shall be born to the house of David, Josiah by name; and on you he shall sacrifice the priests of the high places who burn incense on you, and human bones shall be burned on you.' "

Then he gave a sign the same day, saying, "This is the sign which the Lord has spoken, 'Behold, the altar shall be split apart and the ashes which are on it shall be poured out.' "

Now when the king heard the saying of the man of God, which he cried against the altar in Bethel, Jeroboam stretched out his hand from the altar, saying, "Seize him."

But his hand which he stretched out against him dried up, so that he could not draw it back to himself. The altar also was split apart and the ashes were poured out from the altar, according to the sign which the man of God had given by the word of the Lord.

The king said to the man of God, "Please entreat the Lord your God, and pray for me, that my hand may be **restored** to me."

So the man of God entreated the Lord, and the king's hand was **restored** to him, and it became as it was before.

1 Kings 13:1-6

Moab rebelled against Israel after the death of Ahab. And Ahaziah fell through the lattice in his upper chamber which was in Samaria, and became ill.

So he sent messengers and said to them, "Go, inquire of Baal-zebub, the god of Ekron, whether I will **recover** from this sickness."

But the angel of the Lord said to Elijah the Tishbite, "Arise, go up to meet the messengers of the king of Samaria and say to them, 'Is it because there is no God in Israel that you are going to inquire of Baal-zebub, the god of Ekron?'

"Now therefore thus says the Lord, 'You shall not come down from the bed where you have gone up, but you shall surely die.' "

Then Elijah departed. *2 Kings 1:1-4*

Naaman, captain of the army of the king of Aram, was a great man with his master, and highly respected, because by him the Lord had given victory to Aram. The man was also a valiant warrior, but he was a leper.

Now the Arameans had gone out in bands and had taken captive a little girl

from the land of Israel; and she waited on Naaman's wife. She said to her mistress, "I wish that my master were with the prophet who is in Samaria! Then he would **cure** him of his leprosy."

Naaman went in and told his master, saying, "Thus and thus spoke the girl who is from the land of Israel."

Then the king of Aram said, "Go now, and I will send a letter to the king of Israel." He departed and took with him ten talents of silver and six thousand shekels of gold and ten changes of clothes.

He brought the letter to the king of Israel, saying, "And now as this letter comes to you, behold, I have sent Naaman my servant to you, that you may **cure** him of his leprosy."

When the king of Israel read the letter, he tore his clothes and said, "Am I God, to kill and to make alive, that this man is sending word to me to **cure** a man of his leprosy? But consider now, and see how he is seeking a quarrel against me."

It happened when Elisha the man of God heard that the king of Israel had torn his clothes, that he sent word to the king, saying, "Why have you torn your clothes? Now let him come to me, and he shall know that there is a prophet in Israel."

So Naaman came with his horses and his chariots and stood at the doorway of the house of Elisha. Elisha sent a messenger to him, saying, "Go and wash in the Jordan seven times, and your flesh will be **restored** to you and you will be **clean**."

But Naaman was furious and went away and said, "Behold, I thought, 'He will surely come out to me and stand and call on the name of the Lord his God, and wave his hand over the place and **cure** the leper.' Are not Abanah and Pharpar, the rivers of Damascus, better than all the waters of Israel? Could I not wash in them and be **clean**?" So he turned and went away in a rage.

Then his servants came near and spoke to him and said, "My father, had the prophet told you to do some great thing, would you not have done it? How much more then, when he says to you, 'Wash, and be **clean**'?"

So he went down and dipped himself seven times in the Jordan, according to the word of the man of God; and his flesh was **restored** like the flesh of a little child and he was **clean**.   *2 Kings 5:1-14*

Elisha came to Damascus. Now Ben-hadad king of Aram was sick, and it was told him, saying, "The man of God has come here." The king said to Hazael, "Take a gift in your hand and go to meet the man of God, and inquire of the Lord by him, saying, 'Will I **recover** from this sickness?' "

So Hazael went to meet him and took a gift in his hand, even every kind of good thing of Damascus, forty camels' loads; and he came and stood before him and said, "Your son Ben-hadad king of Aram has sent me to you, saying, 'Will I **recover** from this sickness?' "

Then Elisha said to him, "Go, say to him, 'You will surely **recover**,' but the Lord has shown me that he will certainly die."

He fixed his gaze steadily on him until he was ashamed, and the man of God wept. Hazael said, "Why does my lord weep?"

Then he answered, "Because I know the evil that you will do to the sons of Israel: their strongholds you will set on fire, and their young men you will kill with the sword, and their little ones you will dash in pieces, and their women with child you will rip up."

Then Hazael said, "But what is your servant, who is but a dog, that he should do this great thing?"

And Elisha answered, "The Lord has shown me that you will be king over Aram."

So he departed from Elisha and returned to his master, who said to him, "What did Elisha say to you?"

And he answered, "He told me that you would surely **recover**."

On the following day, he took the cover and dipped it in water and spread it on his face, so that he died. And Hazael became king in his place.   *2 Kings 8:7-15*

Ahaziah was twenty-two years old when he became king, and he reigned one year in Jerusalem. And his mother's name was Athaliah the granddaughter of Omri king of Israel.

He walked in the way of the house of Ahab and did evil in the sight of the Lord, like the house of Ahab had done, because he was a son-in-law of the house of Ahab.

Then he went with Joram the son of Ahab to war against Hazael king of Aram at Ramoth-gilead, and the Arameans wounded Joram. So King Joram returned to be **healed** in Jezreel of the wounds which the Arameans had inflicted on him at Ramah when he fought against Hazael king of Aram.

Then Ahaziah the son of Jehoram king of Judah went down to see Joram the son of Ahab in Jezreel because he was sick.   *2 Kings 8:26-29*

So Jehu the son of Jehoshaphat the son of Nimshi conspired against Joram. Now Joram with all Israel was defending Ramoth-gilead against Hazael king of Aram, but King Joram had returned to Jezreel to be **healed** of the wounds which the Arameans had inflicted on him when he fought with Hazael king of Aram. ~   *2 Kings 9:14-15*

In those days Hezekiah became mortally ill. And Isaiah the prophet the son of Amoz came to him and said to him, "Thus says the Lord, 'Set your house in order, for you shall die and not live.' "

Then he turned his face to the wall and prayed to the Lord, saying, "Remember now, O Lord, I beseech You, how I have walked before You in truth and with a whole heart and have done what is good in Your sight." And Hezekiah wept bitterly.

Before Isaiah had gone out of the middle court, the word of the Lord came to him, saying, "Return and say to Hezekiah the leader of My people, 'Thus says the Lord, the God of your father David, "I have heard your prayer, I have seen your tears; behold, I will **heal** you.

"On the third day you shall go up to the house of the Lord. I will add fifteen years to your life, and I will deliver you and this city from the hand of the king of Assyria; and I will defend this city for My own sake and for My servant David's sake."'"

Then Isaiah said, "Take a cake of figs." And they took and laid it on the boil, and he **recovered**.

Now Hezekiah said to Isaiah, "What will be the sign that the Lord will **heal** me, and that I shall go up to the house of the Lord the third day?"

Isaiah said, "This shall be the sign to you from the Lord, that the Lord will do the thing that He has spoken: Shall the shadow go forward ten steps or go back ten steps?"

So Hezekiah answered, "It is easy for the shadow to decline ten steps; no, but let the shadow turn backward ten steps."

Isaiah the prophet cried to the Lord, and He brought the shadow on the stairway back ten steps by which it had gone down on the stairway of Ahaz.

2 Kings 20:1-11

Solomon finished the house of the Lord and the king's palace, and successfully completed all that he had planned on doing in the house of the Lord and in his palace.

Then the Lord appeared to Solomon at night and said to him, "I have heard your prayer and have chosen this place for Myself as a house of sacrifice.

"If I shut up the heavens so that there is no rain, or if I command the locust to devour the land, or if I send pestilence among My people, and My people who are called by My name humble themselves and pray and seek My face and turn from their wicked ways, then I will hear from heaven, will forgive their sin and will **heal** their land."

2 Chronicles 7:11-14

The inhabitants of Jerusalem made Ahaziah, his youngest son, king in his place, for the band of men who came with the Arabs to the camp had slain all the older sons. So Ahaziah the son of Jehoram king of Judah began to reign.

Ahaziah was twenty-two years old when he became king, and he reigned one year in Jerusalem. And his mother's name was Athaliah, the granddaughter of Omri.

He also walked in the ways of the house of Ahab, for his mother was his counselor to do wickedly. He did evil in the sight of the Lord like the house of Ahab, for they were his counselors after the death of his father, to his destruction. He also walked according to their counsel, and went with Jehoram the son of Ahab king of Israel to wage war against Hazael king of Aram at Ramoth-gilead.

But the Arameans wounded Joram. So he returned to be **healed** in Jezreel of the wounds which they had inflicted on him at Ramah, when he fought against Hazael king of Aram. And Ahaziah, the son of Jehoram king of Judah, went down to see Jehoram the son of Ahab in Jezreel, because he was sick.

Now the destruction of Ahaziah was from God, in that he went to Joram. For when he came, he went out with Jehoram against Jehu the son of Nimshi, whom the Lord had anointed to cut off the house of Ahab.

2 Chronicles 22:1-7

There were many in the assembly who had not consecrated themselves; therefore, the Levites were over the slaughter of the Passover lambs for everyone who was unclean, in order to consecrate them to the Lord. For a multitude of the people, even many from Ephraim and Manasseh, Issachar and Zebulun, had not purified themselves, yet they ate the Passover otherwise than prescribed.

For Hezekiah prayed for them, saying, "May the good Lord pardon everyone who prepares his heart to seek God, the Lord God of his fathers, though not according to the purification rules of the sanctuary."

So the Lord heard Hezekiah and **healed** the people. *2 Chronicles 30:17-20*

Behold, how happy is the man whom God reproves, so do not despise the discipline of the Almighty. For He inflicts pain, and gives relief; He wounds, and His hands also **heal**.

From six troubles He will deliver you, even in seven evil will not touch you.

Job 5:17-19

O Lord, do not rebuke me in Your anger, nor chasten me in Your wrath. Be gracious to me, O Lord, for I am pining away; **heal** me, O Lord, for my bones are dismayed.

Psalm 6:1-2

I will extol You, O Lord, for You have lifted me up, and have not let my enemies rejoice over me. O Lord my God, I cried to You for help, and You **healed** me.

O Lord, You have brought up my soul from Sheol; You have kept me alive, that I would not go down to the pit.

Sing praise to the Lord, you His godly ones, and give thanks to His holy name. For His anger is but for a moment, His favor is for a lifetime; weeping may last for the night, but a shout of joy comes in the morning.

Psalm 30:1-5

O Lord, rebuke me not in Your wrath, and chasten me not in Your burning anger. For Your arrows have sunk deep into me, and Your hand has pressed down on me. There is no soundness in my flesh because of Your indignation; there is no **health** in my bones because of my sin. For my iniquities are gone over my head; as a heavy burden they weigh too much for me.

My wounds grow foul and fester because of my folly. I am bent over and greatly bowed down; I go mourning all day long. For my loins are filled with burning, and there is no soundness in my flesh. I am benumbed and badly crushed; I groan because of the agitation of my heart.

Lord, all my desire is before You; and my sighing is not hidden from You. My heart throbs, my strength fails me; and the light of my eyes, even that has gone from me.

My loved ones and my friends stand aloof from my plague; and my kinsmen stand afar off.

Psalm 38:1-11

How blessed is he who considers the helpless; the Lord will deliver him in a day of trouble. The Lord will protect him and keep him alive, and he shall be called blessed upon the earth; and do not give him over to the desire of his enemies. The Lord will sustain him upon his sickbed; in his illness, You **restore** him to **health**.

As for me, I said, "O Lord, be gracious to me; **heal** my soul, for I have sinned against You."

Psalm 41:1-4

O God, You have rejected us. You have broken us; You have been angry; O, restore us. You have made the land quake, You have split it open; **heal** its breaches, for it totters.

You have made Your people experience hardship; You have given us wine to drink that makes us stagger. *Psalm 60:1-3*

Bless the Lord, O my soul, and all that is within me, bless His holy name.

Bless the Lord, O my soul, and forget none of His benefits; who pardons all your iniquities, who **heals** all your diseases; who redeems your life from the pit, who crowns you with lovingkindness and compassion; who satisfies your years with good things, so that your youth is renewed like the eagle.

The Lord performs righteous deeds and judgments for all who are oppressed.

Psalm 103:1-6

Fools, because of their rebellious way, and because of their iniquities, were afflicted. Their soul abhorred all kinds of food, and they drew near to the gates of death.

Then they cried out to the Lord in their trouble; He saved them out of their distresses. He sent His word and **healed** them, and delivered them from their destructions.

Let them give thanks to the Lord for His lovingkindness, and for His wonders to the sons of men!

Let them also offer sacrifices of thanksgiving, and tell of His works with joyful singing. *Psalm 107:17-22*

Praise the Lord! For it is good to sing praises to our God; for it is pleasant and praise is becoming.

The Lord builds up Jerusalem; He gathers the outcasts of Israel. He **heals** the brokenhearted and binds up their wounds. *Psalm 147:1-3*

Trust in the Lord with all your heart and do not lean on your own understanding. In all your ways acknowledge Him, and He will make your paths straight.

Do not be wise in your own eyes; fear the Lord and turn away from evil. It will be **healing** to your body and refreshment to your bones. *Proverb 3:5-8*

My son, give attention to my words; incline your ear to my sayings. Do not let them depart from your sight; keep them in the midst of your heart. For they are life to those who find them and **health** to all their body.

Watch over your heart with all diligence, for from it flow the springs of life. *Proverb 4:20-23*

A worthless person, a wicked man, is the one who walks with a perverse mouth, who winks with his eyes, who signals with his feet, who points with his fingers; who with perversity in his heart continually devises evil, who spreads strife. Therefore his calamity will come suddenly; instantly he will be broken and there will be no **healing**. *Proverb 6:12-15*

He who speaks truth tells what is right, but a false witness, deceit. There is one who speaks rashly like the thrusts of a sword, but the tongue of the wise brings **healing**.

Truthful lips will be established forever, but a lying tongue is only for a moment. *Proverb 12:17-19*

A wicked messenger falls into adversity, but a faithful envoy brings **healing**. *Proverb 13:17*

The heart of the wise instructs his mouth and adds persuasiveness to his lips.

Pleasant words are a honeycomb, sweet to the soul and **healing** to the bones. *Proverb 16:23-24*

There is an appointed time for everything. And there is a time for every event under heaven - a time to give birth and a time to die; a time to plant and a time to uproot what is planted. A time to kill and a time to **heal**; a time to tear down and a time to build up.

A time to weep and a time to laugh; a time to mourn and a time to dance. *Ecclesiastes 3:1-4*

When a man lays hold of his brother in his father's house, saying, "You have a cloak, you shall be our ruler, and these ruins will be under your charge," he will protest on that day, saying, "I will not be your **healer**, for in my house there is neither bread nor cloak; you should not appoint me ruler of the people."

For Jerusalem has stumbled and Judah has fallen, because their speech and their actions are against the Lord, to rebel against His glorious presence. *Isaiah 3:6-8*

I heard the voice of the Lord, saying, "Whom shall I send, and who will go for Us?"

Then I said, "Here am I. Send me!"

He said, "Go, and tell this people: 'Keep on listening, but do not perceive; keep on looking, but do not understand.'

"Render the hearts of this people insensitive, their ears dull, and their eyes dim, otherwise they might see with their eyes, hear with their ears, understand with their hearts, and return and be **healed**." *Isaiah 6:8-10*

In that day there will be an altar to the Lord in the midst of the land of Egypt, and a pillar to the Lord near its border. It will become a sign and a witness to the Lord of hosts in the land of Egypt; for they will cry to the Lord because of oppressors, and He will send them a Savior and a Champion, and He will deliver them.

Thus the Lord will make Himself known to Egypt, and the Egyptians will know the Lord in that day. They will even worship with sacrifice and offering, and will make a vow to the Lord and perform it.

The Lord will strike Egypt, striking but **healing**; so they will return to the Lord, and He will respond to them and will **heal** them.

In that day there will be a highway from Egypt to Assyria, and the Assyrians will come into Egypt and the Egyptians into Assyria, and the Egyptians will worship with the Assyrians.   *Isaiah 19:19-23*

The light of the moon will be as the light of the sun, and the light of the sun will be seven times brighter, like the light of seven days, on the day the Lord binds up the fracture of His people and **heals** the bruise He has inflicted.   *Isaiah 30:26*

A writing of Hezekiah king of Judah after his illness and **recovery**: I said, "In the middle of my life I am to enter the gates of Sheol; I am to be deprived of the rest of my years.

"I said, 'I will not see the Lord, the Lord in the land of the living; I will look on man no more among the inhabitants of the world.' "   *Isaiah 38:9-11*

"O Lord, by these things men live, and in all these is the life of my spirit; O **restore** me to **health** and let me live! Lo, for my own welfare I had great bitterness; it is You who has kept my soul from the pit of nothingness, for You have cast all my sins behind Your back.

"For Sheol cannot thank You, death cannot praise You; those who go down to the pit cannot hope for Your faithfulness. It is the living who give thanks to You, as I do today; a father tells his sons about Your faithfulness.

"The Lord will surely save me; so we will play my songs on stringed instru-

ments all the days of our life at the house of the Lord."

Now Isaiah had said, "Let them take a cake of figs and apply it to the boil, that he may **recover**."

Then Hezekiah had said, "What is the sign that I shall go up to the house of the Lord?"

At that time Merodach-baladan son of Baladan, king of Babylon, sent letters and a present to Hezekiah, for he heard that he had been sick and had **recovered**.   *Isaiah 38:16 - 39:1*

He was despised and forsaken of men, a man of sorrows and acquainted with grief; and like one from whom men hide their face He was despised, and we did not esteem Him. Surely our griefs He Himself bore, and our sorrows He carried; yet we ourselves esteemed Him stricken, smitten of God, and afflicted.

But He was pierced through for our transgressions, He was crushed for our iniquities; the chastening for our well-being fell upon Him, and by His scourging we are **healed**.

All of us like sheep have gone astray, each of us has turned to his own way; but the Lord has caused the iniquity of us all to fall on Him. He was oppressed and He was afflicted, yet He did not open His mouth; like a lamb that is led to slaughter, and like a sheep that is silent before its shearers, so He did not open His mouth.   *Isaiah 53:3-7*

It will be said, "Build up, build up, prepare the way, remove every obstacle out of the way of My people."

For thus says the high and exalted One who lives forever, whose name is Holy, "I dwell on a high and holy place, and also with the contrite and lowly of spirit in order to revive the spirit of the lowly and to revive the heart of the contrite. For I will not contend forever, nor will I always be angry; for the spirit would grow faint before Me, and the breath of those whom I have made.

"Because of the iniquity of his unjust gain I was angry and struck him; I hid My face and was angry, and he went on turning away, in the way of his heart.

"I have seen his ways, but I will **heal** him; I will lead him and restore comfort to him and to his mourners, creating the praise of the lips. Peace, peace to him who is far and to him who is near," says the Lord, "and I will **heal** him."

But the wicked are like the tossing sea, for it cannot be quiet, and its waters toss up refuse and mud. "There is no peace," says my God, "for the wicked."

Isaiah 57:14-21

"Surely, as a woman treacherously departs from her lover, so you have dealt treacherously with Me, O house of Israel," declares the Lord.

A voice is heard on the bare heights, the weeping and the supplications of the sons of Israel; because they have perverted their way, they have forgotten the Lord their God.

"Return, O faithless sons, I will **heal** your faithlessness."

Behold, we come to You; for You are the Lord our God. Surely, the hills are a deception, a tumult on the mountains. Surely in the Lord our God is the salvation of Israel. *Jeremiah 3:20-23*

"From the least of them even to the greatest of them, everyone is greedy for gain, and from the prophet even to the priest everyone deals falsely. They have **healed** the brokenness of My people superficially, saying, 'Peace, peace,' but there is no peace.

"Were they ashamed because of the abomination they have done? They were not even ashamed at all; they did not even know how to blush.

"Therefore they shall fall among those who fall; at the time that I punish them, they shall be cast down," says the Lord. *Jeremiah 6:13-15*

"The wise men are put to shame, they are dismayed and caught; behold, they have rejected the word of the Lord, and what kind of wisdom do they have? Therefore I will give their wives to others, their fields to new owners; because from the least even to the greatest everyone is greedy for gain; from the prophet even to the priest everyone practices deceit.

"They **heal** the brokenness of the daughter of My people superficially, saying, 'Peace, peace,' but there is no peace.

"Were they ashamed because of the abomination they had done? They certainly were not ashamed, and they did not know how to blush; therefore they shall fall among those who fall; at the time of their punishment they shall be brought down," says the Lord.

"I will surely snatch them away," declares the Lord; "there will be no grapes on the vine and no figs on the fig tree, and the leaf will wither; and what I have given them will pass away."

Why are we sitting still? Assemble yourselves, and let us go into the fortified cities and let us perish there, because the Lord our God has doomed us and given us poisoned water to drink, for we have sinned against the Lord. We waited for peace, but no good came; for a time of **healing**, but behold, terror!

From Dan is heard the snorting of his horses; at the sound of the neighing of his stallions the whole land quakes; for they come and devour the land and its fullness, the city and its inhabitants. "For behold, I am sending serpents against you, adders, for which there is no charm, and they will bite you," declares the Lord.

My sorrow is beyond **healing**, my heart is faint within me! Behold, listen! The cry of the daughter of my people from a distant land: "Is the Lord not in Zion? Is her King not within her?"

Why have they provoked Me with their graven images, with foreign idols? Harvest is past, summer is ended, and we are not saved.

For the brokenness of the daughter of my people I am broken; I mourn, dismay has taken hold of me.

Is there no balm in Gilead? Is there no physician there? Why then has not the **health** of the daughter of my people been **restored**? *Jeremiah 8:9-22*

Have You completely rejected Judah? Or have You loathed Zion? Why have You stricken us so that we are beyond **healing**? We waited for peace, but nothing good came; and for a time of **healing**, but behold, terror!

We know our wickedness, O Lord, the iniquity of our fathers, for we have sinned against You.

Do not despise us, for Your own name's sake; do not disgrace the throne of Your glory; remember and do not annul Your covenant with us.   *Jeremiah 14:19-20*

"Why has my pain been perpetual and my wound incurable, refusing to be **healed**? Will You indeed be to me like a deceptive stream with water that is unreliable?"

Therefore, thus says the Lord, "If you return, then I will **restore** you - before Me you will stand; and if you extract the precious from the worthless, you will become My spokesman. They for their part may turn to you, but as for you, you must not turn to them."   *Jeremiah 15:18-19*

O Lord, the hope of Israel, all who forsake You will be put to shame. Those who turn away on earth will be written down, because they have forsaken the fountain of living water, even the Lord.

Heal me, O Lord, and I will be **healed**; save me and I will be saved, for You are my praise.   *Jeremiah 17:13-14*

"Fear not, O Jacob My servant," declares the Lord, "and do not be dismayed, O Israel; for behold, I will save you from afar and your offspring from the land of their captivity. And Jacob will return and will be quiet and at ease, and no one will make him afraid.

"For I am with you," declares the Lord, "to save you; for I will destroy completely all the nations where I have scattered you, only I will not destroy you completely. But I will chasten you justly and will by no means leave you unpunished."

For thus says the Lord, "Your wound is incurable and your injury is serious. There is no one to plead your cause; no **healing** for your sore, no **recovery** for you. All your lovers have forgotten you, they do not seek you; for I have wounded you with the wound of an enemy, with the punishment of a cruel one, because your iniquity is great and your sins are numerous.

"Therefore all who devour you will be devoured; and all your adversaries, every one of them, will go into captivity; and those who plunder you will be for plunder, and all who prey upon you I will give for prey. For I will **restore** you to **health** and I will **heal** you of your wounds," declares the Lord, "because they have called you an outcast, saying: 'It is Zion; no one cares for her.' "

Thus says the Lord, "Behold, I will restore the fortunes of the tents of Jacob and have compassion on his dwelling places; and the city will be rebuilt on its ruin, and the palace will stand on its rightful place."   *Jeremiah 30:10-18*

The word of the Lord came to Jeremiah the second time, while he was still confined in the court of the guard, saying, "Thus says the Lord who made the earth, the Lord who formed it to establish it, the Lord is His name, 'Call to Me and I will answer you, and I will tell you great and mighty things, which you do not know.'

"For thus says the Lord God of Israel concerning the houses of this city, and concerning the houses of the kings of Judah which are broken down to make a defense against the siege ramps and against the sword, 'While they are coming to fight with the Chaldeans and to fill them with the corpses of men whom I have slain in My anger and in My wrath, and I have hidden My face from this city because of all their wickedness: Behold, I will bring to it **health** and **healing**, and I will **heal** them; and I will reveal to them an abundance of peace and truth. I will restore the fortunes of Judah and the fortunes of Israel and will rebuild them as they were at first.

'I will **cleanse** them from all their iniquity by which they have sinned against Me, and I will pardon all their iniquities by which they have sinned against Me and by which they have transgressed against Me.' "

Jeremiah 33:1-8

Go up to Gilead and obtain balm, O virgin daughter of Egypt! In vain have you multiplied remedies; there is no **healing** for you.

The nations have heard of your shame, and the earth is full of your cry of distress; for one warrior has stumbled over another, and both of them have fallen down together.

Jeremiah 46:11-12

Flee from the midst of Babylon, and each of you save his life! Do not be destroyed in her punishment, for this is the Lord's time of vengeance; He is going to render recompense to her.

Babylon has been a golden cup in the hand of the Lord, intoxicating all the earth. The nations have drunk of her wine; therefore the nations are going mad.

Suddenly Babylon has fallen and been broken; wail over her! Bring balm for her pain; perhaps she may be **healed**.

We applied **healing** to Babylon, but she was not **healed**; forsake her and let us each go to his own country, for her judgment has reached to heaven and towers up to the very skies. *Jeremiah 51:6-9*

How shall I admonish you? To what shall I compare you, O daughter of Jerusalem? To what shall I liken you as I comfort you, O virgin daughter of Zion? For your ruin is as vast as the sea; who can **heal** you?

Your prophets have seen for you false and foolish visions; and they have not exposed your iniquity so as to restore you from captivity, but they have seen for you false and misleading oracles.

Lamentations 2:13-14

"Arise, cry aloud in the night at the beginning of the night watches; pour out your heart like water before the presence of the Lord; lift up your hands to Him for the life of your little ones who are faint because of hunger at the head of every street."

See, O Lord, and look! With whom have You dealt thus? Should women eat their offspring, the little ones who were born **healthy**? Should priest and prophet be slain in the sanctuary of the Lord? On the ground in the streets lie young and old; my virgins and my young men have fallen by the sword.

You have slain them in the day of Your anger, You have slaughtered, not sparing.

Lamentations 2:19-21

In the eleventh year, in the first month, on the seventh of the month, the word of the Lord came to me saying, "Son of man, I have broken the arm of Pharaoh king of Egypt; and, behold, it has not been bound up for **healing** or wrapped with a bandage, that it may be strong to hold the sword.

"Therefore thus says the Lord God, 'Behold, I am against Pharaoh king of Egypt and will break his arms, both the strong and the broken; and I will make the sword fall from his hand. I will scatter the Egyptians among the nations and disperse them among the lands.

'For I will strengthen the arms of the king of Babylon and put My sword in his hand; and I will break the arms of Pharaoh, so that he will groan before him with the groanings of a wounded man. Thus I will strengthen the arms of the king of Babylon, but the arms of Pharaoh will fall.

'Then they will know that I am the Lord, when I put My sword into the hand of the king of Babylon and he stretches it out against the land of Egypt. When I scatter the Egyptians among the nations and disperse them among the lands, then they will know that I am the Lord.' "

Ezekiel 30:20-26

The word of the Lord came to me saying, "Son of man, prophesy against the shepherds of Israel. Prophesy and say to those shepherds, 'Thus says the Lord God, "Woe, shepherds of Israel who have been feeding themselves! Should not the shepherds feed the flock?

"You eat the fat and clothe yourselves with the wool, you slaughter the fat sheep without feeding the flock. Those who are sickly you have not strengthened, the diseased you have not **healed**, the broken you have not bound up, the scattered you have not brought back, nor have you sought for the lost; but with force and with severity you have dominated them."'"   *Ezekiel 34:1-4*

He said to me, "Son of man, have you seen this?" Then he brought me back to the bank of the river.

Now when I had returned, behold, on the bank of the river there were very many trees on the one side and on the other.

Then he said to me, "These waters go out toward the eastern region and go down into the Arabah; then they go toward the sea, being made to flow into the sea, and the waters of the sea become fresh. It will come about that every living creature which swarms in every place where the river goes, will live. And there will be very many fish, for these waters go there and the others become fresh; so everything will live where the river goes.

"And it will come about that fishermen will stand beside it; from Engedi to Eneglaim there will be a place for the spreading of nets. Their fish will be according to their kinds, like the fish of the Great Sea, very many. But its swamps and marshes will not become fresh; they will be left for salt.

"By the river on its bank, on one side and on the other, will grow all kinds of trees for food. Their leaves will not wither and their fruit will not fail. They will bear every month because their water flows from the sanctuary, and their fruit will be for food and their leaves for **healing**."
                        Ezekiel 47:6-12

"The princes of Judah have become like those who move a boundary; on them I will pour out My wrath like water. Ephraim is oppressed, crushed in judgment, because he was determined to follow man's command. Therefore I am like a moth to Ephraim and like rottenness to the house of Judah.

"When Ephraim saw his sickness, and Judah his wound, then Ephraim went to Assyria and sent to King Jareb. But he is unable to **heal** you, or to **cure** you of your wound. For I will be like a lion to Ephraim and like a young lion to the house of Judah. I, even I, will tear to pieces and go away, I will carry away, and there will be none to deliver.

"I will go away and return to My place until they acknowledge their guilt and seek My face; in their affliction they will earnestly seek Me."

Come, let us return to the Lord. For He has torn us, but He will **heal** us; He has wounded us, but He will bandage us. He will revive us after two days; He will raise us up on the third day, that we may live before Him.

So let us know, let us press on to know the Lord. His going forth is as certain as the dawn; and He will come to us like the rain, like the spring rain watering the earth.   *Hosea 5:10 - 6:3*

In the house of Israel I have seen a horrible thing; Ephraim's harlotry is there, Israel has defiled itself. Also, O Judah, there is a harvest appointed for you, when I restore the fortunes of My people.

When I would **heal** Israel, the iniquity of Ephraim is uncovered, and the evil deeds of Samaria, for they deal falsely; the thief enters in, bandits raid outside, and they do not consider in their hearts that I remember all their wickedness. Now their deeds are all around them; they are before My face.   *Hosea 6:10 - 7:2*

When Israel was a youth I loved him, and out of Egypt I called My son. The more they called them, the more they went from them; they kept sacrificing to the Baals and burning incense to idols.

Yet it is I who taught Ephraim to walk, I took them in My arms; but they did not know that I **healed** them. I led them with cords of a man, with bonds of love, and I became to them as one who lifts the yoke from their jaws; and I bent down and fed them.

They will not return to the land of Egypt; but Assyria - he will be their king because they refused to return to Me.
                        Hosea 11:1-5

Return, O Israel, to the Lord your God, for you have stumbled because of your iniquity. Take words with you and return to the Lord.

Say to Him, "Take away all iniquity and receive us graciously, that we may present the fruit of our lips. Assyria will not save us, we will not ride on horses; nor will we say again, 'Our god,' to the work of our hands; for in You the orphan finds mercy."

I will **heal** their apostasy, I will love them freely, for My anger has turned away from them.

I will be like the dew to Israel; he will blossom like the lily, and he will take root like the cedars of Lebanon. His shoots will sprout, and his beauty will be like the olive tree and his fragrance like the cedars of Lebanon. *Hosea 14:1-6*

The Lord said to me, "Take again for yourself the equipment of a foolish shepherd. For behold, I am going to raise up a shepherd in the land who will not care for the perishing, seek the scattered, **heal** the broken, or sustain the one standing, but will devour the flesh of the fat sheep and tear off their hoofs." *Zechariah 11:15-16*

"You will again distinguish between the righteous and the wicked, between one who serves God and one who does not serve Him.

"For behold, the day is coming, burning like a furnace; and all the arrogant and every evildoer will be chaff; and the day that is coming will set them ablaze," says the Lord of hosts, "so that it will leave them neither root nor branch.

"But for you who fear My name, the sun of righteousness will rise with **healing** in its wings; and you will go forth and skip about like calves from the stall. You will tread down the wicked, for they will be ashes under the soles of your feet on the day which I am preparing," says the Lord of hosts. *Malachi 3:18 - 4:3*

NEW TESTAMENT

Jesus was going throughout all Galilee, teaching in their synagogues and proclaiming the gospel of the kingdom, and **healing** every kind of disease and every kind of sickness among the people.

The news about Him spread throughout all Syria; and they brought to Him all who were ill, those suffering with various diseases and pains, demoniacs, epileptics, paralytics; and He **healed** them.

Large crowds followed Him from Galilee and the Decapolis and Jerusalem and Judea and from beyond the Jordan. *Matthew 4:23-25*

When Jesus came down from the mountain, large crowds followed Him.

And a leper came to Him and bowed down before Him, and said, "Lord, if You are willing, You can make me **clean**."

Jesus stretched out His hand and touched him, saying, "I am willing; be **cleansed**." And immediately his leprosy was **cleansed**.

And Jesus said to him, "See that you tell no one; but go, show yourself to the priest and present the offering that Moses commanded, as a testimony to them."

And when Jesus entered Capernaum, a centurion came to Him, imploring Him, and saying, "Lord, my servant is lying paralyzed at home, fearfully tormented."

Jesus said to him, "I will come and **heal** him."

But the centurion said, "Lord, I am not worthy for You to come under my roof, but just say the word, and my servant will be **healed**. For I also am a man under authority, with soldiers under me; and I say to this one, 'Go!' and he goes, and to another, 'Come!' and he comes, and to my slave, 'Do this!' and he does it."

Now when Jesus heard this, He marvelled and said to those who were following, "Truly I say to you, I have not found such great faith with anyone in Israel. I say to you that many will come from east and west, and recline at the table with Abraham, Isaac and Jacob in the kingdom of heaven; but the sons of the kingdom will be cast out into the outer darkness; in that place there will be weeping and gnashing of teeth."

And Jesus said to the centurion, "Go; it shall be done for you as you have believed." And the servant was **healed** that very moment.

When Jesus came into Peter's home, He saw his mother-in-law lying sick in bed with a fever. He touched her hand, and the fever left her; and she got up and waited on Him.

When evening came, they brought to Him many who were demon-possessed; and He cast out the spirits with a word, and **healed** all who were ill. This was to fulfill what was spoken through Isaiah the prophet: "He Himself took our infirmities and carried away our diseases."

Matthew 8:1-17

As Jesus was reclining at the table in the house, behold, many tax collectors and sinners came and were dining with Jesus and His disciples.

When the Pharisees saw this, they said to His disciples, "Why is your Teacher eating with the tax collectors and sinners?"

But when Jesus heard this, He said, "It is not those who are **healthy** who need a physician, but those who are sick. But go and learn what this means: 'I desire compassion, and not sacrifice,' for I did not come to call the righteous, but sinners."   *Matthew 9:10-13*

A woman who had been suffering from a hemorrhage for twelve years, came up behind Him and touched the fringe of His cloak; for she was saying to herself, "If I only touch His garment, I will **get well**."

But Jesus turning and seeing her said, "Daughter, take courage; your faith has **made** you **well**."

At once the woman was **made well**.

Matthew 9:20-22

Jesus was going through all the cities and villages, teaching in their synagogues and proclaiming the gospel of the kingdom, and **healing** every kind of disease and every kind of sickness. Seeing the people, He felt compassion for them, because they were distressed and dispirited like sheep without a shepherd.

Then He said to His disciples, "The harvest is plentiful, but the workers are few. Therefore beseech the Lord of the harvest to send out workers into His harvest."

Jesus summoned His twelve disciples and gave them authority over unclean spirits, to cast them out, and to **heal** every kind of disease and every kind of sickness.   *Matthew 9:35 - 10:1*

These twelve Jesus sent out after instructing them: "Do not go in the way of the Gentiles, and do not enter any city of the Samaritans; but rather go to the lost sheep of the house of Israel. And as you go, preach, saying, 'The kingdom of heaven is at hand.'

"**Heal** the sick, raise the dead, **cleanse** the lepers, cast out demons. Freely you received, freely give."

Matthew 10:5-8

When John, while imprisoned, heard of the works of Christ, he sent word by his disciples and said to Him, "Are You the Expected One, or shall we look for someone else?"

Jesus answered and said to them, "Go and report to John what you hear and see: the blind receive sight and the lame walk, the lepers are **cleansed** and the deaf hear, the dead are raised up, and the poor have the gospel preached to them.

"And blessed is he who does not take offense at Me."   *Matthew 11:2-6*

{Jesus} went into their synagogue. And a man was there whose hand was withered.

And they questioned Jesus, asking, "Is it lawful to **heal** on the Sabbath?" - so that they might accuse Him.

And He said to them, "What man is there among you who has a sheep, and if it falls into a pit on the Sabbath, will he not take hold of it and lift it out? How much more valuable then is a man than a sheep! So then, it is lawful to do good on the Sabbath."

Then He said to the man, "Stretch out your hand!"

He stretched it out, and it was **restored** to normal, like the other.

But the Pharisees went out and conspired against Him, as to how they might destroy Him. But Jesus, aware of this, withdrew from there.

Many followed Him, and He **healed** them all, and warned them not to tell who He was.   *Matthew 12:9-16*

A demon-possessed man who was blind and mute was brought to Jesus, and He **healed** him, so that the mute man spoke and saw.

All the crowds were amazed, and were saying, "This man cannot be the Son of David, can he?"   *Matthew 12:22-23*

I speak to them in parables; because while seeing they do not see, and while hearing they do not hear, nor do they understand. In their case the prophecy of Isaiah is being fulfilled, which says, 'You will keep on hearing, but will not understand; you will keep on seeing, but will not perceive; for the heart of this people has become dull, with their ears they scarcely hear, and they have closed their eyes, otherwise they would see with their eyes, hear with their ears, and understand with their heart and return, and I would **heal** them.'

But blessed are your eyes, because they see; and your ears, because they hear. For truly I say to you that many prophets and righteous men desired to see what you see, and did not see it, and to hear what you hear, and did not hear it.
Matthew 13:13-17

When He went ashore, He saw a large crowd, and felt compassion for them and **healed** their sick.   *Matthew 14:14*

When they had crossed over, they came to land at Gennesaret. And when the men of that place recognized Him, they sent word into all that surrounding district and brought to Him all who were sick; and they implored Him that they might just touch the fringe of His cloak; and as many as touched it were **cured**. *Matthew 14:34-36*

Jesus went away from there, and withdrew into the district of Tyre and Sidon. And a Canaanite woman from that region came out and began to cry out, saying, "Have mercy on me, Lord, Son of David; my daughter is cruelly demon-possessed." But He did not answer her a word.

And His disciples came and implored Him, saying, "Send her away, because she keeps shouting at us."

But He answered and said, "I was sent only to the lost sheep of the house of Israel."

But she came and began to bow down before Him, saying, "Lord, help me!"

And He answered and said, "It is not good to take the children's bread and throw it to the dogs."

But she said, "Yes, Lord; but even the dogs feed on the crumbs which fall from their masters' table."

Then Jesus said to her, "O woman, your faith is great; it shall be done for you as you wish." And her daughter was **healed** at once.

Departing from there, Jesus went along by the Sea of Galilee, and having gone up on the mountain, He was sitting there.

And large crowds came to Him, bringing with them those who were lame, crippled, blind, mute, and many others, and they laid them down at His feet; and He **healed** them.

So the crowd marveled as they saw the mute speaking, the crippled **restored**, and the lame walking, and the blind seeing; and they glorified the God of Israel.
Matthew 15:21-31

When they came to the crowd, a man came up to Jesus, falling on his knees before Him and saying, "Lord, have mercy on my son, for he is a lunatic and is very ill; for he often falls into the fire and often into the water. I brought him to Your disciples, and they could not **cure** him."

And Jesus answered and said, "You unbelieving and perverted generation, how long shall I be with you? How long shall I put up with you? Bring him here to Me."

And Jesus rebuked him, and the demon came out of him, and the boy was **cured** at once.

Then the disciples came to Jesus privately and said, "Why could we not drive it out?"

And He said to them, "Because of the littleness of your faith; for truly I say to you, if you have faith the size of a mustard seed, you will say to this mountain, 'Move from here to there,' and it will move; and nothing will be impossible to you. [But this kind does not go out except by prayer and fasting.]"   *Matthew 17:14-21*

When Jesus had finished these words, He departed from Galilee and came into the region of Judea beyond the Jordan; and large crowds followed Him, and He **healed** them there.   *Matthew 19:1-2*

Jesus entered the temple and drove out all those who were buying and selling in the temple, and overturned the tables of the money changers and the seats of those who were selling doves. And He said to them, "It is written, 'My house shall be called a house of prayer'; but you are making it a robbers' den."

And the blind and the lame came to Him in the temple, and He **healed** them.
Matthew 21:12-14

Simon's mother-in-law was lying sick with a fever; and immediately they spoke to Jesus about her.

And He came to her and raised her up, taking her by the hand, and the fever left her, and she waited on them.

When evening came, after the sun had set, they began bringing to Him all who were ill and those who were demon-possessed. And the whole city had gathered at the door.

And He **healed** many who were ill with various diseases, and cast out many demons; and He was not permitting the demons to speak, because they knew who He was.   *Mark 1:30-34*

He went into their synagogues throughout all Galilee, preaching and casting out the demons.

And a leper came to Jesus, beseeching Him and falling on his knees before Him, and saying, "If You are willing, You can make me **clean**."

Moved with compassion, Jesus stretched out His hand and touched him, and said to him, "I am willing; be **cleansed**." Immediately the leprosy left him and he was **cleansed**.

And He sternly warned him and immediately sent him away, and He said to him, "See that you say nothing to anyone; but go, show yourself to the priest and offer for your **cleansing** what Moses commanded, as a testimony to them."

But he went out and began to proclaim it freely and to spread the news around, to such an extent that Jesus could no longer publicly enter a city, but stayed out in unpopulated areas; and they were coming to Him from everywhere.

When He had come back to Capernaum several days afterward, it was heard that He was at home. And many were gathered together, so that there was no longer room, not even near the door; and He was speaking the word to them.

And they came, bringing to Him a paralytic, carried by four men. Being unable to get to Him because of the crowd, they removed the roof above Him; and when they had dug an opening, they let down the pallet on which the paralytic was lying.

And Jesus seeing their faith said to the paralytic, "Son, your sins are forgiven."

But some of the scribes were sitting there and reasoning in their hearts, "Why does this man speak that way? He is blaspheming; who can forgive sins but God alone?"

Immediately Jesus, aware in His spirit that they were reasoning that way within themselves, said to them, "Why are you reasoning about these things in your hearts? Which is easier, to say to the paralytic, 'Your sins are forgiven'; or to say, 'Get up, and pick up your pallet and walk'?

"But so that you may know that the Son of Man has authority on earth to forgive sins" - He said to the paralytic, "I say to you, get up, pick up your pallet and go home."

And he got up and immediately picked up the pallet and went out in the sight of everyone, so that they were all amazed and were glorifying God, saying, "We have never seen anything like this."

And He went out again by the seashore; and all the people were coming to Him, and He was teaching them.

As He passed by, He saw Levi the son of Alphaeus sitting in the tax booth, and He said to him, "Follow Me!"

And he got up and followed Him.

And it happened that He was reclining at the table in his house, and many tax collectors and sinners were dining with Jesus and His disciples; for there were many of them, and they were following Him.

When the scribes of the Pharisees saw that He was eating with the sinners and tax collectors, they said to His disciples, "Why is He eating and drinking with tax collectors and sinners?"

And hearing this, Jesus said to them, "It is not those who are **healthy** who need a physician, but those who are sick; I did not come to call the righteous, but sinners." *Mark 1:39 - 2:17*

He entered again into a synagogue; and a man was there whose hand was withered. They were watching Him to see if He would **heal** him on the Sabbath, so that they might accuse Him.

He said to the man with the withered hand, "Get up and come forward!"

And He said to them, "Is it lawful to do good or to do harm on the Sabbath, to save a life or to kill?" But they kept silent.

After looking around at them with anger, grieved at their hardness of heart, He said to the man, "Stretch out your hand."

And he stretched it out, and his hand was **restored**.

The Pharisees went out and immediately began conspiring with the Herodians against Him, as to how they might destroy Him.

Jesus withdrew to the sea with His disciples; and a great multitude from Galilee followed; and also from Judea, and from Jerusalem, and from Idumea, and beyond the Jordan, and the vicinity of Tyre and Sidon, a great number of people heard of all that He was doing and came to Him.

And He told His disciples that a boat should stand ready for Him because of the crowd, so that they would not crowd Him; for He had **healed** many, with the result that all those who had afflictions pressed around Him in order to touch Him. *Mark 3:1-10*

When Jesus had crossed over again in the boat to the other side, a large crowd gathered around Him; and so He stayed by the seashore. One of the synagogue officials named Jairus came up, and on seeing Him, fell at His feet and implored Him earnestly, saying, "My little daughter is at the point of death; please come and lay Your hands on her, so that she will **get well** and live."

And He went off with him; and a large crowd was following Him and pressing in on Him.

A woman who had had a hemorrhage for twelve years, and had endured much at the hands of many physicians, and had spent all that she had and was not helped at all, but rather had grown worse - after hearing about Jesus, she came up in the crowd behind Him and touched His cloak. For she thought, "If I just touch His garments, I will **get well**."

Immediately the flow of her blood was dried up; and she felt in her body that she was **healed** of her affliction.

Immediately Jesus, perceiving in

Himself that the power proceeding from Him had gone forth, turned around in the crowd and said, "Who touched My garments?"

And His disciples said to Him, "You see the crowd pressing in on You, and You say, 'Who touched Me?' "

And He looked around to see the woman who had done this. But the woman fearing and trembling, aware of what had happened to her, came and fell down before Him and told Him the whole truth.

And He said to her, "Daughter, your faith has **made** you **well**; go in peace and be **healed** of your affliction."

While He was still speaking, they came from the house of the synagogue official, saying, "Your daughter has died; why trouble the Teacher anymore?"

But Jesus, overhearing what was being spoken, said to the synagogue official, "Do not be afraid any longer, only believe."

And He allowed no one to accompany Him, except Peter and James and John the brother of James.

They came to the house of the synagogue official; and He saw a commotion, and people loudly weeping and wailing.

And entering in, He said to them, "Why make a commotion and weep? The child has not died, but is asleep." They began laughing at Him.

But putting them all out, He took along the child's father and mother and His own companions, and entered the room where the child was.

Taking the child by the hand, He said to her, "Talitha kum!" (which translated means, "Little girl, I say to you, get up!").

Immediately the girl got up and began to walk, for she was twelve years old. And immediately they were completely astounded.

And He gave them strict orders that no one should know about this, and He said that something should be given her to eat. *Mark 5:21-43*

When the Sabbath came, He began to teach in the synagogue; and the many listeners were astonished, saying, "Where did this man get these things, and what is this wisdom given to Him, and such miracles as these performed by His hands?

"Is not this the carpenter, the son of Mary, and brother of James and Joses and Judas and Simon? Are not His sisters here with us?" And they took offense at Him.

Jesus said to them, "A prophet is not without honor except in his hometown and among his own relatives and in his own household." And He could do no miracle there except that He laid His hands on a few sick people and **healed** them. And He wondered at their unbelief.

And He was going around the villages teaching.

And He summoned the twelve and began to send them out in pairs, and gave them authority over the unclean spirits; and He instructed them that they should take nothing for their journey, except a mere staff - no bread, no bag, no money in their belt - but to wear sandals; and He added, "Do not put on two tunics."

And He said to them, "Wherever you enter a house, stay there until you leave town. Any place that does not receive you or listen to you, as you go out from there, shake the dust off the soles of your feet for a testimony against them."

They went out and preached that men should repent. And they were casting out many demons and were anointing with oil many sick people and **healing** them. *Mark 6:2-13*

When they had crossed over they came to land at Gennesaret, and moored to the shore.

When they got out of the boat, immediately the people recognized Him, and ran about that whole country and began to carry here and there on their pallets those who were sick, to the place they heard He was.

Wherever He entered villages, or cities, or countryside, they were laying the sick in the market places, and imploring Him that they might just touch the fringe of His cloak; and as many as touched it were being **cured**. *Mark 6:53-56*

Again He went out from the region of Tyre, and came through Sidon to the Sea of Galilee, within the region of Decapolis.

They brought to Him one who was deaf and spoke with difficulty, and they implored Him to lay His hand on him.

Jesus took him aside from the crowd, by himself, and put His fingers into his ears, and after spitting, He touched his tongue with the saliva; and looking up to heaven with a deep sigh, He said to him, "Ephphatha!" that is, "Be opened!"

And his ears were opened, and the impediment of his tongue was removed, and he began speaking plainly.

Mark 7:31-35

They came to Jericho. And as He was leaving Jericho with His disciples and a large crowd, a blind beggar named Bartimaeus, the son of Timaeus, was sitting by the road.

When he heard that it was Jesus the Nazarene, he began to cry out and say, "Jesus, son of David, have mercy on me!"

Many were sternly telling him to be quiet, but he kept crying out all the more, "Son of David, have mercy on me!"

And Jesus stopped and said, "Call him here."

So they called the blind man, saying to him, "Take courage, stand up! He is calling for you."

Throwing aside his cloak, he jumped up and came to Jesus. And answering him, Jesus said, "What do you want Me to do for you?"

And the blind man said to Him, "Rabboni, I want to regain my sight!"

And Jesus said to him, "Go; your faith has **made** you **well**."

Immediately he regained his sight and began following Him on the road.

Mark 10:46-52

He said to them, "Go into all the world and preach the gospel to all creation. He who has believed and has been baptized shall be saved; but he who has disbelieved shall be condemned.

"These signs will accompany those who have believed: in My name they will cast out demons, they will speak with new tongues; they will pick up serpents, and if they drink any deadly poison, it will not hurt them; they will lay hands on the sick, and they will **recover**."

Mark 16:15-18

{Jesus} came to Nazareth, where He had been brought up; and as was His custom, He entered the synagogue on the Sabbath, and stood up to read. And the book of the prophet Isaiah was handed to Him.

And He opened the book and found the place where it was written, "The Spirit of the Lord is upon Me, because He anointed Me to preach the gospel to the poor. He has sent Me to proclaim release to the captives, and **recovery** of sight to the blind, to set free those who are oppressed, to proclaim the favorable year of the Lord."

And He closed the book, gave it back to the attendant and sat down; and the eyes of all in the synagogue were fixed on Him.

And He began to say to them, "Today this Scripture has been fulfilled in your hearing."

And all were speaking well of Him, and wondering at the gracious words which were falling from His lips; and they were saying, "Is this not Joseph's son?"

And He said to them, "No doubt you will quote this proverb to Me, 'Physician, **heal** yourself! Whatever we heard was done at Capernaum, do here in your hometown as well.' "

And He said, "Truly I say to you, no prophet is welcome in his hometown. But I say to you in truth, there were many widows in Israel in the days of Elijah, when the sky was shut up for three years and six months, when a great famine came over all the land; and yet Elijah was sent to none of them, but only to Zarephath, in the land of Sidon, to a woman who was a widow.

"And there were many lepers in Israel in the time of Elisha the prophet; and none of them was **cleansed**, but only Naaman the Syrian."

Luke 4:16-27

He got up and left the synagogue, and entered Simon's home.   Now Simon's mother-in-law was suffering from a high fever, and they asked Him to help her.

And standing over her, He rebuked the fever, and it left her; and she immediately got up and waited on them.

While the sun was setting, all those who had any who were sick with various diseases brought them to Him; and laying His hands on each one of them, He was **healing** them.

Demons also were coming out of many, shouting, "You are the Son of God!" But rebuking them, He would not allow them to speak, because they knew Him to be the Christ.   *Luke 4:38-41*

While He was in one of the cities, behold, there was a man covered with leprosy; and when he saw Jesus, he fell on his face and implored Him, saying, "Lord, if You are willing, You can make me **clean**."

And He stretched out His hand and touched him, saying, "I am willing; be **cleansed**." And immediately the leprosy left him.

And He ordered him to tell no one, "But go and show yourself to the priest and make an offering for your **cleansing**, just as Moses commanded, as a testimony to them."

But the news about Him was spreading even farther, and large crowds were gathering to hear Him and to be **healed** of their sicknesses.   But Jesus Himself would often slip away to the wilderness and pray.

One day He was teaching; and there were some Pharisees and teachers of the law sitting there, who had come from every village of Galilee and Judea and from Jerusalem; and the power of the Lord was present for Him to perform **healing**.

And some men were carrying on a bed a man who was paralyzed; and they were trying to bring him in and to set him down in front of Him. But not finding any way to bring him in because of the crowd, they went up on the roof and let him down through the tiles with his stretcher, into the middle of the crowd, in front of Jesus. Seeing their faith, He said, "Friend, your sins are forgiven you."

The scribes and the Pharisees began to reason, saying, "Who is this man who speaks blasphemies?   Who can forgive sins, but God alone?"

But Jesus, aware of their reasonings, answered and said to them, "Why are you reasoning in your hearts? Which is easier, to say, 'Your sins have been forgiven you,' or to say, 'Get up and walk'?

"But, so that you may know that the Son of Man has authority on earth to forgive sins," - He said to the paralytic - "I say to you, get up, and pick up your stretcher and go home."

Immediately he got up before them, and picked up what he had been lying on, and went home glorifying God.

They were all struck with astonishment and began glorifying God; and they were filled with fear, saying, "We have seen remarkable things today."

Luke 5:12-26

On another Sabbath He entered the synagogue and was teaching; and there was a man there whose right hand was withered.

The scribes and the Pharisees were watching Him closely to see if He **healed** on the Sabbath, so that they might find reason to accuse Him. But He knew what they were thinking, and He said to the man with the withered hand, "Get up and come forward!"

And he got up and came forward.

And Jesus said to them, "I ask you, is it lawful to do good or to do harm on the Sabbath, to save a life or to destroy it?"

After looking around at them all, He said to him, "Stretch out your hand!" And he did so; and his hand was **restored**.

But they themselves were filled with rage, and discussed together what they might do to Jesus.   *Luke 6:6-11*

Jesus came down with them and stood on a level place; and there was a large crowd of His disciples, and a great throng of people from all Judea and Jerusalem and the coastal region of Tyre and Sidon, who had come to hear Him and to be **healed** of their diseases; and those who were troubled with unclean spirits were being **cured**.

And all the people were trying to touch Him, for power was coming from Him and **healing** them all.   *Luke 6:17-19*

When He had completed all His discourse in the hearing of the people, He went to Capernaum.   And a centurion's slave, who was highly regarded by him, was sick and about to die.

When he heard about Jesus, he sent some Jewish elders asking Him to come and save the life of his slave.

When they came to Jesus, they earnestly implored Him, saying, "He is worthy for You to grant this to him; for he loves our nation and it was he who built us our synagogue."

Now Jesus started on His way with them; and when He was not far from the house, the centurion sent friends, saying to Him, "Lord, do not trouble Yourself further, for I am not worthy for You to come under my roof; for this reason I did not even consider myself worthy to come to You, but just say the word, and my servant will be **healed**.

"For I also am a man placed under authority, with soldiers under me; and I say to this one, 'Go!' and he goes, and to another, 'Come!' and he comes, and to my slave, 'Do this!' and he does it."

Now when Jesus heard this, He marveled at him, and turned and said to the crowd that was following Him, "I say to you, not even in Israel have I found such great faith."

When those who had been sent returned to the house, they found the slave in good **health**.   *Luke 7:1-10*

Summoning two of his disciples, John sent them to the Lord, saying, "Are You the Expected One, or do we look for someone else?"

When the men came to Him, they said, "John the Baptist has sent us to You, to ask, 'Are You the Expected One,

or do we look for someone else?' "

At that very time He **cured** many people of diseases and afflictions and evil spirits; and He gave sight to many who were blind.

And He answered and said to them, "Go and report to John what you have seen and heard: the blind receive sight, the lame walk, the lepers are **cleansed**, and the deaf hear, the dead are raised up, the poor have the gospel preached to them.

"Blessed is he who does not take offense at Me."   *Luke 7:19-23*

Soon afterwards, He began going around from one city and village to another, proclaiming and preaching the kingdom of God. The twelve were with Him, and also some women who had been **healed** of evil spirits and sicknesses: Mary who was called Magdalene, from whom seven demons had gone out, and Joanna the wife of Chuza, Herod's steward, and Susanna, and many others who were contributing to their support out of their private means.   *Luke 8:1-3*

They sailed to the country of the Gerasenes, which is opposite Galilee. And when He came out onto the land, He was met by a man from the city who was possessed with demons; and who had not put on any clothing for a long time, and was not living in a house, but in the tombs.

Seeing Jesus, he cried out and fell before Him, and said in a loud voice, "What business do we have with each other, Jesus, son of the Most High God? I beg You, do not torment me." For He had commanded the unclean spirit to come out of the man. For it had seized him many times; and he was bound with chains and shackles and kept under guard, and yet he would break his bonds and be driven by the demon into the desert.

And Jesus asked him, "What is your name?"

And he said, "Legion"; for many demons had entered him. They were imploring Him not to command them to go away into the abyss. Now there was a herd of many swine feeding there on the mountain; and the demons implored Him to permit them to enter the swine. And He gave them permission.

And the demons came out of the man and entered the swine; and the herd rushed down the steep bank into the lake and was drowned.

When the herdsmen saw what had happened, they ran away and reported it in the city and out in the country.

The people went out to see what had happened; and they came to Jesus, and found the man from whom the demons had gone out, sitting down at the feet of Jesus, clothed and in his right mind; and they became frightened.

Those who had seen it reported to them how the man who was demon-possessed had been **made well**. And all the people of the country of the Gerasenes and the surrounding district asked Him to leave them, for they were gripped with great fear; and He got into a boat and returned.

But the man from whom the demons had gone out was begging Him that he might accompany Him; but He sent him away, saying, "Return to your house and describe what great things God has done for you."

So he went away, proclaiming throughout the whole city what great things Jesus had done for him.

Luke 8:26-39

A woman who had a hemorrhage for twelve years, and could not be **healed** by anyone, came up behind Him and touched the fringe of His cloak, and immediately her hemorrhage stopped.

And Jesus said, "Who is the one who touched Me?"

And while they were all denying it, Peter said, "Master, the people are crowding and pressing in on You."

But Jesus said, "Someone did touch Me, for I was aware that power had gone out of Me."

When the woman saw that she had not escaped notice, she came trembling and fell down before Him, and declared in the presence of all the people the reason why she had touched Him, and how she had been immediately **healed**.

And He said to her, "Daughter, your faith has **made** you **well**; go in peace."

While He was still speaking, someone came from the house of the synagogue official, saying, "Your daughter has died; do not trouble the Teacher anymore."

But when Jesus heard this, He answered him, "Do not be afraid any longer; only believe, and she will be **made well**."

When He came to the house, He did not allow anyone to enter with Him, except Peter and John and James, and the girl's father and mother.

Now they were all weeping and lamenting for her; but He said, "Stop weeping, for she has not died, but is asleep." And they began laughing at Him, knowing that she had died.

He, however, took her by the hand and called, saying, "Child, arise!" And her spirit returned, and she got up immediately; and He gave orders for something to be given her to eat.

Her parents were amazed; but He instructed them to tell no one what had happened.

And He called the twelve together, and gave them power and authority over all the demons and to **heal** diseases. And He sent them out to proclaim the kingdom of God and to perform **healing**.

And He said to them, "Take nothing for your journey, neither a staff, nor a bag, nor bread, nor money; and do not even have two tunics apiece. Whatever house you enter, stay there until you leave that city.

"And as for those who do not receive you, as you go out from that city, shake the dust off your feet as a testimony against them."

Departing, they began going throughout the villages, preaching the gospel and **healing** everywhere.   *Luke 8:43 - 9:6*

When the apostles returned, they gave an account to Him of all that they had done.

Taking them with Him, He withdrew by Himself to a city called Bethsaida. But the crowds were aware of this and followed Him; and welcoming them, He began speaking to them about the kingdom of God and **curing** those who had need of **healing**. *Luke 9:10-11*

On the next day, when they came down from the mountain, a large crowd met Him.

And a man from the crowd shouted, saying, "Teacher, I beg You to look at my son, for he is my only boy, and a spirit seizes him, and he suddenly screams, and it throws him into a convulsion with foaming at the mouth; and only with difficulty does it leave him, mauling him as it leaves. I begged Your disciples to cast it out, and they could not."

And Jesus answered and said, "You unbelieving and perverted generation, how long shall I be with you and put up with you? Bring your son here."

While he was still approaching, the demon slammed him to the ground and threw him into a convulsion. But Jesus rebuked the unclean spirit, and **healed** the boy and gave him back to his father. And they were all amazed at the greatness of God. ~ *Luke 9:37-43*

Whatever city you enter and they receive you, eat what is set before you; and **heal** those in it who are sick, and say to them, "The kingdom of God has come near to you." *Luke 10:8-9*

He was teaching in one of the synagogues on the Sabbath. And there was a woman who for eighteen years had had a sickness caused by a spirit; and she was bent double, and could not straighten up at all.

When Jesus saw her, He called her over and said to her, "Woman, you are freed from your sickness."

And He laid His hands on her; and immediately she was made erect again and began glorifying God.

But the synagogue official, indignant because Jesus had **healed** on the Sabbath, began saying to the crowd in response, "There are six days in which work should be done; so come during them and get **healed**, and not on the Sabbath day."

But the Lord answered him and said, "You hypocrites, does not each of you on the Sabbath untie his ox or his donkey from the stall and lead him away to water him? And this woman, a daughter of Abraham as she is, whom Satan has bound for eighteen long years, should she not have been released from this bond on the Sabbath day?"

As He said this, all His opponents were being humiliated; and the entire crowd was rejoicing over all the glorious things being done by Him. *Luke 13:10-17*

Some Pharisees approached, saying to {Jesus}, "Go away, leave here, for Herod wants to kill You."

And He said to them, "Go and tell that fox, 'Behold, I cast out demons and perform **cures** today and tomorrow, and the third day I reach My goal.' " *Luke 13:31-32*

It happened that when He went into the house of one of the leaders of the Pharisees on the Sabbath to eat bread, they were watching Him closely. And there in front of Him was a man suffering from dropsy.

And Jesus answered and spoke to the lawyers and Pharisees, saying, "Is it lawful to **heal** on the Sabbath, or not?" But they kept silent.

And He took hold of him and **healed** him, and sent him away. And He said to them, "Which one of you will have a son or an ox fall into a well, and will not immediately pull him out on a Sabbath day?"

And they could make no reply to this. *Luke 14:1-6*

While {Jesus} was on the way to Jerusalem, He was passing between Samaria and Galilee.

As He entered a village, ten leprous men who stood at a distance met Him; and they raised their voices, saying, "Jesus, Master, have mercy on us!"

When He saw them, He said to them, "Go and show yourselves to the priests." And as they were going, they were **cleansed**.

Now one of them, when he saw that he had been **healed**, turned back, glorifying God with a loud voice, and he fell on his face at His feet, giving thanks to Him. And he was a Samaritan.

Then Jesus answered and said, "Were there not ten **cleansed**? But the nine - where are they? Was no one found who returned to give glory to God, except this foreigner?"

And He said to him, "Stand up and go; your faith has **made** you **well**."

Luke 17:11-19

As Jesus was approaching Jericho, a blind man was sitting by the road begging. Now hearing a crowd going by, he began to inquire what this was.

They told him that Jesus of Nazareth was passing by. And he called out, saying, "Jesus, son of David, have mercy on me!"

Those who led the way were sternly telling him to be quiet; but he kept crying out all the more, "Son of David, have mercy on me!"

And Jesus stopped and commanded that he be brought to Him; and when he came near, He questioned him, "What do you want Me to do for you?"

And he said, "Lord, I want to regain my sight!"

And Jesus said to him, "Receive your sight; your faith has **made** you **well**."

Immediately he regained his sight and began following Him, glorifying God; and when all the people saw it, they gave praise to God.   *Luke 18:35-43*

While He was still speaking, behold, a crowd came, and the one called Judas, one of the twelve, was preceding them; and he approached Jesus to kiss Him.

But Jesus said to him, "Judas, are you betraying the Son of Man with a kiss?"

When those who were around Him saw what was going to happen, they said,

"Lord, shall we strike with the sword?" And one of them struck the slave of the high priest and cut off his right ear.

But Jesus answered and said, "Stop! No more of this."

And He touched his ear and **healed** him.   *Luke 22:47-51*

{Jesus} came again to Cana of Galilee where He had made the water wine. And there was a royal official whose son was sick at Capernaum. When he heard that Jesus had come out of Judea into Galilee, he went to Him and was imploring Him to come down and **heal** his son; for he was at the point of death.

So Jesus said to him, "Unless you people see signs and wonders, you simply will not believe."

The royal official said to Him, "Sir, come down before my child dies."

Jesus said to him, "Go; your son lives."

The man believed the word that Jesus spoke to him and started off.

As he was now going down, his slaves met him, saying that his son was living. So he inquired of them the hour when he began to get better.

Then they said to him, "Yesterday at the seventh hour the fever left him." So the father knew that it was at that hour in which Jesus said to him, "Your son lives"; and he himself believed and his whole household.

This is again a second sign that Jesus performed when He had come out of Judea into Galilee.

After these things there was a feast of the Jews, and Jesus went up to Jerusalem.

Now there is in Jerusalem by the sheep gate a pool, which is called in Hebrew Bethesda, having five porticoes. In these lay a multitude of those who were sick, blind, lame, and withered, [waiting for the moving of the waters; for an angel of the Lord went down at certain seasons into the pool and stirred up the water; whoever then first, after the stirring up of the water, stepped in was **made well** from whatever disease with which he was afflicted.]

A man was there who had been ill for thirty-eight years. When Jesus saw him lying there, and knew that he had already been a long time in that condition, He said to him, "Do you wish to **get well**?"

The sick man answered Him, "Sir, I have no man to put me into the pool when the water is stirred up, but while I am coming, another steps down before me."

Jesus said to him, "Get up, pick up your pallet and walk." Immediately the man became well, and picked up his pallet and began to walk.

Now it was the Sabbath on that day. So the Jews were saying to the man who was **cured**, "It is the Sabbath, and it is not permissible for you to carry your pallet."

But he answered them, "He who **made** me **well** was the one who said to me, 'Pick up your pallet and walk.' "

They asked him, "Who is the man who said to you, 'Pick up your pallet and walk'?" But the man who was **healed** did not know who it was, for Jesus had slipped away while there was a crowd in that place.

Afterward Jesus found him in the temple and said to him, "Behold, you have become well; do not sin anymore, so that nothing worse happens to you."

The man went away, and told the Jews that it was Jesus who had **made** him **well**.

For this reason the Jews were persecuting Jesus, because He was doing these things on the Sabbath. But He answered them, "My Father is working until now, and I Myself am working."

For this reason therefore the Jews were seeking all the more to kill Him, because He not only was breaking the Sabbath, but also was calling God His own Father, making Himself equal with God.   *John 4:46 - 5:18*

After these things Jesus went away to the other side of the Sea of Galilee (or Tiberias). A large crowd followed Him, because they saw the signs which He was performing on those who were sick.
                    John 6:1-2

{Jesus said,} "For this reason Moses has given you circumcision (not because it is from Moses, but from the fathers), and on the Sabbath you circumcise a man. If a man receives circumcision on the Sabbath so that the Law of Moses will not be broken, are you angry with Me because I **made** an entire man **well** on the Sabbath?

"Do not judge according to appearance, but judge with righteous judgment."
                    John 7:22-24

Though He had performed so many signs before them, yet they were not believing in Him. This was to fulfill the word of Isaiah the prophet which he spoke: "Lord, who has believed our report? And to whom has the arm of the Lord been revealed?"

For this reason they could not believe, for Isaiah said again, "He has blinded their eyes and He hardened their heart, so that they would not see with their eyes and perceive with their heart, and be converted and I **heal** them."

These things Isaiah said because he saw His glory, and he spoke of Him.
                    John 12:37-41

Peter and John were going up to the temple at the ninth hour, the hour of prayer. And a man who had been lame from his mother's womb was being carried along, whom they used to set down every day at the gate of the temple which is called Beautiful, in order to beg alms of those who were entering the temple.

When he saw Peter and John about to go into the temple, he began asking to receive alms. But Peter, along with John, fixed his gaze on him and said, "Look at us!" And he began to give them his attention, expecting to receive something from them.

But Peter said, "I do not possess silver and gold, but what I do have I give to you: In the name of Jesus Christ the Nazarene - walk!"

And seizing him by the right hand, he raised him up; and immediately his feet and his ankles were strengthened. With a leap he stood upright and began to walk; and he entered the temple with them, walking and leaping and praising God.

And all the people saw him walking and praising God; and they were taking note of him as being the one who used to sit at the Beautiful Gate of the temple to beg alms, and they were filled with wonder and amazement at what had happened to him.

While he was clinging to Peter and John, all the people ran together to them at the so-called portico of Solomon, full of amazement.

But when Peter saw this, he replied to the people, "Men of Israel, why are you amazed at this, or why do you gaze at us, as if by our own power or piety we had made him walk? The God of Abraham, Isaac and Jacob, the God of our fathers, has glorified His servant Jesus, the one whom you delivered and disowned in the presence of Pilate, when he had decided to release Him.

"But you disowned the Holy and Righteous One and asked for a murderer to be granted to you, but put to death the Prince of life, the one whom God raised from the dead, a fact to which we are witnesses.

"And on the basis of faith in His name, it is the name of Jesus which has strengthened this man whom you see and know; and the faith which comes through Him has given him this perfect **health** in the presence of you all." *Acts 3:1-16*

Peter, filled with the Holy Spirit, said to them, "Rulers and elders of the people, if we are on trial today for a benefit done to a sick man, as to how this man has been **made well**, let it be known to all of you and to all the people of Israel, that by the name of Jesus Christ the Nazarene, whom you crucified, whom God raised from the dead - by this name this man stands here before you in good **health**.

"He is the stone which was rejected by you, the builders, but which became the chief corner stone. And there is salvation in no one else; for there is no other name under heaven that has been given among men by which we must be saved."

Now as they observed the confidence of Peter and John and understood that they were uneducated and untrained men, they were amazed, and began to recognize them as having been with Jesus. And seeing the man who had been **healed** standing with them, they had nothing to say in reply. ...

... When they had threatened them further, they let them go (finding no basis on which to punish them) on account of the people, because they were all glorifying God for what had happened; for the man was more than forty years old on whom this miracle of **healing** had been performed. *Acts 4:8-14...21-22*

"The kings of the earth took their stand, and the rulers were gathered together against the Lord and against His Christ." For truly in this city there were gathered together against Your holy servant Jesus, whom You anointed, both Herod and Pontius Pilate, along with the Gentiles and the peoples of Israel, to do whatever Your hand and Your purpose predestined to occur.

And now, Lord, take note of their threats, and grant that Your bondservants may speak Your word with all confidence, while You extend Your hand to **heal**, and signs and wonders take place through the name of Your holy servant Jesus. *Acts 4:26-30*

At the hands of the apostles many signs and wonders were taking place among the people; and they were all with one accord in Solomon's portico. But none of the rest dared to associate with them; however, the people held them in high esteem.

And all the more believers in the Lord, multitudes of men and women, were constantly added to their number, to such an extent that they even carried the sick out into the streets and laid them on cots and pallets, so that when Peter came by at least his shadow might fall on any one of them.

Also the people from the cities in the vicinity of Jerusalem were coming together, bringing people who were sick or afflicted with unclean spirits, and they were all being **healed**.

But the high priest rose up, along with all his associates (that is the sect of the Sadducees), and they were filled with jealousy. They laid hands on the apostles and put them in a public jail. *Acts 5:12-18*

Philip went down to the city of Samaria and began proclaiming Christ to them. The crowds with one accord were giving attention to what was said by Philip, as they heard and saw the signs which he was performing.

For in the case of many who had unclean spirits, they were coming out of them shouting with a loud voice; and many who had been paralyzed and lame were **healed**. So there was much rejoicing in that city. *Acts 8:5-8*

As Peter was traveling through all those regions, he came down also to the saints who lived at Lydda. There he found a man named Aeneas, who had been bedridden eight years, for he was paralyzed.

Peter said to him, "Aeneas, Jesus Christ **heals** you; get up and make your bed." Immediately he got up.

And all who lived at Lydda and Sharon saw him, and they turned to the Lord. *Acts 9:32-35*

You know of Jesus of Nazareth, how God anointed Him with the Holy Spirit and with power, and how He went about doing good and **healing** all who were oppressed by the devil, for God was with Him.

We are witnesses of all the things He did both in the land of the Jews and in Jerusalem. ~ *Acts 10:38-39*

At Lystra a man was sitting who had no strength in his feet, lame from his mother's womb, who had never walked. This man was listening to Paul as he spoke, who, when he had fixed his gaze on him and had seen that he had faith to be **made well**, said with a loud voice, "Stand upright on your feet." And he leaped up and began to walk.

When the crowds saw what Paul had done, they raised their voice, saying in the Lycaonian language, "The gods have become like men and have come down to us."

And they began calling Barnabas, Zeus, and Paul, Hermes, because he was the chief speaker. *Acts 14:8-12*

When Paul had gathered a bundle of sticks and laid them on the fire, a viper came out because of the heat and f fastened itself on his hand. When the natives saw the creature hanging from his hand, they began saying to one another, "Undoubtedly this man is a murderer, and though he has been saved from the sea, justice has not allowed him to live." However he shook the creature off into the fire and suffered no harm.

But they were expecting that he was about to swell up or suddenly fall down dead. But after they had waited a long time and had seen nothing unusual happen to him, they changed their minds and began to say that he was a god.

Now in the neighborhood of that place were lands belonging to the leading man of the island, named Publius, who welcomed us and entertained us courteously three days.

And it happened that the father of Publius was lying in bed afflicted with recurrent fever and dysentery; and Paul went in to see him and after he had prayed, he laid his hands on him and **healed** him.

After this had happened, the rest of the people on the island who had diseases were coming to him and getting **cured**. *Acts 28:3-9*

When they had set a day for Paul, they came to him at his lodging in large numbers; and he was explaining to them by solemnly testifying about the kingdom of God and trying to persuade them concerning Jesus, from both the Law of Moses and from the Prophets, from morning until evening.

Some were being persuaded by the things spoken, but others would not believe.

And when they did not agree with one another, they began leaving after Paul had spoken one parting word, "The Holy Spirit rightly spoke through Isaiah the prophet to your fathers, saying, 'Go to this people and say, "You will keep on hearing, but will not understand; and you will keep on seeing, but will not perceive; for the heart of this people has become dull, and with their ears they scarcely hear, and they have closed their eyes; otherwise they might see with their eyes, and hear with their ears, and understand with their heart and return, and I would **heal** them." '

"Therefore let it be known to you that this salvation of God has been sent to the Gentiles; they will also listen."

Acts 28:23-28

There are varieties of gifts, but the same Spirit. And there are varieties of ministries, and the same Lord. There are varieties of effects, but the same God who works all things in all persons. But to each one is given the manifestation of the Spirit for the common good.

For to one is given the word of wisdom through the Spirit, and to another the word of knowledge according to the same Spirit; to another faith by the same Spirit, and to another gifts of **healing** by the one Spirit, and to another the effecting of miracles, and to another prophecy, and to another the distinguishing of spirits, to another various kinds of tongues, and to another the interpretation of tongues.

But one and the same Spirit works all these things, distributing to each one individually just as He wills. For even as the body is one and yet has many members, and all the members of the body, though they are many, are one body, so also is Christ.   *1 Corinthians 12:4-12*

You are Christ's body, and individually members of it. And God has appointed in the church, first apostles, second prophets, third teachers, then miracles, then gifts of **healings**, helps, administrations, various kinds of tongues.

All are not apostles, are they? All are not prophets, are they? All are not teachers, are they? All are not workers of miracles, are they? All do not have gifts of **healings**, do they? All do not speak with tongues, do they? All do not interpret, do they? But earnestly desire the greater gifts. And I show you a still more excellent way.   *1 Corinthians 12:27-31*

All discipline for the moment seems not to be joyful, but sorrowful; yet to those who have been trained by it, afterwards it yields the peaceful fruit of righteousness.

Therefore, strengthen the hands that are weak and the knees that are feeble, and make straight paths for your feet, so that the limb which is lame may not be put out of joint, but rather be **healed**.

Pursue peace with all men, and the sanctification without which no one will see the Lord.   *Hebrews 12:11-14*

Is anyone among you suffering? Then he must pray.

Is anyone cheerful? He is to sing praises.

Is anyone among you sick? Then he must call for the elders of the church and they are to pray over him, anointing him with oil in the name of the Lord; and the prayer offered in faith will **restore** the one who is sick, and the Lord will raise him up, and if he has committed sins, they will be forgiven him.

Therefore, confess your sins to one another, and pray for one another so that you may be **healed**. The effective prayer of a righteous man can accomplish much.

James 5:13-16

You have been called for this purpose, since Christ also suffered for you, leaving you an example for you to follow in His steps, who committed no sin, nor was any deceit found in His mouth; and while being reviled, He did not revile in return; while suffering, He uttered no threats, but kept entrusting Himself to Him who judges righteously; and He Himself bore our sins in His body on the cross, so that we might die to sin and live to righteousness; for by His wounds you were **healed**.

1 Peter 2:21-24

Beloved, I pray that in all respects you may prosper and be in good **health**, just as your soul prospers.

3 John 2

The dragon stood on the sand of the sea-shore. Then I saw a beast coming up out of the sea, having ten horns and seven heads, and on his horns were ten diadems, and on his heads were blasphemous names.

And the beast which I saw was like a leopard, and his feet were like those of a bear, and his mouth like the mouth of a lion. And the dragon gave him his power and his throne and great authority. I saw one of his heads as if it had been slain, and his fatal wound was **healed**.

And the whole earth was amazed and followed after the beast; they worshiped the dragon because he gave his authority to the beast; and they worshiped the beast, saying, "Who is like the beast, and who is able to wage war with him?"

Revelation 13:1-4

I saw another beast coming up out of the earth; and he had two horns like a lamb and he spoke as a dragon. He exercises all the authority of the first beast in his presence. And he makes the earth and those who dwell in it to worship the first beast, whose fatal wound was **healed**.

He performs great signs, so that he even makes fire come down out of heaven to the earth in the presence of men. And he deceives those who dwell on the earth because of the signs which it was given him to perform in the presence of the beast, telling those who dwell on the earth to make an image to the beast who had the wound of the sword and has come to life.

Revelation 13:11-14

Then he showed me a river of the water of life, clear as crystal, coming from the throne of God and of the Lamb, in the middle of its street.

On either side of the river was the tree of life, bearing twelve kinds of fruit, yielding its fruit every month; and the leaves of the tree were for the **healing** of the nations.

There will no longer be any curse; and the throne of God and of the Lamb will be in it, and His bond-servants will serve Him; they will see His face, and His name will be on their foreheads.

Revelation 22:1-4

BLIND
/ BLINDNESSS / BLINDS / BLINDED
+ CANNOT SEE / NOT SEE*^

Definitions

Blind 1. Inability to see, lacking the sense of sight.

2. To make sightless temporarily or permanently, as by injuring, dazzling, or covering the eyes.

3. Inability or unwillingness to perceive or understand.

4. To make something difficult for one to see, perceive or understand; to make dark or obscure.

5. To deprive of discernment, reasoning or understanding.

6. Without the aid of indicators that are usually a source of guidance or judgment.

7. Not based on intelligence, reason, or facts; absolute and unquestioning; *blind faith.*

OLD TESTAMENT

Before they lay down, the men of the city, the men of Sodom, surrounded the house, both young and old, all the people from every quarter; and they called to Lot and said to him, "Where are the men who came to you tonight? Bring them out to us that we may have relations with them."

But Lot went out to them at the doorway, and shut the door behind him, and said, "Please, my brothers, do not act wickedly. Now behold, I have two daughters who have not had relations with man; please let me bring them out to you, and do to them whatever you like; only do nothing to these men, inasmuch as they have come under the shelter of my roof."

But they said, "Stand aside." Furthermore, they said, "This one came in as an alien, and already he is acting like a judge; now we will treat you worse than them." So they pressed hard against Lot and came near to break the door.

But the men reached out their hands and brought Lot into the house with them, and shut the door. They struck the men who were at the doorway of the house with **blindness**, both small and great, so that they wearied themselves trying to find the doorway.   *Genesis 19:4-11*

When Israel saw Joseph's sons, he said, "Who are these?"

Joseph said to his father, "They are my sons, whom God has given me here."

So he said, "Bring them to me, please, that I may bless them."

Now the eyes of Israel were so dim from age that he could **not see**. Then Joseph brought them close to him, and he kissed them and embraced them. Israel said to Joseph, "I never expected to see your face, and behold, God has let me see your children as well." *Genesis 48:8-11*

Moses said to the Lord, "Please, Lord, I have never been eloquent, neither recently nor in time past, nor since You have spoken to Your servant; for I am slow of speech and slow of tongue."

The Lord said to him, "Who has made man's mouth? Or who makes him mute or deaf, or seeing or **blind**? Is it not I, the Lord? Now then go, and I, even I, will be with your mouth, and teach you what you are to say." *Exodus 4:10-12*

You shall not take a bribe, for a bribe **blinds** the clear-sighted and subverts the cause of the just. *Exodus 23:8*

You shall not curse a deaf man, nor place a stumbling block before the **blind**, but you shall revere your God; I am the Lord. *Leviticus 19:14*

The Lord spoke to Moses, saying, "Speak to Aaron, saying, 'No man of your offspring throughout their generations who has a defect shall approach to offer the food of his God. For no one who has a defect shall approach: a **blind** man, or a lame man, or he who has a disfigured face, or any deformed limb, or a man who has a broken foot or broken hand, or a hunchback or a dwarf, or one who has a defect in his eye or eczema or scabs or crushed testicles.

'No man among the descendants of Aaron the priest who has a defect is to come near to offer the Lord's offerings by fire; since he has a defect, he shall not come near to offer the food of his God. He may eat the food of his God, both of the most holy and of the holy, only he shall not go in to the veil or come near the altar because he has a defect, so that he will not profane My sanctuaries. For I am the Lord who sanctifies them.' " *Leviticus 21:16-23*

The Lord spoke to Moses, saying, "Speak to Aaron and to his sons and to all the sons of Israel and say to them, 'Any man of the house of Israel or of the aliens in Israel who presents his offering, whether it is any of their votive or any of their freewill offerings, which they present to the Lord for a burnt offering - for you to be accepted - it must be a male without defect from the cattle, the sheep, or the goats. Whatever has a defect, you shall

not offer, for it will not be accepted for you.

'When a man offers a sacrifice of peace offerings to the Lord to fulfill a special vow or for a freewill offering, of the herd or of the flock, it must be perfect to be accepted; there shall be no defect in it. Those that are **blind** or fractured or maimed or having a running sore or eczema or scabs, you shall not offer to the Lord, nor make of them an offering by fire on the altar to the Lord.' " *Leviticus 22:17-22*

You shall consecrate to the Lord your God all the firstborn males that are born of your herd and of your flock; you shall not work with the firstborn of your herd, nor shear the firstborn of your flock. You and your household shall eat it every year before the Lord your God in the place which the Lord chooses. But if it has any defect, such as lameness or **blindness**, or any serious defect, you shall not sacrifice it to the Lord your God. *Deuteronomy 15:19-21*

You shall not distort justice; you shall not be partial, and you shall not take a bribe, for a bribe **blinds** the eyes of the wise and perverts the words of the righteous. *Deuteronomy 16:19*

Cursed is he who misleads a **blind** person on the road. And all the people shall say, "Amen." *Deuteronomy 27:18*

It shall come about, if you do not obey the Lord your God, to observe to do all His commandments and His statutes with which I charge you today, that all these curses will come upon you and overtake you: Cursed shall you be in the city, and cursed shall you be in the country. ..*<list>*..

The Lord will smite you with madness and with **blindness** and with bewilderment of heart; and you will grope at noon, as the **blind** man gropes in darkness, and you will not prosper in your ways; but you shall only be oppressed and robbed continually, with none to save you. *Deuteronomy 28:15-16 > 28-29*

Moses summoned all Israel and said to them, "You have seen all that the Lord did before your eyes in the land of Egypt to Pharaoh and all his servants and all his land; the great trials which your eyes have seen, those great signs and wonders. Yet to this day the Lord has not given you a heart to know, nor eyes to see, nor ears to hear."   *Deuteronomy 29:2-4*

When Eli heard the noise of the outcry, he said, "What does the noise of this commotion mean?" Then the man came hurriedly and told Eli. Now Eli was ninety-eight years old, and his eyes were set so that he could **not see**.   *1 Samuel 4:14-15*

Samuel said to all Israel, "Behold, I have listened to your voice in all that you said to me and I have appointed a king over you. Now, here is the king walking before you, but I am old and gray, and behold my sons are with you. And I have walked before you from my youth even to this day. Here I am; bear witness against me before the Lord and His anointed.

"Whose ox have I taken, or whose donkey have I taken, or whom have I defrauded? Whom have I oppressed, or from whose hand have I taken a bribe to **blind** my eyes with it? I will restore it to you."

They said, "You have not defrauded us or oppressed us or taken anything from any man's hand."   *1 Samuel 12:1-4*

David was thirty years old when he became king, and he reigned forty years. At Hebron he reigned over Judah seven years and six months, and in Jerusalem he reigned thirty-three years over all Israel and Judah.

Now the king and his men went to Jerusalem against the Jebusites, the inhabitants of the land, and they said to David, "You shall not come in here, but the **blind** and lame will turn you away"; thinking, "David cannot enter here." Nevertheless, David captured the stronghold of Zion, that is the city of David.

David said on that day, "Whoever would strike the Jebusites, let him reach the lame and the **blind**, who are hated by David's soul, through the water tunnel." Therefore they say, "The **blind** or the lame shall not come into the house."

So David lived in the stronghold and called it the city of David. And David built all around from the Millo and inward. David became greater and greater, for the Lord God of hosts was with him.
    2 Samuel 5:4-10

When the attendant of the man of God had risen early and gone out, behold, an army with horses and chariots was circling the city. And his servant said to him, "Alas, my master! What shall we do?" So he answered, "Do not fear, for those who are with us are more than those who are with them."

Then Elisha prayed and said, "O Lord, I pray, open his eyes that he may see." And the Lord opened the servant's eyes and he saw; and behold, the mountain was full of horses and chariots of fire all around Elisha.

When they came down to him, Elisha prayed to the Lord and said, "Strike this people with **blindness**, I pray." So He struck them with **blindness** according to the word of Elisha.

Then Elisha said to them, "This is not the way, nor is this the city; follow me and I will bring you to the man whom you seek." And he brought them to Samaria.

When they had come into Samaria, Elisha said, "O Lord, open the eyes of these men, that they may see."

So the Lord opened their eyes and they saw; and behold, they were in the midst of Samaria.   *2 Kings 6:15-20*

The city was broken into, and all the men of war fled by night by way of the gate between the two walls beside the king's garden, though the Chaldeans were all around the city. And they went by way of the Arabah.

But the army of the Chaldeans pursued the king and overtook him in the plains of Jericho and all his army was scattered from him.

Then they captured the king and

brought him to the king of Babylon at Riblah, and he passed sentence on him. They slaughtered the sons of Zedekiah before his eyes, then put out the eyes of Zedekiah and bound him with bronze fetters and brought him to Babylon.

2 Kings 25:4-7

I put on righteousness, and it clothed me; my justice was like a robe and a turban. I was eyes to the **blind** and feet to the lame. I was a father to the needy, and I investigated the case which I did not know. I broke the jaws of the wicked and snatched the prey from his teeth.

Job 29:14-17

You, O Lord, will not withhold Your compassion from me; Your lovingkindness and Your truth will continually preserve me. For evils beyond number have surrounded me; my iniquities have overtaken me, so that I am **not** able to **see**; they are more numerous than the hairs of my head, and my heart has failed me. Be pleased, O Lord, to deliver me; make haste, O Lord, to help me. *Psalm 40:11-13*

Rise up, O Judge of the earth, render recompense to the proud. How long shall the wicked, O Lord, how long shall the wicked exult? They crush Your people, O Lord, and afflict Your heritage. They slay the widow and the stranger and murder the orphans.

They have said, "The Lord does **not see**, nor does the God of Jacob pay heed."

Pay heed, you senseless among the people; and when will you understand, stupid ones? He who planted the ear, does He not hear? He who formed the eye, does He **not see**?

He who chastens the nations, will He not rebuke, even He who teaches man knowledge? *Psalm 94:2-10*

The idols of the nations are but silver and gold, the work of man's hands. They have mouths, but they do not speak; they have eyes, but they do **not see**; they have ears, but they do not hear, nor is

there any breath at all in their mouths. Those who make them will be like them, yes, everyone who trusts in them.

Psalm 135:15-18

The Lord opens the eyes of the **blind**; the Lord raises up those who are bowed down; the Lord loves the righteous; the Lord protects the strangers; He supports the fatherless and the widow, but He thwarts the way of the wicked. The Lord will reign forever, your God, O Zion, to all generations. Praise the Lord!

Psalm 146:8-10

Be delayed and wait, **blind** yourselves and be **blind**; they become drunk, but not with wine, they stagger, but not with strong drink. For the Lord has poured over you a spirit of deep sleep, He has shut your eyes, the prophets; and He has covered your heads, the seers.

The entire vision will be to you like the words of a sealed book, which when they give it to the one who is literate, saying, "Please read this," he will say, "I cannot, for it is sealed." Then the book will be given to the one who is illiterate, saying, "Please read this." And he will say, "I cannot read." *Isaiah 29:9-12*

Is it not yet just a little while before Lebanon will be turned into a fertile field, and the fertile field will be considered as a forest?

On that day the deaf will hear words of a book, and out of their gloom and darkness the eyes of the **blind** will see. The afflicted also will increase their gladness in the Lord, and the needy of mankind will rejoice in the Holy One of Israel.

Isaiah 29:17-19

Behold, a king will reign righteously and princes will rule justly. Each will be like a refuge from the wind and a shelter from the storm, like streams of water in a dry country, like the shade of a huge rock in a parched land.

Then the eyes of those who see will not be **blinded**, and the ears of those who hear will listen. The mind of the hasty will discern the truth, and the tongue of the stammerers will hasten to speak clearly.   *Isaiah 32:1-4*

Encourage the exhausted, and strengthen the feeble. Say to those with anxious heart, "Take courage, fear not. Behold, your God will come with vengeance; the recompense of God will come, but He will save you."

Then the eyes of the **blind** will be opened and the ears of the deaf will be unstopped. Then the lame will leap like a deer, and the tongue of the mute will shout for joy. For waters will break forth in the wilderness and streams in the Arabah.   *Isaiah 35:3-6*

Thus says God the Lord, who created the heavens and stretched them out, who spread out the earth and its offspring, who gives breath to the people on it and spirit to those who walk in it, "I am the Lord, I have called You in righteousness, I will also hold You by the hand and watch over You, and I will appoint You as a covenant to the people, as a light to the nations, to open **blind** eyes, to bring out prisoners from the dungeon and those who dwell in darkness from the prison."   *Isaiah 42:5-7*

The Lord will go forth like a warrior, He will arouse His zeal like a man of war. He will utter a shout, yes, He will raise a war cry. He will prevail against His enemies.

"I have kept silent for a long time, I have kept still and restrained Myself. Now like a woman in labor I will groan, I will both gasp and pant. I will lay waste the mountains and hills and wither all their vegetation; I will make the rivers into coastlands and dry up the ponds.

"I will lead the **blind** by a way they do not know, in paths they do not know I will guide them. I will make darkness into light before them and rugged places into plains. These are the things I will do, and I will not leave them undone."

They will be turned back and be utterly put to shame, who trust in idols, who say to molten images, "You are our gods."

Hear, you deaf! And look, you **blind**, that you may see. Who is **blind** but My servant, or so deaf as My messenger whom I send?

Who is so **blind** as he that is at peace with Me, or so **blind** as the servant of the Lord? You have seen many things, but you do not observe them; your ears are open, but none hears.   *Isaiah 42:13-20*

Do not fear, for I am with you; I will bring your offspring from the east, and gather you from the west. I will say to the north, "Give them up!" And to the south, "Do not hold them back."

Bring My sons from afar and My daughters from the ends of the earth, everyone who is called by My name, and whom I have created for My glory, whom I have formed, even whom I have made. Bring out the people who are **blind**, even though they have eyes, and the deaf, even though they have ears.   *Isaiah 43:5-8*

Surely he cuts cedars for himself, and takes a cypress or an oak and raises it for himself among the trees of the forest. He plants a fir, and the rain makes it grow. Then it becomes something for a man to burn, so he takes one of them and warms himself; he also makes a fire to bake bread. He also makes a god and worships it; he makes it a graven image and falls down before it.

Half of it he burns in the fire; over this half he eats meat as he roasts a roast and is satisfied. He also warms himself and says, "Aha! I am warm, I have seen the fire."

But the rest of it he makes into a god, his graven image. He falls down before it and worships; he also prays to it and says, "Deliver me, for you are my god."

They do not know, nor do they understand, for He has smeared over their eyes so that they **cannot see** and their hearts so that they cannot comprehend. No one recalls, nor is there knowledge or understanding to say, "I have burned half of it in the fire and also have baked bread over its coals. I roast meat and eat it. Then I make the rest of it into an abomination, I fall down before a block of wood!"

He feeds on ashes; a deceived heart has turned him aside. And he cannot deliver himself, nor say, "Is there not a lie in my right hand?"

Remember these things, O Jacob, and Israel, for you are My servant; I have formed you, you are My servant, O Israel, you will not be forgotten by Me.

Isaiah 44:14-21

The Lord God, who gathers the dispersed of Israel, declares, "Yet others I will gather to them, to those already gathered. All you beasts of the field, all you beasts in the forest, come to eat. His watchmen are **blind**, all of them know nothing. All of them are mute dogs unable to bark, dreamers lying down, who love to slumber; and the dogs are greedy, they are not satisfied.

"And they are shepherds who have no understanding; they have all turned to their own way, each one to his unjust gain, to the last one. 'Come,' they say, 'let us get wine, and let us drink heavily of strong drink; and tomorrow will be like today, only more so.' " *Isaiah 56:8-12*

Their feet run to evil, and they hasten to shed innocent blood; their thoughts are thoughts of iniquity, devastation and destruction are in their highways. They do not know the way of peace, and there is no justice in their tracks; they have made their paths crooked, whoever treads on them does not know peace. Therefore justice is far from us, and righteousness does not overtake us; we hope for light, but behold, darkness, for brightness, but we walk in gloom.

We grope along the wall like **blind** men, we grope like those who have no eyes; we stumble at midday as in the twilight, among those who are vigorous we are like dead men. All of us growl like bears, and moan sadly like doves; we hope for justice, but there is none, for salvation, but it is far from us.

For our transgressions are multiplied before You, and our sins testify against us; for our transgressions are with us, and we know our iniquities: transgressing and denying the Lord, and turning away from our God, speaking oppression and revolt, conceiving in and uttering from the heart lying words.

Justice is turned back, and righteousness stands far away; for truth has stumbled in the street, and uprightness cannot enter. Yes, truth is lacking; and he who turns aside from evil makes himself a prey. ~ *Isaiah 59:7-15*

"It shall come about when they say, 'Why has the Lord our God done all these things to us?' then you shall say to them, 'As you have forsaken Me and served foreign gods in your land, so you will serve strangers in a land that is not yours.'

"Declare this in the house of Jacob and proclaim it in Judah, saying, 'Now hear this, O foolish and senseless people, who have eyes but do **not see**; who have ears but do not hear. Do you not fear Me?' declares the Lord. 'Do you not tremble in My presence?

"For I have placed the sand as a boundary for the sea, an eternal decree, so it cannot cross over it. Though the waves toss, yet they cannot prevail; though they roar, yet they cannot cross over it.

'But this people has a stubborn and rebellious heart; they have turned aside and departed. They do not say in their heart, "Let us now fear the Lord our God, who gives rain in its season, both the autumn rain and the spring rain, who keeps for us the appointed weeks of the harvest."'" *Jeremiah 5:19-24*

Thus says the Lord, "Sing aloud with gladness for Jacob, and shout among the chief of the nations; proclaim, give praise and say, 'O Lord, save Your people, the remnant of Israel.'

"Behold, I am bringing them from the north country, and I will gather them from the remote parts of the earth, among them the **blind** and the lame, the woman with child and she who is in labor with child, together; a great company, they will return here. With weeping they will come, and by supplication I will lead them; I will make them walk by streams of waters, on a straight path in which they will not stumble; for I am a father to Israel, and Ephraim is My firstborn."   *Jeremiah 31:7-9*

The king of Babylon slew the sons of Zedekiah before his eyes at Riblah; the king of Babylon also slew all the nobles of Judah. He then **blinded** Zedekiah's eyes and bound him in fetters of bronze to bring him to Babylon. The Chaldeans also burned with fire the king's palace and the houses of the people, and they broke down the walls of Jerusalem.   *Jeremiah 39:6-8*

The king of Babylon slaughtered the sons of Zedekiah before his eyes, and he also slaughtered all the princes of Judah in Riblah. Then he **blinded** the eyes of Zedekiah; and the king of Babylon bound him with bronze fetters and brought him to Babylon and put him in prison until the day of his death.   *Jeremiah 52:10-11*

The Lord has accomplished His wrath, He has poured out His fierce anger; and He has kindled a fire in Zion which has consumed its foundations. The kings of the earth did not believe, nor did any of the inhabitants of the world, that the adversary and the enemy could enter the gates of Jerusalem.

Because of the sins of her prophets and the iniquities of her priests, who have shed in her midst the blood of the righteous; they wandered, **blind**, in the streets; they were defiled with blood so that no one could touch their garments. "Depart! Unclean!" they cried of themselves. "Depart, depart, do not touch!"

So they fled and wandered; men among the nations said, "They shall not continue to dwell with us." The presence of the Lord has scattered them, He will not continue to regard them; they did not honor the priests, they did not favor the elders.

Yet our eyes failed, looking for help was useless; in our watching we have watched for a nation that could not save.   *Lamentations 4:11-17*

The word of the Lord came to me, saying, "Son of man, you live in the midst of the rebellious house, who have eyes to see but do **not see**, ears to hear but do not hear; for they are a rebellious house.

"Therefore, son of man, prepare for yourself baggage for exile and go into exile by day in their sight; even go into exile from your place to another place in their sight. Perhaps they will understand though they are a rebellious house."   *Ezekiel 12:1-3*

"O king, the Most High God granted sovereignty, grandeur, glory and majesty to Nebuchadnezzar your father. Because of the grandeur which He bestowed on him, all the peoples, nations and men of every language feared and trembled before him; whomever he wished he killed and whomever he wished he spared alive; and whomever he wished he elevated and whomever he wished he humbled.

"But when his heart was lifted up and his spirit became so proud that he behaved arrogantly, he was deposed from his royal throne and his glory was taken away from him. He was also driven away from mankind, and his heart was made like that of beasts, and his dwelling place was with the wild donkeys. He was given grass to eat like cattle, and his body was drenched with the dew of heaven until he recognized that the Most High God is ruler over the realm of mankind and that He sets over it whomever He wishes.

"Yet you, his son, Belshazzar, have not humbled your heart, even though you knew all this, but you have exalted yourself against the Lord of heaven; and they have brought the vessels of His house before you, and you and your nobles, your wives and your concubines have been drinking wine from them; and you have praised the gods of silver and gold, of bronze, iron, wood and stone, which do **not see**, hear or understand. But the God in whose hand are your life-breath and your ways, you have not glorified."   *Daniel 5:18-23*

Near is the great day of the Lord, near and coming very quickly; listen, the day of the Lord! In it the warrior cries out bitterly. A day of wrath is that day, a day of trouble and distress, a day of destruction and desolation, a day of darkness and gloom, a day of clouds and thick darkness, a day of trumpet and battle cry against the fortified cities and the high corner towers.

I will bring distress on men so that they will walk like the **blind**, because they have sinned against the Lord; and their blood will be poured out like dust and their flesh like dung. *Zephaniah 1:14-17*

The Lord said to me, "Take again for yourself the equipment of a foolish shepherd. For behold, I am going to raise up a shepherd in the land who will not care for the perishing, seek the scattered, heal the broken, or sustain the one standing, but will devour the flesh of the fat sheep and tear off their hoofs.

"Woe to the worthless shepherd who leaves the flock! A sword will be on his arm and on his right eye! His arm will be totally withered and his right eye will be **blind**."

The burden of the word of the Lord concerning Israel. Thus declares the Lord who stretches out the heavens, lays the foundation of the earth, and forms the spirit of man within him, "Behold, I am going to make Jerusalem a cup that causes reeling to all the peoples around; and when the siege is against Jerusalem, it will also be against Judah.

"It will come about in that day that I will make Jerusalem a heavy stone for all the peoples; all who lift it will be severely injured. And all the nations of the earth will be gathered against it.

"In that day," declares the Lord, "I will strike every horse with bewilderment and his rider with madness. But I will watch over the house of Judah, while I strike every horse of the peoples with **blindness**.

"Then the clans of Judah will say in their hearts, 'A strong support for us are the inhabitants of Jerusalem through the Lord of hosts, their God.' "
Zechariah 11:15 - 12:5

"A son honors his father, and a servant his master. Then if I am a father, where is My honor? And if I am a master, where is My respect?" says the Lord of hosts to you, "O priests who despise My name.

"But you say, 'How have we despised Your name?' You are presenting defiled food upon My altar. But you say, 'How have we defiled You?' In that you say, 'The table of the Lord is to be despised.'

"But when you present the **blind** for sacrifice, is it not evil? And when you present the lame and sick, is it not evil? Why not offer it to your governor? Would he be pleased with you? Or would he receive you kindly?" says the Lord of hosts.

"But now will you not entreat God's favor, that He may be gracious to us? With such an offering on your part, will He receive any of you kindly?" says the Lord of hosts. *Malachi 1:6-9*

NEW TESTAMENT

As Jesus went on from there, two **blind** men followed Him, crying out, "Have mercy on us, Son of David!"

When He entered the house, the **blind** men came up to Him, and Jesus said to them, "Do you believe that I am able to do this?"

They said to Him, "Yes, Lord."

Then He touched their eyes, saying, "It shall be done to you according to your faith." And their eyes were opened. And Jesus sternly warned them: "See that no one knows about this!" But they went out and spread the news about Him throughout all that land.   *Matthew 9:27-31*

When John, while imprisoned, heard of the works of Christ, he sent word by his disciples and said to Him, "Are You the Expected One, or shall we look for someone else?"

Jesus answered and said to them, "Go and report to John what you hear and see: The **blind** receive sight and the lame walk, the lepers are cleansed and the deaf hear, the dead are raised up, and the poor have the gospel preached to them."   *Matthew 11:2-5*

A demon-possessed man who was **blind** and mute was brought to Jesus, and He healed him, so that the mute man spoke and saw. All the crowds were amazed, and were saying, "This man cannot be the Son of David, can he?"

But when the Pharisees heard this, they said, "This man casts out demons only by Beelzebul the ruler of the demons."   *Matthew 12:22-24*

The disciples came and said to Him, "Why do You speak to them in parables?" Jesus answered them, "To you it has been granted to know the mysteries of the kingdom of heaven, but to them it has not been granted. For whoever has, to him more shall be given, and he will have an abundance; but whoever does not have, even what he has shall be taken away from him.

"Therefore I speak to them in parables; because while seeing they do **not see**, and while hearing they do not hear, nor do they understand. In their case the prophecy of Isaiah is being fulfilled, which says, 'You will keep on hearing, but will not understand; you will keep on seeing, but will not perceive; for the heart of this people has become dull, with their ears they scarcely hear, and they have closed their eyes, otherwise they would see with their eyes, hear with their ears, and understand with their heart and return, and I would heal them.'

"But blessed are your eyes, because they see; and your ears, because they hear. For truly I say to you that many prophets and righteous men desired to see what you see, and did **not see** it, and to hear what you hear, and did not hear it."   *Matthew 13:10-17*

After Jesus called the crowd to Him, He said to them, "Hear and understand. It is not what enters into the mouth that defiles the man, but what proceeds out of the mouth, this defiles the man."

Then the disciples came and said to Him, "Do You know that the Pharisees were offended when they heard this statement?"

But He answered and said, "Every plant which My heavenly Father did not plant shall be uprooted. Let them alone; they are **blind** guides of the **blind**. And if a **blind** man guides a **blind** man, both will fall into a pit."   *Matthew 15:10-14*

Departing from there, Jesus went along by the Sea of Galilee, and having gone up on the mountain, He was sitting there. And large crowds came to Him, bringing with them those who were lame, crippled, **blind**, mute, and many others, and they laid them down at His feet; and He healed them. So the crowd marveled as they saw the mute speaking, the crippled restored, and the lame walking, and the **blind** seeing; and they glorified the God of Israel.   *Matthew 15:29-31*

As they were leaving Jericho, a large crowd followed Him. And two **blind** men sitting by the road, hearing that Jesus was passing by, cried out, "Lord, have mercy on us, Son of David!"

The crowd sternly told them to be quiet, but they cried out all the more, "Lord, Son of David, have mercy on us!"

And Jesus stopped and called them, and said, "What do you want Me to do for you?"

They said to Him, "Lord, we want our eyes to be opened."

Moved with compassion, Jesus touched their eyes; and immediately they regained their sight and followed Him.

Matthew 20:29-34

The **blind** and the lame came to Him in the temple, and He healed them.

Matthew 21:14

Woe to you, scribes and Pharisees, hypocrites, because you travel around on sea and land to make one proselyte; and when he becomes one, you make him twice as much a son of hell as yourselves.

Woe to you, **blind** guides, who say, "Whoever swears by the temple, that is nothing; but whoever swears by the gold of the temple is obligated."

You fools and **blind** men! Which is more important, the gold or the temple that sanctified the gold?

And, "Whoever swears by the altar, that is nothing, but whoever swears by the offering on it, he is obligated." You **blind** men, which is more important, the offering, or the altar that sanctifies the offering?

Therefore, whoever swears by the altar, swears both by the altar and by everything on it. And whoever swears by the temple, swears both by the temple and by Him who dwells within it.

And whoever swears by heaven, swears both by the throne of God and by Him who sits upon it.

Woe to you, scribes and Pharisees, hypocrites! For you tithe mint and dill and cummin, and have neglected the weightier provisions of the law: Justice and mercy and faithfulness; but these are the things you should have done without neglecting the others.

You **blind** guides, who strain out a gnat and swallow a camel! Woe to you, scribes and Pharisees, hypocrites! For you clean the outside of the cup and of the dish, but inside they are full of robbery and self-indulgence. You **blind** Pharisee, first clean the inside of the cup and of the dish, so that the outside of it may become clean also.

Woe to you, scribes and Pharisees, hypocrites! For you are like whitewashed tombs which on the outside appear beautiful, but inside they are full of dead men's bones and all uncleanness.

So you, too, outwardly appear righteous to men, but inwardly you are full of hypocrisy and lawlessness.

Matthew 23:15-28

As soon as He was alone, His followers, along with the twelve, began asking Him about the parables.

And He was saying to them, "To you has been given the mystery of the kingdom of God, but those who are outside get everything in parables, so that while seeing, they may see and not perceive, and while hearing, they may hear and not understand, otherwise they might return and be forgiven."

And He said to them, "Do you not understand this parable? How will you understand all the parables?" *Mark 4:10-13*

And He was giving orders to them, saying, "Watch out! Beware of the leaven of the Pharisees and the leaven of Herod." They began to discuss with one another the fact that they had no bread.

And Jesus, aware of this, said to them, "Why do you discuss the fact that you have no bread? Do you not yet see or understand? Do you have a hardened heart? Having eyes, do you **not see**? And having ears, do you not hear?

"And do you not remember, when I broke the five loaves for the five thousand, how many baskets full of broken pieces you picked up?"

They said to Him, "Twelve."

"When I broke the seven for the four thousand, how many large baskets full of broken pieces did you pick up?"

And they said to Him, "Seven."

And He was saying to them, "Do you not yet understand?"

And they came to Bethsaida. And they brought a **blind** man to Jesus and implored Him to touch him. Taking the **blind** man by the hand, He brought him out of the village; and after spitting on his eyes and laying His hands on him, He asked him, "Do you see anything?"

And he looked up and said, "I see men, for I see them like trees, walking around."

Then again He laid His hands on his eyes; and he looked intently and was restored, and began to see everything clearly.   *Mark 8:15-25*

Then they came to Jericho. And as He was leaving Jericho with His disciples and a large crowd, a **blind** beggar named Bartimaeus, the son of Timaeus, was sitting by the road. When he heard that it was Jesus the Nazarene, he began to cry out and say, "Jesus, Son of David, have mercy on me!"

Many were sternly telling him to be quiet, but he kept crying out all the more, "Son of David, have mercy on me!"

And Jesus stopped and said, "Call him here."

So they called the **blind** man, saying to him, "Take courage, stand up! He is calling for you." Throwing aside his cloak, he jumped up and came to Jesus.

And answering him, Jesus said, "What do you want Me to do for you?"

And the **blind** man said to Him, "Rabboni, I want to regain my sight!"

And Jesus said to him, "Go; your faith has made you well." Immediately he regained his sight and began following Him on the road.   *Mark 10:46-52*

He came to Nazareth, where He had been brought up; and as was His custom, He entered the synagogue on the Sab-

bath, and stood up to read. And the book of the prophet Isaiah was handed to Him.

And He opened the book and found the place where it was written, "The Spirit of the Lord is upon Me, because He anointed Me to preach the gospel to the poor. He has sent Me to proclaim release to the captives, and recovery of sight to the **blind**, to set free those who are oppressed, to proclaim the favorable year of the Lord."

And He closed the book, gave it back to the attendant and sat down; and the eyes of all in the synagogue were fixed on Him.

And He began to say to them, "Today this Scripture has been fulfilled in your hearing."   *Luke 4:16-21*

He also spoke a parable to them: A **blind** man cannot guide a **blind** man, can he? Will they not both fall into a pit?   *Luke 6:39*

Summoning two of his disciples, John sent them to the Lord, saying, "Are You the Expected One, or do we look for someone else?"

When the men came to Him, they said, "John the Baptist has sent us to You, to ask, 'Are You the Expected One, or do we look for someone else?' "

At that very time He cured many people of diseases and afflictions and evil spirits; and He gave sight to many who were **blind**.

And He answered and said to them, "Go and report to John what you have seen and heard: The **blind** receive sight, the lame walk, the lepers are cleansed, and the deaf hear, the dead are raised up, the poor have the gospel preached to them."   *Luke 7:19-22*

His disciples began questioning Him as to what this parable meant.

And He said, "To you it has been granted to know the mysteries of the kingdom of God, but to the rest it is in parables, so that seeing they may **not see**, and hearing they may not understand."

Luke 8:9-10

He also went on to say to the one who had invited Him, "When you give a luncheon or a dinner, do not invite your friends or your brothers or your relatives or rich neighbors, otherwise they may also invite you in return and that will be your repayment. But when you give a reception, invite the poor, the crippled, the lame, the **blind**, and you will be blessed, since they do not have the means to repay you; for you will be repaid at the resurrection of the righteous."

When one of those who were reclining at the table with Him heard this, he said to Him, "Blessed is everyone who will eat bread in the kingdom of God!"

But He said to him, "A man was giving a big dinner, and he invited many; and at the dinner hour he sent his slave to say to those who had been invited, 'Come; for everything is ready now.'

"But they all alike began to make excuses. The first one said to him, 'I have bought a piece of land and I need to go out and look at it; please consider me excused.'

Another one said, 'I have bought five yoke of oxen, and I am going to try them out; please consider me excused.'

Another one said, 'I have married a wife, and for that reason I cannot come.' And the slave came back and reported this to his master.

"Then the head of the household became angry and said to his slave, 'Go out at once into the streets and lanes of the city and bring in here the poor and crippled and **blind** and lame.'

And the slave said, 'Master, what you commanded has been done, and still there is room.'

"And the master said to the slave, 'Go out into the highways and along the hedges, and compel them to come in, so that my house may be filled. For I tell you, none of those men who were invited shall taste of my dinner.' " *Luke 14:12-24*

As Jesus was approaching Jericho, a **blind** man was sitting by the road begging. Now hearing a crowd going by, he began to inquire what this was. They told him that Jesus of Nazareth was passing by. And he called out, saying, "Jesus, Son of David, have mercy on me!"

Those who led the way were sternly telling him to be quiet; but he kept crying out all the more, "Son of David, have mercy on me!"

And Jesus stopped and commanded that he be brought to Him; and when he came near, He questioned him, "What do you want Me to do for you?"

And he said, "Lord, I want to regain my sight!"

And Jesus said to him, "Receive your sight; your faith has made you well."

Immediately he regained his sight and began following Him, glorifying God; and when all the people saw it, they gave praise to God. *Luke 18:35-43*

After these things there was a feast of the Jews, and Jesus went up to Jerusalem. Now there is in Jerusalem by the sheep gate a pool, which is called in Hebrew Bethesda, having five porticoes. In these lay a multitude of those who were sick, **blind**, lame, and withered, [waiting for the moving of the waters; for an angel of the Lord went down at certain seasons into the pool and stirred up the water; whoever then first, after the stirring up of the water, stepped in was made well from whatever disease with which he was afflicted.] *John 5:1-4*

As He passed by, He saw a man **blind** from birth. And His disciples asked Him, "Rabbi, who sinned, this man or his parents, that he would be born **blind**?"

Jesus answered, "It was neither that this man sinned, nor his parents; but it was so that the works of God might be displayed in him.

"We must work the works of Him who sent Me as long as it is day; night is coming when no one can work. While I am in the world, I am the Light of the world."

When He had said this, He spat on the ground, and made clay of the spittle, and applied the clay to his eyes, and said to him, "Go, wash in the pool of Siloam" (which is translated, Sent).

So he went away and washed, and came back seeing. Therefore the neighbors, and those who previously saw him as a beggar, were saying, "Is not this the one who used to sit and beg?" Others were saying, "This is he," still others were saying, "No, but he is like him." He kept saying, "I am the one."

So they were saying to him, "How then were your eyes opened?"

He answered, "The man who is called Jesus made clay, and anointed my eyes, and said to me, 'Go to Siloam and wash'; so I went away and washed, and I received sight."

They said to him, "Where is He?" He said, "I do not know."

They brought to the Pharisees the man who was formerly **blind**.

Now it was a Sabbath on the day when Jesus made the clay and opened his eyes. Then the Pharisees also were asking him again how he received his sight. And he said to them, "He applied clay to my eyes, and I washed, and I see."

Therefore some of the Pharisees were saying, "This man is not from God, because He does not keep the Sabbath." But others were saying, "How can a man who is a sinner perform such signs?" And there was a division among them.

So they said to the **blind** man again, "What do you say about Him, since He opened your eyes?"

And he said, "He is a prophet."

The Jews then did not believe it of him, that he had been **blind** and had received sight, until they called the parents of the very one who had received his sight, and questioned them, saying, "Is this your son, who you say was born **blind**? Then how does he now see?"

His parents answered them and said, "We know that this is our son, and that he was born **blind**; but how he now sees, we do not know; or who opened his eyes, we do not know.

"Ask him; he is of age, he will speak for himself."

His parents said this because they were afraid of the Jews; for the Jews had already agreed that if anyone confessed Him to be Christ, he was to be put out of the synagogue. For this reason his parents said, "He is of age; ask him."

So a second time they called the man who had been **blind**, and said to him, "Give glory to God; we know that this man is a sinner."

He then answered, "Whether He is a sinner, I do not know; one thing I do know, that though I was **blind**, now I see."

So they said to him, "What did He do to you? How did He open your eyes?"

He answered them, "I told you already and you did not listen; why do you want to hear it again? You do not want to become His disciples too, do you?"

They reviled him and said, "You are His disciple, but we are disciples of Moses. We know that God has spoken to Moses, but as for this man, we do not know where He is from."

The man answered and said to them, "Well, here is an amazing thing, that you do not know where He is from, and yet He opened my eyes. We know that God does not hear sinners; but if anyone is God-fearing and does His will, He hears him.

"Since the beginning of time it has never been heard that anyone opened the eyes of a person born **blind**. If this man were not from God, He could do nothing."

They answered him, "You were born entirely in sins, and are you teaching us?" So they put him out.

Jesus heard that they had put him out, and finding him, He said, "Do you believe in the Son of Man?"

He answered, "Who is He, Lord, that I may believe in Him?"

Jesus said to him, "You have both seen Him, and He is the one who is talking with you."

And he said, "Lord, I believe." And he worshiped Him.

And Jesus said, "For judgment I came into this world, so that those who do **not see** may see, and that those who see may become **blind**."

Those of the Pharisees who were

with Him heard these things and said to Him, "We are not **blind** too, are we?"

Jesus said to them, "If you were **blind**, you would have no sin; but since you say, 'We see,' your sin remains."

John 9:1-41

"For this reason the Father loves Me, because I lay down My life so that I may take it again. No one has taken it away from Me, but I lay it down on My own initiative. I have authority to lay it down, and I have authority to take it up again. This commandment I received from My Father."

A division occurred again among the Jews because of these words. Many of them were saying, "He has a demon and is insane. Why do you listen to Him?"

Others were saying, "These are not the sayings of one demon-possessed. A demon cannot open the eyes of the **blind**, can he?"

John 10:17-21

When Mary came where Jesus was, she saw Him, and fell at His feet, saying to Him, "Lord, if You had been here, my brother would not have died."

When Jesus therefore saw her weeping, and the Jews who came with her also weeping, He was deeply moved in spirit and was troubled, and said, "Where have you laid him?"

They said to Him, "Lord, come and see."

Jesus wept. So the Jews were saying, "See how He loved him!"

But some of them said, "Could not this man, who opened the eyes of the **blind** man, have kept this man also from dying?"

John 11:32-37

Jesus said to them, "For a little while longer the Light is among you. Walk while you have the Light, so that darkness will not overtake you; he who walks in the darkness does not know where he goes.

"While you have the Light, believe in the Light, so that you may become sons of Light." These things Jesus spoke, and He went away and hid Himself from them. But though He had performed so

many signs before them, yet they were not believing in Him. This was to fulfill the word of Isaiah the prophet which he spoke: "Lord, who has believed our report? And to whom has the arm of the Lord been revealed?"

For this reason they could not believe, for Isaiah said again, "He has **blinded** their eyes and He hardened their heart, so that they would **not see** with their eyes and perceive with their heart, and be converted and I heal them."

These things Isaiah said because he saw His glory, and he spoke of Him.

John 12:35-41

When they had gone through the whole island as far as Paphos, they found a magician, a Jewish false prophet whose name was Bar-Jesus, who was with the proconsul, Sergius Paulus, a man of intelligence. This man summoned Barnabas and Saul and sought to hear the word of God.

But Elymas the magician (for so his name is translated) was opposing them, seeking to turn the proconsul away from the faith.

But Saul, who was also known as Paul, filled with the Holy Spirit, fixed his gaze on him, and said, "You who are full of all deceit and fraud, you son of the devil, you enemy of all righteousness, will you not cease to make crooked the straight ways of the Lord? Now, behold, the hand of the Lord is upon you, and you will be **blind** and **not see** the sun for a time."

And immediately a mist and a darkness fell upon him, and he went about seeking those who would lead him by the hand.

Then the proconsul believed when he saw what had happened, being amazed at the teaching of the Lord. *Acts 13:6-12*

When they had set a day for Paul, they came to him at his lodging in large numbers; and he was explaining to them by solemnly testifying about the kingdom of God and trying to persuade them concerning Jesus, from both the Law of

Moses and from the Prophets, from morning until evening. Some were being persuaded by the things spoken, but others would not believe.

And when they did not agree with one another, they began leaving after Paul had spoken one parting word, "The Holy Spirit rightly spoke through Isaiah the prophet to your fathers, saying, 'Go to this people and say, "You will keep on hearing, but will not understand; and you will keep on seeing, but will not perceive; for the heart of this people has become dull, and with their ears they scarcely hear, and they have closed their eyes; otherwise they might see with their eyes, and hear with their ears, and understand with their heart and return, and I would heal them." '

"Therefore let it be known to you that this salvation of God has been sent to the Gentiles; they will also listen."

Acts 28:23-28

There is no partiality with God. For all who have sinned without the Law will also perish without the Law, and all who have sinned under the Law will be judged by the Law; for it is not the hearers of the Law who are just before God, but the doers of the Law will be justified.

For when Gentiles who do not have the Law do instinctively the things of the Law, these, not having the Law, are a law to themselves, in that they show the work of the Law written in their hearts, their conscience bearing witness and their thoughts alternately accusing or else defending them, on the day when, according to my gospel, God will judge the secrets of men through Christ Jesus.

But if you bear the name "Jew" and rely upon the Law and boast in God, and know His will and approve the things that are essential, being instructed out of the Law, and are confident that you yourself are a guide to the **blind**, a light to those who are in darkness, a corrector of the foolish, a teacher of the immature, having in the Law the embodiment of knowledge and of the truth, you, therefore, who teach another, do you not teach yourself? You who preach that one shall not steal, do you steal?

Romans 2:11-21

God has not rejected His people whom He foreknew. Or do you not know what the Scripture says in the passage about Elijah, how he pleads with God against Israel? "Lord, they have killed Your prophets, they have torn down Your altars, and I alone am left, and they are seeking my life."

But what is the divine response to him? "I have kept for Myself seven thousand men who have not bowed the knee to Baal." In the same way then, there has also come to be at the present time a remnant according to God's gracious choice. But if it is by grace, it is no longer on the basis of works, otherwise grace is no longer grace.

What then? What Israel is seeking, it has not obtained, but those who were chosen obtained it, and the rest were hardened; just as it is written, "God gave them a spirit of stupor, eyes to **see not** and ears to hear not, down to this very day."

And David says, "Let their table become a snare and a trap, and a stumbling block and a retribution to them. Let their eyes be darkened to **see not**, and bend their backs forever."

I say then, they did not stumble so as to fall, did they? May it never be! But by their transgression salvation has come to the Gentiles, to make them jealous.

Romans 11:2-11

Since we have this ministry, as we received mercy, we do not lose heart, but we have renounced the things hidden because of shame, not walking in craftiness or adulterating the word of God, but by the manifestation of truth commending ourselves to every man's conscience in the sight of God.

And even if our gospel is veiled, it is veiled to those who are perishing, in whose case the god of this world has **blinded** the minds of the unbelieving so that they might **not see** the light of the gospel of the glory of Christ, who is the image of God.

For we do not preach ourselves but Christ Jesus as Lord, and ourselves as your bond-servants for Jesus' sake. For God, who said, "Light shall shine out of darkness," is the One who has shone in our hearts to give the Light of the knowledge of the glory of God in the face of Christ. *2 Corinthians 4:1-6*

For this very reason also, applying all diligence, in your faith supply moral excellence, and in your moral excellence, knowledge, and in your knowledge, self-control, and in your self-control, perseverance, and in your perseverance, godliness, and in your godliness, brotherly kindness, and in your brotherly kindness, love.

For if these qualities are yours and are increasing, they render you neither useless nor unfruitful in the true knowledge of our Lord Jesus Christ. For he who lacks these qualities is **blind** or short-sighted, having forgotten his purification from his former sins.

Therefore, brethren, be all the more diligent to make certain about His calling and choosing you; for as long as you practice these things, you will never stumble; for in this way the entrance into the eternal kingdom of our Lord and Savior Jesus Christ will be abundantly supplied to you. *2 Peter 1:5-11*

The one who says he is in the Light and yet hates his brother is in the darkness until now. The one who loves his brother abides in the Light and there is no cause for stumbling in him. But the one who hates his brother is in the darkness and walks in the darkness, and does not know where he is going because the darkness has **blinded** his eyes. *1 John 2:9-11*

To the angel of the church in Laodicea write: The Amen, the faithful and true Witness, the Beginning of the creation of God, says this: "I know your deeds, that you are neither cold nor hot; I wish that you were cold or hot. So because you are lukewarm, and neither hot nor cold, I will spit you out of My mouth.

"Because you say, 'I am rich, and have become wealthy, and have need of nothing,' and you do not know that you are wretched and miserable and poor and **blind** and naked, I advise you to buy from Me gold refined by fire so that you may become rich, and white garments so that you may clothe yourself, and that the shame of your nakedness will not be revealed; and eye salve to anoint your eyes so that you may see.

"Those whom I love, I reprove and discipline; therefore be zealous and repent. Behold, I stand at the door and knock; if anyone hears My voice and opens the door, I will come in to him and will dine with him, and he with Me." *Revelation 3:14-20*

The rest of mankind, who were not killed by these plagues, did not repent of the works of their hands, so as not to worship demons, and the idols of gold and of silver and of brass and of stone and of wood, which **can neither see** nor hear nor walk; and they did not repent of their murders nor of their sorceries nor of their immorality nor of their thefts. *Revelation 9:20-21*

MIRACLE
/ MIRACLES / MIRACULOUS + WONDER* / WONDERS*

Definitions

Miracle 1. An extraordinary occurrence that surpasses all known natural forces or human powers and is ascribed to a divine or supernatural cause, especially to God.

2. An event or effect in the physical world that deviates from the known laws of nature.

3. A superb or surpassing example of something; a wonder; a marvel.

Miraculous 1. Of the nature of a miracle; marvelous; wonderful.

2. Performed by or involving a supernatural power or agency.

3. Having or seeming to have the power to work or effect miracles.

Wonder 1. A remarkable or extraordinary phenomenon, deed, or event; a miracle or a marvel.

2. A cause of surprise, astonishment or admiration.

OLD TESTAMENT

"Go and gather the elders of Israel together and say to them, 'The Lord, the God of your fathers, the God of Abraham, Isaac and Jacob, has appeared to me, saying, "I am indeed concerned about you and what has been done to you in Egypt.

"So I said, I will bring you up out of the affliction of Egypt to the land of the Canaanite and the Hittite and the Amorite and the Perizzite and the Hivite and the Jebusite, to a land flowing with milk and honey.

"They will pay heed to what you say; and you with the elders of Israel will come to the king of Egypt and you will say to him, 'The Lord, the God of the Hebrews, has met with us. So now, please, let us go a three days' journey into the wilderness, that we may sacrifice to the Lord our God.' But I know that the king of Egypt will not permit you to go, except under compulsion.

"So I will stretch out My hand and strike Egypt with all My **miracles** which I shall do in the midst of it; and after that he will let you go. I will grant this people favor in the sight of the Egyptians; and it shall be that when you go, you will not go empty-handed. But every woman shall ask of her neighbor and the woman who lives in her house, articles of silver and articles of gold, and clothing; and you will put them on your sons and daughters. Thus you will plunder the Egyptians.'""

Then Moses said, "What if they will not believe me or listen to what I say? For they may say, 'The Lord has not appeared to you.'"

The Lord said to him, "What is that in your hand?" And he said, "A staff."

Then He said, "Throw it on the ground." So he threw it on the ground, and it became a serpent; and Moses fled from it.

But the Lord said to Moses, "Stretch out your hand and grasp it by its tail" - so he stretched out his hand and caught it, and it became a staff in his hand - that they may believe that the Lord, the God of their fathers, the God of Abraham, the God of Isaac, and the God of Jacob, has appeared to you."

The Lord furthermore said to him, "Now put your hand into your bosom." So he put his hand into his bosom, and when he took it out, behold, his hand was leprous like snow.

Then He said, "Put your hand into your bosom again." So he put his hand into his bosom again, and when he took it out of his bosom, behold, it was restored like the rest of his flesh.

"If they will not believe you or heed the witness of the first sign, they may believe the witness of the last sign. But if they will not believe even these two signs or heed what you say, then you shall take some water from the Nile and pour it on the dry ground; and the water which you take from the Nile will become blood on the dry ground." *Exodus 3:16 - 4:9*

The Lord said to Moses, "When you go back to Egypt see that you perform before Pharaoh all the **wonders** which I have put in your power; but I will harden his heart so that he will not let the people go.

"Then you shall say to Pharaoh, 'Thus says the Lord, "Israel is My son, My firstborn. So I said to you, 'Let My son go that he may serve Me'; but you have refused to let him go. Behold, I will kill your son, your firstborn."'" *Exodus 4:21-23*

The Lord said to Moses, "See, I make you as God to Pharaoh, and your brother Aaron shall be your prophet.

"You shall speak all that I command you, and your brother Aaron shall speak to Pharaoh that he let the sons of Israel go out of his land. But I will harden Pharaoh's heart that I may multiply My signs and My **wonders** in the land of Egypt.

"When Pharaoh does not listen to you, then I will lay My hand on Egypt and bring out My hosts, My people the sons of Israel, from the land of Egypt by great judgments.

"The Egyptians shall know that I am the Lord, when I stretch out My hand on Egypt and bring out the sons of Israel from their midst."

So Moses and Aaron did it; as the Lord commanded them, thus they did. Moses was eighty years old and Aaron eighty-three, when they spoke to Pharaoh.

Now the Lord spoke to Moses and Aaron, saying, "When Pharaoh speaks to you, saying, 'Work a **miracle**,' then you shall say to Aaron, 'Take your staff and throw it down before Pharaoh, that it may become a serpent.' "

So Moses and Aaron came to Pharaoh, and thus they did just as the Lord had commanded; and Aaron threw his staff down before Pharaoh and his servants, and it became a serpent.

Then Pharaoh also called for the wise men and the sorcerers, and they also, the magicians of Egypt, did the same with their secret arts. For each one threw down his staff and they turned into serpents. But Aaron's staff swallowed up their staffs.

Yet Pharaoh's heart was hardened, and he did not listen to them, as the Lord had said. *Exodus 7:1-13*

The Lord said to Moses, "Pharaoh will not listen to you, so that My **wonders** will be multiplied in the land of Egypt."

Moses and Aaron performed all these **wonders** before Pharaoh; yet the Lord hardened Pharaoh's heart, and he did not let the sons of Israel go out of his land. *Exodus 11:9-10*

Your right hand, O Lord, is majestic in power, Your right hand, O Lord, shatters the enemy. And in the greatness of Your excellence You overthrow those who rise up against You; You send forth Your burning anger, and it consumes them as chaff. At the blast of Your nostrils the waters were piled up, the flowing waters stood up like a heap; the deeps were congealed in the heart of the sea.

The enemy said, "I will pursue, I will overtake, I will divide the spoil; my desire shall be gratified against them; I will draw out my sword, my hand will destroy them." You blew with Your wind, the sea covered them; they sank like lead in the mighty waters.

Who is like You among the gods, O Lord? Who is like You, majestic in holiness, awesome in praises, working **wonders**? You stretched out Your right hand, the earth swallowed them.

Exodus 15:6-12

God said, "Behold, I am going to make a covenant. Before all your people I will perform **miracles** which have not been produced in all the earth nor among any of the nations; and all the people among whom you live will see the working of the Lord, for it is a fearful thing that I am going to perform with you." *Exodus 34:10*

Ask now concerning the former days which were before you, since the day that God created man on the earth, and inquire from one end of the heavens to the other. Has anything been done like this great thing, or has anything been heard like it? Has any people heard the voice of God speaking from the midst of the fire, as you have heard it, and survived?

Or has a god tried to go to take for himself a nation from within another nation by trials, by signs and **wonders** and by war and by a mighty hand and by an outstretched arm and by great terrors, as the Lord your God did for you in Egypt before your eyes?

To you it was shown that you might know that the Lord, He is God; there is no other besides Him. Out of the heavens He let you hear His voice to discipline you; and on earth He let you see His great fire, and you heard His words from the midst of the fire. Because He loved your fathers, therefore He chose their descendants after them.

And He personally brought you from Egypt by His great power, driving out from before you nations greater and mightier than you, to bring you in and to give you their land for an inheritance, as it is today.

Know therefore today, and take it to your heart, that the Lord, He is God in heaven above and on the earth below; there is no other. So you shall keep His statutes and His commandments which I am giving you today, that it may go well with you and with your children after you, and that you may live long on the land which the Lord your God is giving you for all time. *Deuteronomy 4:32-40*

When your son asks you in time to come, saying, "What do the testimonies and the statutes and the judgments mean which the Lord our God commanded you?" then you shall say to your son, "We were slaves to Pharaoh in Egypt, and the Lord brought us from Egypt with a mighty hand.

"Moreover, the Lord showed great and distressing signs and **wonders** before our eyes against Egypt, Pharaoh and all his household; He brought us out from there in order to bring us in, to give us the land which He had sworn to our fathers." *Deuteronomy 6:20-23*

You shall consume all the peoples whom the Lord your God will deliver to you; your eye shall not pity them, nor shall you serve their gods, for that would be a snare to you.

If you should say in your heart, "These nations are greater than I; how can I dispossess them?" you shall not be afraid of them; you shall well remember what the Lord your God did to Pharaoh and to all Egypt: the great trials which your eyes saw and the signs and the **wonders** and the mighty hand and the outstretched arm by which the Lord your God brought you out. So shall the Lord your God do to all the peoples of whom you are afraid.

Moreover, the Lord your God will send the hornet against them, until those who are left and hide themselves from you perish. You shall not dread them, for the Lord your God is in your midst, a great and awesome God.

Deuteronomy 7:16-21

If a prophet or a dreamer of dreams arises among you and gives you a sign or a **wonder**, and the sign or the **wonder** comes true, concerning which he spoke to you, saying, "Let us go after other gods (whom you have not known) and let us serve them," you shall not listen to the words of that prophet or that dreamer of dreams; for the Lord your God is testing you to find out if you love the Lord your God with all your heart and with all your soul.

You shall follow the Lord your God and fear Him; and you shall keep His commandments, listen to His voice, serve Him, and cling to Him. *Deuteronomy 13:1-4*

The Egyptians treated us harshly and afflicted us, and imposed hard labor on us.

Then we cried to the Lord, the God of our fathers, and the Lord heard our voice and saw our affliction and our toil and our oppression; and the Lord brought us out of Egypt with a mighty hand and an outstretched arm and with great terror and with signs and **wonders**; and He has brought us to this place and has given us this land, a land flowing with milk and honey. *Deuteronomy 26:6-9*

Moses summoned all Israel and said to them, "You have seen all that the Lord did before your eyes in the land of Egypt to Pharaoh and all his servants and all his land; the great trials which your eyes have seen, those great signs and **wonders**. Yet to this day the Lord has not given you a heart to know, nor eyes to see, nor ears to hear.

"I have led you forty years in the wilderness; your clothes have not worn out on you, and your sandal has not worn out on your foot." *Deuteronomy 29:2-5*

Joshua the son of Nun was filled with the spirit of wisdom, for Moses had laid his hands on him; and the sons of Israel listened to him and did as the Lord had commanded Moses.

Since that time no prophet has risen in Israel like Moses, whom the Lord knew face to face, for all the signs and **wonders** which the Lord sent him to perform in the land of Egypt against Pharaoh, all his servants, and all his land, and for all the mighty power and for all the great terror which Moses performed in the sight of all Israel. *Deuteronomy 34:9-12*

Joshua said to the people, "Consecrate yourselves, for tomorrow the Lord will do **wonders** among you."

And Joshua spoke to the priests, saying, "Take up the ark of the covenant and cross over ahead of the people." So they took up the ark of the covenant and went ahead of the people.

Now the Lord said to Joshua, "This day I will begin to exalt you in the sight of all Israel, that they may know that just as I have been with Moses, I will be with you." *Joshua 3:5-7*

The angel of the Lord appeared to him and said to him, "The Lord is with you, O valiant warrior."

Then Gideon said to him, "O my lord, if the Lord is with us, why then has all this happened to us? And where are all His **miracles** which our fathers told us about, saying, 'Did not the Lord bring us up from Egypt?' But now the Lord has abandoned us and given us into the hand of Midian."

The Lord looked at him and said, "Go in this your strength and deliver Israel from the hand of Midian. Have I not sent you?"

He said to Him, "O Lord, how shall I deliver Israel? Behold, my family is the least in Manasseh, and I am the youngest in my father's house."

But the Lord said to him, "Surely I will be with you, and you shall defeat Midian as one man."

So Gideon said to Him, "If now I have found favor in Your sight, then show me a sign that it is You who speak with me. Please do not depart from here, until I come back to You, and bring out my offering and lay it before You."

And He said, "I will remain until you return."

Then Gideon went in and prepared a

young goat and unleavened bread from an ephah of flour; he put the meat in a basket and the broth in a pot, and brought them out to him under the oak and presented them.

The angel of God said to him, "Take the meat and the unleavened bread and lay them on this rock, and pour out the broth." And he did so.

Then the angel of the Lord put out the end of the staff that was in his hand and touched the meat and the unleavened bread; and fire sprang up from the rock and consumed the meat and the unleavened bread. Then the angel of the Lord vanished from his sight.

When Gideon saw that he was the angel of the Lord, he said, "Alas, O Lord God! For now I have seen the angel of the Lord face to face."

The Lord said to him, "Peace to you, do not fear; you shall not die."

Then Gideon built an altar there to the Lord and named it The Lord is Peace. To this day it is still in Ophrah of the Abiezrites.   *Judges 6:12-24*

Then Gideon said to God, "If You will deliver Israel through me, as You have spoken, behold, I will put a fleece of wool on the threshing floor. If there is dew on the fleece only, and it is dry on all the ground, then I will know that You will deliver Israel through me, as You have spoken." And it was so.

When he arose early the next morning and squeezed the fleece, he drained the dew from the fleece, a bowl full of water.

Then Gideon said to God, "Do not let Your anger burn against me that I may speak once more; please let me make a test once more with the fleece, let it now be dry only on the fleece, and let there be dew on all the ground."

God did so that night; for it was dry only on the fleece, and dew was on all the ground.   *Judges 6:36-40*

Manoah said to the angel of the Lord, "What is your name, so that when your words come to pass, we may honor you?"

But the angel of the Lord said to him, "Why do you ask my name, seeing it is wonderful?"

So Manoah took the young goat with the grain offering and offered it on the rock to the Lord, and He performed **wonders** while Manoah and his wife looked on. For it came about when the flame went up from the altar toward heaven, that the angel of the Lord ascended in the flame of the altar.

When Manoah and his wife saw this, they fell on their faces to the ground.
                    Judges 13:17-20

Oh give thanks to the Lord, call upon His name; make known His deeds among the peoples. Sing to Him, sing praises to Him; speak of all His **wonders**. Glory in His holy name; let the heart of those who seek the Lord be glad.

Seek the Lord and His strength; seek His face continually. Remember His wonderful deeds which He has done, His marvels and the judgments from His mouth, O seed of Israel His servant, sons of Jacob, His chosen ones!
                    1 Chronicles 16:8-13

It was Hezekiah who stopped the upper outlet of the waters of Gihon and directed them to the west side of the city of David. And Hezekiah prospered in all that he did. Even in the matter of the envoys of the rulers of Babylon, who sent to him to inquire of the **wonder** that had happened in the land, God left him alone only to test him, that He might know all that was in his heart.   *2 Chronicles 32:30-31*

You saw the affliction of our fathers in Egypt, and heard their cry by the Red Sea. Then You performed signs and **wonders** against Pharaoh, against all his servants and all the people of his land; for You knew that they acted arrogantly toward them, and made a name for Yourself as it is this day.

You divided the sea before them, so they passed through the midst of the sea on dry ground; and their pursuers You hurled into the depths, like a stone into raging waters. And with a pillar of cloud You led them by day, and with a pillar of fire by night to light for them the way in which they were to go.

Then You came down on Mount Sinai, and spoke with them from heaven; You gave them just ordinances and true laws, good statutes and commandments. So You made known to them Your holy sabbath, and laid down for them commandments, statutes and law, through Your servant Moses.

You provided bread from heaven for them for their hunger, You brought forth water from a rock for them for their thirst, and You told them to enter in order to possess the land which You swore to give them. *Nehemiah 9:9-15*

Man is born for trouble, as sparks fly upward. But as for me, I would seek God, and I would place my cause before God; who does great and unsearchable things, **wonders** without number. He gives rain on the earth and sends water on the fields, so that He sets on high those who are lowly, and those who mourn are lifted to safety.

He frustrates the plotting of the shrewd, so that their hands cannot attain success. He captures the wise by their own shrewdness, and the advice of the cunning is quickly thwarted. *Job 5:7-13*

Listen to this, O Job, stand and consider the **wonders** of God. Do you know how God establishes them, and makes the lightning of His cloud to shine? Do you know about the layers of the thick clouds, the **wonders** of one perfect in knowledge, you whose garments are hot, when the land is still because of the south wind? *Job 37:14-17*

I will give thanks to the Lord with all my heart; I will tell of all Your **wonders**. I will be glad and exult in You; I will sing praise to Your name, O Most High. *Psalm 9:1-2*

I hate the assembly of evildoers, and I will not sit with the wicked. I shall wash my hands in innocence, and I will go about

Your altar, O Lord, that I may proclaim with the voice of thanksgiving and declare all Your **wonders**. *Psalm 26:5-7*

Many, O Lord my God, are the **wonders** which You have done, and Your thoughts toward us; there is none to compare with You. If I would declare and speak of them, they would be too numerous to count. *Psalm 40:5*

Blessed be the Lord God, the God of Israel, who alone works **wonders**. And blessed be His glorious name forever; and may the whole earth be filled with His glory. Amen, and Amen. *Psalm 72:18-19*

I shall remember the deeds of the Lord; surely I will remember Your **wonders** of old. I will meditate on all Your work and muse on Your deeds. Your way, O God, is holy; what god is great like our God?

You are the God who works **wonders**; You have made known Your strength among the peoples. You have by Your power redeemed Your people, the sons of Jacob and Joseph. *Psalm 77:11-15*

The sons of Ephraim were archers equipped with bows, yet they turned back in the day of battle. They did not keep the covenant of God and refused to walk in His law; they forgot His deeds and His **miracles** that He had shown them.

He wrought **wonders** before their fathers in the land of Egypt, in the field of Zoan. He divided the sea and caused them to pass through, and He made the waters stand up like a heap. Then He led them with the cloud by day and all the night with a light of fire.

He split the rocks in the wilderness and gave them abundant drink like the ocean depths. He brought forth streams also from the rock and caused waters to run down like rivers. Yet they still continued to sin against Him, to rebel against the Most High in the desert.

And in their heart they put God to the test by asking food according to their desire.

Then they spoke against God; they said, "Can God prepare a table in the wilderness? Behold, He struck the rock so that waters gushed out, and streams were overflowing; can He give bread also? Will He provide meat for His people?"

Therefore the Lord heard and was full of wrath; and a fire was kindled against Jacob and anger also mounted against Israel, because they did not believe in God and did not trust in His salvation.

Yet He commanded the clouds above and opened the doors of heaven; He rained down manna upon them to eat and gave them food from heaven. Man did eat the bread of angels; He sent them food in abundance. He caused the east wind to blow in the heavens and by His power He directed the south wind.

When He rained meat upon them like the dust, even winged fowl like the sand of the seas, then He let them fall in the midst of their camp, round about their dwellings.

So they ate and were well filled, and their desire He gave to them.
Psalm 78:9-29

Will You perform **wonders** for the dead? Will the departed spirits rise and praise You?

Will Your lovingkindness be declared in the grave, Your faithfulness in Abaddon? Will Your **wonders** be made known in the darkness? And Your righteousness in the land of forgetfulness? *Psalm 88:10-12*

The heavens will praise Your **wonders**, O Lord; Your faithfulness also in the assembly of the holy ones. For who in the skies is comparable to the Lord? Who among the sons of the mighty is like the Lord, a God greatly feared in the council of the holy ones, and awesome above all those who are around Him? *Psalm 89:5-7*

Oh give thanks to the Lord, call upon His name; make known His deeds among the peoples. Sing to Him, sing praises to Him; speak of all His **wonders**. Glory in His holy name; let the heart of those who seek the Lord be glad.

Seek the Lord and His strength; seek His face continually. Remember His **wonders** which He has done, His marvels and the judgments uttered by His mouth, O seed of Abraham, His servant, O sons of Jacob, His chosen ones! He is the Lord our God; His judgments are in all the earth. *Psalm 105:1-7*

Israel also came into Egypt; thus Jacob sojourned in the land of Ham. And He caused His people to be very fruitful, and made them stronger than their adversaries.

He turned their heart to hate His people, to deal craftily with His servants. He sent Moses His servant, and Aaron, whom He had chosen. They performed His wondrous acts among them, and **miracles** in the land of Ham. He sent darkness and made it dark; and they did not rebel against His words.

He turned their waters into blood and caused their fish to die. Their land swarmed with frogs even in the chambers of their kings.

He spoke, and there came a swarm of flies and gnats in all their territory. He gave them hail for rain, and flaming fire in their land.

He struck down their vines also and their fig trees, and shattered the trees of their territory. He spoke, and locusts came, and young locusts, even without number, and ate up all vegetation in their land, and ate up the fruit of their ground. He also struck down all the first-born in their land, the first fruits of all their vigor.

Then He brought them out with silver and gold, and among His tribes there was not one who stumbled. Egypt was glad when they departed, for the dread of them had fallen upon them.

He spread a cloud for a covering, and fire to illumine by night. They asked, and He brought quail, and satisfied them with the bread of heaven. He opened the rock and water flowed out; it ran in the dry places like a river. *Psalm 105:23-41*

We have sinned like our fathers, we have committed iniquity, we have behaved wickedly. Our fathers in Egypt did not understand Your **wonders**; they did not remember Your abundant kindnesses, but rebelled by the sea, at the Red Sea.

Nevertheless He saved them for the sake of His name, that He might make His power known.

Thus He rebuked the Red Sea and it dried up, and He led them through the deeps, as through the wilderness. So He saved them from the hand of the one who hated them, and redeemed them from the hand of the enemy. The waters covered their adversaries; not one of them was left. Then they believed His words; they sang His praise.

They quickly forgot His works; they did not wait for His counsel, but craved intensely in the wilderness, and tempted God in the desert. So He gave them their request, but sent a wasting disease among them.

When they became envious of Moses in the camp, and of Aaron, the holy one of the Lord, the earth opened and swallowed up Dathan, and engulfed the company of Abiram. And a fire blazed up in their company; the flame consumed the wicked.

They made a calf in Horeb and worshiped a molten image. Thus they exchanged their glory for the image of an ox that eats grass.

They forgot God their Savior, who had done great things in Egypt, **wonders** in the land of Ham and awesome things by the Red Sea.

Therefore He said that He would destroy them, had not Moses His chosen one stood in the breach before Him, to turn away His wrath from destroying them. *Psalm 106:6-23*

They wandered in the wilderness in a desert region; they did not find a way to an inhabited city. They were hungry and thirsty; their soul fainted within them.

Then they cried out to the Lord in their trouble; He delivered them out of their distresses. He led them also by a straight way, to go to an inhabited city. Let them give thanks to the Lord for His lovingkindness, and for His **wonders** to the sons of men! For He has satisfied the thirsty soul, and the hungry soul He has filled with what is good.

There were those who dwelt in darkness and in the shadow of death, prisoners in misery and chains, because they had rebelled against the words of God and spurned the counsel of the Most High. Therefore He humbled their heart with labor; they stumbled and there was none to help.

Then they cried out to the Lord in their trouble; He saved them out of their distresses. He brought them out of darkness and the shadow of death and broke their bands apart. Let them give thanks to the Lord for His lovingkindness, and for His **wonders** to the sons of men! For He has shattered gates of bronze and cut bars of iron asunder.

Fools, because of their rebellious way, and because of their iniquities, were afflicted. Their soul abhorred all kinds of food, and they drew near to the gates of death.

Then they cried out to the Lord in their trouble; He saved them out of their distresses. He sent His word and healed them, and delivered them from their destructions. Let them give thanks to the Lord for His lovingkindness, and for His **wonders** to the sons of men!

Let them also offer sacrifices of thanksgiving, and tell of His works with joyful singing. Those who go down to the sea in ships, who do business on great waters; they have seen the works of the Lord, and His **wonders** in the deep. For He spoke and raised up a stormy wind, which lifted up the waves of the sea. *Psalm 107:4-25*

Let them give thanks to the Lord for His lovingkindness, and for His **wonders** to the sons of men! Let them extol Him also in the congregation of the people, and praise Him at the seat of the elders.

He changes rivers into a wilderness and springs of water into a thirsty ground;

a fruitful land into a salt waste, because of the wickedness of those who dwell in it.

Psalm 107:31-34

Great are the works of the Lord; they are studied by all who delight in them. Splendid and majestic is His work, and His righteousness endures forever. He has made His **wonders** to be remembered; the Lord is gracious and compassionate. He has given food to those who fear Him; He will remember His covenant forever.

He has made known to His people the power of His works, in giving them the heritage of the nations. The works of His hands are truth and justice; all His precepts are sure.

Psalm 111:2-7

My soul cleaves to the dust; revive me according to Your word. I have told of my ways, and You have answered me; teach me Your statutes. Make me understand the way of Your precepts, so I will meditate on Your **wonders**.

Psalm 119:25-27

For I know that the Lord is great and that our Lord is above all gods. Whatever the Lord pleases, He does, in heaven and in earth, in the seas and in all deeps. He causes the vapors to ascend from the ends of the earth; who makes lightnings for the rain, who brings forth the wind from His treasuries.

He smote the firstborn of Egypt, both of man and beast. He sent signs and **wonders** into your midst, O Egypt, upon Pharaoh and all his servants. He smote many nations and slew mighty kings, ~

Psalm 135:5-10

Give thanks to the Lord of lords, for His lovingkindness is everlasting.

To Him who alone does great **wonders**, for His lovingkindness is everlasting; to Him who made the heavens with skill, for His lovingkindness is everlasting;

to Him who spread out the earth above the waters, for His lovingkindness is everlasting;

to Him who made the great lights, for His lovingkindness is everlasting:

the sun to rule by day, for His loving-

kindness is everlasting,

the moon and stars to rule by night, for His lovingkindness is everlasting.

to Him who smote the Egyptians in their firstborn, for His lovingkindness is everlasting,

and brought Israel out from their midst, for His lovingkindness is everlasting, with a strong hand and an outstretched arm, for His lovingkindness is everlasting.

To Him who divided the Red Sea asunder, for His lovingkindness is everlasting, ~

Psalm 136:3-13

Behold, I and the children whom the Lord has given me are for signs and **wonders** in Israel from the Lord of hosts, who dwells on Mount Zion.

Isaiah 8:18

O Lord, You are my God; I will exalt You, I will give thanks to Your name; for You have worked **wonders**, plans formed long ago, with perfect faithfulness. For You have made a city into a heap, a fortified city into a ruin; a palace of strangers is a city no more, it will never be rebuilt. Therefore a strong people will glorify You; cities of ruthless nations will revere You.

Isaiah 25:1-3

Ah Lord God! Behold, You have made the heavens and the earth by Your great power and by Your outstretched arm! Nothing is too difficult for You, who shows lovingkindness to thousands, but repays the iniquity of fathers into the bosom of their children after them, O great and mighty God.

The Lord of hosts is His name; great in counsel and mighty in deed, whose eyes are open to all the ways of the sons of men, giving to everyone according to his ways and according to the fruit of his deeds; who has set signs and **wonders** in the land of Egypt, and even to this day both in Israel and among mankind; and You have made a name for Yourself, as at this day.

You brought Your people Israel out of the land of Egypt with signs and with **wonders**, and with a strong hand and

with an outstretched arm and with great terror; and gave them this land, which You swore to their forefathers to give them, a land flowing with milk and honey.
Jeremiah 32:17-22

Nebuchadnezzar the king to all the peoples, nations, and men of every language that live in all the earth: "May your peace abound! It has seemed good to me to declare the signs and **wonders** which the Most High God has done for me. How great are His signs and how mighty are His **wonders**!

"His kingdom is an everlasting kingdom and His dominion is from generation to generation."
Daniel 4:1-3

Darius the king wrote to all the peoples, nations and men of every language who were living in all the land: "May your peace abound! I make a decree that in all the dominion of my kingdom men are to fear and tremble before the God of Daniel; for He is the living God and enduring forever, and His kingdom is one which will not be destroyed, and His dominion will be forever.

"He delivers and rescues and performs signs and **wonders** in heaven and on earth, who has also delivered Daniel from the power of the lions."
Daniel 6:25-27

I, Daniel, looked and behold, two others were standing, one on this bank of the river and the other on that bank of the river.

And one said to the man dressed in linen, who was above the waters of the river, "How long will it be until the end of these **wonders**?"

I heard the man dressed in linen, who was above the waters of the river, as he raised his right hand and his left toward heaven, and swore by Him who lives forever that it would be for a time, times, and half a time; and as soon as they finish shattering the power of the holy people, all these events will be completed.
Daniel 12:5-7

It will come about after this that I will pour out My Spirit on all mankind; and your sons and daughters will prophesy, your old men will dream dreams, your young men will see visions. Even on the male and female servants I will pour out My Spirit in those days.

I will display **wonders** in the sky and on the earth, blood, fire and columns of smoke. The sun will be turned into darkness and the moon into blood before the great and awesome day of the Lord comes.

And it will come about that whoever calls on the name of the Lord will be delivered; for on Mount Zion and in Jerusalem there will be those who escape, as the Lord has said, even among the survivors whom the Lord calls.
Joel 2:28-32

As in the days when you came out from the land of Egypt, I will show you **miracles**. Nations will see and be ashamed of all their might. They will put their hand on their mouth, their ears will be deaf.
Micah 7:15-16

NEW TESTAMENT

Not everyone who says to Me, "Lord, Lord," will enter the kingdom of heaven, but he who does the will of My Father who is in heaven will enter.

Many will say to Me on that day, "Lord, Lord, did we not prophesy in Your name, and in Your name cast out demons, and in Your name perform many **miracles**?"

And then I will declare to them, "I never knew you; depart from Me, you who practice lawlessness."   *Matthew 7:21-23*

He began to denounce the cities in which most of His **miracles** were done, because they did not repent. "Woe to you, Chorazin! Woe to you, Bethsaida! For if the **miracles** had occurred in Tyre and Sidon which occurred in you, they would have repented long ago in sackcloth and ashes.

"Nevertheless I say to you, it will be more tolerable for Tyre and Sidon in the day of judgment than for you.

"And you, Capernaum, will not be exalted to heaven, will you? You will descend to Hades; for if the **miracles** had occurred in Sodom which occurred in you, it would have remained to this day.

"Nevertheless I say to you that it will be more tolerable for the land of Sodom in the day of judgment, than for you."   *Matthew 11:20-24*

When Jesus had finished these parables, He departed from there. He came to His hometown and began teaching them in their synagogue, so that they were astonished, and said, "Where did this man get this wisdom and these **miraculous** powers? Is not this the carpenter's son?

"Is not His mother called Mary, and His brothers, James and Joseph and Simon and Judas? And His sisters, are they not all with us?

"Where then did this man get all these things?" And they took offense at Him.

But Jesus said to them, "A prophet is not without honor except in his hometown

and in his own household." And He did not do many **miracles** there because of their unbelief.

At that time Herod the tetrarch heard the news about Jesus, and said to his servants, "This is John the Baptist; he has risen from the dead, and that is why **miraculous** powers are at work in him."   *Matthew 13:53 - 14:2*

There will be a great tribulation, such as has not occurred since the beginning of the world until now, nor ever will. Unless those days had been cut short, no life would have been saved; but for the sake of the elect those days will be cut short.

Then if anyone says to you, "Behold, here is the Christ," or "There He is," do not believe him. For false Christs and false prophets will arise and will show great signs and **wonders**, so as to mislead, if possible, even the elect.

Behold, I have told you in advance.   *Matthew 24:21-25*

Jesus went out from there and came into His hometown; and His disciples followed Him.

When the Sabbath came, He began to teach in the synagogue; and the many listeners were astonished, saying, "Where did this man get these things, and what is this wisdom given to Him, and such **miracles** as these performed by His hands?

"Is not this the carpenter, the son of Mary, and brother of James and Joses and Judas and Simon? Are not His sisters here with us?" And they took offense at Him.

Jesus said to them, "A prophet is not without honor except in his hometown and among his own relatives and in his own household."

And He could do no **miracle** there except that He laid His hands on a few sick people and healed them. And He wondered at their unbelief. ~   *Mark 6:1-6*

They went out and preached that men should repent. And they were casting out many demons and were anointing with oil many sick people and healing them.

And King Herod heard of it, for His name had become well known; and people were saying, "John the Baptist has risen from the dead, and that is why these **miraculous** powers are at work in Him."

But others were saying, "He is Elijah." And others were saying, "He is a prophet, like one of the prophets of old."

But when Herod heard of it, he kept saying, "John, whom I beheaded, has risen!"   *Mark 6:12-16*

When it was already quite late, His disciples came to Him and said, "This place is desolate and it is already quite late; send them away so that they may go into the surrounding countryside and villages and buy themselves something to eat."

But He answered them, "You give them something to eat!"

And they said to Him, "Shall we go and spend two hundred denarii on bread and give them something to eat?"

And He said to them, "How many loaves do you have? Go look!"

And when they found out, they said, "Five, and two fish."

And He commanded them all to sit down by groups on the green grass. They sat down in groups of hundreds and of fifties.

And He took the five loaves and the two fish, and looking up toward heaven, He blessed the food and broke the loaves and He kept giving them to the disciples to set before them; and He divided up the two fish among them all.

They all ate and were satisfied, and they picked up twelve full baskets of the broken pieces, and also of the fish. There were five thousand men who ate the loaves.

Immediately Jesus made His disciples get into the boat and go ahead of Him to the other side to Bethsaida, while He Himself was sending the crowd away. After bidding them farewell, He left for the mountain to pray.

When it was evening, the boat was in the middle of the sea, and He was alone on the land. Seeing them straining at the oars, for the wind was against them, at about the fourth watch of the night He came to them, walking on the sea; and He intended to pass by them.

But when they saw Him walking on the sea, they supposed that it was a ghost, and cried out; for they all saw Him and were terrified. But immediately He spoke with them and said to them, "Take courage; it is I, do not be afraid."

Then He got into the boat with them, and the wind stopped; and they were utterly astonished, for they had not gained any insight from the incident of the loaves, but their heart was hardened.
                          Mark 6:35-52

In those days, when there was again a large crowd and they had nothing to eat, Jesus called His disciples and said to them, "I feel compassion for the people because they have remained with Me now three days and have nothing to eat. If I send them away hungry to their homes, they will faint on the way; and some of them have come from a great distance."

And His disciples answered Him, "Where will anyone be able to find enough bread here in this desolate place to satisfy these people?"

And He was asking them, "How many loaves do you have?" And they said, "Seven."

And He directed the people to sit down on the ground; and taking the seven loaves, He gave thanks and broke them, and started giving them to His disciples to serve to them, and they served them to the people. They also had a few small fish; and after He had blessed them, He ordered these to be served as well.

And they ate and were satisfied; and they picked up seven large baskets full of what was left over of the broken pieces. About four thousand were there; and He sent them away.   *Mark 8:1-9*

John said to Him, "Teacher, we saw someone casting out demons in Your name, and we tried to prevent him because he was not following us."

But Jesus said, "Do not hinder him,

for there is no one who will perform a **miracle** in My name, and be able soon afterward to speak evil of Me. For he who is not against us is for us." *Mark 9:38-40*

Those days will be a time of tribulation such as has not occurred since the beginning of the creation which God created until now, and never will. Unless the Lord had shortened those days, no life would have been saved; but for the sake of the elect, whom He chose, He shortened the days.

And then if anyone says to you, "Behold, here is the Christ"; or, "Behold, He is there"; do not believe him; for false Christs and false prophets will arise, and will show signs and **wonders**, in order to lead astray, if possible, the elect.

"But take heed; behold, I have told you everything in advance. *Mark 13:19-23*

The day was ending, and the twelve came and said to Him, "Send the crowd away, that they may go into the surrounding villages and countryside and find lodging and get something to eat; for here we are in a desolate place."

But He said to them, "You give them something to eat!"

And they said, "We have no more than five loaves and two fish, unless perhaps we go and buy food for all these people." (For there were about five thousand men.)

And He said to His disciples, "Have them sit down to eat in groups of about fifty each." They did so, and had them all sit down.

Then He took the five loaves and the two fish, and looking up to heaven, He blessed them, and broke them, and kept giving them to the disciples to set before the people.

And they all ate and were satisfied; and the broken pieces which they had left over were picked up, twelve baskets full. *Luke 9:12-17*

Whatever city you enter and they do not receive you, go out into its streets and say, "Even the dust of your city which clings to our feet we wipe off in protest against you; yet be sure of this, that the kingdom of God has come near."

I say to you, it will be more tolerable in that day for Sodom than for that city. Woe to you, Chorazin! Woe to you, Bethsaida! For if the **miracles** had been performed in Tyre and Sidon which occurred in you, they would have repented long ago, sitting in sackcloth and ashes. But it will be more tolerable for Tyre and Sidon in the judgment than for you. *Luke 10:10-14*

As soon as He was approaching, near the descent of the Mount of Olives, the whole crowd of the disciples began to praise God joyfully with a loud voice for all the **miracles** which they had seen, shouting: "Blessed is the King who comes in the name of the Lord; peace in heaven and glory in the highest!" *Luke 19:37-38*

When He was in Jerusalem at the Passover, during the feast, many believed in His name, observing His signs which He was doing. *John 2:23*

When He came to Galilee, the Galileans received Him, having seen all the things that He did in Jerusalem at the feast; for they themselves also went to the feast. Therefore He came again to Cana of Galilee where He had made the water wine.

And there was a royal official whose son was sick at Capernaum. When he heard that Jesus had come out of Judea into Galilee, he went to Him and was imploring Him to come down and heal his son; for he was at the point of death.

So Jesus said to him, "Unless you people see signs and **wonders**, you simply will not believe." *John 4:45-48*

Jesus answered them and said, "Truly, truly, I say to you, you seek Me, not because you saw signs, but because you ate of the loaves and were filled.

"Do not work for the food which perishes, but for the food which endures to eternal life, which the Son of Man will give to you, for on Him the Father, God, has set His seal."

Therefore they said to Him, "What shall we do, so that we may work the works of God?"

Jesus answered and said to them, "This is the work of God, that you believe in Him whom He has sent."

So they said to Him, "What then do You do for a sign, so that we may see, and believe You? What work do You perform? Our fathers ate the manna in the wilderness; as it is written, 'He gave them bread out of heaven to eat.' "

Jesus then said to them, "Truly, truly, I say to you, it is not Moses who has given you the bread out of heaven, but it is My Father who gives you the true bread out of heaven. For the bread of God is that which comes down out of heaven, and gives life to the world." *John 6:26-33*

A certain man was sick, Lazarus of Bethany, the village of Mary and her sister Martha. It was the Mary who anointed the Lord with ointment, and wiped His feet with her hair, whose brother Lazarus was sick.

So the sisters sent word to Him, saying, "Lord, behold, he whom You love is sick."

But when Jesus heard this, He said, "This sickness is not to end in death, but for the glory of God, so that the Son of God may be glorified by it." …

… Jesus wept. So the Jews were saying, "See how He loved him!"

But some of them said, "Could not this man, who opened the eyes of the blind man, have kept this man also from dying?"

So Jesus, again being deeply moved within, came to the tomb. Now it was a cave, and a stone was lying against it.

Jesus said, "Remove the stone."

Martha, the sister of the deceased, said to Him, "Lord, by this time there will be a stench, for he has been dead four days."

Jesus said to her, "Did I not say to you that if you believe, you will see the glory of God?" So they removed the stone.

Then Jesus raised His eyes, and said, "Father, I thank You that You have heard Me. I knew that You always hear Me; but because of the people standing around I said it, so that they may believe that You sent Me."

When He had said these things, He cried out with a loud voice, "Lazarus, come forth."

The man who had died came forth, bound hand and foot with wrappings, and his face was wrapped around with a cloth. Jesus said to them, "Unbind him, and let him go."

Therefore many of the Jews who came to Mary, and saw what He had done, believed in Him. *John 11:1-4...35-45*

The people, who were with Him when He called Lazarus out of the tomb and raised him from the dead, continued to testify about Him. For this reason also the people went and met Him, because they heard that He had performed this sign. *John 12:17-18*

"It shall be in the last days," God says, "that I will pour forth of My Spirit on all mankind; and your sons and your daughters shall prophesy, and your young men shall see visions, and your old men shall dream dreams; even on My bondslaves, both men and women, I will in those days pour forth of My Spirit and they shall prophesy.

"And I will grant **wonders** in the sky above and signs on the earth below, blood, and fire, and vapor of smoke. The sun will be turned into darkness and the moon into blood, before the great and glorious day of the Lord shall come. And it shall be that everyone who calls on the name of the Lord will be saved."

Men of Israel, listen to these words: Jesus the Nazarene, a man attested to you by God with **miracles** and **wonders** and signs which God performed through Him in your midst, just as you yourselves know - this Man, delivered over by the predetermined plan and foreknowledge of God, you nailed to a cross by the hands of godless men and put Him to death.

But God raised Him up again, putting an end to the agony of death, since it was impossible for Him to be held in its power.

Acts 2:17-24

Those who had received his word were baptized; and that day there were added about three thousand souls. They were continually devoting themselves to the apostles' teaching and to fellowship, to the breaking of bread and to prayer.

Everyone kept feeling a sense of awe; and many **wonders** and signs were taking place through the apostles.

Acts 2:41-43

As they observed the confidence of Peter and John and understood that they were uneducated and untrained men, they were amazed, and began to recognize them as having been with Jesus. And seeing the man who had been healed standing with them, they had nothing to say in reply.

But when they had ordered them to leave the Council, they began to confer with one another, saying, "What shall we do with these men? For the fact that a noteworthy **miracle** has taken place through them is apparent to all who live in Jerusalem, and we cannot deny it.

"But so that it will not spread any further among the people, let us warn them to speak no longer to any man in this name."

And when they had summoned them, they commanded them not to speak or teach at all in the name of Jesus.

But Peter and John answered and said to them, "Whether it is right in the sight of God to give heed to you rather than to God, you be the judge; for we cannot stop speaking about what we have seen and heard."

When they had threatened them further, they let them go (finding no basis on which to punish them) on account of the people, because they were all glorifying God for what had happened; for the man was more than forty years old on whom this **miracle** of healing had been performed.

Acts 4:13-22

"Lord, take note of their threats, and grant that Your bond-servants may speak Your word with all confidence, while You extend Your hand to heal, and signs and **wonders** take place through the name of Your holy servant Jesus."

And when they had prayed, the place where they had gathered together was shaken, and they were all filled with the Holy Spirit and began to speak the word of God with boldness.

Acts 4:29-31

At the hands of the apostles many signs and **wonders** were taking place among the people; and they were all with one accord in Solomon's portico. But none of the rest dared to associate with them; however, the people held them in high esteem.

And all the more believers in the Lord, multitudes of men and women, were constantly added to their number, to such an extent that they even carried the sick out into the streets and laid them on cots and pallets, so that when Peter came by at least his shadow might fall on any one of them.

Also the people from the cities in the vicinity of Jerusalem were coming together, bringing people who were sick or afflicted with unclean spirits, and they were all being healed.

Acts 5:12-16

The word of God kept on spreading; and the number of the disciples continued to increase greatly in Jerusalem, and a great many of the priests were becoming obedient to the faith. And Stephen, full of grace and power, was performing great **wonders** and signs among the people.

Acts 6:7-8

This Moses whom they disowned, saying, "Who made you a ruler and a judge?" is the one whom God sent to be both a ruler and a deliverer with the help of the angel who appeared to him in the thorn bush.

This man led them out, performing **wonders** and signs in the land of Egypt and in the Red Sea and in the wilderness for forty years.

Acts 7:35-36

There was a man named Simon, who formerly was practicing magic in the city and astonishing the people of Samaria, claiming to be someone great; and they all, from smallest to greatest, were giving attention to him, saying, "This man is what is called the Great Power of God." And they were giving him attention because he had for a long time astonished them with his magic arts.

But when they believed Philip preaching the good news about the kingdom of God and the name of Jesus Christ, they were being baptized, men and women alike. Even Simon himself believed; and after being baptized, he continued on with Philip, and as he observed signs and great **miracles** taking place, he was constantly amazed. *Acts 8:9-13*

In Iconium they entered the synagogue of the Jews together, and spoke in such a manner that a large number of people believed, both of Jews and of Greeks. But the Jews who disbelieved stirred up the minds of the Gentiles and embittered them against the brethren.

Therefore they spent a long time there speaking boldly with reliance upon the Lord, who was testifying to the word of His grace, granting that signs and **wonders** be done by their hands.

But the people of the city were divided; and some sided with the Jews, and some with the apostles. *Acts 14:1-4*

"God, who knows the heart, testified to them giving them the Holy Spirit, just as He also did to us; and He made no distinction between us and them, cleansing their hearts by faith. Now therefore why do you put God to the test by placing upon the neck of the disciples a yoke which neither our fathers nor we have been able to bear?

"But we believe that we are saved through the grace of the Lord Jesus, in the same way as they also are."

All the people kept silent, and they were listening to Barnabas and Paul as they were relating what signs and **wonders** God had done through them among the Gentiles. *Acts 15:8-12*

God was performing extraordinary **miracles** by the hands of Paul, so that handkerchiefs or aprons were even carried from his body to the sick, and the diseases left them and the evil spirits went out. But also some of the Jewish exorcists, who went from place to place, attempted to name over those who had the evil spirits the name of the Lord Jesus, saying, "I adjure you by Jesus whom Paul preaches." *Acts 19:11-13*

In Christ Jesus I have found reason for boasting in things pertaining to God. For I will not presume to speak of anything except what Christ has accomplished through me, resulting in the obedience of the Gentiles by word and deed, in the power of signs and **wonders**, in the power of the Spirit; so that from Jerusalem and round about as far as Illyricum I have fully preached the gospel of Christ. *Romans 15:17-19*

There are varieties of gifts, but the same Spirit. And there are varieties of ministries, and the same Lord. There are varieties of effects, but the same God who works all things in all persons. But to each one is given the manifestation of the Spirit for the common good.

For to one is given the word of wisdom through the Spirit, and to another the word of knowledge according to the same Spirit; to another faith by the same Spirit, and to another gifts of healing by the one Spirit, and to another the effecting of **miracles**, and to another prophecy, and to another the distinguishing of spirits, to another various kinds of tongues, and to another the interpretation of tongues.

But one and the same Spirit works all these things, distributing to each one individually just as He wills. For by one Spirit we were all baptized into one body, whether Jews or Greeks, whether slaves or free, and we were all made to drink of one Spirit. For the body is not one member, but many. *1 Corinthians 12:4-14*

You are Christ's body, and individually members of it. And God has appointed in the church, first apostles, second prophets, third teachers, then **miracles**, then gifts of healings, helps, administrations, various kinds of tongues.

All are not apostles, are they? All are not prophets, are they? All are not teachers, are they? All are not workers of **miracles**, are they?

All do not have gifts of healings, do they? All do not speak with tongues, do they? All do not interpret, do they?

But earnestly desire the greater gifts. And I show you a still more excellent way.

1 Corinthians 12:27-31

The signs of a true apostle were performed among you with all perseverance, by signs and **wonders** and **miracles**.

2 Corinthians 12:12

You foolish Galatians, who has bewitched you, before whose eyes Jesus Christ was publicly portrayed as crucified? This is the only thing I want to find out from you: did you receive the Spirit by the works of the Law, or by hearing with faith?

Are you so foolish? Having begun by the Spirit, are you now being perfected by the flesh? Did you suffer so many things in vain - if indeed it was in vain?

So then, does He who provides you with the Spirit and works **miracles** among you, do it by the works of the Law, or by hearing with faith? Even so Abraham believed God, and it was reckoned to him as righteousness.

Therefore, be sure that it is those who are of faith who are sons of Abraham.

Galatians 3:1-7

The mystery of lawlessness is already at work; only he who now restrains will do so until he is taken out of the way.

Then that lawless one will be revealed whom the Lord will slay with the breath of His mouth and bring to an end by the appearance of His coming; that is, the one whose coming is in accord with the activity of Satan, with all power and signs and false **wonders**, and with all the deception of wickedness for those who perish, because they did not receive the love of the truth so as to be saved.

For this reason God will send upon them a deluding influence so that they will believe what is false, in order that they all may be judged who did not believe the truth, but took pleasure in wickedness.

2 Thessalonians 2:7-12

We must pay much closer attention to what we have heard, so that we do not drift away from it.

For if the word spoken through angels proved unalterable, and every transgression and disobedience received a just penalty, how will we escape if we neglect so great a salvation?

After it was at the first spoken through the Lord, it was confirmed to us by those who heard, God also testifying with them, both by signs and **wonders** and by various **miracles** and by gifts of the Holy Spirit according to His own will.

Hebrews 2:1-4

PRAY
/ PRAYS / PRAYING / PRAYED / PRAYER(S)

Definitions

Pray 1. To offer devout petition, supplication, praise or thanks, etc. to God or an object of worship; to entreat; to implore.

2. To offer a prayer; to engage in prayer.

3. To make earnest petition or entreaty to a person, deity or God.

4. To make entreaty for; to invite; to appeal; to crave.

Prayer 1. The act or practice of praying to God or an object of worship.

2. A spiritual communion with God or an object of worship, as in supplication, praise, thanksgiving, or adoration.

3. A devout, solemn and humble petition to God or an object of worship.

4. An earnest request to someone for something; an entreaty; a petition.

5. A formula or sequence of words used when praying.

6. Something prayed for.

OLD TESTAMENT

Abraham journeyed from there toward the land of the Negev, and settled between Kadesh and Shur; then he sojourned in Gerar. Abraham said of Sarah his wife, "She is my sister." So Abimelech king of Gerar sent and took Sarah.

But God came to Abimelech in a dream of the night, and said to him, "Behold, you are a dead man because of the woman whom you have taken, for she is married."

Now Abimelech had not come near her; and he said, "Lord, will You slay a nation, even though blameless? Did he not himself say to me, 'She is my sister'? And she herself said, 'He is my brother.' In the integrity of my heart and the innocence of my hands I have done this."

Then God said to him in the dream, "Yes, I know that in the integrity of your heart you have done this, and I also kept you from sinning against Me; therefore I did not let you touch her. Now therefore, restore the man's wife, for he is a proph-et, and he will **pray** for you and you will live.

But if you do not restore her, know that you shall surely die, you and all who are yours." ...

... Abimelech then took sheep and oxen and male and female servants, and gave them to Abraham, and restored his wife Sarah to him.

Abimelech said, "Behold, my land is before you; settle wherever you please."

To Sarah he said, "Behold, I have given your brother a thousand pieces of silver; behold, it is your vindication before all who are with you, and before all men you are cleared."

Abraham **prayed** to God, and God healed Abimelech and his wife and his maids, so that they bore children. For the Lord had closed fast all the wombs of the household of Abimelech because of Sarah, Abraham's wife.

Genesis 20:1-7...14-18

These are the records of the generations of Isaac, Abraham's son: Abraham became the father of Isaac; and Isaac was forty years old when he took Rebekah, the daughter of Bethuel the Aramean of Paddan-aram, the sister of Laban the Aramean, to be his wife.

Isaac **prayed** to the Lord on behalf of his wife, because she was barren; and the Lord answered him and Rebekah his wife conceived. But the children struggled together within her; and she said, "If it is so, why then am I this way?" So she went to inquire of the Lord.

The Lord said to her, "Two nations are in your womb; and two peoples will be separated from your body; and one people shall be stronger than the other; and the older shall serve the younger."

When her days to be delivered were fulfilled, behold, there were twins in her womb.   *Genesis 25:19-24*

Jacob said, "O God of my father Abraham and God of my father Isaac, O Lord, who said to me, 'Return to your country and to your relatives, and I will prosper you,' I am unworthy of all the lovingkindness and of all the faithfulness which You have shown to Your servant; for with my staff only I crossed this Jordan, and now I have become two companies.

"Deliver me, I **pray**, from the hand of my brother, from the hand of Esau; for I fear him, that he will come and attack me and the mothers with the children. For Thou didst say, 'I will surely prosper you, and make your descendants as the sand of the sea, which cannot be numbered for multitude.' "   *Genesis 32:9-12*

When all the people saw the pillar of cloud standing at the entrance of the tent, all the people would arise and worship, each at the entrance of his tent.

Then Moses said to the Lord, "See, You say to me, 'Bring up this people!' But You Yourself have not let me know whom You will send with me.

"Moreover, You have said, 'I have known you by name, and you have also found favor in My sight.'

"Now therefore, I **pray** You, if I have found favor in Your sight, let me know Your ways that I may know You, so that I

may find favor in Your sight. Consider too, that this nation is Your people."

And He said, "My presence shall go with you, and I will give you rest."

Then he said to Him, "If Your presence does not go with us, do not lead us up from here. For how then can it be known that I have found favor in Your sight, I and Your people? Is it not by Your going with us, so that we, I and Your people, may be distinguished from all the other people who are upon the face of the earth?"

The Lord said to Moses, "I will also do this thing of which you have spoken; for you have found favor in My sight and I have known you by name."

Then Moses said, "I **pray** You, show me Your glory!"

And He said, "I Myself will make all My goodness pass before you, and will proclaim the name of the Lord before you; and I will be gracious to whom I will be gracious, and will show compassion on whom I will show compassion."

But He said, "You cannot see My face, for no man can see Me and live!"
                    Exodus 33:10-20

The Lord descended in the cloud and stood there with him as he called upon the name of the Lord.

Then the Lord passed by in front of him and proclaimed, "The Lord, the Lord God, compassionate and gracious, slow to anger, and abounding in lovingkindness and truth; who keeps lovingkindness for thousands, who forgives iniquity, transgression and sin; yet He will by no means leave the guilty unpunished, visiting the iniquity of fathers on the children and on the grandchildren to the third and fourth generations."

Moses made haste to bow low toward the earth and worship. He said, "If now I have found favor in Your sight, O Lord, I **pray**, let the Lord go along in our midst, even though the people are so obstinate, and pardon our iniquity and our sin, and take us as Your own possession."

Then God said, "Behold, I am going to make a covenant. Before all your people I will perform miracles which have not been produced in all the earth nor among any of the nations; and all the people among whom you live will see the working of the Lord, for it is a fearful thing that I am going to perform with you.

"Be sure to observe what I am commanding you this day: Behold, I am going to drive out the Amorite before you, and the Canaanite, the Hittite, the Perizzite, the Hivite and the Jebusite." *Exodus 34:5-11*

The people became like those who complain of adversity in the hearing of the Lord; and when the Lord heard it, His anger was kindled, and the fire of the Lord burned among them and consumed some of the outskirts of the camp.

The people therefore cried out to Moses, and Moses **prayed** to the Lord and the fire died out. So the name of that place was called Taberah, because the fire of the Lord burned among them.
Numbers 11:1-3

The anger of the Lord burned against them and He departed. But when the cloud had withdrawn from over the tent, behold, Miriam was leprous, as white as snow. As Aaron turned toward Miriam, behold, she was leprous.

Then Aaron said to Moses, "Oh, my lord, I beg you, do not account this sin to us, in which we have acted foolishly and in which we have sinned. Oh, do not let her be like one dead, whose flesh is half eaten away when he comes from his mother's womb!"

Moses cried out to the Lord, saying, "O God, heal her, I **pray**!" But the Lord said to Moses, "If her father had but spit in her face, would she not bear her shame for seven days? Let her be shut up for seven days outside the camp, and afterward she may be received again."

So Miriam was shut up outside the camp for seven days, and the people did not move on until Miriam was received again.
Numbers 12:9-15

If You slay this people as one man, then the nations who have heard of Your fame will say, "Because the Lord could not bring this people into the land which He promised them by oath, therefore He slaughtered them in the wilderness."

But now, I **pray**, let the power of the Lord be great, just as You have declared, "The Lord is slow to anger and abundant in lovingkindness, forgiving iniquity and transgression; but He will by no means clear the guilty, visiting the iniquity of the fathers on the children to the third and the fourth generations."

Pardon, I **pray**, the iniquity of this people according to the greatness of Your lovingkindness, just as You also have forgiven this people, from Egypt even until now.

So the Lord said, "I have pardoned them according to your word; but indeed, as I live, all the earth will be filled with the glory of the Lord." *Numbers 14:15-21*

I also pleaded with the Lord at that time, saying, "O Lord God, You have begun to show Your servant Your greatness and Your strong hand; for what god is there in heaven or on earth who can do such works and mighty acts as Yours? Let me, I **pray**, cross over and see the fair land that is beyond the Jordan, that good hill country and Lebanon."

But the Lord was angry with me on your account, and would not listen to me; and the Lord said to me, "Enough! Speak to Me no more of this matter. Go up to the top of Pisgah and lift up your eyes to the west and north and south and east, and see it with your eyes, for you shall not cross over this Jordan.

"But charge Joshua and encourage him and strengthen him, for he shall go across at the head of this people, and he will give them as an inheritance the land which you will see." *Deuteronomy 3:23-28*

I turned and came down from the mountain while the mountain was burning with fire, and the two tablets of the covenant were in my two hands. And I saw that you had indeed sinned against the Lord your God. You had made for yourselves a molten calf; you had turned aside quickly from the way which the Lord had commanded you.

I took hold of the two tablets and threw them from my hands and smashed them before your eyes. I fell down before the Lord, as at the first, forty days and nights; I neither ate bread nor drank water, because of all your sin which you had committed in doing what was evil in the sight of the Lord to provoke Him to anger.

For I was afraid of the anger and hot displeasure with which the Lord was wrathful against you in order to destroy you, but the Lord listened to me that time also.

The Lord was angry enough with Aaron to destroy him; so I also **prayed** for Aaron at the same time.

I took your sinful thing, the calf which you had made, and burned it with fire and crushed it, grinding it very small until it was as fine as dust; and I threw its dust into the brook that came down from the mountain.

Again at Taberah and at Massah and at Kibroth-hattaavah you provoked the Lord to wrath. When the Lord sent you from Kadesh-barnea, saying, "Go up and possess the land which I have given you," then you rebelled against the command of the Lord your God; you neither believed Him nor listened to His voice. You have been rebellious against the Lord from the day I knew you.

"So I fell down before the Lord the forty days and nights, which I did because the Lord had said He would destroy you.

"I **prayed** to the Lord and said, "O Lord God, do not destroy Your people, even Your inheritance, whom You have redeemed through Your greatness, whom You have brought out of Egypt with a mighty hand.

"Remember Your servants, Abraham, Isaac, and Jacob; do not look at the stubbornness of this people or at their wickedness or their sin." *Deuteronomy 9:15-27*

Elkanah her husband said to her, "Hannah, why do you weep and why do you not eat and why is your heart sad? Am I not better to you than ten sons?"

Then Hannah rose after eating and drinking in Shiloh. Now Eli the priest was sitting on the seat by the doorpost of the temple of the Lord.

She, greatly distressed, **prayed** to the Lord and wept bitterly. She made a vow and said, "O Lord of hosts, if You will indeed look on the affliction of Your maidservant and remember me, and not forget Your maidservant, but will give Your maidservant a son, then I will give him to the Lord all the days of his life, and a razor shall never come on his head."

Now it came about, as she continued **praying** before the Lord, that Eli was watching her mouth. As for Hannah, she was speaking in her heart, only her lips were moving, but her voice was not heard. So Eli thought she was drunk.

Then Eli said to her, "How long will you make yourself drunk? Put away your wine from you."

But Hannah replied, "No, my lord, I am a woman oppressed in spirit; I have drunk neither wine nor strong drink, but I have poured out my soul before the Lord. Do not consider your maidservant as a worthless woman, for I have spoken until now out of my great concern and provocation."

Then Eli answered and said, "Go in peace; and may the God of Israel grant your petition that you have asked of Him." She said, "Let your maidservant find favor in your sight."

So the woman went her way and ate, and her face was no longer sad. Then they arose early in the morning and worshiped before the Lord, and returned again to their house in Ramah.

And Elkanah had relations with Hannah his wife, and the Lord remembered her. It came about in due time, after Hannah had conceived, that she gave birth to a son; and she named him Samuel, saying, "Because I have asked him of the Lord."

Then the man Elkanah went up with all his household to offer to the Lord the yearly sacrifice and pay his vow. But Hannah did not go up, for she said to her husband, "I will not go up until the child is weaned; then I will bring him, that he may appear before the Lord and stay there forever."

Elkanah her husband said to her, "Do what seems best to you. Remain until you have weaned him; only may the Lord confirm His word."

So the woman remained and nursed her son until she weaned him.

Now when she had weaned him, she took him up with her, with a three-year-old bull and one ephah of flour and a jug of wine, and brought him to the house of the Lord in Shiloh, although the child was young. Then they slaughtered the bull, and brought the boy to Eli.

She said, "Oh, my lord! As your soul lives, my lord, I am the woman who stood here beside you, **praying** to the Lord. For this boy I **prayed**, and the Lord has given me my petition which I asked of Him. So I have also dedicated him to the Lord; as long as he lives he is dedicated to the Lord." And he worshiped the Lord there.

Then Hannah **prayed** and said, "My heart exults in the Lord; my horn is exalted in the Lord, my mouth speaks boldly against my enemies, because I rejoice in Your salvation.

"There is no one holy like the Lord, indeed, there is no one besides You, nor is there any rock like our God."

1 Samuel 1:8 - 2:2

Samuel spoke to all the house of Israel, saying, "If you return to the Lord with all your heart, remove the foreign gods and the Ashtaroth from among you and direct your hearts to the Lord and serve Him alone; and He will deliver you from the hand of the Philistines."

So the sons of Israel removed the Baals and the Ashtaroth and served the Lord alone.

Then Samuel said, "Gather all Israel to Mizpah and I will **pray** to the Lord for you." They gathered to Mizpah, and drew water and poured it out before the Lord, and fasted on that day and said there, "We have sinned against the Lord." And Samuel judged the sons of Israel at Mizpah.

Now when the Philistines heard that the sons of Israel had gathered to Mizpah, the lords of the Philistines went up against Israel. And when the sons of Israel heard it, they were afraid of the Philistines.

Then the sons of Israel said to Samuel, "Do not cease to cry to the Lord our God for us, that He may save us from the hand of the Philistines."

Samuel took a suckling lamb and offered it for a whole burnt offering to the Lord; and Samuel cried to the Lord for Israel and the Lord answered him.

1 Samuel 7:3-9

It came about when Samuel was old that he appointed his sons judges over Israel. Now the name of his firstborn was Joel, and the name of his second, Abijah; they were judging in Beersheba.

His sons, however, did not walk in his ways, but turned aside after dishonest gain and took bribes and perverted justice.

Then all the elders of Israel gathered together and came to Samuel at Ramah; and they said to him, "Behold, you have grown old, and your sons do not walk in your ways. Now appoint a king for us to judge us like all the nations."

But the thing was displeasing in the sight of Samuel when they said, "Give us a king to judge us."

And Samuel **prayed** to the Lord.

The Lord said to Samuel, "Listen to the voice of the people in regard to all that they say to you, for they have not rejected you, but they have rejected Me from being king over them. Like all the deeds which they have done since the day that I brought them up from Egypt even to this day - in that they have forsaken Me and served other gods - so they are doing to you also."

1 Samuel 8:1-8

"Is it not the wheat harvest today? I will call to the Lord, that He may send thunder and rain. Then you will know and see that your wickedness is great which you have done in the sight of the Lord by asking for yourselves a king."

So Samuel called to the Lord, and the Lord sent thunder and rain that day; and all the people greatly feared the Lord and Samuel.

Then all the people said to Samuel, "**Pray** for your servants to the Lord your God, so that we may not die, for we have added to all our sins this evil by asking for ourselves a king."

Samuel said to the people, "Do not fear. You have committed all this evil, yet do not turn aside from following the Lord, but serve the Lord with all your heart. You must not turn aside, for then you would go after futile things which can not profit or deliver, because they are futile. For the Lord will not abandon His people on account of His great name, because the Lord has been pleased to make you a people for Himself.

"Moreover, as for me, far be it from me that I should sin against the Lord by ceasing to **pray** for you; but I will instruct you in the good and right way. Only fear the Lord and serve Him in truth with all your heart; for consider what great things He has done for you.

"But if you still do wickedly, both you and your king will be swept away."

1 Samuel 12:17-25

David said, "O Lord God of Israel, Your servant has heard for certain that Saul is seeking to come to Keilah to destroy the city on my account. Will the men of Keilah surrender me into his hand? Will Saul come down just as Your servant has heard? O Lord God of Israel, I **pray**, tell Your servant."

And the Lord said, "He will come down."

Then David said, "Will the men of Keilah surrender me and my men into the hand of Saul?"

And the Lord said, "They will surrender you."

Then David and his men, about six hundred, arose and departed from Keilah, and they went wherever they could go. When it was told Saul that David had escaped from Keilah, he gave up the pursuit.

1 Samuel 23:10-13

You, O Lord of hosts, the God of Israel, have made a revelation to Your servant, saying, "I will build you a house"; therefore Your servant has found courage to **pray** this **prayer** to You.

"Now, O Lord God, You are God, and Your words are truth, and You have promised this good thing to Your servant.

2 Samuel 7:27-28

David went up the ascent of the Mount of Olives, and wept as he went, and his head was covered and he walked barefoot.

Then all the people who were with him each covered his head and went up weeping as they went.

Now someone told David, saying, "Ahithophel is among the conspirators with Absalom."

And David said, "O Lord, I **pray**, make the counsel of Ahithophel foolishness."

2 Samuel 15:30-31

They buried the bones of Saul and Jonathan his son in the country of Benjamin in Zela, in the grave of Kish his father; thus they did all that the king commanded, and after that God was moved by **prayer** for the land.

2 Samuel 21:14

David built there an altar to the Lord and offered burnt offerings and peace offerings. Thus the Lord was moved by **prayer** for the land, and the plague was held back from Israel.

2 Samuel 24:25

Solomon stood before the altar of the Lord in the presence of all the assembly of Israel and spread out his hands toward heaven. He said, "O Lord, the God of Israel, there is no God like You in heaven above or on earth beneath, keeping covenant and showing lovingkindness to Your servants who walk before You with all their heart, who have kept with Your servant, my father David, that which You have promised him; indeed, You have spoken with Your mouth and have fulfilled it with Your hand as it is this day.

"Now therefore, O Lord, the God of Israel, keep with Your servant David my father that which You have promised him, saying, 'You shall not lack a man to sit on the throne of Israel, if only your sons take heed to their way to walk before Me as you have walked.'

"Now therefore, O God of Israel, let Your word, I **pray**, be confirmed which You have spoken to Your servant, my father David. But will God indeed dwell on the earth? Behold, heaven and the highest heaven cannot contain You, how much less this house which I have built!

"Yet have regard to the **prayer** of Your servant and to his supplication, O Lord my God, to listen to the cry and to the **prayer** which Your servant **prays** before You today; that Your eyes may be open toward this house night and day, toward the place of which You have said, 'My name shall be there,' to listen to the **prayer** which Your servant shall **pray** toward this place. Listen to the supplication of Your servant and of Your people Israel, when they **pray** toward this place; hear in heaven Your dwelling place; hear and forgive.

"If a man sins against his neighbor and is made to take an oath, and he comes and takes an oath before Your altar in this house, then hear in heaven and act and judge Your servants, condemning the wicked by bringing his way on his own head and justifying the righteous by giving him according to his righteousness.

"When Your people Israel are defeated before an enemy, because they have sinned against You, if they turn to You again and confess Your name and **pray** and make supplication to You in this house, then hear in heaven, and forgive the sin of Your people Israel, and bring them back to the land which You gave to their fathers.

"When the heavens are shut up and there is no rain, because they have sinned against You, and they **pray** toward this place and confess Your name and turn from their sin when You afflict them, then hear in heaven and forgive the sin of

Your servants and of Your people Israel, indeed, teach them the good way in which they should walk. And send rain on Your land, which You have given Your people for an inheritance.

"If there is famine in the land, if there is pestilence, if there is blight or mildew, locust or grasshopper, if their enemy besieges them in the land of their cities, whatever plague, whatever sickness there is, whatever **prayer** or supplication is made by any man or by all Your people Israel, each knowing the affliction of his own heart, and spreading his hands toward this house; then hear in heaven Your dwelling place, and forgive and act and render to each according to all his ways, whose heart You know, for You alone know the hearts of all the sons of men, that they may fear You all the days that they live in the land which You have given to our fathers.

"Also concerning the foreigner who is not of Your people Israel, when he comes from a far country for Your name's sake (for they will hear of Your great name and Your mighty hand, and of Your outstretched arm); when he comes and **prays** toward this house, hear in heaven Your dwelling place, and do according to all for which the foreigner calls to You, in order that all the peoples of the earth may know Your name, to fear You, as do Your people Israel, and that they may know that this house which I have built is called by Your name.

"When Your people go out to battle against their enemy, by whatever way You shall send them, and they **pray** to the Lord toward the city which You have chosen and the house which I have built for Your name, then hear in heaven their **prayer** and their supplication, and maintain their cause.

"When they sin against You (for there is no man who does not sin) and You are angry with them and deliver them to an enemy, so that they take them away captive to the land of the enemy, far off or near; if they take thought in the land where they have been taken captive, and repent and make supplication to You in the land of those who have taken them captive, saying, 'We have sinned and have committed iniquity, we have acted wickedly'; if they return to You with all their heart and with all their soul in the land of their enemies who have taken them captive, and **pray** to You toward their land which You have given to their fathers, the city which You have chosen, and the house which I have built for Your name; then hear their **prayer** and their supplication in heaven Your dwelling place, and maintain their cause, and forgive Your people who have sinned against You and all their transgressions which they have transgressed against You, and make them objects of compassion before those who have taken them captive, that they may have compassion on them (for they are Your people and Your inheritance which You have brought forth from Egypt, from the midst of the iron furnace), that Your eyes may be open to the supplication of Your servant and to the supplication of Your people Israel, to listen to them whenever they call to You. For You have separated them from all the peoples of the earth as Your inheritance, as You spoke through Moses Your servant, when You brought our fathers forth from Egypt, O Lord God."

When Solomon had finished **praying** this entire **prayer** and supplication to the Lord, he arose from before the altar of the Lord, from kneeling on his knees with his hands spread toward heaven.

And he stood and blessed all the assembly of Israel with a loud voice, saying: "Blessed be the Lord, who has given rest to His people Israel, according to all that He promised; not one word has failed of all His good promise, which He promised through Moses His servant."

1 Kings 8:22-56

It came about when Solomon had finished building the house of the Lord, and the king's house, and all that Solomon desired to do, that the Lord appeared to Solomon a second time, as He had appeared to him at Gibeon.

The Lord said to him, "I have heard your **prayer** and your supplication, which you have made before Me; I have consecrated this house which you have built by putting My name there forever, and My eyes and My heart will be there perpetually.

"As for you, if you will walk before Me as your father David walked, in integrity of heart and uprightness, doing according to all that I have commanded you and will keep My statutes and My ordinances, then I will establish the throne of your kingdom over Israel forever, just as I promised to your father David, saying, 'You shall not lack a man on the throne of Israel.' "

1 Kings 9:1-5

Behold, there came a man of God from Judah to Bethel by the word of the Lord, while Jeroboam was standing by the altar to burn incense. He cried against the altar by the word of the Lord, and said, "O altar, altar, thus says the Lord, 'Behold, a son shall be born to the house of David, Josiah by name; and on you he shall sacrifice the priests of the high places who burn incense on you, and human bones shall be burned on you.' "

Then he gave a sign the same day, saying, "This is the sign which the Lord has spoken, 'Behold, the altar shall be split apart and the ashes which are on it shall be poured out.' "

Now when the king heard the saying of the man of God, which he cried against the altar in Bethel, Jeroboam stretched out his hand from the altar, saying, "Seize him." But his hand which he stretched out against him dried up, so that he could not draw it back to himself.

The altar also was split apart and the ashes were poured out from the altar, according to the sign which the man of God had given by the word of the Lord.

The king said to the man of God, "Please entreat the Lord your God, and **pray** for me, that my hand may be restored to me."

So the man of God entreated the Lord, and the king's hand was restored to him, and it became as it was before.

1 Kings 13:1-6

It came about after these things that the son of the woman, the mistress of the house, became sick; and his sickness was so severe that there was no breath left in him. So she said to Elijah, "What do I have to do with you, O man of God? You have come to me to bring my iniquity to remembrance and to put my son to death!"

He said to her, "Give me your son." Then he took him from her bosom and carried him up to the upper room where he was living, and laid him on his own bed.

He called to the Lord and said, "O Lord my God, have You also brought calamity to the widow with whom I am staying, by causing her son to die?"

Then he stretched himself upon the child three times, and called to the Lord and said, "O Lord my God, I **pray** You, let this child's life return to him."

The Lord heard the voice of Elijah, and the life of the child returned to him and he revived.

Elijah took the child and brought him down from the upper room into the house and gave him to his mother; and Elijah said, "See, your son is alive."

Then the woman said to Elijah, "Now I know that you are a man of God and that the word of the Lord in your mouth is truth." *1 Kings 17:17-24*

Gehazi passed on before them and laid the staff on the lad's face, but there was no sound or response. So he returned to meet him and told him, "The lad has not awakened."

When Elisha came into the house, behold the lad was dead and laid on his bed. So he entered and shut the door behind them both and **prayed** to the Lord.

And he went up and lay on the child, and put his mouth on his mouth and his eyes on his eyes and his hands on his hands, and he stretched himself on him; and the flesh of the child became warm.

Then he returned and walked in the house once back and forth, and went up and stretched himself on him; and the lad sneezed seven times and the lad opened his eyes.

He called Gehazi and said, "Call this Shunammite." So he called her. And when she came in to him, he said, "Take up your son."

Then she went in and fell at his feet and bowed herself to the ground, and she took up her son and went out.
2 Kings 4:31-37

When the attendant of the man of God had risen early and gone out, behold, an army with horses and chariots was circling the city.

And his servant said to him, "Alas, my master! What shall we do?"

So he answered, "Do not fear, for those who are with us are more than those who are with them."

Then Elisha **prayed** and said, "O Lord, I **pray**, open his eyes that he may see."

And the Lord opened the servant's yes and he saw; and behold, the mountain was full of horses and chariots of fire all around Elisha.

When they came down to him, Elisha **prayed** to the Lord and said, "Strike this people with blindness, I **pray**."

So He struck them with blindness according to the word of Elisha.

Then Elisha said to them, "This is not the way, nor is this the city; follow me and I will bring you to the man whom you seek." And he brought them to Samaria.

When they had come into Samaria, Elisha said, "O Lord, open the eyes of these men, that they may see."

So the Lord opened their eyes and they saw; and behold, they were in the midst of Samaria. *2 Kings 6:15-20*

They said to him, "Thus says Hezekiah, 'This day is a day of distress, rebuke, and rejection; for children have come to birth and there is no strength to deliver. Perhaps the Lord your God will hear all the words of Rabshakeh, whom his master the king of Assyria has sent to reproach the living God, and will rebuke the words which the Lord your God has heard. Therefore, offer a **prayer** for the remnant that is left.' "

So the servants of King Hezekiah came to Isaiah. Isaiah said to them, "Thus you shall say to your master, 'Thus says the Lord, "Do not be afraid because of the words that you have heard, with which the servants of the king of Assyria have blasphemed Me.

"Behold, I will put a spirit in him so that he will hear a rumor and return to his own land. And I will make him fall by the sword in his own land."" *2 Kings 19:3-7*

Then Hezekiah took the letter from the hand of the messengers and read it, and he went up to the house of the Lord and spread it out before the Lord. Hezekiah **prayed** before the Lord and said, "O Lord, the God of Israel, who are enthroned above the cherubim, You are the God, You alone, of all the kingdoms of the earth. You have made heaven and earth. Incline Your ear, O Lord, and hear; open Your eyes, O Lord, and see; and listen to the words of Sennacherib, which he has sent to reproach the living God.

"Truly, O Lord, the kings of Assyria have devastated the nations and their lands and have cast their gods into the fire, for they were not gods but the work of men's hands, wood and stone. So they have destroyed them. Now, O Lord our God, I **pray**, deliver us from his hand that all the kingdoms of the earth may know that You alone, O Lord, are God."

Then Isaiah the son of Amoz sent to Hezekiah saying, "Thus says the Lord, the God of Israel, 'Because you have **prayed** to Me about Sennacherib king of Assyria, I have heard you.' "
2 Kings 19:14-20

In those days Hezekiah became mortally ill. And Isaiah the prophet the son of Amoz came to him and said to him, "Thus says the Lord, 'Set your house in order, for you shall die and not live.' "

Then he turned his face to the wall and **prayed** to the Lord, saying, "Remember now, O Lord, I beseech You, how I have walked before You in truth and with a whole heart and have done what is good in Your sight." And Hezekiah wept bitterly.

Before Isaiah had gone out of the middle court, the word of the Lord came to him, saying, "Return and say to Hezekiah the leader of My people, 'Thus says the Lord, the God of your father David, "I have heard your **prayer**, I have seen your tears; behold, I will heal you. On the third day you shall go up to the house of the Lord. I will add fifteen years to your life, and I will deliver you and this city from the hand of the king of Assyria; and I will defend this city for My own sake and for My servant David's sake."''

Then Isaiah said, "Take a cake of figs." And they took and laid it on the boil, and he recovered. *2 Kings 20:1-7*

The sons of Reuben and the Gadites and the half-tribe of Manasseh, consisting of valiant men, men who bore shield and sword and shot with bow and were skillful in battle, were 44,760, who went to war. They made war against the Hagrites, Jetur, Naphish and Nodab.

They were helped against them, and the Hagrites and all who were with them were given into their hand; for they cried out to God in the battle, and He answered their **prayers** because they trusted in Him. *1 Chronicles 5:18-20*

O Lord, let the word that You have spoken concerning Your servant and concerning his house be established forever, and do as You have spoken. Let Your name be established and magnified forever, saying, "The Lord of hosts is the God of Israel, even a God to Israel; and the house of David Your servant is established before You."

For You, O my God, have revealed to Your servant that You will build for him a house; therefore Your servant has found courage to **pray** before You.
1 Chronicles 17:23-25

"O Lord, the God of Israel, let Your word be confirmed which You have spoken to Your servant David. But will God indeed dwell with mankind on the earth? Behold, heaven and the highest heaven cannot contain You; how much less this house which I have built.

"Yet have regard to the **prayer** of Your servant and to his supplication, O Lord my God, to listen to the cry and to the **prayer** which Your servant **prays** before You; that Your eye may be open toward this house day and night, toward the place of which You have said that You would put Your name there, to listen to the **prayer** which Your servant shall **pray** toward this place.

"Listen to the supplications of Your servant and of Your people Israel when they **pray** toward this place; hear from Your dwelling place, from heaven; hear and forgive.

"If a man sins against his neighbor and is made to take an oath, and he comes and takes an oath before Your altar in this house, then hear from heaven and act and judge Your servants, punishing the wicked by bringing his way on his own head and justifying the righteous by giving him according to his righteousness.

"If Your people Israel are defeated before an enemy because they have sinned against You, and they return to You and confess Your name, and **pray** and make supplication before You in this house, then hear from heaven and forgive the sin of Your people Israel, and bring them back to the land which You have given to them and to their fathers.

"When the heavens are shut up and there is no rain because they have sinned against You, and they **pray** toward this place and confess Your name, and turn from their sin when You afflict them; then hear in heaven and forgive the sin of Your servants and Your people Israel, indeed, teach them the good way in which they should walk. And send rain on Your land which You have given to Your people for an inheritance.

"If there is famine in the land, if there is pestilence, if there is blight or mildew, if there is locust or grasshopper, if their enemies besiege them in the land of their cities, whatever plague or whatever sickness there is, whatever **prayer** or suppli-

cation is made by any man or by all Your people Israel, each knowing his own affliction and his own pain, and spreading his hands toward this house, then hear from heaven Your dwelling place, and forgive, and render to each according to all his ways, whose heart You know for You alone know the hearts of the sons of men, that they may fear You, to walk in Your ways as long as they live in the land which You have given to our fathers.

"Also concerning the foreigner who is not from Your people Israel, when he comes from a far country for Your great name's sake and Your mighty hand and Your outstretched arm, when they come and **pray** toward this house, then hear from heaven, from Your dwelling place, and do according to all for which the foreigner calls to You, in order that all the peoples of the earth may know Your name, and fear You as do Your people Israel, and that they may know that this house which I have built is called by Your name.

"When Your people go out to battle against their enemies, by whatever way You shall send them, and they **pray** to You toward this city which You have chosen and the house which I have built for Your name, then hear from heaven their **prayer** and their supplication, and maintain their cause.

"When they sin against You (for there is no man who does not sin) and You are angry with them and deliver them to an enemy, so that they take them away captive to a land far off or near, if they take thought in the land where they are taken captive, and repent and make supplication to You in the land of their captivity, saying, 'We have sinned, we have committed iniquity and have acted wickedly'; if they return to You with all their heart and with all their soul in the land of their captivity, where they have been taken captive, and **pray** toward their land which You have given to their fathers and the city which You have chosen, and toward the house which I have built for Your name, then hear from heaven, from Your dwelling place, their **prayer** and supplications, and maintain their cause and forgive Your people who have sinned against You.

"Now, O my God, I **pray**, let Your eyes be open and Your ears attentive to the **prayer** offered in this place.

"Now therefore arise, O Lord God, to Your resting place, You and the ark of Your might; let Your priests, O Lord God, be clothed with salvation and let Your godly ones rejoice in what is good. O Lord God, do not turn away the face of Your anointed; remember Your loving-kindness to Your servant David."

Now when Solomon had finished **praying**, fire came down from heaven and consumed the burnt offering and the sacrifices, and the glory of the Lord filled the house. The priests could not enter into the house of the Lord because the glory of the Lord filled the Lord's house.

All the sons of Israel, seeing the fire come down and the glory of the Lord upon the house, bowed down on the pavement with their faces to the ground, and they worshiped and gave praise to the Lord, saying, "Truly He is good, truly His lovingkindness is everlasting." Then the king and all the people offered sacrifice before the Lord.   *2 Chronicles 6:13 - 7:4*

Solomon finished the house of the Lord and the king's palace, and successfully completed all that he had planned on doing in the house of the Lord and in his palace. Then the Lord appeared to Solomon at night and said to him, "I have heard your **prayer** and have chosen this place for Myself as a house of sacrifice.

"If I shut up the heavens so that there is no rain, or if I command the locust to devour the land, or if I send pestilence among My people, and My people who are called by My name humble themselves and **pray** and seek My face and turn from their wicked ways, then I will hear from heaven, will forgive their sin and will heal their land.

"Now My eyes will be open and My ears attentive to the **prayer** offered in this place. For now I have chosen and consecrated this house that My name may be

there forever, and My eyes and My heart will be there perpetually."
          2 Chronicles 7:11-16

There were many in the assembly who had not consecrated themselves; therefore, the Levites were over the slaughter of the Passover lambs for everyone who was unclean, in order to consecrate them to the Lord. For a multitude of the people, even many from Ephraim and Manasseh, Issachar and Zebulun, had not purified themselves, yet they ate the Passover otherwise than prescribed.

For Hezekiah **prayed** for them, saying, "May the good Lord pardon everyone who prepares his heart to seek God, the Lord God of his fathers, though not according to the purification rules of the sanctuary."

So the Lord heard Hezekiah and healed the people.   *2 Chronicles 30:17-20*

The whole assembly decided to celebrate the feast another seven days, so they celebrated the seven days with joy. For Hezekiah king of Judah had contributed to the assembly 1,000 bulls and 7,000 sheep, and the princes had contributed to the assembly 1,000 bulls and 10,000 sheep; and a large number of priests consecrated themselves.

All the assembly of Judah rejoiced, with the priests and the Levites and all the assembly that came from Israel, both the sojourners who came from the land of Israel and those living in Judah. So there was great joy in Jerusalem, because there was nothing like this in Jerusalem since the days of Solomon the son of David, king of Israel.

Then the Levitical priests arose and blessed the people; and their voice was heard and their **prayer** came to His holy dwelling place, to heaven.
          2 Chronicles 30:23-27

They called this out with a loud voice in the language of Judah to the people of Jerusalem who were on the wall, to frighten and terrify them, so that they might take the city. They spoke of the God of

Jerusalem as of the gods of the peoples of the earth, the work of men's hands.

But King Hezekiah and Isaiah the prophet, the son of Amoz, **prayed** about this and cried out to heaven. And the Lord sent an angel who destroyed every mighty warrior, commander and officer in the camp of the king of Assyria.

So he returned in shame to his own land. And when he had entered the temple of his god, some of his own children killed him there with the sword.

So the Lord saved Hezekiah and the inhabitants of Jerusalem from the hand of Sennacherib the king of Assyria and from the hand of all others, and guided them on every side. And many were bringing gifts to the Lord at Jerusalem and choice presents to Hezekiah king of Judah, so that he was exalted in the sight of all nations thereafter.

In those days Hezekiah became mortally ill; and he **prayed** to the Lord, and the Lord spoke to him and gave him a sign. But Hezekiah gave no return for the benefit he received, because his heart was proud; therefore wrath came on him and on Judah and Jerusalem.

However, Hezekiah humbled the pride of his heart, both he and the inhabitants of Jerusalem, so that the wrath of the Lord did not come on them in the days of Hezekiah.   *2 Chronicles 32:18-26*

Manasseh misled Judah and the inhabitants of Jerusalem to do more evil than the nations whom the Lord destroy-ed before the sons of Israel. The Lord spoke to Manasseh and his people, but they paid no attention.

Therefore the Lord brought the commanders of the army of the king of Assyria against them, and they captured Manasseh with hooks, bound him with bronze chains and took him to Babylon.

When he was in distress, he entreated the Lord his God and humbled himself greatly before the God of his fathers. When he **prayed** to Him, He was moved by his entreaty and heard his supplication, and brought him again to Jerusalem to his kingdom.

Then Manasseh knew that the Lord was God.   *2 Chronicles 33:9-13*

The rest of the acts of Manasseh even his **prayer** to his God, and the words of the seers who spoke to him in the name of the Lord God of Israel, behold, they are among the records of the kings of Israel.

His **prayer** also and how God was entreated by him, and all his sin, his unfaithfulness, and the sites on which he built high places and erected the Asherim and the carved images, before he humbled himself, behold, they are written in the records of the Hozai.

So Manasseh slept with his fathers, and they buried him in his own house. And Amon his son became king in his place.   *2 Chronicles 33:18-20*

Leave this work on the house of God alone; let the governor of the Jews and the elders of the Jews rebuild this house of God on its site.

Moreover, I issue a decree concerning what you are to do for these elders of Judah in the rebuilding of this house of God: The full cost is to be paid to these people from the royal treasury out of the taxes of the provinces beyond the River, and that without delay.

Whatever is needed, both young bulls, rams, and lambs for a burnt offering to the God of heaven, and wheat, salt, wine and anointing oil, as the priests in Jerusalem request, it is to be given to them daily without fail, that they may offer acceptable sacrifices to the God of heaven and **pray** for the life of the king and his sons.   *Ezra 6:7-10*

"After all that has come upon us for our evil deeds and our great guilt, since You our God have requited us less than our iniquities deserve, and have given us an escaped remnant as this, shall we again break Your commandments and intermarry with the peoples who commit these abominations? Would You not be angry with us to the point of destruction, until there is no remnant nor any who escape?

"O Lord God of Israel, You are righteous, for we have been left an escaped remnant, as it is this day; behold, we are before You in our guilt, for no one can stand before You because of this."

Now while Ezra was **praying** and making confession, weeping and prostrating himself before the house of God, a very large assembly, men, women and children, gathered to him from Israel; for the people wept bitterly.   *Ezra 9:13 - 10:1*

The words of Nehemiah the son of Hacaliah. Now it happened in the month Chislev, in the twentieth year, while I was in Susa the capitol, that Hanani, one of my brothers, and some men from Judah came; and I asked them concerning the Jews who had escaped and had survived the captivity, and about Jerusalem.

They said to me, "The remnant there in the province who survived the captivity are in great distress and reproach, and the wall of Jerusalem is broken down and its gates are burned with fire."

When I heard these words, I sat down and wept and mourned for days; and I was fasting and **praying** before the God of heaven.

I said, "I beseech You, O Lord God of heaven, the great and awesome God, who preserves the covenant and loving-kindness for those who love Him and keep His commandments, let Your ear now be attentive and Your eyes open to hear the **prayer** of Your servant which I am **praying** before You now, day and night, on behalf of the sons of Israel Your servants, confessing the sins of the sons of Israel which we have sinned against You; I and my father's house have sinned.

"We have acted very corruptly against You and have not kept the commandments, nor the statutes, nor the ordinances which You commanded Your servant Moses.

"Remember the word which You commanded Your servant Moses, saying, 'If you are unfaithful I will scatter you among the peoples; but if you return to Me and keep My commandments and do them, though those of you who have been

scattered were in the most remote part of the heavens, I will gather them from there and will bring them to the place where I have chosen to cause My name to dwell.'

"They are Your servants and Your people whom You redeemed by Your great power and by Your strong hand. O Lord, I beseech You, may Your ear be attentive to the **prayer** of Your servant and the **prayer** of Your servants who delight to revere Your name, and make Your servant successful today and grant him compassion before this man." ~
Nehemiah 1:1-11

The king said to me, "What would you request?" So I **prayed** to the God of heaven. I said to the king, "If it please the king, and if your servant has found favor before you, send me to Judah, to the city of my fathers' tombs, that I may rebuild it."
Nehemiah 2:4-5

When Sanballat, Tobiah, the Arabs, the Ammonites and the Ashdodites heard that the repair of the walls of Jerusalem went on, and that the breaches began to be closed, they were very angry. All of them conspired together to come and fight against Jerusalem and to cause a disturbance in it. But we **prayed** to our God, and because of them we set up a guard against them day and night.
Nehemiah 4:7-9

I have sewed sackcloth over my skin and thrust my horn in the dust. My face is flushed from weeping, and deep darkness is on my eyelids, although there is no violence in my hands, and my **prayer** is pure.   *Job 16:15-17*

Please receive instruction from His mouth and establish His words in your heart. If you return to the Almighty, you will be restored; if you remove unrighteousness far from your tent, and place your gold in the dust, and the gold of Ophir among the stones of the brooks, then the Almighty will be your gold and choice silver to you.

For then you will delight in the Almighty and lift up your face to God. You

will **pray** to Him, and He will hear you; and you will pay your vows. You will also decree a thing, and it will be established for you; and light will shine on your ways.
Job 22:22-28

Man is also chastened with pain on his bed, and with unceasing complaint in his bones; so that his life loathes bread, and his soul favorite food. His flesh wastes away from sight, and his bones which were not seen stick out. Then his soul draws near to the pit, and his life to those who bring death.

If there is an angel as mediator for him, one out of a thousand, to remind a man what is right for him, then let him be gracious to him, and say, "Deliver him from going down to the pit, I have found a ransom"; let his flesh become fresher than in youth, let him return to the days of his youthful vigor; then he will **pray** to God, and He will accept him, that he may see His face with joy, and He may restore His righteousness to man.

He will sing to men and say, "I have sinned and perverted what is right, and it is not proper for me. He has redeemed my soul from going to the pit, and my life shall see the light."

Behold, God does all these oftentimes with men, to bring back his soul from the pit, that he may be enlightened with the light of life. *Job 33:19-30*

It came about after the Lord had spoken these words to Job, that the Lord said to Eliphaz the Temanite, "My wrath is kindled against you and against your two friends, because you have not spoken of Me what is right as My servant Job has.

"Now therefore, take for yourselves seven bulls and seven rams, and go to My servant Job, and offer up a burnt offering for yourselves, and My servant Job will **pray** for you. For I will accept him so that I may not do with you according to your folly, because you have not spoken of Me what is right, as My servant Job has."

So Eliphaz the Temanite and Bildad the Shuhite and Zophar the Naamathite

went and did as the Lord told them; and the Lord accepted Job.

The Lord restored the fortunes of Job when he **prayed** for his friends, and the Lord increased all that Job had twofold.
Job 42:7-10

Answer me when I call, O God of my righteousness! You have relieved me in my distress; be gracious to me and hear my **prayer**. *Psalm 4:1*

Give ear to my words, O Lord, consider my groaning. Heed the sound of my cry for help, my King and my God, for to You I **pray**.

In the morning, O Lord, You will hear my voice; in the morning I will order my **prayer** to You and eagerly watch.
Psalm 5:1-3

I am weary with my sighing; every night I make my bed swim, I dissolve my couch with my tears. My eye has wasted away with grief; it has become old because of all my adversaries.

Depart from me, all you who do iniquity, for the Lord has heard the voice of my weeping.

The Lord has heard my supplication, the Lord receives my **prayer**. All my enemies will be ashamed and greatly dismayed; they shall turn back, they will suddenly be ashamed. *Psalm 6:6-10*

Hear a just cause, O Lord, give heed to my cry; give ear to my **prayer**, which is not from deceitful lips. Let my judgment come forth from Your presence; let Your eyes look with equity.

You have tried my heart; You have visited me by night; You have tested me and You find nothing; I have purposed that my mouth will not transgress.

As for the deeds of men, by the word of Your lips I have kept from the paths of the violent. My steps have held fast to Your paths. My feet have not slipped.

I have called upon You, for You will answer me, O God; incline Your ear to me, hear my speech. Wondrously show Your lovingkindness, O Savior of those who take refuge at Your right hand from those who rise up against them.

Psalm 17:1-7

When I kept silent about my sin, my body wasted away through my groaning all day long. For day and night Your hand was heavy upon me; my vitality was drained away as with the fever heat of summer.

I acknowledged my sin to You, and my iniquity I did not hide; I said, "I will confess my transgressions to the Lord"; and You forgave the guilt of my sin. Therefore, let everyone who is godly **pray** to You in a time when You may be found; surely in a flood of great waters they will not reach him. *Psalm 32:3-6*

Malicious witnesses rise up; they ask me of things that I do not know. They repay me evil for good, to the bereavement of my soul. But as for me, when they were sick, my clothing was sackcloth; I humbled my soul with fasting, and my **prayer** kept returning to my bosom. I went about as though it were my friend or brother; I bowed down mourning, as one who sorrows for a mother. *Psalm 35:11-14*

Now, Lord, for what do I wait? My hope is in You. Deliver me from all my transgressions; make me not the reproach of the foolish. I have become mute, I do not open my mouth, because it is You who have done it.

Remove Your plague from me; because of the opposition of Your hand I am perishing. With reproofs You chasten a man for iniquity; You consume as a moth what is precious to him; surely every man is a mere breath.

Hear my **prayer**, O Lord, and give ear to my cry; do not be silent at my tears; for I am a stranger with You, a sojourner like all my fathers. *Psalm 39:7-12*

The Lord will command His lovingkindness in the daytime; and His song will be with me in the night, a **prayer** to the God of my life. I will say to God my rock, "Why have You forgotten me? Why do I go mourning because of the oppression of the enemy?" *Psalm 42:8-9*

Save me, O God, by Your name, and vindicate me by Your power. Hear my **prayer**, O God; give ear to the words of my mouth. For strangers have risen against me and violent men have sought my life; they have not set God before them.

Behold, God is my helper; the Lord is the sustainer of my soul. He will recompense the evil to my foes; destroy them in Your faithfulness. Willingly I will sacrifice to You; I will give thanks to Your name, O Lord, for it is good. *Psalm 54:1-6*

Give ear to my **prayer**, O God; and do not hide Yourself from my supplication. Give heed to me and answer me; I am restless in my complaint and am surely distracted, because of the voice of the enemy, because of the pressure of the wicked; for they bring down trouble upon me and in anger they bear a grudge against me.

Psalm 55:1-3

Hear my cry, O God; give heed to my **prayer**. From the end of the earth I call to You when my heart is faint; lead me to the rock that is higher than I. For You have been a refuge for me, a tower of strength against the enemy. Let me dwell in Your tent forever; let me take refuge in the shelter of Your wings. *Psalm 61:1-4*

There will be silence before You, and praise in Zion, O God, and to You the vow will be performed. You who hear **prayer**, to You all men come. Iniquities prevail against me; as for our transgressions, You forgive them.

How blessed is the one whom You choose and bring near to You to dwell in Your courts. We will be satisfied with the goodness of Your house, Your holy temple.

By awesome deeds You answer us in righteousness, O God of our salvation, You who are the trust of all the ends of the earth and of the farthest sea; ~

Psalm 65:1-5

Come and hear, all who fear God, and I will tell of what He has done for my soul.

I cried to Him with my mouth, and He was extolled with my tongue.

If I regard wickedness in my heart, the Lord will not hear; but certainly God has heard; He has given heed to the voice of my **prayer**. Blessed be God, who has not turned away my **prayer** nor His lovingkindness from me. *Psalm 66:16-20*

When I wept in my soul with fasting, it became my reproach. When I made sackcloth my clothing, I became a byword to them. Those who sit in the gate talk about me, and I am the song of the drunkards. But as for me, my **prayer** is to You, O Lord, at an acceptable time; O God, in the greatness of Your lovingkindness, answer me with Your saving truth.

Deliver me from the mire and do not let me sink; may I be delivered from my foes and from the deep waters. May the flood of water not overflow me nor the deep swallow me up, nor the pit shut its mouth on me.

Answer me, O Lord, for Your lovingkindness is good; according to the greatness of Your compassion, turn to me, and do not hide Your face from Your servant, for I am in distress; answer me quickly. Oh draw near to my soul and redeem it; ransom me because of my enemies! *Psalm 69:10-18*

Let all kings bow down before him, all nations serve him. For he will deliver the needy when he cries for help, the afflicted also, and him who has no helper. He will have compassion on the poor and needy, and the lives of the needy he will save.

He will rescue their life from oppression and violence, and their blood will be precious in his sight; so may he live, and may the gold of Sheba be given to him; and let them **pray** for him continually; let them bless him all day long. *Psalm 72:11-15*

Blessed be the Lord God, the God of Israel, who alone works wonders. And blessed be His glorious name forever; and may the whole earth be filled with His glory. Amen, and Amen. The **prayers** of David the son of Jesse are ended. *Psalm 72:18-20*

O God, restore us and cause Your face to shine upon us, and we will be saved. O Lord God of hosts, how long will You be angry with the **prayer** of Your people?

You have fed them with the bread of tears, and You have made them to drink tears in large measure. You make us an object of contention to our neighbors, and our enemies laugh among themselves.

O God of hosts, restore us and cause Your face to shine upon us, and we will be saved. *Psalm 80:3-7*

O Lord God of hosts, hear my **prayer**; give ear, O God of Jacob! Behold our shield, O God, and look upon the face of Your anointed. *Psalm 84:8-9*

Incline Your ear, O Lord, and answer me; for I am afflicted and needy. Preserve my soul, for I am a godly man; O You my God, save Your servant who trusts in You. Be gracious to me, O Lord, for to You I cry all day long.

Make glad the soul of Your servant, for to You, O Lord, I lift up my soul. For You, Lord, are good, and ready to forgive, and abundant in lovingkindness to all who call upon You. Give ear, O Lord, to my **prayer**; and give heed to the voice of my supplications! In the day of my trouble I shall call upon You, for You will answer me. *Psalm 86:1-7*

O Lord, the God of my salvation, I have cried out by day and in the night before You. Let my **prayer** come before You; incline Your ear to my cry! For my soul has had enough troubles, and my life has drawn near to Sheol. *Psalm 88:1-3*

I, O Lord, have cried out to You for help, and in the morning my **prayer** comes before You. O Lord, why do You reject my soul? Why do You hide Your face from me?

I was afflicted and about to die from my youth on; I suffer Your terrors; I am overcome. Your burning anger has passed over me; Your terrors have destroyed me. *Psalm 88:13-16*

Hear my **prayer**, O Lord! And let my cry for help come to You. Do not hide Your face from me in the day of my distress; incline Your ear to me; in the day when I call answer me quickly. For my days have been consumed in smoke, and my bones have been scorched like a hearth. My heart has been smitten like grass and has withered away, indeed, I forget to eat my bread.   *Psalm 102:1-4*

The nations will fear the name of the Lord and all the kings of the earth Your glory. For the Lord has built up Zion; He has appeared in His glory.

He has regarded the **prayer** of the destitute and has not despised their **prayer**. This will be written for the generation to come, that a people yet to be created may praise the Lord.

For He looked down from His holy height; from heaven the Lord gazed upon the earth, to hear the groaning of the prisoner, to set free those who were doomed to death, that men may tell of the name of the Lord in Zion and His praise in Jerusalem, when the peoples are gathered together, and the kingdoms, to serve the Lord.   *Psalm 102:15-22*

O God of my praise, do not be silent! For they have opened the wicked and deceitful mouth against me; they have spoken against me with a lying tongue. They have also surrounded me with words of hatred, and fought against me without cause. In return for my love they act as my accusers; but I am in **prayer**.

Thus they have repaid me evil for good and hatred for my love. Appoint a wicked man over him, and let an accuser stand at his right hand. When he is judged, let him come forth guilty, and let his **prayer** become sin. Let his days be few; let another take his office. Let his children be fatherless and his wife a widow.   *Psalm 109:1-9*

Pray for the peace of Jerusalem: May they prosper who love you. May peace be within your walls, and prosperity within your palaces. For the sake of my broth-

ers and my friends, I will now say, "May peace be within you."   *Psalm 122:6-8*

O Lord, I call upon You; hasten to me! Give ear to my voice when I call to You! May my **prayer** be counted as incense before You; the lifting up of my hands as the evening offering.

Set a guard, O Lord, over my mouth; keep watch over the door of my lips. Do not incline my heart to any evil thing, to practice deeds of wickedness with men who do iniquity; and do not let me eat of their delicacies.

Let the righteous smite me in kindness and reprove me; it is oil upon the head; do not let my head refuse it, for still my **prayer** is against their wicked deeds. Their judges are thrown down by the sides of the rock, and they hear my words, for they are pleasant. *Psalm 141:1-6*

Hear my **prayer**, O Lord, give ear to my supplications! Answer me in Your faithfulness, in Your righteousness! And do not enter into judgment with Your servant, for in Your sight no man living is righteous.

For the enemy has persecuted my soul; he has crushed my life to the ground; he has made me dwell in dark places, like those who have long been dead. Therefore my spirit is overwhelmed within me; my heart is appalled within me.

I remember the days of old; I meditate on all Your doings; I muse on the work of Your hands. I stretch out my hands to You; my soul longs for You, as a parched land. Answer me quickly, O Lord, my spirit fails; do not hide Your face from me, or I will become like those who go down to the pit.

Let me hear Your lovingkindness in the morning; for I trust in You; teach me the way in which I should walk; for to You I lift up my soul. Deliver me, O Lord, from my enemies; I take refuge in You.
                      Psalm 143:1-9

The sacrifice of the wicked is an abomination to the Lord, but the **prayer** of the upright is His delight. The way of the wicked is an abomination to the Lord, but

He loves one who pursues righteousness.
Proverb 15:8 -9

The heart of the righteous ponders how to answer, but the mouth of the wicked pours out evil things. The Lord is far from the wicked, but He hears the **prayer** of the righteous. *Proverb 15:28-29*

He who turns away his ear from listening to the law, even his **prayer** is an abomination. *Proverb 28:9*

Bring your worthless offerings no longer, incense is an abomination to Me. New moon and sabbath, the calling of assemblies - I cannot endure iniquity and the solemn assembly. I hate your new moon festivals and your appointed feasts, they have become a burden to Me; I am weary of bearing them.

So when you spread out your hands in **prayer**, I will hide My eyes from you; yes, even though you multiply **prayers**, I will not listen. Your hands are covered with blood.

Wash yourselves, make yourselves clean; remove the evil of your deeds from My sight. Cease to do evil, learn to do good; seek justice, reprove the ruthless, defend the orphan, plead for the widow.
Isaiah 1:13-17

It will come about when Moab presents himself, when he wearies himself upon his high place and comes to his sanctuary to **pray**, that he will not prevail. This is the word which the Lord spoke earlier concerning Moab.

But now the Lord speaks, saying, "Within three years, as a hired man would count them, the glory of Moab will be degraded along with all his great population, and his remnant will be very small and impotent." *Isaiah 16:12-14*

O Lord, they sought You in distress; they could only whisper a **prayer**, Your chastening was upon them. As the pregnant woman approaches the time to give birth, she writhes and cries out in her labor pains, thus were we before You, O Lord.
Isaiah 26:16-17

Perhaps the Lord your God will hear the words of Rabshakeh, whom his master the king of Assyria has sent to reproach the living God, and will rebuke the words which the Lord your God has heard. Therefore, offer a **prayer** for the remnant that is left. *Isaiah 37:4*

Hezekiah took the letter from the hand of the messengers and read it, and he went up to the house of the Lord and spread it out before the Lord.

Hezekiah **prayed** to the Lord saying, "O Lord of hosts, the God of Israel, who is enthroned above the cherubim, You are the God, You alone, of all the kingdoms of the earth. You have made heaven and earth. Incline Your ear, O Lord, and hear; open Your eyes, O Lord, and see; and listen to all the words of Sennacherib, who sent them to reproach the living God.

"Truly, O Lord, the kings of Assyria have devastated all the countries and their lands, and have cast their gods into the fire, for they were not gods but the work of men's hands, wood and stone. So they have destroyed them.

"Now, O Lord our God, deliver us from his hand that all the kingdoms of the earth may know that You alone, Lord, are God."

Then Isaiah the son of Amoz sent word to Hezekiah, saying, "Thus says the Lord, the God of Israel, 'Because you have **prayed** to Me about Sennacherib king of Assyria, this is the word that the Lord has spoken against him: "She has despised you and mocked you, the virgin daughter of Zion; she has shaken her head behind you, the daughter of Jerusalem!"'" *Isaiah 37:14-22*

In those days Hezekiah became mortally ill. And Isaiah the prophet the son of Amoz came to him and said to him, "Thus says the Lord, 'Set your house in order, for you shall die and not live.' "

Then Hezekiah turned his face to the wall and **prayed** to the Lord, and said, "Remember now, O Lord, I beseech You, how I have walked before You in truth and with a whole heart, and have done what is good in Your sight." And Hezekiah wept bitterly.

Then the word of the Lord came to Isaiah, saying, "Go and say to Hezekiah, 'Thus says the Lord, the God of your father David, "I have heard your **prayer**, I have seen your tears; behold, I will add fifteen years to your life. I will deliver you and this city from the hand of the king of Assyria; and I will defend this city."

'This shall be the sign to you from the Lord, that the Lord will do this thing that He has spoken: Behold, I will cause the shadow on the stairway, which has gone down with the sun on the stairway of Ahaz, to go back ten steps.' "

So the sun's shadow went back ten steps on the stairway on which it had gone down.   *Isaiah 38:1-8*

Surely he cuts cedars for himself, and takes a cypress or an oak and raises it for himself among the trees of the forest. He plants a fir, and the rain makes it grow. Then it becomes something for a man to burn, so he takes one of them and warms himself; he also makes a fire to bake bread.

He also makes a god and worships it; he makes it a graven image and falls down before it. Half of it he burns in the fire; over this half he eats meat as he roasts a roast and is satisfied.

He also warms himself and says, "Aha! I am warm, I have seen the fire."

But the rest of it he makes into a god, his graven image. He falls down before it and worships; he also **prays** to it and says, "Deliver me, for you are my god."

They do not know, nor do they understand, for He has smeared over their eyes so that they cannot see and their hearts so that they cannot comprehend.

No one recalls, nor is there knowledge or understanding to say, "I have burned half of it in the fire and also have baked bread over its coals. I roast meat and eat it. Then I make the rest of it into an abomination, I fall down before a block of wood!"

He feeds on ashes; a deceived heart has turned him aside. And he cannot deliver himself, nor say, "Is there not a lie in my right hand?"   *Isaiah 44:14-20*

Gather yourselves and come; draw near together, you fugitives of the nations; they have no knowledge, who carry about their wooden idol and **pray** to a god who cannot save.

Declare and set forth your case; indeed, let them consult together. Who has announced this from of old? Who has long since declared it? Is it not I, the Lord? And there is no other God besides Me, a righteous God and a Savior; there is none except Me. Turn to Me and be saved, all the ends of the earth; for I am God, and there is no other.   *Isaiah 45:20-22*

Thus says the Lord, "To the eunuchs who keep My sabbaths, and choose what pleases Me, and hold fast My covenant, to them I will give in My house and within My walls a memorial, and a name better than that of sons and daughters; I will give them an everlasting name which will not be cut off.

"Also the foreigners who join themselves to the Lord, to minister to Him, and to love the name of the Lord, to be His servants, every one who keeps from profaning the sabbath and holds fast My covenant; even those I will bring to My holy mountain and make them joyful in My house of **prayer**. Their burnt offerings and their sacrifices will be acceptable on My altar; for My house will be called a house of **prayer** for all the peoples."

The Lord God, who gathers the dispersed of Israel, declares, "Yet others I will gather to them, to those already gathered."   *Isaiah 56:4-8*

"Now, because you have done all these things," declares the Lord, "and I spoke to you, rising up early and speaking, but you did not hear, and I called you but you did not answer, therefore, I will do to the house which is called by My name, in which you trust, and to the place which I gave you and your fathers, as I did to Shiloh. I will cast you out of My sight, as I have cast out all your brothers, all the offspring of Ephraim.

"As for you, do not **pray** for this people, and do not lift up cry or **prayer** for them, and do not intercede with Me; for I do not hear you.

"Do you not see what they are doing in the cities of Judah and in the streets of Jerusalem? The children gather wood, and the fathers kindle the fire, and the women knead dough to make cakes for the queen of heaven; and they pour out drink offerings to other gods in order to spite Me. Do they spite Me?" declares the Lord. "Is it not themselves they spite, to their own shame?"

Therefore thus says the Lord God, "Behold, My anger and My wrath will be poured out on this place, on man and on beast and on the trees of the field and on the fruit of the ground; and it will burn and not be quenched." *Jeremiah 7:13-20*

The Lord said to me, "A conspiracy has been found among the men of Judah and among the inhabitants of Jerusalem. They have turned back to the iniquities of their ancestors who refused to hear My words, and they have gone after other gods to serve them; the house of Israel and the house of Judah have broken My covenant which I made with their fathers."

Therefore thus says the Lord, "Behold I am bringing disaster on them which they will not be able to escape; though they will cry to Me, yet I will not listen to them. Then the cities of Judah and the inhabitants of Jerusalem will go and cry to the gods to whom they burn incense, but they surely will not save them in the time of their disaster.

"For your gods are as many as your cities, O Judah; and as many as the streets of Jerusalem are the altars you have set up to the shameful thing, altars to burn incense to Baal.

"Therefore do not **pray** for this people, nor lift up a cry or **prayer** for them; for I will not listen when they call to Me because of their disaster. What right has My beloved in My house when she has done many vile deeds? Can the sacrificial flesh take away from you your disas-

ter, so that you can rejoice?"
Jeremiah 11:9-15

Thus says the Lord to this people, "Even so they have loved to wander; they have not kept their feet in check. Therefore the Lord does not accept them; now He will remember their iniquity and call their sins to account."

So the Lord said to me, "Do not **pray** for the welfare of this people. When they fast, I am not going to listen to their cry; and when they offer burnt offering and grain offering, I am not going to accept them. Rather I am going to make an end of them by the sword, famine and pestilence." *Jeremiah 14:10-12*

Thus says the Lord of hosts, the God of Israel, to all the exiles whom I have sent into exile from Jerusalem to Babylon, "Build houses and live in them; and plant gardens and eat their produce. Take wives and become the fathers of sons and daughters, and take wives for your sons and give your daughters to husbands, that they may bear sons and daughters; and multiply there and do not decrease.

"Seek the welfare of the city where I have sent you into exile, and **pray** to the Lord on its behalf; for in its welfare you will have welfare." *Jeremiah 29:4-7*

Thus says the Lord, "When seventy years have been completed for Babylon, I will visit you and fulfill My good word to you, to bring you back to this place. For I know the plans that I have for you," declares the Lord, "plans for welfare and not for calamity to give you a future and a hope. Then you will call upon Me and come and **pray** to Me, and I will listen to you.

"You will seek Me and find Me when you search for Me with all your heart. I will be found by you," declares the Lord, "and I will restore your fortunes and will gather you from all the nations and from all the places where I have driven you," declares the Lord, "and I will bring you back to the place from where I sent you into exile." *Jeremiah 29:10-14*

I commanded Baruch in their presence, saying, "Thus says the Lord of hosts, the God of Israel, 'Take these deeds, this sealed deed of purchase and this open deed, and put them in an earthenware jar, that they may last a long time.' For thus says the Lord of hosts, the God of Israel, 'Houses and fields and vineyards will again be bought in this land.' "

After I had given the deed of purchase to Baruch the son of Neriah, then I **prayed** to the Lord, saying, "Ah Lord God! Behold, You have made the heavens and the earth by Your great power and by Your outstretched arm! Nothing is too difficult for You, who shows lovingkindness to thousands, but repays the iniquity of fathers into the bosom of their children after them, O great and mighty God." ~ *Jeremiah 32:13-18*

Zedekiah the son of Josiah whom Nebuchadnezzar king of Babylon had made king in the land of Judah, reigned as king in place of Coniah the son of Jehoiakim. But neither he nor his servants nor the people of the land listened to the words of the Lord which He spoke through Jeremiah the prophet.

Yet King Zedekiah sent Jehucal the son of Shelemiah, and Zephaniah the son of Maaseiah, the priest, to Jeremiah the prophet, saying, "Please **pray** to the Lord our Go on our behalf." *Jeremiah 37:1-3*

All the commanders of the forces, Johanan the son of Kareah, Jezaniah the son of Hoshaiah, and all the people both small and great approached and said to Jeremiah the prophet, "Please let our petition come before you, and **pray** for us to the Lord your God, that is for all this remnant; because we are left but a few out of many, as your own eyes now see us, that the Lord your God may tell us the way in which we should walk and the thing that we should do."

Then Jeremiah the prophet said to them, "I have heard you. Behold, I am going to **pray** to the Lord your God in accordance with your words; and I will tell you the whole message which the Lord will answer you. I will not keep back a word from you."

Then they said to Jeremiah, "May the Lord be a true and faithful witness against us if we do not act in accordance with the whole message with which the Lord your God will send you to us. Whether it is pleasant or unpleasant, we will listen to the voice of the Lord our God to whom we are sending you, so that it may go well with us when we listen to the voice of the Lord our God."

Now at the end of ten days the word of the Lord came to Jeremiah.
Jeremiah 42:1-7

"All the men who set their mind to go to Egypt to reside there will die by the sword, by famine and by pestilence; and they will have no survivors or refugees from the calamity that I am going to bring on them."

For thus says the Lord of hosts, the God of Israel, "As My anger and wrath have been poured out on the inhabitants of Jerusalem, so My wrath will be poured out on you when you enter Egypt. And you will become a curse, an object of horror, an imprecation and a reproach; and you will see this place no more.

"The Lord has spoken to you, O remnant of Judah, 'Do not go into Egypt!' You should clearly understand that today I have testified against you. For you have only deceived yourselves; for it is you who sent me to the Lord your God, saying, '**Pray** for us to the Lord our God; and whatever the Lord our God says, tell us so, and we will do it.'

"So I have told you today, but you have not obeyed the Lord your God, even in whatever He has sent me to tell you. Therefore you should now clearly understand that you will die by the sword, by famine and by pestilence, in the place where you wish to go to reside."
Jeremiah 42:17-22

I am the man who has seen affliction because of the rod of His wrath. He has driven me and made me walk in darkness and not in light. Surely against me He has turned His hand repeatedly all the day. He has caused my flesh and my skin to waste away, He has broken my bones. He has besieged and encompassed me with bitterness and hardship.

In dark places He has made me dwell, like those who have long been dead. He has walled me in so that I cannot go out; He has made my chain heavy. Even when I cry out and call for help, He shuts out my **prayer**.

He has blocked my ways with hewn stone; He has made my paths crooked.

Lamentations 3:1-9

Why should any living mortal, or any man, offer complaint in view of his sins? Let us examine and probe our ways, and let us return to the Lord. We lift up our heart and hands toward God in heaven; we have transgressed and rebelled, You have not pardoned.

You have covered Yourself with anger and pursued us; You have slain and have not spared. You have covered Yourself with a cloud so that no **prayer** can pass through. You have made us mere offscouring and refuse In the midst of the peoples. All our enemies have opened their mouths against us.

Lamentations 3:39-46

My enemies without cause hunted me down like a bird; they have silenced me in the pit and have placed a stone on me. Waters flowed over my head; I said, "I am cut off!"

I called on Your name, O Lord, out of the lowest pit. You have heard my voice, "Do not hide Your ear from my **prayer** for relief, from my cry for help."

You drew near when I called on You; You said, "Do not fear!"

O Lord, You have pleaded my soul's cause; You have redeemed my life. O Lord, You have seen my oppression; judge my case. You have seen all their vengeance, all their schemes against me.

Lamentations 3:52-60

The commissioners and satraps came by agreement to the king and spoke to him as follows: "King Darius, live forever! All the commissioners of the kingdom, the prefects and the satraps, the high officials and the governors have consulted together that the king should establish a statute and enforce an injunction that anyone who makes a petition to any god or man besides you, O king, for thirty days, shall be cast into the lions' den.

"Now, O king, establish the injunction and sign the document so that it may not be changed, according to the law of the Medes and Persians, which may not be revoked." Therefore King Darius signed the document, that is, the injunction.

Now when Daniel knew that the document was signed, he entered his house (now in his roof chamber he had windows open toward Jerusalem); and he continued kneeling on his knees three times a day, **praying** and giving thanks before his God, as he had been doing previously.

Then these men came by agreement and found Daniel making petition and supplication before his God. Then they approached and spoke before the king about the king's injunction, "Did you not sign an injunction that any man who makes a petition to any god or man besides you, O king, for thirty days, is to be cast into the lions' den?"

The king replied, "The statement is true, according to the law of the Medes and Persians, which may not be revoked."

Then they answered and spoke before the king, "Daniel, who is one of the exiles from Judah, pays no attention to you, O king, or to the injunction which you signed, but keeps making his petition three times a day."

Then, as soon as the king heard this statement, he was deeply distressed and set his mind on delivering Daniel; and even until sunset he kept exerting himself to rescue him.

Daniel 6:6-14

In the first year of Darius the son of Ahasuerus, of Median descent, who was made king over the kingdom of the Chaldeans -

in the first year of his reign, I, Daniel, observed in the books the number of the years which was revealed as the word of the Lord to Jeremiah the prophet for the completion of the desolations of Jerusalem, namely, seventy years.

So I gave my attention to the Lord God to seek Him by **prayer** and supplications, with fasting, sackcloth and ashes.

I **prayed** to the Lord my God and confessed and said, "Alas, O Lord, the great and awesome God, who keeps His covenant and lovingkindness for those who love Him and keep His commandments, we have sinned, committed iniquity, acted wickedly and rebelled, even turning aside from Your commandments and ordinances. Moreover, we have not listened to Your servants the prophets, who spoke in Your name to our kings, our princes, our fathers and all the people of the land."   *Daniel 9:1-6*

"O Lord our God, who have brought Your people out of the land of Egypt with a mighty hand and have made a name for Yourself, as it is this day - we have sinned, we have been wicked. O Lord, in accordance with all Your righteous acts, let now Your anger and Your wrath turn away from Your city Jerusalem, Your holy mountain; for because of our sins and the iniquities of our fathers, Jerusalem and Your people have become a reproach to all those around us.

"So now, our God, listen to the **prayer** of Your servant and to his supplications, and for Your sake, O Lord, let Your face shine on Your desolate sanctuary. O my God, incline Your ear and hear!

"Open Your eyes and see our desolations and the city which is called by Your name; for we are not presenting our supplications before You on account of any merits of our own, but on account of Your great compassion. O Lord, hear! O Lord, forgive! O Lord, listen and take action! For Your own sake, O my God, do not delay, because Your city and Your people are called by Your name."

Now while I was speaking and **praying**, and confessing my sin and the sin of my people Israel, and presenting my supplication before the Lord my God in behalf of the holy mountain of my God, while I was still speaking in **prayer**, then the man Gabriel, whom I had seen in the vision previously, came to me in my extreme weariness about the time of the evening offering.

He gave me instruction and talked with me and said, "O Daniel, I have now come forth to give you insight with understanding. At the beginning of your supplications the command was issued, and I have come to tell you, for you are highly esteemed; so give heed to the message and gain understanding of the vision."
    Daniel 9:15-23

The word of the Lord came to Jonah the son of Amittai saying, "Arise, go to Nineveh the great city and cry against it, for their wickedness has come up before Me."

But Jonah rose up to flee to Tarshish from the presence of the Lord. So he went down to Joppa, found a ship which was going to Tarshish, paid the fare and went down into it to go with them to Tarshish from the presence of the Lord.

The Lord hurled a great wind on the sea and there was a great storm on the sea so that the ship was about to break up.

Then the sailors became afraid and every man cried to his god, and they threw the cargo which was in the ship into the sea to lighten it for them. But Jonah had gone below into the hold of the ship, lain down and fallen sound asleep.

So the captain approached him and said, "How is it that you are sleeping? Get up, call on your god. Perhaps your god will be concerned about us so that we will not perish."

Each man said to his mate, "Come, let us cast lots so we may learn on whose account this calamity has struck us." So they cast lots and the lot fell on Jonah.

Then they said to him, "Tell us, now! On whose account has this calamity struck us? What is your occupation? And where do you come from? What is your country? From what people are you?"

He said to them, "I am a Hebrew, and I fear the Lord God of heaven who made the sea and the dry land."

Then the men became extremely frightened and they said to him, "How could you do this?" For the men knew that he was fleeing from the presence of the Lord, because he had told them.

So they said to him, "What should we do to you that the sea may become calm for us?" - for the sea was becoming increasingly stormy.

He said to them, "Pick me up and throw me into the sea. Then the sea will become calm for you, for I know that on account of me this great storm has come upon you."

However, the men rowed desperately to return to land but they could not, for the sea was becoming even stormier against them.

Then they called on the Lord and said, "We earnestly **pray**, O Lord, do not let us perish on account of this man's life and do not put innocent blood on us; for You, O Lord, have done as You have pleased."

So they picked up Jonah, threw him into the sea, and the sea stopped its raging. Then the men feared the Lord greatly, and they offered a sacrifice to the Lord and made vows.

And the Lord appointed a great fish to swallow Jonah, and Jonah was in the stomach of the fish three days and three nights.

Then Jonah **prayed** to the Lord his God from the stomach of the fish, and he said, "I called out of my distress to the Lord, and He answered me. I cried for help from the depth of Sheol; You heard my voice. For You had cast me into the deep, into the heart of the seas, and the current engulfed me. All Your breakers and billows passed over me.

"So I said, 'I have been expelled from Your sight. Nevertheless I will look again toward Your holy temple.' Water encompassed me to the point of death. The great deep engulfed me, weeds were

wrapped around my head.

"I descended to the roots of the mountains. The earth with its bars was around me forever, but You have brought up my life from the pit, O Lord my God.

"While I was fainting away, I remembered the Lord, and my **prayer** came to You, into Your holy temple. Those who regard vain idols forsake their faithfulness, but I will sacrifice to You with the voice of thanksgiving.

"That which I have vowed I will pay. Salvation is from the Lord."

Then the Lord commanded the fish, and it vomited Jonah up onto the dry land.
Jonah 1:1 - 2:10

When God saw their deeds, that they turned from their wicked way, then God relented concerning the calamity which He had declared He would bring upon them. And He did not do it. But it greatly displeased Jonah and he became angry.

He **prayed** to the Lord and said, "Please Lord, was not this what I said while I was still in my own country? Therefore in order to forestall this I fled to Tarshish, for I knew that You are a gracious and compassionate God, slow to anger and abundant in lovingkindness, and one who relents concerning calamity.

"Therefore now, O Lord, please take my life from me, for death is better to me than life."

The Lord said, "Do you have good reason to be angry?" *Jonah 3:10 - 4:4*

A **prayer** of Habakkuk the prophet, according to Shigionoth.

"Lord, I have heard the report about You and I fear. O Lord, revive Your work in the midst of the years, in the midst of the years make it known; in wrath remember mercy.

"God comes from Teman, and the Holy One from Mount Paran. His splendor covers the heavens, and the earth is full of His praise." *Habakkuk 3:1-3*

NEW TESTAMENT

You have heard that it was said, "You shall love your neighbor and hate your enemy." But I say to you, love your enemies and **pray** for those who persecute you, so that you may be sons of your Father who is in heaven; for He causes His sun to rise on the evil and the good, and sends rain on the righteous and the unrighteous.

For if you love those who love you, what reward do you have? Do not even the tax collectors do the same? If you greet only your brothers, what more are you doing than others? Do not even the Gentiles do the same?   *Matthew 5:43-47*

When you **pray**, you are not to be like the hypocrites; for they love to stand and **pray** in the synagogues and on the street corners so that they may be seen by men. Truly I say to you, they have their reward in full.

But you, when you **pray**, go into your inner room, close your door and **pray** to your Father who is in secret, and your Father who sees what is done in secret will reward you.

And when you are **praying**, do not use meaningless repetition as the Gentiles do, for they suppose that they will be heard for their many words. So do not be like them; for your Father knows what you need before you ask Him.

Pray, then, in this way: "Our Father who is in heaven, hallowed be Your name. Your kingdom come. Your will be done, on earth as it is in heaven.

"Give us this day our daily bread. And forgive us our debts, as we also have forgiven our debtors.

"And do not lead us into temptation, but deliver us from evil. [For Yours is the kingdom and the power and the glory forever. Amen.]"

For if you forgive others for their transgressions, your heavenly Father will also forgive you. But if you do not forgive others, then your Father will not forgive your transgressions.   *Matthew 6:5-15*

After He had sent the crowds away, He went up on the mountain by Himself to **pray**; and when it was evening, He was there alone.   *Matthew 14:23*

When they came to the crowd, a man came up to Jesus, falling on his knees before Him and saying, "Lord, have mercy on my son, for he is a lunatic and is very ill; for he often falls into the fire and often into the water. I brought him to Your disciples, and they could not cure him."

And Jesus answered and said, "You unbelieving and perverted generation, how long shall I be with you? How long shall I put up with you? Bring him here to Me."

And Jesus rebuked him, and the demon came out of him, and the boy was cured at once.

Then the disciples came to Jesus privately and said, "Why could we not drive it out?"

And He said to them, "Because of the littleness of your faith; for truly I say to you, if you have faith the size of a mustard seed, you will say to this mountain, 'Move from here to there,' and it will move; and nothing will be impossible to you. [But this kind does not go out except by **prayer** and fasting.]"   *Matthew 17:14-21*

Some children were brought to Him so that He might lay His hands on them and **pray**; and the disciples rebuked them.

But Jesus said, "Let the children alone, and do not hinder them from coming to Me; for the kingdom of heaven belongs to such as these."

After laying His hands on them, He departed from there.   *Matthew 19:13-15*

Jesus entered the temple and drove out all those who were buying and selling in the temple, and overturned the tables of the money changers and the seats of those who were selling doves.

And He said to them, "It is written, 'My house shall be called a house of **prayer**'; but you are making it a robbers' den."   *Matthew 21:12-13*

In the morning, when He was returning to the city, He became hungry. Seeing a lone fig tree by the road, He came to it and found nothing on it except leaves only; and He said to it, "No longer shall there ever be any fruit from you." And at once the fig tree withered.

Seeing this, the disciples were amazed and asked, "How did the fig tree wither all at once?"

And Jesus answered and said to them, "Truly I say to you, if you have faith and do not doubt, you will not only do what was done to the fig tree, but even if you say to this mountain, 'Be taken up and cast into the sea,' it will happen.

And all things you ask in **prayer**, believing, you will receive."

Matthew 21:18-22

Whoever exalts himself shall be humbled; and whoever humbles himself shall be exalted.

But woe to you, scribes and Pharisees, hypocrites, because you shut off the kingdom of heaven from people; for you do not enter in yourselves, nor do you allow those who are entering to go in.

[Woe to you, scribes and Pharisees, hypocrites, because you devour widows' houses, and for a pretense you make long **prayers**; therefore you will receive greater condemnation.]   *Matthew 23:12-14*

They will deliver you to tribulation, and will kill you, and you will be hated by all nations because of My name. At that time many will fall away and will betray one another and hate one another. Many false prophets will arise and will mislead many.

Because lawlessness is increased, most people's love will grow cold. But the one who endures to the end, he will be saved.

This gospel of the kingdom shall be preached in the whole world as a testimony to all the nations, and then the end will come.

Therefore when you see the abomination of desolation which was spoken of through Daniel the prophet, standing in the holy place (let the reader understand), then those who are in Judea must flee to the mountains.

Whoever is on the housetop must not go down to get the things out that are in his house. Whoever is in the field must not turn back to get his cloak. But woe to those who are pregnant and to those who are nursing babies in those days!

But **pray** that your flight will not be in the winter, or on a Sabbath. For then there will be a great tribulation, such as has not occurred since the beginning of the world until now, nor ever will.

Matthew 24:9-21

Jesus came with them to a place called Gethsemane, and said to His disciples, "Sit here while I go over there and **pray**."

And He took with Him Peter and the two sons of Zebedee, and began to be grieved and distressed.

Then He said to them, "My soul is deeply grieved, to the point of death; remain here and keep watch with Me."

And He went a little beyond them, and fell on His face and **prayed**, saying, "My Father, if it is possible, let this cup pass from Me; yet not as I will, but as You will."

And He came to the disciples and found them sleeping, and said to Peter, "So, you men could not keep watch with Me for one hour? Keep watching and **praying** that you may not enter into temptation; the spirit is willing, but the flesh is weak."

He went away again a second time and **prayed**, saying, "My Father, if this cannot pass away unless I drink it, Your will be done."

Again He came and found them sleeping, for their eyes were heavy. And He left them again, and went away and **prayed** a third time, saying the same thing once more.

Then He came to the disciples and said to them, "Are you still sleeping and resting? Behold, the hour is at hand and the Son of Man is being betrayed into the hands of sinners. Get up, let us be going; behold, the one who betrays Me is at hand!" *Matthew 26:36-46*

In the early morning, while it was still dark, Jesus got up, left the house, and went away to a secluded place, and was **praying** there.

Simon and his companions searched for Him; they found Him, and said to Him, "Everyone is looking for You." He said to them, "Let us go somewhere else to the towns nearby, so that I may preach there also; for that is what I came for."

And He went into their synagogues throughout all Galilee, preaching and casting out the demons. *Mark 1:35-39*

Jesus made His disciples get into the boat and go ahead of Him to the other side to Bethsaida, while He Himself was sending the crowd away. After bidding them farewell, He left for the mountain to **pray**. *Mark 6:45-46*

They brought the boy to Him. When he saw Him, immediately the spirit threw him into a convulsion, and falling to the ground, he began rolling around and foaming at the mouth.

And He asked his father, "How long has this been happening to him?" And he said, "From childhood. It has often thrown him both into the fire and into the water to destroy him. But if You can do anything, take pity on us and help us!"

And Jesus said to him, " 'If You can?' All things are possible to him who believes."

Immediately the boy's father cried out and said, "I do believe; help my unbelief."

When Jesus saw that a crowd was rapidly gathering, He rebuked the unclean spirit, saying to it, "You deaf and mute spirit, I command you, come out of him and do not enter him again."

After crying out and throwing him into terrible convulsions, it came out; and the boy became so much like a corpse that most of them said, "He is dead!"

But Jesus took him by the hand and raised him; and he got up. When He came into the house, His disciples began questioning Him privately, "Why could we not drive it out?"

And He said to them, "This kind cannot come out by anything but **prayer**." *Mark 9:20-29*

They came to Jerusalem. And He entered the temple and began to drive out those who were buying and selling in the temple, and overturned the tables of the money changers and the seats of those who were selling doves; and He would not permit anyone to carry merchandise through the temple.

And He began to teach and say to them, "Is it not written, 'My house shall be called a house of **prayer** for all the nations'? But you have made it a robbers' den." The chief priests and the scribes heard this, and began seeking how to destroy Him; for they were afraid of Him, for the whole crowd was astonished at His teaching.

When evening came, they would go out of the city. As they were passing by in the morning, they saw the fig tree withered from the roots up.

Being reminded, Peter said to Him, "Rabbi, look, the fig tree which You cursed has withered."

And Jesus answered saying to them, "Have faith in God. Truly I say to you, whoever says to this mountain, 'Be taken up and cast into the sea,' and does not doubt in his heart, but believes that what he says is going to happen, it will be granted him.

"Therefore I say to you, all things for which you **pray** and ask, believe that you have received them, and they will be granted you.

"Whenever you stand **praying**, forgive, if you have anything against anyone, so that your Father who is in heaven will also forgive you your transgressions. [But if you do not forgive, neither will your Father who is in heaven forgive your transgressions.]" *Mark 11:15-26*

In His teaching He was saying: "Beware of the scribes who like to walk around in long robes, and like respectful greetings in the market places, and chief seats in the synagogues and places of honor at banquets, who devour widows' houses, and for appearance's sake offer long **prayers**; these will receive greater condemnation." *Mark 12:38-40*

When they arrest you and hand you over, do not worry beforehand about what you are to say, but say whatever is given you in that hour; for it is not you who speak, but it is the Holy Spirit.

Brother will betray brother to death, and a father his child; and children will rise up against parents and have them put to death. You will be hated by all because of My name, but the one who endures to the end, he will be saved.

But when you see the abomination of desolation standing where it should not be (let the reader understand), then those who are in Judea must flee to the mountains. The one who is on the housetop must not go down, or go in to get anything out of his house; and the one who is in the field must not turn back to get his coat.

But woe to those who are pregnant and to those who are nursing babies in those days!

But **pray** that it may not happen in the winter. For those days will be a time of tribulation such as has not occurred since the beginning of the creation which God created until now, and never will.

Unless the Lord had shortened those days, no life would have been saved; but for the sake of the elect, whom He chose, He shortened the days. *Mark 13:11-20*

They came to a place named Gethsemane; and He said to His disciples, "Sit here until I have **prayed**."

And He took with Him Peter and James and John, and began to be very distressed and troubled. And He said to them, "My soul is deeply grieved to the point of death; remain here and keep watch."

And He went a little beyond them, and fell to the ground and began to **pray** that if it were possible, the hour might pass Him by.

And He was saying, "Abba! Father! All things are possible for You; remove this cup from Me; yet not what I will, but what You will."

And He came and found them sleeping, and said to Peter, "Simon, are you asleep? Could you not keep watch for one hour? Keep watching and **praying** that you may not come into temptation; the spirit is willing, but the flesh is weak."

Again He went away and **prayed**, saying the same words. And again He came and found them sleeping, for their eyes were very heavy; and they did not know what to answer Him.

And He came the third time, and said to them, "Are you still sleeping and resting? It is enough; the hour has come; behold, the Son of Man is being betrayed into the hands of sinners. Get up, let us be going; behold, the one who betrays Me is at hand!" *Mark 14:32-42*

In the days of Herod, king of Judea, there was a priest named Zacharias, of the division of Abijah; and he had a wife from the daughters of Aaron, and her name was Elizabeth. They were both righteous in the sight of God, walking blamelessly in all the commandments and requirements of the Lord. But they had no child, because Elizabeth was barren, and they were both advanced in years.

Now it happened that while he was performing his priestly service before God in the appointed order of his division, according to the custom of the priestly office, he was chosen by lot to enter the temple of the Lord and burn incense. And the whole multitude of the people were in **prayer** outside at the hour of the incense offering.

And an angel of the Lord appeared to him, standing to the right of the altar of incense.

Zacharias was troubled when he saw the angel, and fear gripped him. But the angel said to him, "Do not be afraid, Zacharias, for your petition has been heard, and your wife Elizabeth will bear you a son, and you will give him the name John." *Luke 1:5-13*

There was a prophetess, Anna the daughter of Phanuel, of the tribe of Asher. She was advanced in years and had lived with her husband seven years after her marriage, and then as a widow to the age of eighty-four. She never left the temple, serving night and day with fastings and **prayers**.

At that very moment she came up and began giving thanks to God, and continued to speak of Him to all those who were looking for the redemption of Jerusalem.   *Luke 2:36-38*

When all the people were baptized, Jesus was also baptized, and while He was **praying**, heaven was opened, and the Holy Spirit descended upon Him in bodily form like a dove, and a voice came out of heaven, "You are My beloved Son, in You I am well-pleased."   *Luke 3:21-22*

While He was in one of the cities, behold, there was a man covered with leprosy; and when he saw Jesus, he fell on his face and implored Him, saying, "Lord, if You are willing, You can make me clean."

And He stretched out His hand and touched him, saying, "I am willing; be cleansed." And immediately the leprosy left him.

And He ordered him to tell no one, "But go and show yourself to the priest and make an offering for your cleansing, just as Moses commanded, as a testimony to them."

But the news about Him was spreading even farther, and large crowds were gathering to hear Him and to be healed of their sicknesses. But Jesus Himself would often slip away to the wilderness and **pray**.   *Luke 5:12-16*

They said to Him, "The disciples of John often fast and offer **prayers**, the disciples of the Pharisees also do the same, but Yours eat and drink."

And Jesus said to them, "You cannot make the attendants of the bridegroom fast while the bridegroom is with them, can you? But the days will come; and when the bridegroom is taken away from them, then they will fast in those days."
                        Luke 5:33-35

It was at this time that He went off to the mountain to **pray**, and He spent the whole night in **prayer** to God.

And when day came, He called His disciples to Him and chose twelve of them, whom He also named as apostles: Simon, whom He also named Peter, and Andrew his brother; and James and John; and Philip and Bartholomew; and Matthew and Thomas; James the son of Alphaeus, and Simon who was called the Zealot; Judas the son of James, and Judas Iscariot, who became a traitor.
                        Luke 6:12-16

Woe to you who are well-fed now, for you shall be hungry. Woe to you who laugh now, for you shall mourn and weep.

Woe to you when all men speak well of you, for their fathers used to treat the false prophets in the same way.

But I say to you who hear, love your enemies, do good to those who hate you, bless those who curse you, **pray** for those who mistreat you.

Whoever hits you on the cheek, offer him the other also; and whoever takes away your coat, do not withhold your shirt from him either.

Give to everyone who asks of you, and whoever takes away what is yours, do not demand it back. Treat others the same way you want them to treat you.

If you love those who love you, what credit is that to you? For even sinners love those who love them.

If you do good to those who do good to you, what credit is that to you? For even sinners do the same.   *Luke 6:25-33*

It happened that while He was **praying** alone, the disciples were with Him, and He questioned them, saying, "Who do the people say that I am?"

They answered and said, "John the Baptist, and others say Elijah; but others, that one of the prophets of old has risen again."

And He said to them, "But who do

you say that I am?"

And Peter answered and said, "The Christ of God." *Luke 9:18-20*

Some eight days after these sayings, He took along Peter and John and James, and went up on the mountain to **pray**. And while He was **praying**, the appearance of His face became different, and His clothing became white and gleaming.

And behold, two men were talking with Him; and they were Moses and Elijah, who, appearing in glory, were speaking of His departure which He was about to accomplish at Jerusalem. *Luke 9:28-31*

It happened that while Jesus was **praying** in a certain place, after He had finished, one of His disciples said to Him, "Lord, teach us to **pray** just as John also taught his disciples."

And He said to them, "When you **pray**, say: 'Father, hallowed be Your name. Your kingdom come.

"Give us each day our daily bread. And forgive us our sins, for we ourselves also forgive everyone who is indebted to us. And lead us not into temptation.' " *Luke 11:1-4*

He was telling them a parable to show that at all times they ought to **pray** and not to lose heart, saying, "In a certain city there was a judge who did not fear God and did not respect man. There was a widow in that city, and she kept coming to him, saying, 'Give me legal protection from my opponent.'

"For a while he was unwilling; but afterward he said to himself, 'Even though I do not fear God nor respect man, yet because this widow bothers me, I will give her legal protection, otherwise by continually coming she will wear me out.' "

And the Lord said, "Hear what the unrighteous judge said; now, will not God bring about justice for His elect who cry to Him day and night, and will He delay long over them? I tell you that He will bring about justice for them quickly. However, when the Son of Man comes, will He find faith on the earth?"

And He also told this parable to some people who trusted in themselves that they were righteous, and viewed others with contempt: "Two men went up into the temple to **pray**, one a Pharisee and the other a tax collector.

"The Pharisee stood and was **praying** this to himself: 'God, I thank You that I am not like other people: swindlers, unjust, adulterers, or even like this tax collector. I fast twice a week; I pay tithes of all that I get.'

"But the tax collector, standing some distance away, was even unwilling to lift up his eyes to heaven, but was beating his breast, saying, 'God, be merciful to me, the sinner!'

"I tell you, this man went to his house justified rather than the other; for everyone who exalts himself will be humbled, but he who humbles himself will be exalted." *Luke 18:1-14*

Jesus entered the temple and began to drive out those who were selling, saying to them, "It is written, 'And My house shall be a house of **prayer**,' but you have made it a robbers' den."

And He was teaching daily in the temple; but the chief priests and the scribes and the leading men among the people were trying to destroy Him, and they could not find anything that they might do, for all the people were hanging on to every word He said. *Luke 19:45-48*

While all the people were listening, He said to the disciples, "Beware of the scribes, who like to walk around in long robes, and love respectful greetings in the market places, and chief seats in the synagogues and places of honor at banquets, who devour widows' houses, and for appearance's sake offer long **prayers**. These will receive greater condemnation." *Luke 20:45-47*

Be on guard, so that your hearts will not be weighted down with dissipation and drunkenness and the worries of life, and that day will not come on you suddenly like a trap; for it will come upon all those who dwell on the face of all the earth.

But keep on the alert at all times, **praying** that you may have strength to escape all these things that are about to take place, and to stand before the Son of Man. *Luke 21:34-36*

"Simon, Simon, behold, Satan has demanded permission to sift you like wheat; but I have **prayed** for you, that your faith may not fail; and you, when once you have turned again, strengthen your brothers."

But he said to Him, "Lord, with You I am ready to go both to prison and to death!" And He said, "I say to you, Peter, the rooster will not crow today until you have denied three times that you know Me." *Luke 22:31-34*

He came out and proceeded as was His custom to the Mount of Olives; and the disciples also followed Him. When He arrived at the place, He said to them, "**Pray** that you may not enter into temptation."

And He withdrew from them about a stone's throw, and He knelt down and began to **pray**, saying, "Father, if You are willing, remove this cup from Me; yet not My will, but Yours be done."

Now an angel from heaven appeared to Him, strengthening Him. And being in agony He was **praying** very fervently; and His sweat became like drops of blood, falling down upon the ground.

When He rose from **prayer**, He came to the disciples and found them sleeping from sorrow, and said to them, "Why are you sleeping? Get up and **pray** that you may not enter into temptation."

While He was still speaking, behold, a crowd came, and the one called Judas, one of the twelve, was preceding them; and he approached Jesus to kiss Him. But Jesus said to him, "Judas, are you betraying the Son of Man with a kiss?" *Luke 22:39-48*

They returned to Jerusalem from the mount called Olivet, which is near Jerusalem, a Sabbath day's journey away.

When they had entered the city, they went up to the upper room where they were staying; that is, Peter and John and James and Andrew, Philip and Thomas, Bartholomew and Matthew, James the son of Alphaeus, and Simon the Zealot, and Judas the son of James.

These all with one mind were continually devoting themselves to **prayer**, along with the women, and Mary the mother of Jesus, and with His brothers. *Acts 1:12-14*

"It is necessary that of the men who have accompanied us all the time that the Lord Jesus went in and out among us - beginning with the baptism of John until the day that He was taken up from us - one of these must become a witness with us of His resurrection."

So they put forward two men, Joseph called Barsabbas (who was also called Justus), and Matthias. And they **prayed** and said, "You, Lord, who know the hearts of all men, show which one of these two You have chosen to occupy this ministry and apostleship from which Judas turned aside to go to his own place."

And they drew lots for them, and the lot fell to Matthias; and he was added to the eleven apostles. *Acts 1:21-26*

"Let all the house of Israel know for certain that God has made Him both Lord and Christ - this Jesus whom you crucified."

Now when they heard this, they were pierced to the heart, and said to Peter and the rest of the apostles, "Brethren, what shall we do?"

Peter said to them, "Repent, and each of you be baptized in the name of Jesus Christ for the forgiveness of your sins; and you will receive the gift of the Holy Spirit. For the promise is for you and your children and for all who are far off, as many as the Lord our God will call to Himself."

And with many other words he solemnly testified and kept on exhorting them, saying, "Be saved from this perverse generation!"

So then, those who had received his

word were baptized; and that day there were added about three thousand souls. They were continually devoting themselves to the apostles' teaching and to fellowship, to the breaking of bread and to **prayer**.

Everyone kept feeling a sense of awe; and many wonders and signs were taking place through the apostles.

Acts 2:36-43

Peter and John were going up to the temple at the ninth hour, the hour of **prayer**. And a man who had been lame from his mother's womb was being carried along, whom they used to set down every day at the gate of the temple which is called Beautiful, in order to beg alms of those who were entering the temple.

When he saw Peter and John about to go into the temple, he began asking to receive alms. But Peter, along with John, fixed his gaze on him and said, "Look at us!" And he began to give them his attention, expecting to receive something from them.

But Peter said, "I do not possess silver and gold, but what I do have I give to you: In the name of Jesus Christ the Nazarene - walk!" And seizing him by the right hand, he raised him up; and immediately his feet and his ankles were strengthened.

With a leap he stood upright and began to walk; and he entered the temple with them, walking and leaping and praising God. *Acts 3:1-8*

"Lord, take note of their threats, and grant that Your bond-servants may speak Your word with all confidence, while You extend Your hand to heal, and signs and wonders take place through the name of Your holy servant Jesus."

And when they had **prayed**, the place where they had gathered together was shaken, and they were all filled with the Holy Spirit and began to speak the word of God with boldness. *Acts 4:29-31*

At this time while the disciples were increasing in number, a complaint arose on the part of the Hellenistic Jews against the native Hebrews, because their widows were being overlooked in the daily serving of food.

So the twelve summoned the congregation of the disciples and said, "It is not desirable for us to neglect the word of God in order to serve tables. Therefore, brethren, select from among you seven men of good reputation, full of the Spirit and of wisdom, whom we may put in charge of this task.

"But we will devote ourselves to **prayer** and to the ministry of the word."

The statement found approval with the whole congregation; and they chose Stephen, a man full of faith and of the Holy Spirit, and Philip, Prochorus, Nicanor, Timon, Parmenas and Nicolas, a proselyte from Antioch. And these they brought before the apostles; and after **praying**, they laid their hands on them.

The word of God kept on spreading; and the number of the disciples continued to increase greatly in Jerusalem, and a great many of the priests were becoming obedient to the faith. *Acts 6:1-7*

When the apostles in Jerusalem heard that Samaria had received the word of God, they sent them Peter and John, who came down and **prayed** for them that they might receive the Holy Spirit. For He had not yet fallen upon any of them; they had simply been baptized in the name of the Lord Jesus.

Then they began laying their hands on them, and they were receiving the Holy Spirit.

Now when Simon saw that the Spirit was bestowed through the laying on of the apostles' hands, he offered them money, saying, "Give this authority to me as well, so that everyone on whom I lay my hands may receive the Holy Spirit."

But Peter said to him, "May your silver perish with you, because you thought you could obtain the gift of God with money! You have no part or portion in this matter, for your heart is not right before God. Therefore repent of this wickedness of yours, and **pray** the Lord that, if possible, the intention of your heart may be forgiven you. For I see that you are in the gall of bitterness and in the bondage of iniquity."

But Simon answered and said, "**Pray** to the Lord for me yourselves, so that nothing of what you have said may come upon me."   *Acts 8:14-24*

There was a disciple at Damascus named Ananias; and the Lord said to him in a vision, "Ananias." And he said, "Here I am, Lord."

And the Lord said to him, "Get up and go to the street called Straight, and inquire at the house of Judas for a man from Tarsus named Saul, for he is **praying**, and he has seen in a vision a man named Ananias come in and lay his hands on him, so that he might regain his sight."

But Ananias answered, "Lord, I have heard from many about this man, how much harm he did to Your saints at Jerusalem; and here he has authority from the chief priests to bind all who call on Your name."

But the Lord said to him, "Go, for he is a chosen instrument of Mine, to bear My name before the Gentiles and kings and the sons of Israel; for I will show him how much he must suffer for My name's sake."

So Ananias departed and entered the house, and after laying his hands on him said, "Brother Saul, the Lord Jesus, who appeared to you on the road by which you were coming, has sent me so that you may regain your sight and be filled with the Holy Spirit."

And immediately there fell from his eyes something like scales, and he regained his sight, and he got up and was baptized; and he took food and was strengthened.

Now for several days he was with the disciples who were at Damascus, and immediately he began to proclaim Jesus in the synagogues, saying, "He is the Son of God."   *Acts 9:10-20*

In Joppa there was a disciple named Tabitha (which translated in Greek is called Dorcas); this woman was abounding with deeds of kindness and charity which she continually did. And it happened at that time that she fell sick and died; and when they had washed her body, they laid it in an upper room.

Since Lydda was near Joppa, the disciples, having heard that Peter was there, sent two men to him, imploring him, "Do not delay in coming to us." So Peter arose and went with them.

When he arrived, they brought him into the upper room; and all the widows stood beside him, weeping and showing all the tunics and garments that Dorcas used to make while she was with them.

But Peter sent them all out and knelt down and **prayed**, and turning to the body, he said, "Tabitha, arise."

And she opened her eyes, and when she saw Peter, she sat up.

And he gave her his hand and raised her up; and calling the saints and widows, he presented her alive.

It became known all over Joppa, and many believed in the Lord.   *Acts 9:36-42*

There was a man at Caesarea named Cornelius, a centurion of what was called the Italian cohort, a devout man and one who feared God with all his household, and gave many alms to the Jewish people and **prayed** to God continually.

About the ninth hour of the day he clearly saw in a vision an angel of God who had just come in and said to him, "Cornelius!" And fixing his gaze on him and being much alarmed, he said, "What is it, Lord?"

And he said to him, "Your **prayers** and alms have ascended as a memorial before God. Now dispatch some men to Joppa and send for a man named Simon, who is also called Peter; he is staying with a tanner named Simon, whose house is by the sea."

When the angel who was speaking to him had left, he summoned two of his servants and a devout soldier of those who were his personal attendants, and after he had explained everything to them, he sent them to Joppa.

On the next day, as they were on their way and approaching the city, Peter went up on the housetop about the sixth hour to **pray**.

But he became hungry and was desiring to eat; but while they were making preparations, he fell into a trance; and he saw the sky opened up, and an object like a great sheet coming down, lowered by four corners to the ground, and there were in it all kinds of four-footed animals and crawling creatures of the earth and birds of the air.

A voice came to him, "Get up, Peter, kill and eat!"

But Peter said, "By no means, Lord, for I have never eaten anything unholy and unclean."

Again a voice came to him a second time, "What God has cleansed, no longer consider unholy."

This happened three times, and immediately the object was taken up into the sky.   *Acts 10:1-16*

Cornelius said, "Four days ago to this hour, I was **praying** in my house during the ninth hour; and behold, a man stood before me in shining garments, and he said, 'Cornelius, your **prayer** has been heard and your alms have been remembered before God. Therefore send to Joppa and invite Simon, who is also called Peter, to come to you; he is staying at the house of Simon the tanner by the sea.'

"So I sent for you immediately, and you have been kind enough to come. Now then, we are all here present before God to hear all that you have been commanded by the Lord."   *Acts 10:30-33*

The apostles and the brethren who were throughout Judea heard that the Gentiles also had received the word of God.

And when Peter came up to Jerusalem, those who were circumcised took issue with him, saying, "You went to uncircumcised men and ate with them."

But Peter began speaking and proceeded to explain to them in orderly sequence, saying, "I was in the city of Joppa **praying**; and in a trance I saw a vision, an object coming down like a great sheet lowered by four corners from the sky; and it came right down to me, and when I had fixed my gaze on it and was observing it I saw the four-footed animals of the earth and the wild beasts and the crawling creatures and the birds of the air. I also heard a voice saying to me, 'Get up, Peter; kill and eat.'

"But I said, 'By no means, Lord, for nothing unholy or unclean has ever entered my mouth.'

"But a voice from heaven answered a second time, 'What God has cleansed, no longer consider unholy.' This happened three times, and everything was drawn back up into the sky.

"And behold, at that moment three men appeared at the house in which we were staying, having been sent to me from Caesarea."   *Acts 11:1-11*

About that time Herod the king laid hands on some who belonged to the church in order to mistreat them. And he had James the brother of John put to death with a sword. When he saw that it pleased the Jews, he proceeded to arrest Peter also.

Now it was during the days of Unleavened Bread. When he had seized him, he put him in prison, delivering him to four squads of soldiers to guard him, intending after the Passover to bring him out before the people. So Peter was kept in the prison, but **prayer** for him was being made fervently by the church to God.

On the very night when Herod was about to bring him forward, Peter was sleeping between two soldiers, bound with two chains, and guards in front of the door were watching over the prison. And behold, an angel of the Lord suddenly appeared and a light shone in the cell; and he struck Peter's side and woke him up, saying, "Get up quickly." And his chains fell off his hands.

And the angel said to him, "Gird yourself and put on your sandals." And he did so.

And he said to him, "Wrap your cloak around you and follow me." And he went out and continued to follow, and he did not know that what was being done by the angel was real, but thought he was seeing a vision.

When they had passed the first and second guard, they came to the iron gate that leads into the city, which opened for them by itself; and they went out and went along one street, and immediately the angel departed from him.

When Peter came to himself, he said, "Now I know for sure that the Lord has sent forth His angel and rescued me from the hand of Herod and from all that the Jewish people were expecting."

And when he realized this, he went to the house of Mary, the mother of John who was also called Mark, where many were gathered together and were **praying**. *Acts 12:1-12*

There were at Antioch, in the church that was there, prophets and teachers: Barnabas, and Simeon who was called Niger, and Lucius of Cyrene, and Manaen who had been brought up with Herod the tetrarch, and Saul. While they were ministering to the Lord and fasting, the Holy Spirit said, "Set apart for Me Barnabas and Saul for the work to which I have called them."

Then, when they had fasted and **prayed** and laid their hands on them, they sent them away. So, being sent out by the Holy Spirit, they went down to Seleucia and from there they sailed to Cyprus. *Acts 13:1-4*

After they had preached the gospel to that city and had made many disciples, they returned to Lystra and to Iconium and to Antioch, strengthening the souls of the disciples, encouraging them to continue in the faith, and saying, "Through many tribulations we must enter the kingdom of God."

When they had appointed elders for them in every church, having **prayed** with fasting, they commended them to the Lord in whom they had believed. *Acts 14:21-23*

A vision appeared to Paul in the night: a man of Macedonia was standing and appealing to him, and saying, "Come over to Macedonia and help us." When he had seen the vision, immediately we sought to go into Macedonia, concluding that God had called us to preach the gospel to them.

So putting out to sea from Troas, we ran a straight course to Samothrace, and on the day following to Neapolis; and from there to Philippi, which is a leading city of the district of Macedonia, a Roman colony; and we were staying in this city for some days.

And on the Sabbath day we went outside the gate to a riverside, where we were supposing that there would be a place of **prayer**; and we sat down and began speaking to the women who had assembled.

A woman named Lydia, from the city of Thyatira, a seller of purple fabrics, a worshiper of God, was listening; and the Lord opened her heart to respond to the things spoken by Paul.

And when she and her household had been baptized, she urged us, saying, "If you have judged me to be faithful to the Lord, come into my house and stay." And she prevailed upon us.

It happened that as we were going to the place of **prayer**, a slave-girl having a spirit of divination met us, who was bringing her masters much profit by fortune-telling.

Following after Paul and us, she kept crying out, saying, "These men are bond-servants of the Most High God, who are proclaiming to you the way of salvation." She continued doing this for many days.
~ *Acts 16:9-18*

The crowd rose up together against them, and the chief magistrates tore their robes off them and proceeded to order them to be beaten with rods.

When they had struck them with many blows, they threw them into prison, commanding the jailer to guard them securely; and he, having received such a command, threw them into the inner prison and fastened their feet in the stocks.

But about midnight Paul and Silas were **praying** and singing hymns of praise to God, and the prisoners were listening to them; and suddenly there came a great earthquake, so that the foundations of the prison house were shaken; and immediately all the doors were opened and everyone's chains were unfastened. *Acts 16:22-26*

"I have coveted no one's silver or gold or clothes. You yourselves know that these hands ministered to my own needs and to the men who were with me. In everything I showed you that by working hard in this manner you must help the weak and remember the words of the Lord Jesus, that He Himself said, 'It is more blessed to give than to receive.' "

When he had said these things, he knelt down and **prayed** with them all. And they began to weep aloud and embraced Paul, and repeatedly kissed him, grieving especially over the word which he had spoken, that they would not see his face again. And they were accompanying him to the ship. *Acts 20:33-38*

When our days there were ended, we left and started on our journey, while they all, with wives and children, escorted us until we were out of the city.

After kneeling down on the beach and **praying**, we said farewell to one another. Then we went on board the ship, and they returned home again. *Acts 21:5-6*

It happened when I returned to Jerusalem and was **praying** in the temple, that I fell into a trance, and I saw Him saying to me, "Make haste, and get out of Jerusalem quickly, because they will not accept your testimony about Me."

And I said, "Lord, they themselves understand that in one synagogue after another I used to imprison and beat those who believed in You.

"And when the blood of Your witness Stephen was being shed, I also was standing by approving, and watching out for the coats of those who were slaying him."

And He said to me, "Go! For I will send you far away to the Gentiles." *Acts 22:17-21*

The father of Publius was lying in bed afflicted with recurrent fever and dysentery; and Paul went in to see him and after he had **prayed**, he laid his hands on him and healed him.

After this had happened, the rest of the people on the island who had diseases were coming to him and getting cured. *Acts 28:8-9*

First, I thank my God through Jesus Christ for you all, because your faith is being proclaimed throughout the whole world. For God, whom I serve in my spirit in the preaching of the gospel of His Son, is my witness as to how unceasingly I make mention of you, always in my **prayers** making request, if perhaps now at last by the will of God I may succeed in coming to you. *Romans 1:8-10*

In hope we have been saved, but hope that is seen is not hope; for who hopes for what he already sees? But if we hope for what we do not see, with perseverance we wait eagerly for it.

In the same way the Spirit also helps our weakness; for we do not know how to **pray** as we should, but the Spirit Himself intercedes for us with groanings too deep for words; and He who searches the hearts knows what the mind of the Spirit is, because He intercedes for the saints according to the will of God. *Romans 8:24-27*

Brethren, my heart's desire and my **prayer** to God for them is for their salvation. For I testify about them that they have a zeal for God, but not in accordance with knowledge.

For not knowing about God's righteousness and seeking to establish their own, they did not subject themselves to the righteousness of God.

For Christ is the end of the law for righteousness to everyone who believes.

Romans 10:1-4

Let love be without hypocrisy. Abhor what is evil; cling to what is good. Be devoted to one another in brotherly love; give preference to one another in honor; not lagging behind in diligence, fervent in spirit, serving the Lord; rejoicing in hope, persevering in tribulation, devoted to **prayer**, contributing to the needs of the saints, practicing hospitality.

Bless those who persecute you; bless and do not curse. Rejoice with those who rejoice, and weep with those who weep.

Romans 12:9-15

I urge you, brethren, by our Lord Jesus Christ and by the love of the Spirit, to strive together with me in your **prayers** to God for me, that I may be rescued from those who are disobedient in Judea, and that my service for Jerusalem may prove acceptable to the saints; so that I may come to you in joy by the will of God and find refreshing rest in your company. Now the God of peace be with you all. Amen.   *Romans 15:30-33*

The husband must fulfill his duty to his wife, and likewise also the wife to her husband. The wife does not have authority over her own body, but the husband does; and likewise also the husband does not have authority over his own body, but the wife does.

Stop depriving one another, except by agreement for a time, so that you may devote yourselves to **prayer**, and come together again so that Satan will not tempt you because of your lack of self-control. But this I say by way of concession, not of command.   *1 Corinthians 7:3-6*

I praise you because you remember me in everything and hold firmly to the traditions, just as I delivered them to you. But I want you to understand that Christ is the head of every man, and the man is the head of a woman, and God is the head of

Christ.

Every man who has something on his head while **praying** or prophesying disgraces his head. But every woman who has her head uncovered while **praying** or prophesying disgraces her head, for she is one and the same as the woman whose head is shaved. For if a woman does not cover her head, let her also have her hair cut off; but if it is disgraceful for a woman to have her hair cut off or her head shaved, let her cover her head.

For a man ought not to have his head covered, since he is the image and glory of God; but the woman is the glory of man. For man does not originate from woman, but woman from man; for indeed man was not created for the woman's sake, but woman for the man's sake. Therefore the woman ought to have a symbol of authority on her head, because of the angels.

However, in the Lord, neither is woman independent of man, nor is man independent of woman. For as the woman originates from the man, so also the man has his birth through the woman; and all things originate from God.

Judge for yourselves: Is it proper for a woman to **pray** to God with her head uncovered? Does not even nature itself teach you that if a man has long hair, it is a dishonor to him, but if a woman has long hair, it is a glory to her? For her hair is given to her for a covering.

But if one is inclined to be contentious, we have no other practice, nor have the churches of God.   *1 Corinthians 11:2-16*

There are, perhaps, a great many kinds of languages in the world, and no kind is without meaning. If then I do not know the meaning of the language, I will be to the one who speaks a barbarian, and the one who speaks will be a barbarian to me. So also you, since you are zealous of spiritual gifts, seek to abound for the edification of the church.

Therefore let one who speaks in a tongue **pray** that he may interpret. For if I **pray** in a tongue, my spirit **prays**, but my mind is unfruitful. What is the outcome then?

I will **pray** with the spirit and I will **pray** with the mind also; I will sing with the spirit and I will sing with the mind also. Otherwise if you bless in the spirit only, how will the one who fills the place of the ungifted say the "Amen" at your giving of thanks, since he does not know what you are saying? For you are giving thanks well enough, but the other person is not edified. *1 Corinthians 14:10-17*

We do not want you to be unaware, brethren, of our affliction which came to us in Asia, that we were burdened excessively, beyond our strength, so that we despaired even of life; indeed, we had the sentence of death within ourselves so that we would not trust in ourselves, but in God who raises the dead; who delivered us from so great a peril of death, and will deliver us, He on whom we have set our hope.

And He will yet deliver us, you also joining in helping us through your **prayers**, so that thanks may be given by many persons on our behalf for the favor bestowed on us through the **prayers** of many. *2 Corinthians 1:8-11*

Because of the proof given by this ministry, they will glorify God for your obedience to your confession of the gospel of Christ and for the liberality of your contribution to them and to all, while they also, by **prayer** on your behalf, yearn for you because of the surpassing grace of God in you. Thanks be to God for His indescribable gift! *2 Corinthians 9:13-15*

We **pray** to God that you do no wrong; not that we ourselves may appear approved, but that you may do what is right, even though we may appear unapproved. For we can do nothing against the truth, but only for the truth.

For we rejoice when we ourselves are weak but you are strong; this we also **pray** for, that you be made complete. *2 Corinthians 13:7-9*

I too, having heard of the faith in the Lord Jesus which exists among you and your love for all the saints, do not cease giving thanks for you, while making mention of you in my **prayers**; that the God of our Lord Jesus Christ, the Father of glory, may give to you a spirit of wisdom and of revelation in the knowledge of Him.

I **pray** that the eyes of your heart may be enlightened, so that you will know what is the hope of His calling, what are the riches of the glory of His inheritance in the saints, and what is the surpassing greatness of His power toward us who believe. ~ *Ephesians 1:15-19*

With all **prayer** and petition **pray** at all times in the Spirit, and with this in view, be on the alert with all perseverance and petition for all the saints, and **pray** on my behalf, that utterance may be given to me in the opening of my mouth, to make known with boldness the mystery of the gospel, for which I am an ambassador in chains; that in proclaiming it I may speak boldly, as I ought to speak. *Ephesians 6:18-20*

I thank my God in all my remembrance of you, always offering **prayer** with joy in my every **prayer** for you all, in view of your participation in the gospel from the first day until now. For I am confident of this very thing, that He who began a good work in you will perfect it until the day of Christ Jesus.

For it is only right for me to feel this way about you all, because I have you in my heart, since both in my imprisonment and in the defense and confirmation of the gospel, you all are partakers of grace with me.

For God is my witness, how I long for you all with the affection of Christ Jesus. And this I **pray**, that your love may abound still more and more in real knowledge and all discernment, so that you may approve the things that are excellent, in order to be sincere and blameless until the day of Christ; having been filled with the fruit of righteousness which comes through Jesus Christ, to the glory and praise of God. *Philippians 1:3-11*

What then? Only that in every way, whether in pretense or in truth, Christ is proclaimed; and in this I rejoice.

Yes, and I will rejoice, for I know that this will turn out for my deliverance through your **prayers** and the provision of the Spirit of Jesus Christ, according to my earnest expectation and hope, that I will not be put to shame in anything, but that with all boldness, Christ will even now, as always, be exalted in my body, whether by life or by death. For to me, to live is Christ and to die is gain. *Philippians 1:18-21*

Rejoice in the Lord always; again I will say, rejoice! Let your gentle spirit be known to all men. The Lord is near.

Be anxious for nothing, but in everything by **prayer** and supplication with thanksgiving let your requests be made known to God. And the peace of God, which surpasses all comprehension, will guard your hearts and your minds in Christ Jesus. *Philippians 4:4-7*

Paul, an apostle of Jesus Christ by the will of God, and Timothy our brother, to the saints and faithful brethren in Christ who are at Colossae: Grace to you and peace from God our Father.

We give thanks to God, the Father of our Lord Jesus Christ, **praying** always for you, since we heard of your faith in Christ Jesus and the love which you have for all the saints; because of the hope laid up for you in heaven, of which you previously heard in the word of truth, the gospel which has come to you, just as in all the world also it is constantly bearing fruit and increasing, even as it has been doing in you also since the day you heard of it and understood the grace of God in truth; just as you learned it from Epaphras, our beloved fellow bond-servant, who is a faithful servant of Christ on our behalf, and he also informed us of your love in the Spirit.

For this reason also, since the day we heard of it, we have not ceased to **pray** for you and to ask that you may be filled with the knowledge of His will in all spiritual wisdom and understanding, so that you will walk in a manner worthy of the Lord, to please Him in all respects, bearing fruit in every good work and increasing in the knowledge of God; strengthened with all power, according to His glorious might, for the attaining of all steadfastness and patience; joyously giving thanks to the Father, who has qualified us to share in the inheritance of the saints in Light. *Colossians 1:1-12*

Devote yourselves to **prayer**, keeping alert in it with an attitude of thanksgiving; **praying** at the same time for us as well, that God will open up to us a door for the word, so that we may speak forth the mystery of Christ, for which I have also been imprisoned; that I may make it clear in the way I ought to speak. *Colossians 4:2-4*

Epaphras, who is one of your number, a bond-slave of Jesus Christ, sends you his greetings, always laboring earnestly for you in his **prayers**, that you may stand perfect and fully assured in all the will of God. *Colossians 4:12*

Paul and Silvanus and Timothy, to the church of the Thessalonians in God the Father and the Lord Jesus Christ: Grace to you and peace. We give thanks to God always for all of you, making mention of you in our **prayers**; constantly bearing in mind your work of faith and labor of love and steadfastness of hope in our Lord Jesus Christ in the presence of our God and Father, knowing, brethren beloved by God, His choice of you; for our gospel did not come to you in word only, but also in power and in the Holy Spirit and with full conviction; just as you know what kind of men we proved to be among you for your sake. *1 Thessalonians 1:1-5*

What thanks can we render to God for you in return for all the joy with which we rejoice before our God on your account, as we night and day keep **praying** most earnestly that we may see your face, and may complete what is lacking in your faith? *1 Thessalonians 3:9-10*

Rejoice always; **pray** without ceasing; in everything give thanks; for this is God's will for you in Christ Jesus.

Do not quench the Spirit; do not despise prophetic utterances. But examine everything carefully; hold fast to that which is good; abstain from every form of evil.

Now may the God of peace Himself sanctify you entirely; and may your spirit and soul and body be preserved complete, without blame at the coming of our Lord Jesus Christ. Faithful is He who calls you, and He also will bring it to pass.

Brethren, **pray** for us. Greet all the brethren with a holy kiss. *1 Thessalonians 5:16-26*

To this end also we **pray** for you always, that our God will count you worthy of your calling, and fulfill every desire for goodness and the work of faith with power, so that the name of our Lord Jesus will be glorified in you, and you in Him, according to the grace of our God and the Lord Jesus Christ. *2 Thessalonians 1:11-12*

Finally, brethren, **pray** for us that the word of the Lord will spread rapidly and be glorified, just as it did also with you; and that we will be rescued from perverse and evil men; for not all have faith.

But the Lord is faithful, and He will strengthen and protect you from the evil one. *2 Thessalonians 3:1-3*

First, I urge that entreaties and **prayers**, petitions and thanksgivings, be made on behalf of all men, for kings and all who are in authority, so that we may lead a tranquil and quiet life in all godliness and dignity. This is good and acceptable in the sight of God our Savior, who desires all men to be saved and to come to the knowledge of the truth.

For there is one God, and one mediator also between God and men, the man Christ Jesus, who gave Himself as a ransom for all, the testimony given at the proper time.

For this I was appointed a preacher and an apostle (I am telling the truth, I am not lying) as a teacher of the Gentiles in faith and truth. Therefore I want the men in every place to **pray**, lifting up holy hands, without wrath and dissension. *1 Timothy 2:1-8*

The Spirit explicitly says that in later times some will fall away from the faith, paying attention to deceitful spirits and doctrines of demons, by means of the hypocrisy of liars seared in their own conscience as with a branding iron, men who forbid marriage and advocate abstaining from foods which God has created to be gratefully shared in by those who believe and know the truth.

For everything created by God is good, and nothing is to be rejected if it is received with gratitude; for it is sanctified by means of the word of God and **prayer**.

In pointing out these things to the brethren, you will be a good servant of Christ Jesus, constantly nourished on the words of the faith and of the sound doctrine which you have been following. *1 Timothy 4:1-6*

Honor widows who are widows indeed; but if any widow has children or grandchildren, they must first learn to practice piety in regard to their own family and to make some return to their parents; for this is acceptable in the sight of God.

Now she who is a widow indeed and who has been left alone, has fixed her hope on God and continues in entreaties and **prayers** night and day. But she who gives herself to wanton pleasure is dead even while she lives.

Prescribe these things as well, so that they may be above reproach. *1 Timothy 5:3-7*

Paul, an apostle of Christ Jesus by the will of God, according to the promise of life in Christ Jesus, to Timothy, my beloved son: Grace, mercy and peace from God the Father and Christ Jesus our Lord.

I thank God, whom I serve with a

clear conscience the way my forefathers did, as I constantly remember you in my **prayers** night and day, longing to see you, even as I recall your tears, so that I may be filled with joy.   *2 Timothy 1:1-4*

Grace to you and peace from God our Father and the Lord Jesus Christ. I thank my God always, making mention of you in my **prayers**, because I hear of your love and of the faith which you have toward the Lord Jesus and toward all the saints; and I **pray** that the fellowship of your faith may become effective through the knowledge of every good thing which is in you for Christ's sake.   *Philemon 3-6*

Having confidence in your obedience, I write to you, since I know that you will do even more than what I say.

At the same time also prepare me a lodging, for I hope that through your **prayers** I will be given to you.   *Philemon 21-22*

No one takes the honor to himself, but receives it when he is called by God, even as Aaron was.

So also Christ did not glorify Himself so as to become a high priest, but He who said to Him, "You are My Son, today I have begotten You"; just as He says also in another passage, "You are a priest forever according to the order of Melchizedek."

In the days of His flesh, He offered up both **prayers** and supplications with loud crying and tears to the One able to save Him from death, and He was heard because of His piety.

Although He was a Son, He learned obedience from the things which He suffered. And having been made perfect, He became to all those who obey Him the source of eternal salvation, being designated by God as a high priest according to the order of Melchizedek.   *Hebrews 5:4-10*

Pray for us, for we are sure that we have a good conscience, desiring to conduct ourselves honorably in all things. And I urge you all the more to do this, so that I

may be restored to you the sooner.

Now the God of peace, who brought up from the dead the great Shepherd of the sheep through the blood of the eternal covenant, even Jesus our Lord, equip you in every good thing to do His will, working in us that which is pleasing in His sight, through Jesus Christ, to whom be the glory forever and ever. Amen.   *Hebrews 13:18-21*

Is anyone among you suffering? Then he must **pray**. Is anyone cheerful? He is to sing praises. Is anyone among you sick? Then he must call for the elders of the church and they are to **pray** over him, anointing him with oil in the name of the Lord; and the **prayer** offered in faith will restore the one who is sick, and the Lord will raise him up, and if he has committed sins, they will be forgiven him.

Therefore, confess your sins to one another, and **pray** for one another so that you may be healed.

The effective **prayer** of a righteous man can accomplish much. Elijah was a man with a nature like ours, and he **prayed** earnestly that it would not rain, and it did not rain on the earth for three years and six months.

Then he **prayed** again, and the sky poured rain and the earth produced its fruit.   *James 5:13-18*

You husbands in the same way, live with your wives in an understanding way, as with someone weaker, since she is a woman; and show her honor as a fellow heir of the grace of life, so that your **prayers** will not be hindered.

To sum up, all of you be harmonious, sympathetic, brotherly, kindhearted, and humble in spirit; not returning evil for evil or insult for insult, but giving a blessing instead; for you were called for the very purpose that you might inherit a blessing.

For, "The one who desires life, to love and see good days, must keep his tongue from evil and his lips from speaking deceit. He must turn away from evil and do good; he must seek peace and pursue it.

For the eyes of the Lord are toward the righteous, and His ears attend to their **prayer**, but the face of the Lord is against those who do evil."
1 Peter 3:7-12

The end of all things is near; therefore, be of sound judgment and sober spirit for the purpose of **prayer**.

Above all, keep fervent in your love for one another, because love covers a multitude of sins. Be hospitable to one another without complaint.

As each one has received a special gift, employ it in serving one another as good stewards of the manifold grace of God.
1 Peter 4:7-10

Beloved, I **pray** that in all respects you may prosper and be in good health, just as your soul prospers. For I was very glad when brethren came and testified to your truth, that is, how you are walking in truth.

I have no greater joy than this, to hear of my children walking in the truth.
3 John 2-4

You, beloved, ought to remember the words that were spoken beforehand by the apostles of our Lord Jesus Christ, that they were saying to you, "In the last time there will be mockers, following after their own ungodly lusts." These are the ones who cause divisions, worldly-minded, devoid of the Spirit.

But you, beloved, building yourselves up on your most holy faith, **praying** in the Holy Spirit, keep yourselves in the love of God, waiting anxiously for the mercy of our Lord Jesus Christ to eternal life.
Jude 17-21

I saw between the throne (with the four living creatures) and the elders a Lamb standing, as if slain, having seven horns and seven eyes, which are the seven Spirits of God, sent out into all the earth.

And He came and took the book out of the right hand of Him who sat on the throne.

When He had taken the book, the four living creatures and the twenty-four elders fell down before the Lamb, each one holding a harp and golden bowls full of incense, which are the **prayers** of the saints.

And they sang a new song, saying, "Worthy are You to take the book and to break its seals; for You were slain, and purchased for God with Your blood men from every tribe and tongue and people and nation. You have made them to be a kingdom and priests to our God; and they will reign upon the earth." *Revelation 5:6-10*

When the Lamb broke the seventh seal, there was silence in heaven for about half an hour.

And I saw the seven angels who stand before God, and seven trumpets were given to them.

Another angel came and stood at the altar, holding a golden censer; and much incense was given to him, so that he might add it to the **prayers** of all the saints on the golden altar which was before the throne. And the smoke of the incense, with the **prayers** of the saints, went up before God out of the angel's hand.

Then the angel took the censer and filled it with the fire of the altar, and threw it to the earth; and there followed peals of thunder and sounds and flashes of lightning and an earthquake.

And the seven angels who had the seven trumpets prepared themselves to sound them. *Revelation 8:1-6*

FAITH

/ FAITHLESS / FAITHLESSNESS

Definitions

Faith 1. Belief that is not based on proof.

2. Belief in God or a Supreme being.

3. Belief in the doctrines or teachings of religion.

4. A system of belief; a religion.

5. The act or state of having confidence or trust in a person or thing.

6. Belief in anything as a code of ethics or standard of merit.

7. Fidelity to one's promise, oath, allegiance, etc.

Faithless 1. Lacking trust or belief, especially in God or religion.

2. Being without a faith or lacking strong convictions.

3. Not adhering to allegiance, promises, vows, or duty.

4. False to promises and agreements; not trustworthy; unreliable.

OLD TESTAMENT

The Lord spoke to Moses that very same day, saying, "Go up to this mountain of the Abarim, Mount Nebo, which is in the land of Moab opposite Jericho, and look at the land of Canaan, which I am giving to the sons of Israel for a possession.

"Then die on the mountain where you ascend, and be gathered to your people, as Aaron your brother died on Mount Hor and was gathered to his people, because you broke **faith** with Me in the midst of the sons of Israel at the waters of Meri-bahkadesh, in the wilderness of Zin, because you did not treat Me as holy in the midst of the sons of Israel.

"For you shall see the land at a distance, but you shall not go there, into the land which I am giving the sons of Israel."
Deuteronomy 32:48-52

Will the wild ox consent to serve you, or will he spend the night at your manger?

Can you bind the wild ox in a furrow with ropes, or will he harrow the valleys after you? Will you trust him because his strength is great and leave your labor to him?

Will you have **faith** in him that he will return your grain and gather it from your threshing floor?
Job 39:9-12

How blessed is he whose help is the God of Jacob, whose hope is in the Lord his God, who made heaven and earth, the sea and all that is in them; who keeps **faith** forever; who executes justice for the oppressed; who gives food to the hungry. The Lord sets the prisoners free.
Psalm 146:5-7

Give me your heart, my son, and let your eyes delight in my ways. For a harlot is a deep pit and an adulterous woman is a narrow well.

Surely she lurks as a robber, and increases the **faithless** among men.
Proverb 23:26-28

Like a bad tooth and an unsteady foot is confidence in a **faithless** man in time of trouble.
Proverb 25:19

The Lord said to me in the days of Josiah the king, "Have you seen what **faithless** Israel did? She went up on every high hill and under every green tree, and she was a harlot there. I thought, 'After she has done all these things she will return to Me'; but she did not return, and her treacherous sister Judah saw it.

"And I saw that for all the adulteries of **faithless** Israel, I had sent her away and given her a writ of divorce, yet her treacherous sister Judah did not fear; but she went and was a harlot also.

"Because of the lightness of her harlotry, she polluted the land and committed adultery with stones and trees. Yet in spite of all this her treacherous sister Judah did not return to Me with all her heart, but rather in deception," declares the Lord.

And the Lord said to me, "**Faithless** Israel has proved herself more righteous than treacherous Judah.

"Go and proclaim these words toward the north and say, 'Return, **faithless** Israel,' declares the Lord; 'I will not look upon you in anger.

'For I am gracious,' declares the Lord; 'I will not be angry forever. Only acknowledge your iniquity, that you have transgressed against the Lord your God and have scattered your favors to the strangers under every green tree, and you have not obeyed My voice,' declares the Lord.

'Return, O **faithless** sons,' declares the Lord; 'for I am a master to you, and I will take you one from a city and two from a family, and I will bring you to Zion.

'Then I will give you shepherds after My own heart, who will feed you on knowledge and understanding.' " *Jeremiah 3:6-15*

A voice is heard on the bare heights, the weeping and the supplications of the sons of Israel; because they have perverted their way, they have forgotten the Lord their God.

"Return, O **faithless** sons, I will heal your **faithlessness**."

Behold, we come to You; for You are the Lord our God.

Surely, the hills are a deception, a tumult on the mountains. Surely in the Lord our God is the salvation of Israel.
Jeremiah 3:21-23

Set up for yourself roadmarks, place for yourself guideposts; direct your mind to the highway, the way by which you went.

Return, O virgin of Israel, return to these your cities. How long will you go here and there, O **faithless** daughter? For the Lord has created a new thing in the earth - a woman will encompass a man. *Jeremiah 31:21-22*

Israel is a luxuriant vine; he produces fruit for himself. The more his fruit, the more altars he made; the richer his land, the better he made the sacred pillars.

Their heart is **faithless**; now they must bear their guilt. The Lord will break down their altars and destroy their sacred pillars. *Hosea 10:1-2*

Behold, as for the proud one, his soul is not right within him; but the righteous will live by his **faith**. *Habakkuk 2:4*

NEW TESTAMENT

I say to you, do not be worried about your life, as to what you will eat or what you will drink; nor for your body, as to what you will put on. Is not life more than food, and the body more than clothing?

Look at the birds of the air, that they do not sow, nor reap nor gather into barns, and yet your heavenly Father feeds them. Are you not worth much more than they?

And who of you by being worried can add a single hour to his life?

And why are you worried about clothing? Observe how the lilies of the field grow; they do not toil nor do they spin, yet I say to you that not even Solomon in all his glory clothed himself like one of these.

But if God so clothes the grass of the field, which is alive today and tomorrow is thrown into the furnace, will He not much more clothe you? You of little **faith**!

Do not worry then, saying, "What will we eat?" or "What will we drink?" or "What will we wear for clothing?" For the Gentiles eagerly seek all these things; for your heavenly Father knows that you need all these things.

But seek first His kingdom and His righteousness, and all these things will be added to you.

So do not worry about tomorrow; for tomorrow will care for itself. Each day has enough trouble of its own.

Matthew 6:25-34

When Jesus entered Capernaum, a centurion came to Him, imploring Him, and saying, "Lord, my servant is lying paralyzed at home, fearfully tormented."

Jesus said to him, "I will come and heal him."

But the centurion said, "Lord, I am not worthy for You to come under my roof, but just say the word, and my servant will be healed. For I also am a man under authority, with soldiers under me; and I say to this one, 'Go!' and he goes, and to another, 'Come!' and he comes, and to my slave, 'Do this!' and he does it."

Now when Jesus heard this, He marveled and said to those who were following, "Truly I say to you, I have not found such great **faith** with anyone in Israel.

'I say to you that many will come from east and west, and recline at the table with Abraham, Isaac and Jacob in the kingdom of heaven; but the sons of the kingdom will be cast out into the outer darkness; in that place there will be weeping and gnashing of teeth."

And Jesus said to the centurion, "Go; it shall be done for you as you have believed."

And the servant was healed that very moment. *Matthew 8:5-13*

When He got into the boat, His disciples followed Him.

And behold, there arose a great storm on the sea, so that the boat was being covered with the waves; but Jesus Himself was asleep.

And they came to Him and woke Him, saying, "Save us, Lord; we are perishing!"

He said to them, "Why are you afraid, you men of little **faith**?"

Then He got up and rebuked the winds and the sea, and it became perfectly calm.

The men were amazed, and said, "What kind of a man is this, that even the winds and the sea obey Him?"

Matthew 8:23-27

They brought to Him a paralytic lying on a bed. Seeing their **faith**, Jesus said to the paralytic, "Take courage, son; your sins are forgiven." *Matthew 9:2*

A woman who had been suffering from a hemorrhage for twelve years, came up behind Him and touched the fringe of His cloak; for she was saying to herself, "If I only touch His garment, I will get well."

But Jesus turning and seeing her said, "Daughter, take courage; your **faith** has made you well." At once the woman was made well. *Matthew 9:20-22*

As Jesus went on from there, two blind men followed Him, crying out, "Have mercy on us, Son of David!"

When He entered the house, the blind men came up to Him, and Jesus said to them, "Do you believe that I am able to do this?"

They said to Him, "Yes, Lord."

Then He touched their eyes, saying, "It shall be done to you according to your **faith**." And their eyes were opened. ~

Matthew 9:27-30

In the fourth watch of the night He came to them, walking on the sea.

When the disciples saw Him walking on the sea, they were terrified, and said, "It is a ghost!" And they cried out in fear.

But immediately Jesus spoke to them, saying, "Take courage, it is I; do not be afraid."

Peter said to Him, "Lord, if it is You, command me to come to You on the water."

And He said, "Come!"

And Peter got out of the boat, and walked on the water and came toward Jesus. But seeing the wind, he became frightened, and beginning to sink, he cried out, "Lord, save me!"

Immediately Jesus stretched out His hand and took hold of him, and said to him, "You of little **faith**, why did you doubt?"

When they got into the boat, the wind stopped.

And those who were in the boat worshiped Him, saying, "You are certainly God's Son!" *Matthew 14:25-33*

Jesus went away from there, and withdrew into the district of Tyre and Sidon.

And a Canaanite woman from that region came out and began to cry out, saying, "Have mercy on me, Lord, Son of David; my daughter is cruelly demon-possessed." But He did not answer her a word.

And His disciples came and implored Him, saying, "Send her away, because she keeps shouting at us."

But He answered and said, "I was sent only to the lost sheep of the house of Israel."

But she came and began to bow down before Him, saying, "Lord, help me!"

And He answered and said, "It is not good to take the children's bread and throw it to the dogs."

But she said, "Yes, Lord; but even the dogs feed on the crumbs which fall from their masters' table."

Then Jesus said to her, "O woman, your **faith** is great; it shall be done for you as you wish."

And her daughter was healed at once. *Matthew 15:21-28*

The disciples came to the other side of the sea, but they had forgotten to bring any bread.

And Jesus said to them, "Watch out and beware of the leaven of the Pharisees and Sadducees."

They began to discuss this among themselves, saying, "He said that because we did not bring any bread."

But Jesus, aware of this, said, "You men of little **faith**, why do you discuss among yourselves that you have no bread? Do you not yet understand or remember the five loaves of the five thousand, and how many baskets full you picked up?

'Or the seven loaves of the four thousand, and how many large baskets full you picked up? How is it that you do not understand that I did not speak to you concerning bread? But beware of the leaven of the Pharisees and Sadducees."

Then they understood that He did not say to beware of the leaven of bread, but of the teaching of the Pharisees and Sadducees. *Matthew 16:5-12*

When they came to the crowd, a man came up to Jesus, falling on his knees before Him and saying, "Lord, have mercy on my son, for he is a lunatic and is very ill; for he often falls into the fire and often into the water. I brought him to Your disciples, and they could not cure him."

And Jesus answered and said, "You unbelieving and perverted generation, how long shall I be with you? How long shall I put up with you? Bring him here to Me."

And Jesus rebuked him, and the demon came out of him, and the boy was cured at once.

Then the disciples came to Jesus privately and said, "Why could we not drive it out?"

And He said to them, "Because of the littleness of your **faith**; for truly I say to you, if you have **faith** the size of a mustard seed, you will say to this mountain, 'Move from here to there,' and it will move; and nothing will be impossible to you.

[But this kind does not go out except by prayer and fasting.]"   *Matthew 17:14-21*

In the morning, when He was returning to the city, He became hungry. Seeing a lone fig tree by the road, He came to it and found nothing on it except leaves only; and He said to it, "No longer shall there ever be any fruit from you." And at once the fig tree withered.

Seeing this, the disciples were amazed and asked, "How did the fig tree wither all at once?"

And Jesus answered and said to them, "Truly I say to you, if you have **faith** and do not doubt, you will not only do what was done to the fig tree, but even if you say to this mountain, 'Be taken up and cast into the sea,' it will happen.

'And all things you ask in prayer, believing, you will receive."   *Matthew 21:18-22*

When He came back to Capernaum several days afterward, it was heard that He was at home. And many were gathered together, so that there was no longer room, not even near the door; and He was speaking the word to them.

And they came, bringing to Him a paralytic, carried by four men.

Being unable to get to Him because of the crowd, they removed the roof above Him; and when they had dug an opening, they let down the pallet on which the paralytic was lying.

And Jesus seeing their **faith** said to the paralytic, "Son, your sins are forgiven."   *Mark 2:1-5*

When evening came, He said to them, "Let us go over to the other side."

Leaving the crowd, they took Him along with them in the boat, just as He was; and other boats were with Him.

And there arose a fierce gale of wind, and the waves were breaking over the boat so much that the boat was already filling up.

Jesus Himself was in the stern, asleep on the cushion; and they woke Him and said to Him, "Teacher, do You not care that we are perishing?"

And He got up and rebuked the wind and said to the sea, "Hush, be still." And the wind died down and it became perfectly calm.

And He said to them, "Why are you afraid? Do you still have no **faith**?"

They became very much afraid and said to one another, "Who then is this, that even the wind and the sea obey Him?"   *Mark 4:35-41*

A woman who had had a hemorrhage for twelve years, and had endured much at the hands of many physicians, and had spent all that she had and was not helped at all, but rather had grown worse - after hearing about Jesus, she came up in the crowd behind Him and touched His cloak. For she thought, "If I just touch His garments, I will get well."

Immediately the flow of her blood was dried up; and she felt in her body that she was healed of her affliction.

Immediately Jesus, perceiving in Himself that the power proceeding from Him had gone forth, turned around in the crowd and said, "Who touched My garments?"

And His disciples said to Him, "You see the crowd pressing in on You, and You say, 'Who touched Me?' "

And He looked around to see the woman who had done this.

But the woman fearing and trembling, aware of what had happened to her, came and fell down before Him and told

Him the whole truth.

And He said to her, "Daughter, your **faith** has made you well; go in peace and be healed of your affliction." *Mark 5:25-34*

They came to Jericho. And as He was leaving Jericho with His disciples and a large crowd, a blind beggar named Bartimaeus, the son of Timaeus, was sitting by the road.

When he heard that it was Jesus the Nazarene, he began to cry out and say, "Jesus, Son of David, have mercy on me!"

Many were sternly telling him to be quiet, but he kept crying out all the more, "Son of David, have mercy on me!"

And Jesus stopped and said, "Call him here."

So they called the blind man, saying to him, "Take courage, stand up! He is calling for you."

Throwing aside his cloak, he jumped up and came to Jesus.

And answering him, Jesus said, "What do you want Me to do for you?"

And the blind man said to Him, "Rabboni, I want to regain my sight!"

And Jesus said to him, "Go; your **faith** has made you well."

Immediately he regained his sight and began following Him on the road.
Mark 10:46-52

As they were passing by in the morning, they saw the fig tree withered from the roots up.

Being reminded, Peter said to Him, "Rabbi, look, the fig tree which You cursed has withered."

Jesus answered saying to them, "Have **faith** in God.

'Truly I say to you, whoever says to this mountain, 'Be taken up and cast into the sea,' and does not doubt in his heart, but believes that what he says is going to happen, it will be granted him.

"Therefore I say to you, all things for which you pray and ask, believe that you have received them, and they will be granted you." *Mark 11:20-24*

One day He was teaching; and there were some Pharisees and teachers of the law sitting there, who had come from every village of Galilee and Judea and from Jerusalem; and the power of the Lord was present for Him to perform healing.

And some men were carrying on a bed a man who was paralyzed; and they were trying to bring him in and to set him down in front of Him.

But not finding any way to bring him in because of the crowd, they went up on the roof and let him down through the tiles with his stretcher, into the middle of the crowd, in front of Jesus.

Seeing their **faith**, He said, "Friend, your sins are forgiven you." *Luke 5:17-20*

When He had completed all His discourse in the hearing of the people, He went to Capernaum.

And a centurion's slave, who was highly regarded by him, was sick and about to die. When he heard about Jesus, he sent some Jewish elders asking Him to come and save the life of his slave.

When they came to Jesus, they earnestly implored Him, saying, "He is worthy for You to grant this to him; for he loves our nation and it was he who built us our synagogue."

Now Jesus started on His way with them; and when He was not far from the house, the centurion sent friends, saying to Him, "Lord, do not trouble Yourself further, for I am not worthy for You to come under my roof; for this reason I did not even consider myself worthy to come to You, but just say the word, and my servant will be healed. For I also am a man placed under authority, with soldiers under me; and I say to this one, 'Go!' and he goes, and to another, 'Come!' and he comes, and to my slave, 'Do this!' and he does it."

Now when Jesus heard this, He marveled at him, and turned and said to the crowd that was following Him, "I say to you, not even in Israel have I found such great **faith**."

When those who had been sent returned to the house, they found the slave in good health.   *Luke 7:1-10*

One of the Pharisees was requesting Him to dine with him, and He entered the Pharisee's house and reclined at the table.

And there was a woman in the city who was a sinner; and when she learned that He was reclining at the table in the Pharisee's house, she brought an alabaster vial of perfume, and standing behind Him at His feet, weeping, she began to wet His feet with her tears, and kept wiping them with the hair of her head, and kissing His feet and anointing them with the perfume.

Now when the Pharisee who had invited Him saw this, he said to himself, "If this man were a prophet He would know who and what sort of person this woman is who is touching Him, that she is a sinner."

And Jesus answered him, "Simon, I have something to say to you."

And he replied, "Say it, Teacher."

"A moneylender had two debtors: one owed five hundred denarii, and the other fifty. When they were unable to repay, he graciously forgave them both. So which of them will love him more?"

Simon answered and said, "I suppose the one whom he forgave more."

And He said to him, "You have judged correctly."

Turning toward the woman, He said to Simon, "Do you see this woman? I entered your house; you gave Me no water for My feet, but she has wet My feet with her tears and wiped them with her hair.

"You gave Me no kiss; but she, since the time I came in, has not ceased to kiss My feet. You did not anoint My head with oil, but she anointed My feet with perfume.

"For this reason I say to you, her sins, which are many, have been forgiven, for she loved much; but he who is forgiven little, loves little."

Then He said to her, "Your sins have been forgiven."

Those who were reclining at the table with Him began to say to themselves, "Who is this man who even forgives sins?"

And He said to the woman, "Your **faith** has saved you; go in peace."   *Luke 7:36-50*

On one of those days Jesus and His disciples got into a boat, and He said to them, "Let us go over to the other side of the lake." So they launched out.

But as they were sailing along He fell asleep; and a fierce gale of wind descended on the lake, and they began to be swamped and to be in danger.

They came to Jesus and woke Him up, saying, "Master, Master, we are perishing!"

And He got up and rebuked the wind and the surging waves, and they stopped, and it became calm.

And He said to them, "Where is your **faith**?"

They were fearful and amazed, saying to one another, "Who then is this, that He commands even the winds and the water, and they obey Him?"   *Luke 8:22-25*

A woman who had a hemorrhage for twelve years, and could not be healed by anyone, came up behind Him and touched the fringe of His cloak, and immediately her hemorrhage stopped.

And Jesus said, "Who is the one who touched Me?"

And while they were all denying it, Peter said, "Master, the people are crowding and pressing in on You."

But Jesus said, "Someone did touch Me, for I was aware that power had gone out of Me."

When the woman saw that she had not escaped notice, she came trembling and fell down before Him, and declared in the presence of all the people the reason why she had touched Him, and how she had been immediately healed.

And He said to her, "Daughter, your **faith** has made you well; go in peace."   *Luke 8:43-48*

He said to His disciples, "For this reason I say to you, do not worry about your life, as to what you will eat; nor for your body, as to what you will put on. For life is more than food, and the body more than clothing.

"Consider the ravens, for they neither sow nor reap; they have no storeroom nor barn, and yet God feeds them; how much more valuable you are than the birds!

"And which of you by worrying can add a single hour to his life's span? If then you cannot do even a very little thing, why do you worry about other matters?

"Consider the lilies, how they grow: they neither toil nor spin; but I tell you, not even Solomon in all his glory clothed himself like one of these.

"But if God so clothes the grass in the field, which is alive today and tomorrow is thrown into the furnace, how much more will He clothe you? You men of little **faith**!

"And do not seek what you will eat and what you will drink, and do not keep worrying. For all these things the nations of the world eagerly seek; but your Father knows that you need these things. But seek His kingdom, and these things will be added to you.

"Do not be afraid, little flock, for your Father has chosen gladly to give you the kingdom.

"Sell your possessions and give to charity; make yourselves money belts which do not wear out, an unfailing treasure in heaven, where no thief comes near nor moth destroys." *Luke 12:22-31*

"Be on your guard! If your brother sins, rebuke him; and if he repents, forgive him.

And if he sins against you seven times a day, and returns to you seven times, saying, 'I repent,' forgive him."

The apostles said to the Lord, "Increase our **faith**!"

And the Lord said, "If you had **faith** like a mustard seed, you would say to this mulberry tree, 'Be uprooted and be planted in the sea'; and it would obey you." *Luke 17:3-6*

While He was on the way to Jerusalem, He was passing between Samaria and Galilee.

As He entered a village, ten leprous men who stood at a distance met Him; and they raised their voices, saying, "Jesus, Master, have mercy on us!"

When He saw them, He said to them, "Go and show yourselves to the priests." And as they were going, they were cleansed.

Now one of them, when he saw that he had been healed, turned back, glorifying God with a loud voice, and he fell on his face at His feet, giving thanks to Him. And he was a Samaritan.

Then Jesus answered and said, "Were there not ten cleansed? But the nine - where are they? Was no one found who returned to give glory to God, except this foreigner?"

And He said to him, "Stand up and go; your **faith** has made you well." *Luke 17:11-19*

He was telling them a parable to show that at all times they ought to pray and not to lose heart, saying, "In a certain city there was a judge who did not fear God and did not respect man. There was a widow in that city, and she kept coming to him, saying, 'Give me legal protection from my opponent.'

"For a while he was unwilling; but afterward he said to himself, 'Even though I do not fear God nor respect man, yet because this widow bothers me, I will give her legal protection, otherwise by continually coming she will wear me out.' "

And the Lord said, "Hear what the unrighteous judge said; now, will not God bring about justice for His elect who cry to Him day and night, and will He delay long over them? "I tell you that He will bring about justice for them quickly.

"However, when the Son of Man comes, will He find **faith** on the earth?" *Luke 18:1-8*

As Jesus was approaching Jericho, a blind man was sitting by the road begging.

Now hearing a crowd going by, he began to inquire what this was. They told him that Jesus of Nazareth was passing by.

And he called out, saying, "Jesus, Son of David, have mercy on me!"

Those who led the way were sternly telling him to be quiet; but he kept crying out all the more, "Son of David, have mercy on me!"

And Jesus stopped and commanded that he be brought to Him; and when he came near, He questioned him, "What do you want Me to do for you?"

And he said, "Lord, I want to regain my sight!"

And Jesus said to him, "Receive your sight; your **faith** has made you well."

Immediately he regained his sight and began following Him, glorifying God; and when all the people saw it, they gave praise to God.   *Luke 18:35-43*

"Simon, Simon, behold, Satan has demanded permission to sift you like wheat; but I have prayed for you, that your **faith** may not fail; and you, when once you have turned again, strengthen your brothers."

But he said, "Lord, with You I am ready to go both to prison and to death!"

And He said, "I say to you, Peter, the rooster will not crow today until you have denied three times that you know Me."
                                        Luke 22:31-34

Peter and John were going up to the temple at the ninth hour, the hour of prayer. And a man who had been lame from his mother's womb was being carried along, whom they used to set down every day at the gate of the temple which is called Beautiful, in order to beg alms of those who were entering the temple.

When he saw Peter and John about to go into the temple, he began asking to receive alms.

But Peter, along with John, fixed his gaze on him and said, "Look at us!"

And he began to give them his attention, expecting to receive something from them.

But Peter said, "I do not possess silver and gold, but what I do have I give to you: In the name of Jesus Christ the Nazarene - walk!"

And seizing him by the right hand, he raised him up; and immediately his feet and his ankles were strengthened.

With a leap he stood upright and began to walk; and he entered the temple with them, walking and leaping and praising God.

And all the people saw him walking and praising God; and they were taking note of him as being the one who used to sit at the Beautiful Gate of the temple to beg alms, and they were filled with wonder and amazement at what had happened to him.

While he was clinging to Peter and John, all the people ran together to them at the so-called portico of Solomon, full of amazement.

But when Peter saw this, he replied to the people, "Men of Israel, why are you amazed at this, or why do you gaze at us, as if by our own power or piety we had made him walk?

"The God of Abraham, Isaac and Jacob, the God of our fathers, has glorified His servant Jesus, the one whom you delivered and disowned in the presence of Pilate, when he had decided to release Him.

"But you disowned the Holy and Righteous One and asked for a murderer to be granted to you, but put to death the Prince of life, the one whom God raised from the dead, a fact to which we are witnesses.

"And on the basis of **faith** in His name, it is the name of Jesus which has strengthened this man whom you see and know; and the **faith** which comes through Him has given him this perfect health in the presence of you all."   *Acts 3:1-16*

At this time while the disciples were increasing in number, a complaint arose on the part of the Hellenistic Jews against the native Hebrews, because their widows were being overlooked in the daily serving of food.

So the twelve summoned the congregation of the disciples and said, "It is not desirable for us to neglect the word of God in order to serve tables. Therefore, brethren, select from among you seven men of good reputation, full of the Spirit and of wisdom, whom we may put in charge of this task.

"But we will devote ourselves to prayer and to the ministry of the word."

The statement found approval with the whole congregation; and they chose Stephen, a man full of **faith** and of the Holy Spirit, and Philip, Prochorus, Nicanor, Timon, Parmenas and Nicolas, a proselyte from Antioch. And these they brought before the apostles; and after praying, they laid their hands on them.

The word of God kept on spreading; and the number of the disciples continued to increase greatly in Jerusalem, and a great many of the priests were becoming obedient to the **faith**.

And Stephen, full of grace and power, was performing great wonders and signs among the people. *Acts 6:1-8*

The news about them reached the ears of the church at Jerusalem, and they sent Barnabas off to Antioch.

Then when he arrived and witnessed the grace of God, he rejoiced and began to encourage them all with resolute heart to remain true to the Lord; for he was a good man, and full of the Holy Spirit and of **faith**.

And considerable numbers were brought to the Lord. *Acts 11:22-24*

When they had gone through the whole island as far as Paphos, they found a magician, a Jewish false prophet whose name was Bar-Jesus, who was with the proconsul, Sergius Paulus, a man of intelligence.

This man summoned Barnabas and Saul and sought to hear the word of God. But Elymas the magician (for so his name is translated) was opposing them, seeking to turn the proconsul away from the **faith**.

But Saul, who was also known as Paul, filled with the Holy Spirit, fixed his gaze on him, and said, "You who are full of all deceit and fraud, you son of the devil, you enemy of all righteousness, will you not cease to make crooked the straight ways of the Lord?

"Now, behold, the hand of the Lord is upon you, and you will be blind and not see the sun for a time."

And immediately a mist and a darkness fell upon him, and he went about seeking those who would lead him by the hand.

Then the proconsul believed when he saw what had happened, being amazed at the teaching of the Lord. *Acts 13:6-12*

At Lystra a man was sitting who had no strength in his feet, lame from his mother's womb, who had never walked.

This man was listening to Paul as he spoke, who, when he had fixed his gaze on him and had seen that he had **faith** to be made well, said with a loud voice, "Stand upright on your feet."

And he leaped up and began to walk. *Acts 14:8-10*

Jews came from Antioch and Iconium, and having won over the crowds, they stoned Paul and dragged him out of the city, supposing him to be dead. But while the disciples stood around him, he got up and entered the city.

The next day he went away with Barnabas to Derbe.

After they had preached the gospel to that city and had made many disciples, they returned to Lystra and to Iconium and to Antioch, strengthening the souls of the disciples, encouraging them to continue in the **faith**, and saying, "Through many tribulations we must enter the kingdom of God." *Acts 14:19-22*

When they had arrived and gathered the church together, they began to report all things that God had done with them and how He had opened a door of **faith** to the Gentiles. *Acts 14:27*

When they arrived at Jerusalem, they were received by the church and the apostles and the elders, and they reported all that God had done with them.

But some of the sect of the Pharisees who had believed stood up, saying, "It is necessary to circumcise them and to direct them to observe the Law of Moses."

The apostles and the elders came together to look into this matter.

After there had been much debate, Peter stood up and said to them, "Brethren, you know that in the early days God made a choice among you, that by my mouth the Gentiles would hear the word of the gospel and believe.

"And God, who knows the heart, testified to them giving them the Holy Spirit, just as He also did to us; and He made no distinction between us and them, cleansing their hearts by **faith**.

"Now therefore why do you put God to the test by placing upon the neck of the disciples a yoke which neither our fathers nor we have been able to bear?

"But we believe that we are saved through the grace of the Lord Jesus, in the same way as they also are."   *Acts 15:4-11*

While they were passing through the cities, they were delivering the decrees which had been decided upon by the apostles and elders who were in Jerusalem, for them to observe.

So the churches were being strengthened in the **faith**, and were increasing in number daily.   *Acts 16:4-5*

He said to them, "You yourselves know, from the first day that I set foot in Asia, how I was with you the whole time, serving the Lord with all humility and with tears and with trials which came upon me through the plots of the Jews; how I did not shrink from declaring to you anything that was profitable, and teaching you publicly and from house to house, solemnly testifying to both Jews and Greeks of repentance toward God and **faith** in our Lord Jesus Christ."   *Acts 20:18-21*

Felix, having a more exact knowledge about the Way, put them off, saying, "When Lysias the commander comes down, I will decide your case."

Then he gave orders to the centurion for him to be kept in custody and yet have some freedom, and not to prevent any of his friends from ministering to him.

But some days later Felix arrived with Drusilla, his wife who was a Jewess, and sent for Paul and heard him speak about **faith** in Christ Jesus.

But as he was discussing righteousness, self-control and the judgment to come, Felix became frightened and said, "Go away for the present, and when I find time I will summon you."   *Acts 24:22-25*

I was journeying to Damascus with the authority and commission of the chief priests, at midday, O King, I saw on the way a light from heaven, brighter than the sun, shining all around me and those who were journeying with me.

And when we had all fallen to the ground, I heard a voice saying to me in the Hebrew dialect, "Saul, Saul, why are you persecuting Me? It is hard for you to kick against the goads."

And I said, "Who are You, Lord?"

And the Lord said, "I am Jesus whom you are persecuting. But get up and stand on your feet; for this purpose I have appeared to you, to appoint you a minister and a witness not only to the things which you have seen, but also to the things in which I will appear to you; rescuing you from the Jewish people and from the Gentiles, to whom I am sending you, to open their eyes so that they may turn from darkness to light and from the dominion of Satan to God, that they may receive forgiveness of sins and an inheritance among those who have been sanctified by **faith** in Me."   *Acts 26:12-18*

Paul, a bond-servant of Christ Jesus, called as an apostle, set apart for the gospel of God, which He promised beforehand through His prophets in the holy Scriptures, concerning His Son, who was born of a descendant of David according to the flesh, who was declared the Son of God with power by the resurrection from the dead, according to the Spirit of holiness, Jesus Christ our Lord, through whom we have received grace and apostleship to bring about the obedience of **faith** among all the Gentiles for His name's sake, among whom you also are the called of Jesus Christ; to all who are beloved of God in Rome, called as saints: Grace to you and peace from God our Father and the Lord Jesus Christ.

First, I thank my God through Jesus Christ for you all, because your **faith** is being proclaimed throughout the whole world. For God, whom I serve in my spirit in the preaching of the gospel of His Son, is my witness as to how unceasingly I make mention of you, always in my prayers making request, if perhaps now at last by the will of God I may succeed in coming to you.

For I long to see you so that I may impart some spiritual gift to you, that you may be established; that is, that I may be encouraged together with you while among you, each of us by the other's **faith**, both yours and mine. ...

... I am under obligation both to Greeks and to barbarians, both to the wise and to the foolish. So, for my part, I am eager to preach the gospel to you also who are in Rome.

For I am not ashamed of the gospel, for it is the power of God for salvation to everyone who believes, to the Jew first and also to the Greek. For in it the righteousness of God is revealed from **faith** to **faith**; as it is written, "But the righteous man shall live by **faith**."

Romans 1:1-12...14-17

We know that whatever the Law says, it speaks to those who are under the Law, so that every mouth may be closed and all the world may become accountable to God; because by the works of the Law no flesh will be justified in His sight; for through the Law comes the knowledge of sin.

But now apart from the Law the righteousness of God has been manifested, being witnessed by the Law and the Prophets, even the righteousness of God

through **faith** in Jesus Christ for all those who believe; for there is no distinction; for all have sinned and fall short of the glory of God, being justified as a gift by His grace through the redemption which is in Christ Jesus; whom God displayed publicly as a propitiation in His blood through **faith**.

This was to demonstrate His righteousness, because in the forbearance of God He passed over the sins previously committed; for the demonstration, I say, of His righteousness at the present time, so that He would be just and the justifier of the one who has **faith** in Jesus.

Where then is boasting? It is excluded. By what kind of law? Of works? No, but by a law of **faith**.

For we maintain that a man is justified by **faith** apart from works of the Law. Or is God the God of Jews only? Is He not the God of Gentiles also? Yes, of Gentiles also, since indeed God who will justify the circumcised by **faith** and the uncircumcised through **faith** is one.

Do we then nullify the Law through **faith**? May it never be! On the contrary, we establish the Law.

What then shall we say that Abraham, our forefather according to the flesh, has found? For if Abraham was justified by works, he has something to boast about, but not before God.

For what does the Scripture say? "Abraham believed God, and it was credited to him as righteousness."

Now to the one who works, his wage is not credited as a favor, but as what is due.

But to the one who does not work, but believes in Him who justifies the ungodly, his **faith** is credited as righteousness, just as David also speaks of the blessing on the man to whom God credits righteousness apart from works: Is this blessing then on the circumcised, or on the uncircumcised also? For we say, "**Faith** was credited to Abraham as righteousness."

How then was it credited? While he was circumcised, or uncircumcised?

Not while circumcised, but while uncircumcised; and he received the sign of circumcision, a seal of the righteousness of the **faith** which he had while uncircumcised, so that he might be the father of all who believe without being circumcised, that righteousness might be credited to them, and the father of circumcision to those who not only are of the circumcision, but who also follow in the steps of the **faith** of our father Abraham which he had while uncircumcised.

For the promise to Abraham or to his descendants that he would be heir of the world was not through the Law, but through the righteousness of **faith**. For if those who are of the Law are heirs, **faith** is made void and the promise is nullified; for the Law brings about wrath, but where there is no law, there also is no violation.

For this reason it is by **faith**, in order that it may be in accordance with grace, so that the promise will be guaranteed to all the descendants, not only to those who are of the Law, but also to those who are of the **faith** of Abraham, who is the father of us all, (as it is written, "A father of many nations have I made you") in the presence of Him whom he believed, even God, who gives life to the dead and calls into being that which does not exist.

In hope against hope he believed, so that he might become a father of many nations according to that which had been spoken, "So shall your descendants be."

Without becoming weak in **faith** he contemplated his own body, now as good as dead since he was about a hundred years old, and the deadness of Sarah's womb; yet, with respect to the promise of God, he did not waver in unbelief but grew strong in **faith**, giving glory to God, and being fully assured that what God had promised, He was able also to perform.

Therefore it was also credited to him as righteousness. Now not for his sake only was it written that it was credited to him, but for our sake also, to whom it will be credited, as those who believe in Him who raised Jesus our Lord from the dead, He who was delivered over because of our transgressions, and was raised because of our justification.

Therefore, having been justified by **faith**, we have peace with God through our Lord Jesus Christ, through whom also we have obtained our introduction by **faith** into this grace in which we stand; and we exult in hope of the glory of God.

Romans 3:19 - 5:2

Isaiah cries out concerning Israel, "Though the number of the sons of Israel be like the sand of the sea, it is the remnant that will be saved; for the Lord will execute His word on the earth, thoroughly and quickly."

And just as Isaiah foretold, "Unless the Lord of Sabaoth had left to us a posterity, we would have become like Sodom, and would have resembled Gomorrah."

What shall we say then? That Gentiles, who did not pursue righteousness, attained righteousness, even the righteousness which is by **faith**; but Israel, pursuing a law of righteousness, did not arrive at that law.

Why? Because they did not pursue it by **faith**, but as though it were by works.

They stumbled over the stumbling stone, just as it is written, "Behold, I lay in Zion a stone of stumbling and a rock of offense, and he who believes in Him will not be disappointed." *Romans 9:27-33*

Christ is the end of the law for righteousness to everyone who believes. For Moses writes that the man who practices the righteousness which is based on law shall live by that righteousness.

But the righteousness based on **faith** speaks as follows: "Do not say in your heart, 'Who will ascend into heaven?' (that is, to bring Christ down), or 'Who will descend into the abyss?' (that is, to bring Christ up from the dead)."

But what does it say? "The word is near you, in your mouth and in your heart" - that is, the word of **faith** which we are preaching, that if you confess with your mouth Jesus as Lord, and believe in your heart that God raised Him from the dead, you will be saved; for with the heart a person believes, resulting in righteousness, and with the mouth he confesses, resulting in salvation.

For the Scripture says, "Whoever believes in Him will not be disappointed."

For there is no distinction between Jew and Greek; for the same Lord is Lord of all, abounding in riches for all who call on Him; for "Whoever will call on the name of the Lord will be saved."

How then will they call on Him in whom they have not believed? How will they believe in Him whom they have not heard? And how will they hear without a preacher? How will they preach unless they are sent?

Just as it is written, "How beautiful are the feet of those who bring good news of good things!"

However, they did not all heed the good news; for Isaiah says, "Lord, who has believed our report?"

So **faith** comes from hearing, and hearing by the word of Christ.

Romans 10:4-17

If some of the branches were broken off, and you, being a wild olive, were grafted in among them and became partaker with them of the rich root of the olive tree, do not be arrogant toward the branches; but if you are arrogant, remember that it is not you who supports the root, but the root supports you.

You will say then, "Branches were broken off so that I might be grafted in." Quite right, they were broken off for their unbelief, but you stand by your **faith**.

Do not be conceited, but fear; for if God did not spare the natural branches, He will not spare you, either.

Behold then the kindness and severity of God; to those who fell, severity, but to you, God's kindness, if you continue in His kindness; otherwise you also will be cut off.

And they also, if they do not continue in their unbelief, will be grafted in, for God is able to graft them in again.

Romans 11:17-23

I urge you, brethren, by the mercies of God, to present your bodies a living and holy sacrifice, acceptable to God, which is your spiritual service of worship.

And do not be conformed to this world, but be transformed by the renewing of your mind, so that you may prove what the will of God is, that which is good and acceptable and perfect.

For through the grace given to me I say to everyone among you not to think more highly of himself than he ought to think; but to think so as to have sound judgment, as God has allotted to each a measure of **faith**.

For just as we have many members in one body and all the members do not have the same function, so we, who are many, are one body in Christ, and individually members one of another.

Since we have gifts that differ according to the grace given to us, each of us is to exercise them accordingly: if prophecy, according to the proportion of his **faith**; if service, in his serving; or he who teaches, in his teaching; or he who exhorts, in his exhortation; he who gives, with liberality; he who leads, with diligence; he who shows mercy, with cheerfulness.

Romans 12:1-8

Accept the one who is weak in **faith**, but not for the purpose of passing judgment on his opinions.

One person has **faith** that he may eat all things, but he who is weak eats vegetables only. The one who eats is not to regard with contempt the one who does not eat, and the one who does not eat is not to judge the one who eats, for God has accepted him.

Who are you to judge the servant of another? To his own master he stands or falls; and he will stand, for the Lord is able to make him stand. *Romans 14:1-4*

Do not tear down the work of God for the sake of food. All things indeed are clean, but they are evil for the man who eats and gives offense.

It is good not to eat meat or to drink wine, or to do anything by which your brother stumbles. The **faith** which you have, have as your own conviction before

God.

Happy is he who does not condemn himself in what he approves.

But he who doubts is condemned if he eats, because his eating is not from **faith**; and whatever is not from **faith** is sin.   *Romans 14:20-23*

To Him who is able to establish you according to my gospel and the preaching of Jesus Christ, according to the revelation of the mystery which has been kept secret for long ages past, but now is manifested, and by the Scriptures of the prophets, according to the commandment of the eternal God, has been made known to all the nations, leading to obedience of **faith**; to the only wise God, through Jesus Christ, be the glory forever. Amen.
Romans 16:25-27

When I came to you, brethren, I did not come with superiority of speech or of wisdom, proclaiming to you the testimony of God. For I determined to know nothing among you except Jesus Christ, and Him crucified.

I was with you in weakness and in fear and in much trembling, and my message and my preaching were not in persuasive words of wisdom, but in demonstration of the Spirit and of power, so that your **faith** would not rest on the wisdom of men, but on the power of God.
1 Corinthians 2:1-5

There are varieties of gifts, but the same Spirit. And there are varieties of ministries, and the same Lord.

There are varieties of effects, but the same God who works all things in all persons. But to each one is given the manifestation of the Spirit for the common good.

For to one is given the word of wisdom through the Spirit, and to another the word of knowledge according to the same Spirit; to another **faith** by the same Spirit, and to another gifts of healing by the one Spirit, and to another the effecting of miracles, and to another prophecy, and to another the distinguishing of spirits, to another various kinds of tongues, and to another the interpretation of tongues.

But one and the same Spirit works all these things, distributing to each one individually just as He wills.
1 Corinthians 12:4-11

If I speak with the tongues of men and of angels, but do not have love, I have become a noisy gong or a clanging cymbal. If I have the gift of prophecy, and know all mysteries and all knowledge; and if I have all **faith**, so as to remove mountains, but do not have love, I am nothing.
1 Corinthians 13:1-2

Faith, hope, love, abide these three; but the greatest of these is love.
1 Corinthians 13:13

If Christ is preached, that He has been raised from the dead, how do some among you say that there is no resurrection of the dead?

But if there is no resurrection of the dead, not even Christ has been raised; and if Christ has not been raised, then our preaching is vain, your **faith** also is vain. Moreover we are even found to be false witnesses of God, because we testified against God that He raised Christ, whom He did not raise, if in fact the dead are not raised.

For if the dead are not raised, not even Christ has been raised; and if Christ has not been raised, your **faith** is worthless; you are still in your sins. Then those also who have fallen asleep in Christ have perished.

If we have hoped in Christ in this life only, we are of all men most to be pitied.

But now Christ has been raised from the dead, the first fruits of those who are asleep. For since by a man came death, by a man also came the resurrection of the dead.

For as in Adam all die, so also in Christ all will be made alive.
1 Corinthians 15:12-22

Be on the alert, stand firm in the **faith**, act like men, be strong. Let all that you do be done in love.   *1 Corinthians 16:13-14*

I call God as witness to my soul, that to spare you I did not come again to Corinth. Not that we lord it over your **faith**, but are workers with you for your joy; for in your **faith** you are standing firm.

2 Corinthians 1:23-24

Having the same spirit of **faith**, according to what is written, "I believed, therefore I spoke," we also believe, therefore we also speak, knowing that He who raised the Lord Jesus will raise us also with Jesus and will present us with you.

For all things are for your sakes, so that the grace which is spreading to more and more people may cause the giving of thanks to abound to the glory of God.

2 Corinthians 4:13-15

He who prepared us for this very purpose is God, who gave to us the Spirit as a pledge.

Therefore, being always of good courage, and knowing that while we are at home in the body we are absent from the Lord - for we walk by **faith**, not by sight - we are of good courage, I say, and prefer rather to be absent from the body and to be at home with the Lord.

Therefore we also have as our ambition, whether at home or absent, to be pleasing to Him.

2 Corinthians 5:5-9

Just as you abound in everything, in **faith** and utterance and knowledge and in all earnestness and in the love we inspired in you, see that you abound in this gracious work also.

I am not speaking this as a command, but as proving through the earnestness of others the sincerity of your love also.

2 Corinthians 8:7-8

We are not overextending ourselves, as if we did not reach to you, for we were the first to come even as far as you in the gospel of Christ; not boasting beyond our measure, that is, in other men's labors, but with the hope that as your **faith** grows, we will be, within our sphere, enlarged even more by you, so as to preach the gospel even to the regions beyond

you, and not to boast in what has been accomplished in the sphere of another.

But he who boasts is to boast in the Lord. For it is not he who commends himself that is approved, but he whom the Lord commends.

2 Corinthians 10:14-18

Test yourselves to see if you are in the **faith**; examine yourselves!

Or do you not recognize this about yourselves, that Jesus Christ is in you - unless indeed you fail the test?

2 Corinthians 13:5

I went into the regions of Syria and Cilicia. I was still unknown by sight to the churches of Judea which were in Christ; but only, they kept hearing, "He who once persecuted us is now preaching the **faith** which he once tried to destroy."

But it was because of the false brethren secretly brought in, who had sneaked in to spy out our liberty which we have in Christ Jesus, in order to bring us into bondage.

Galatians 1:21-24

We are Jews by nature and not sinners from among the Gentiles; nevertheless knowing that a man is not justified by the works of the Law but through **faith** in Christ Jesus, even we have believed in Christ Jesus, so that we may be justified by **faith** in Christ and not by the works of the Law; since by the works of the Law no flesh will be justified.

But if, while seeking to be justified in Christ, we ourselves have also been found sinners, is Christ then a minister of sin? May it never be! For if I rebuild what I have once destroyed, I prove myself to be a transgressor.

For through the Law I died to the Law, so that I might live to God. I have been crucified with Christ; and it is no longer I who live, but Christ lives in me; and the life which I now live in the flesh I live by **faith** in the Son of God, who loved me and gave Himself up for me.

I do not nullify the grace of God, for if righteousness comes through the Law, then Christ died needlessly.

You foolish Galatians, who has bewitched you, before whose eyes Jesus Christ was publicly portrayed as crucified?

This is the only thing I want to find out from you: Did you receive the Spirit by the works of the Law, or by hearing with **faith**?

Are you so foolish? Having begun by the Spirit, are you now being perfected by the flesh? Did you suffer so many things in vain - if indeed it was in vain?

So then, does He who provides you with the Spirit and works miracles among you, do it by the works of the Law, or by hearing with **faith**?

Even so Abraham believed God, and it was reckoned to him as righteousness. Therefore, be sure that it is those who are of **faith** who are sons of Abraham.

The Scripture, foreseeing that God would justify the Gentiles by **faith**, preached the gospel beforehand to Abraham, saying, "All the nations will be blessed in you." So then those who are of **faith** are blessed with Abraham, the believer.

For as many as are of the works of the Law are under a curse; for it is written, "Cursed is everyone who does not abide by all things written in the book of the law, to perform them."

Now that no one is justified by the Law before God is evident; for, "The righteous man shall live by **faith**."

However, the Law is not of **faith**; on the contrary, "He who practices them shall live by them."

Christ redeemed us from the curse of the Law, having become a curse for us - for it is written, "Cursed is everyone who hangs on a tree" - in order that in Christ Jesus the blessing of Abraham might come to the Gentiles, so that we would receive the promise of the Spirit through **faith**.

Brethren, I speak in terms of human relations: even though it is only a man's covenant, yet when it has been ratified, no one sets it aside or adds conditions to it.

Now the promises were spoken to Abraham and to his seed. He does not say, "And to seeds," as referring to many, but rather to one, "And to your seed," that is, Christ.

What I am saying is this: the Law, which came four hundred and thirty years later, does not invalidate a covenant previously ratified by God, so as to nullify the promise.

For if the inheritance is based on law, it is no longer based on a promise; but God has granted it to Abraham by means of a promise.

Why the Law then? It was added because of transgressions, having been ordained through angels by the agency of a mediator, until the seed would come to whom the promise had been made. Now a mediator is not for one party only; whereas God is only one.

Is the Law then contrary to the promises of God? May it never be! For if a law had been given which was able to impart life, then righteousness would indeed have been based on law.

But the Scripture has shut up everyone under sin, so that the promise by **faith** in Jesus Christ might be given to those who believe.

But before **faith** came, we were kept in custody under the law, being shut up to the **faith** which was later to be revealed.

Therefore the Law has become our tutor to lead us to Christ, so that we may be justified by **faith**.

But now that **faith** has come, we are no longer under a tutor. For you are all sons of God through **faith** in Christ Jesus. For all of you who were baptized into Christ have clothed yourselves with Christ.

There is neither Jew nor Greek, there is neither slave nor free man, there is neither male nor female; for you are all one in Christ Jesus.

And if you belong to Christ, then you are Abraham's descendants, heirs according to promise. *Galatians 2:15 - 3:29*

It was for freedom that Christ set us free; therefore keep standing firm and do not be subject again to a yoke of slavery.

Behold I, Paul, say to you that if you

receive circumcision, Christ will be of no benefit to you.

And I testify again to every man who receives circumcision, that he is under obligation to keep the whole Law.

You have been severed from Christ, you who are seeking to be justified by law; you have fallen from grace. For we through the Spirit, by **faith**, are waiting for the hope of righteousness.

For in Christ Jesus neither circumcision nor uncircumcision means anything, but **faith** working through love.

Galatians 5:1-6

Do not be deceived, God is not mocked; for whatever a man sows, this he will also reap.

For the one who sows to his own flesh will from the flesh reap corruption, but the one who sows to the Spirit will from the Spirit reap eternal life.

Let us not lose heart in doing good, for in due time we will reap if we do not grow weary. So then, while we have opportunity, let us do good to all people, and especially to those who are of the household of the **faith**.

Galatians 6:7-10

In Him, you also, after listening to the message of truth, the gospel of your salvation - having also believed, you were sealed in Him with the Holy Spirit of promise, who is given as a pledge of our inheritance, with a view to the redemption of God's own possession, to the praise of His glory.

For this reason I too, having heard of the **faith** in the Lord Jesus which exists among you and your love for all the saints, do not cease giving thanks for you, while making mention of you in my prayers; that the God of our Lord Jesus Christ, the Father of glory, may give to you a spirit of wisdom and of revelation in the knowledge of Him.

Ephesians 1:13-17

You were dead in your trespasses and sins, in which you formerly walked according to the course of this world, according to the prince of the power of the air, of the spirit that is now working in the

sons of disobedience.

Among them we too all formerly lived in the lusts of our flesh, indulging the desires of the flesh and of the mind, and were by nature children of wrath, even as the rest.

But God, being rich in mercy, because of His great love with which He loved us, even when we were dead in our transgressions, made us alive together with Christ (by grace you have been saved), and raised us up with Him, and seated us with Him in the heavenly places in Christ Jesus, so that in the ages to come He might show the surpassing riches of His grace in kindness toward us in Christ Jesus.

For by grace you have been saved through **faith**; and that not of yourselves, it is the gift of God; not as a result of works, so that no one may boast.

For we are His workmanship, created in Christ Jesus for good works, which God prepared beforehand so that we would walk in them.

Ephesians 2:1-10

To me, the very least of all saints, this grace was given, to preach to the Gentiles the unfathomable riches of Christ, and to bring to light what is the administration of the mystery which for ages has been hidden in God who created all things; so that the manifold wisdom of God might now be made known through the church to the rulers and the authorities in the heavenly places.

This was in accordance with the eternal purpose which He carried out in Christ Jesus our Lord, in whom we have boldness and confident access through **faith** in Him. Therefore I ask you not to lose heart at my tribulations on your behalf, for they are your glory.

For this reason I bow my knees before the Father, from whom every family in heaven and on earth derives its name, that He would grant you, according to the riches of His glory, to be strengthened with power through His Spirit in the inner man, so that Christ may dwell in your hearts through **faith**; and that you, being rooted and grounded in love, may be able to comprehend with all the saints what is the breadth and length and height and depth, and to know the love of Christ which surpasses knowledge, that you may be filled up to all the fullness of God.

Ephesians 3:8-19

There is one body and one Spirit, just as also you were called in one hope of your calling; one Lord, one **faith**, one baptism, one God and Father of all who is over all and through all and in all.

But to each one of us grace was given according to the measure of Christ's gift.   *Ephesians 4:4-7*

He gave some as apostles, and some as prophets, and some as evangelists, and some as pastors and teachers, for the equipping of the saints for the work of service, to the building up of the body of Christ; until we all attain to the unity of the **faith**, and of the knowledge of the Son of God, to a mature man, to the measure of the stature which belongs to the fullness of Christ.   *Ephesians 4:11-13*

Be strong in the Lord and in the strength of His might. Put on the full armor of God, so that you will be able to stand firm against the schemes of the devil.

For our struggle is not against flesh and blood, but against the rulers, against the powers, against the world forces of this darkness, against the spiritual forces of wickedness in the heavenly places. Therefore, take up the full armor of God, so that you will be able to resist in the evil day, and having done everything, to stand firm.

Stand firm therefore, having girded your loins with truth, and having put on the breastplate of righteousness, and having shod your feet with the preparation of the gospel of peace; in addition to all, taking up the shield of **faith** with which you will be able to extinguish all the flaming arrows of the evil one.

And take the helmet of salvation, and the sword of the Spirit, which is the word of God.   *Ephesians 6:10-17*

Peace be to the brethren, and love with **faith**, from God the Father and the Lord Jesus Christ.

Grace be with all those who love our Lord Jesus Christ with incorruptible love.

Ephesians 6:23 -24

To me, to live is Christ and to die is gain. But if I am to live on in the flesh, this will mean fruitful labor for me; and I do not know which to choose.

But I am hard-pressed from both directions, having the desire to depart and be with Christ, for that is very much better; yet to remain on in the flesh is more necessary for your sake.

Convinced of this, I know that I will remain and continue with you all for your progress and joy in the **faith**, so that your proud confidence in me may abound in Christ Jesus through my coming to you again.

Only conduct yourselves in a manner worthy of the gospel of Christ, so that whether I come and see you or remain absent, I will hear of you that you are standing firm in one spirit, with one mind striving together for the **faith** of the gospel; in no way alarmed by your opponents - which is a sign of destruction for them, but of salvation for you, and that too, from God.

For to you it has been granted for Christ's sake, not only to believe in Him, but also to suffer for His sake, experiencing the same conflict which you saw in me, and now hear to be in me.

Philippians 1:21-30

Even if I am being poured out as a drink offering upon the sacrifice and service of your **faith**, I rejoice and share my joy with you all.

You too, I urge you, rejoice in the same way and share your joy with me.

Philippians 2:17-18

Whatever things were gain to me, those things I have counted as loss for the sake of Christ.

More than that, I count all things to be loss in view of the surpassing value of knowing Christ Jesus my Lord, for whom I have suffered the loss of all things, and count them but rubbish so that I may gain Christ, and may be found in Him, not having a righteousness of my own derived from the Law, but that which is through **faith** in Christ, the righteousness which comes from God on the basis of **faith**, that I may know Him and the power of His resurrection and the fellowship of His sufferings, being conformed to His death; in order that I may attain to the resurrection from the dead.

Not that I have already obtained it or have already become perfect, but I press on so that I may lay hold of that for which also I was laid hold of by Christ Jesus.

Brethren, I do not regard myself as having laid hold of it yet; but one thing I do: forgetting what lies behind and reaching forward to what lies ahead, I press on toward the goal for the prize of the upward call of God in Christ Jesus.

Philippians 3:7-14

We give thanks to God, the Father of our Lord Jesus Christ, praying always for you, since we heard of your **faith** in Christ Jesus and the love which you have for all the saints; because of the hope laid up for you in heaven, of which you previously heard in the word of truth, the gospel which has come to you, just as in all the world also it is constantly bearing fruit and increasing, even as it has been doing in you also since the day you heard of it and understood the grace of God in truth; just as you learned it from Epaphras, our beloved fellow bond-servant, who is a faithful servant of Christ on our behalf, and he also informed us of your love in the Spirit.

Colossians 1:3-8

Although you were formerly alienated and hostile in mind, engaged in evil deeds, yet He has now reconciled you in His fleshly body through death, in order to present you before Him holy and blameless and beyond reproach - if indeed you continue in the **faith** firmly established and steadfast, and not moved away from the hope of the gospel that you have heard, which was proclaimed in all creation under

heaven, and of which I, Paul, was made a minister.

Colossians 1:21-23

Even though I am absent in body, nevertheless I am with you in spirit, rejoicing to see your good discipline and the stability of your **faith** in Christ.

Therefore as you have received Christ Jesus the Lord, so walk in Him, having been firmly rooted and now being built up in Him and established in your **faith**, just as you were instructed, and overflowing with gratitude.

See to it that no one takes you captive through philosophy and empty deception, according to the tradition of men, according to the elementary principles of the world, rather than according to Christ.

For in Him all the fullness of Deity dwells in bodily form, and in Him you have been made complete, and He is the head over all rule and authority; and in Him you were also circumcised with a circumcision made without hands, in the removal of the body of the flesh by the circumcision of Christ; having been buried with Him in baptism, in which you were also raised up with Him through **faith** in the working of God, who raised Him from the dead.

Colossians 2:5-12

Paul and Silvanus and Timothy, to the church of the Thessalonians in God the Father and the Lord Jesus Christ: Grace to you and peace.

We give thanks to God always for all of you, making mention of you in our prayers; constantly bearing in mind your work of **faith** and labor of love and steadfastness of hope in our Lord Jesus Christ in the presence of our God and Father, knowing, brethren beloved by God, His choice of you; for our gospel did not come to you in word only, but also in power and in the Holy Spirit and with full conviction; just as you know what kind of men we proved to be among you for your sake.

You also became imitators of us and of the Lord, having received the word in much tribulation with the joy of the Holy Spirit, so that you became an example to all the believers in Macedonia and in

Achaia.

For the word of the Lord has sounded forth from you, not only in Macedonia and Achaia, but also in every place your **faith** toward God has gone forth, so that we have no need to say anything.

For they themselves report about us what kind of a reception we had with you, and how you turned to God from idols to serve a living and true God, and to wait for His Son from heaven, whom He raised from the dead, that is Jesus, who rescues us from the wrath to come.

1 Thessalonians 1:1-10

When we could endure it no longer, we thought it best to be left behind at Athens alone, and we sent Timothy, our brother and God's fellow worker in the gospel of Christ, to strengthen and encourage you as to your **faith**, so that no one would be disturbed by these afflictions; for you yourselves know that we have been destined for this.

For indeed when we were with you, we kept telling you in advance that we were going to suffer affliction; and so it came to pass, as you know.

For this reason, when I could endure it no longer, I also sent to find out about your **faith**, for fear that the tempter might have tempted you, and our labor would be in vain.

But now that Timothy has come to us from you, and has brought us good news of your **faith** and love, and that you always think kindly of us, longing to see us just as we also long to see you, for this reason, brethren, in all our distress and affliction we were comforted about you through your **faith**; for now we really live, if you stand firm in the Lord.

For what thanks can we render to God for you in return for all the joy with which we rejoice before our God on your account, as we night and day keep praying most earnestly that we may see your face, and may complete what is lacking in your **faith**? *1 Thessalonians 3:1-10*

You, brethren, are not in darkness, that the day would overtake you like a thief;

for you are all sons of light and sons of day.

We are not of night nor of darkness; so then let us not sleep as others do, but let us be alert and sober. For those who sleep do their sleeping at night, and those who get drunk get drunk at night.

But since we are of the day, let us be sober, having put on the breastplate of **faith** and love, and as a helmet, the hope of salvation.

For God has not destined us for wrath, but for obtaining salvation through our Lord Jesus Christ, who died for us, so that whether we are awake or asleep, we will live together with Him.

Therefore encourage one another and build up one another, just as you also are doing. *1 Thessalonians 5:4-11*

Grace to you and peace from God the Father and the Lord Jesus Christ.

We ought always to give thanks to God for you, brethren, as is only fitting, because your **faith** is greatly enlarged, and the love of each one of you toward one another grows ever greater; therefore, we ourselves speak proudly of you among the churches of God for your perseverance and **faith** in the midst of all your persecutions and afflictions which you endure.

This is a plain indication of God's righteous judgment so that you will be considered worthy of the kingdom of God, for which indeed you are suffering.

2 Thessalonians 1:2-5

We pray for you always, that our God will count you worthy of your calling, and fulfill every desire for goodness and the work of **faith** with power, so that the name of our Lord Jesus will be glorified in you, and you in Him, according to the grace of our God and the Lord Jesus Christ.

2 Thessalonians 1:11-12

We should always give thanks to God for you, brethren beloved by the Lord, because God has chosen you from the beginning for salvation through sanctification by the Spirit and **faith** in the truth.

It was for this He called you through

our gospel, that you may gain the glory of our Lord Jesus Christ.

So then, brethren, stand firm and hold to the traditions which you were taught, whether by word of mouth or by letter from us.

Now may our Lord Jesus Christ Himself and God our Father, who has loved us and given us eternal comfort and good hope by grace, comfort and strengthen your hearts in every good work and word.

Finally, brethren, pray for us that the word of the Lord will spread rapidly and be glorified, just as it did also with you; and that we will be rescued from perverse and evil men; for not all have **faith**.

But the Lord is faithful, and He will strengthen and protect you from the evil one.   *2 Thessalonians 2:13 - 3:3*

Paul, an apostle of Christ Jesus according to the commandment of God our Savior, and of Christ Jesus, who is our hope, to Timothy, my true child in the **faith**: Grace, mercy and peace from God the Father and Christ Jesus our Lord.

As I urged you upon my departure for Macedonia, remain on at Ephesus so that you may instruct certain men not to teach strange doctrines, nor to pay attention to myths and endless genealogies, which give rise to mere speculation rather than furthering the administration of God which is by **faith**.

But the goal of our instruction is love from a pure heart and a good conscience and a sincere **faith**.

For some men, straying from these things, have turned aside to fruitless discussion, wanting to be teachers of the Law, even though they do not understand either what they are saying or the matters about which they make confident assertions.   *1 Timothy 1:1-7*

I thank Christ Jesus our Lord, who has strengthened me, because He considered me faithful, putting me into service, even though I was formerly a blasphemer and a persecutor and a violent aggressor.

Yet I was shown mercy because I acted ignorantly in unbelief; and the grace of our Lord was more than abundant, with the **faith** and love which are found in Christ Jesus.

It is a trustworthy statement, deserving full acceptance, that Christ Jesus came into the world to save sinners, among whom I am foremost of all.

Yet for this reason I found mercy, so that in me as the foremost, Jesus Christ might demonstrate His perfect patience as an example for those who would believe in Him for eternal life.   *1 Timothy 1:12-16*

This command I entrust to you, Timothy, my son, in accordance with the prophecies previously made concerning you, that by them you fight the good fight, keeping **faith** and a good conscience, which some have rejected and suffered shipwreck in regard to their **faith**.

Among these are Hymenaeus and Alexander, whom I have handed over to Satan, so that they will be taught not to blaspheme.

First of all, then, I urge that entreaties and prayers, petitions and thanksgivings, be made on behalf of all men, for kings and all who are in authority, so that we may lead a tranquil and quiet life in all godliness and dignity.

This is good and acceptable in the sight of God our Savior, who desires all men to be saved and to come to the knowledge of the truth.

For there is one God, and one mediator also between God and men, the man Christ Jesus, who gave Himself as a ransom for all, the testimony given at the proper time.

For this I was appointed a preacher and an apostle (I am telling the truth, I am not lying) as a teacher of the Gentiles in **faith** and truth. Therefore I want the men in every place to pray, lifting up holy hands, without wrath and dissension.

Likewise, I want women to adorn themselves with proper clothing, modestly and discreetly, not with braided hair and gold or pearls or costly garments, but rather by means of good works, as is proper for women making a claim to godliness.

A woman must quietly receive instruction with entire submissiveness. But I do not allow a woman to teach or exercise authority over a man, but to remain quiet. For it was Adam who was first created, and then Eve. And it was not Adam who was deceived, but the woman being deceived, fell into transgression.

But women will be preserved through the bearing of children if they continue in **faith** and love and sanctity with self-restraint.   *1 Timothy 1:18 - 2:15*

Deacons likewise must be men of dignity, not double-tongued, or addicted to much wine or fond of sordid gain, but holding to the mystery of the **faith** with a clear conscience. ...

...Deacons must be husbands of only one wife, and good managers of their children and their own households.

For those who have served well as deacons obtain for themselves a high standing and great confidence in the **faith** that is in Christ Jesus.

1 Timothy 3:8-9...12-13

By common confession, great is the mystery of godliness: He who was revealed in the flesh, was vindicated in the Spirit, seen by angels, proclaimed among the nations, believed on in the world, taken up in glory.

But the Spirit explicitly says that in later times some will fall away from the **faith**, paying attention to deceitful spirits and doctrines of demons, by means of the hypocrisy of liars seared in their own conscience as with a branding iron, men who forbid marriage and advocate abstaining from foods which God has created to be gratefully shared in by those who believe and know the truth.

For everything created by God is good, and nothing is to be rejected if it is received with gratitude; for it is sanctified by means of the word of God and prayer.

In pointing out these things to the brethren, you will be a good servant of Christ Jesus, constantly nourished on the words of the **faith** and of the sound doc-

trine which you have been following. ...

... Prescribe and teach these things. Let no one look down on your youthfulness, but rather in speech, conduct, love, **faith** and purity, show yourself an example of those who believe.

1 Timothy 4:1-6...11-12

If anyone does not provide for his own, and especially for those of his household, he has denied the **faith** and is worse than an unbeliever.   *1 Timothy 5:8*

Godliness actually is a means of great gain when accompanied by contentment. For we have brought nothing into the world, so we cannot take anything out of it either.

If we have food and covering, with these we shall be content.

But those who want to get rich fall into temptation and a snare and many foolish and harmful desires which plunge men into ruin and destruction.

For the love of money is a root of all sorts of evil, and some by longing for it have wandered away from the **faith** and pierced themselves with many griefs.

But flee from these things, you man of God, and pursue righteousness, godliness, **faith**, love, perseverance and gentleness.

Fight the good fight of **faith**; take hold of the eternal life to which you were called, and you made the good confession in the presence of many witnesses.

1 Timothy 6:6-12

O Timothy, guard what has been entrusted to you, avoiding worldly and empty chatter and the opposing arguments of what is falsely called "knowledge" - which some have professed and thus gone astray from the **faith**. Grace be with you.

1 Timothy 6:20-21

Paul, an apostle of Christ Jesus by the will of God, according to the promise of life in Christ Jesus, to Timothy, my beloved son: Grace, mercy and peace from God the Father and Christ Jesus our Lord.

I thank God, whom I serve with a clear conscience the way my forefathers did, as I constantly remember you in my prayers night and day, longing to see you, even as I recall your tears, so that I may be filled with joy. For I am mindful of the sincere **faith** within you, which first dwelt in your grandmother Lois and your mother Eunice, and I am sure that it is in you as well.   *2 Timothy 1:1-5*

Retain the standard of sound words which you have heard from me, in the **faith** and love which are in Christ Jesus.

Guard, through the Holy Spirit who dwells in us, the treasure which has been entrusted to you.   *2 Timothy 1:13-14*

I endure all things for the sake of those who are chosen, so that they also may obtain the salvation which is in Christ Jesus and with it eternal glory.

It is a trustworthy statement: for if we died with Him, we will also live with Him; if we endure, we will also reign with Him; if we deny Him, He also will deny us; if we are **faithless**, He remains faithful, for He cannot deny Himself.

Remind them of these things, and solemnly charge them in the presence of God not to wrangle about words, which is useless and leads to the ruin of the hearers.

Be diligent to present yourself approved to God as a workman who does not need to be ashamed, accurately handling the word of truth.

The Lord grant mercy to the house of Onesiphorus, for he often refreshed me and was not ashamed of my chains; but when he was in Rome, he eagerly searched for me and found me - men who have gone astray from the truth saying that the resurrection has already taken place, and they upset the **faith** of some.

Nevertheless, the firm foundation of God stands, having this seal, "The Lord knows those who are His," and, "Everyone who names the name of the Lord is to abstain from wickedness."

Now in a large house there are not only gold and silver vessels, but also vessels of wood and of earthenware, and some to honor and some to dishonor.

Therefore, if anyone cleanses himself from these things, he will be a vessel for honor, sanctified, useful to the Master, prepared for every good work.

Now flee from youthful lusts and pursue righteousness, **faith**, love and peace, with those who call on the Lord from a pure heart.   *2 Timothy 2:10-22*

Just as Jannes and Jambres opposed Moses, so these men also oppose the truth, men of depraved mind, rejected in regard to the **faith**.

But they will not make further progress; for their folly will be obvious to all, just as Jannes's and Jambres's folly was also.

Now you followed my teaching, conduct, purpose, **faith**, patience, love, perseverance, persecutions, and sufferings, such as happened to me at Antioch, at Iconium and at Lystra; what persecutions I endured, and out of them all the Lord rescued me! Indeed, all who desire to live godly in Christ Jesus will be persecuted. But evil men and impostors will proceed from bad to worse, deceiving and being deceived.

You, however, continue in the things you have learned and become convinced of, knowing from whom you have learned them, and that from childhood you have known the sacred writings which are able to give you the wisdom that leads to salvation through **faith** which is in Christ Jesus.

All Scripture is inspired by God and profitable for teaching, for reproof, for correction, for training in righteousness; so that the man of God may be adequate, equipped for every good work.
                              2 Timothy 3:8-17

Be sober in all things, endure hardship, do the work of an evangelist, fulfill your ministry. For I am already being poured out as a drink offering, and the time of my departure has come.

I have fought the good fight, I have finished the course, I have kept the **faith**;

in the future there is laid up for me the crown of righteousness, which the Lord, the righteous Judge, will award to me on that day; and not only to me, but also to all who have loved His appearing.

2 Timothy 4:5-8

Paul, a bond-servant of God and an apostle of Jesus Christ, for the **faith** of those chosen of God and the knowledge of the truth which is according to godliness, in the hope of eternal life, which God, who cannot lie, promised long ages ago, but at the proper time manifested, even His word, in the proclamation with which I was entrusted according to the commandment of God our Savior, to Titus, my true child in a common **faith**: Grace and peace from God the Father and Christ Jesus our Savior. *Titus 1:1-4*

This testimony is true. For this reason reprove them severely so that they may be sound in the **faith**, not paying attention to Jewish myths and commandments of men who turn away from the truth.

To the pure, all things are pure; but to those who are defiled and unbelieving, nothing is pure, but both their mind and their conscience are defiled. They profess to know God, but by their deeds they deny Him, being detestable and disobedient and worthless for any good deed.

But as for you, speak the things which are fitting for sound doctrine. Older men are to be temperate, dignified, sensible, sound in **faith**, in love, in perseverance. *Titus 1:13 - 2:2*

Urge bondslaves to be subject to their own masters in everything, to be well-pleasing, not argumentative, not pilfering, but showing all good **faith** so that they will adorn the doctrine of God our Savior in every respect.

For the grace of God has appeared, bringing salvation to all men, instructing us to deny ungodliness and worldly desires and to live sensibly, righteously and godly in the present age, looking for the blessed hope and the appearing of the glory of our great God and Savior, Christ

Jesus, who gave Himself for us to redeem us from every lawless deed, and to purify for Himself a people for His own possession, zealous for good deeds. *Titus 2:9-14*

All who are with me greet you. Greet those who love us in the **faith**. Grace be with you all. *Titus 3:15*

I thank my God always, making mention of you in my prayers, because I hear of your love and of the **faith** which you have toward the Lord Jesus and toward all the saints; and I pray that the fellowship of your **faith** may become effective through the knowledge of every good thing which is in you for Christ's sake. *Philemon 4-6*

Take care, brethren, that there not be in any one of you an evil, unbelieving heart that falls away from the living God. But encourage one another day after day, as long as it is still called "Today," so that none of you will be hardened by the deceitfulness of sin.

For we have become partakers of Christ, if we hold fast the beginning of our assurance firm until the end, while it is said, "Today if you hear His voice, do not harden your hearts, as when they provoked Me."

For who provoked Him when they had heard? Indeed, did not all those who came out of Egypt led by Moses?

And with whom was He angry for forty years? Was it not with those who sinned, whose bodies fell in the wilderness?

And to whom did He swear that they would not enter His rest, but to those who were disobedient?

So we see that they were not able to enter because of unbelief. Therefore, let us fear if, while a promise remains of entering His rest, any one of you may seem to have come short of it.

For indeed we have had good news preached to us, just as they also; but the word they heard did not profit them, because it was not united by **faith** in those who heard.

For we who have believed enter that

rest, just as He has said, "As I swore in My wrath, they shall not enter My rest," although His works were finished from the foundation of the world. *Hebrews 3:14 - 4:3*

Leaving the elementary teaching about the Christ, let us press on to maturity, not laying again a foundation of repentance from dead works and of **faith** toward God, of instruction about washings and laying on of hands, and the resurrection of the dead and eternal judgment. And this we will do, if God permits.

For in the case of those who have once been enlightened and have tasted of the heavenly gift and have been made partakers of the Holy Spirit, and have tasted the good word of God and the powers of the age to come, and then have fallen away, it is impossible to renew them again to repentance, since they again crucify to themselves the Son of God and put Him to open shame.

Hebrews 6:1-6

We desire that each one of you show the same diligence so as to realize the full assurance of hope until the end, so that you will not be sluggish, but imitators of those who through **faith** and patience inherit the promises.

For when God made the promise to Abraham, since He could swear by no one greater, He swore by Himself, saying, "I will surely bless you and I will surely multiply you." And so, having patiently waited, he obtained the promise.

For men swear by one greater than themselves, and with them an oath given as confirmation is an end of every dispute. In the same way God, desiring even more to show to the heirs of the promise the unchangeableness of His purpose, interposed with an oath, so that by two unchangeable things in which it is impossible for God to lie, we who have taken refuge would have strong encouragement to take hold of the hope set before us.

This hope we have as an anchor of the soul, a hope both sure and steadfast and one which enters within the veil,

where Jesus has entered as a forerunner for us, having become a high priest forever according to the order of Melchizedek.

Hebrews 6:11-15

Brethren, since we have confidence to enter the holy place by the blood of Jesus, by a new and living way which He inaugurated for us through the veil, that is, His flesh, and since we have a great priest over the house of God, let us draw near with a sincere heart in full assurance of **faith**, having our hearts sprinkled clean from an evil conscience and our bodies washed with pure water.

Let us hold fast the confession of our hope without wavering, for He who promised is faithful; and let us consider how to stimulate one another to love and good deeds, not forsaking our own assembling together, as is the habit of some, but encouraging one another; and all the more as you see the day drawing near.

Hebrews 10:19-25

It is a terrifying thing to fall into the hands of the living God. But remember the former days, when, after being enlightened, you endured a great conflict of sufferings, partly by being made a public spectacle through reproaches and tribulations, and partly by becoming sharers with those who were so treated.

For you showed sympathy to the prisoners and accepted joyfully the seizure of your property, knowing that you have for yourselves a better possession and a lasting one. Therefore, do not throw away your confidence, which has a great reward.

For you have need of endurance, so that when you have done the will of God, you may receive what was promised. "For yet in a very little while, He who is coming will come, and will not delay.

"But My righteous one shall live by **faith**; and if he shrinks back, My soul has no pleasure in him."

But we are not of those who shrink back to destruction, but of those who have **faith** to the preserving of the soul.

Now **faith** is the assurance of things

hoped for, the conviction of things not seen. For by it the men of old gained approval.

By **faith** we understand that the worlds were prepared by the word of God, so that what is seen was not made out of things which are visible.

By **faith** Abel offered to God a better sacrifice than Cain, through which he obtained the testimony that he was righteous, God testifying about his gifts, and through **faith**, though he is dead, he still speaks.

By **faith** Enoch was taken up so that he would not see death; and he was not found because God took him up; for he obtained the witness that before his being taken up he was pleasing to God.

And without **faith** it is impossible to please Him, for he who comes to God must believe that He is and that He is a rewarder of those who seek Him.

By **faith** Noah, being warned by God about things not yet seen, in reverence prepared an ark for the salvation of his household, by which he condemned the world, and became an heir of the righteousness which is according to **faith**.

By **faith** Abraham, when he was called, obeyed by going out to a place which he was to receive for an inheritance; and he went out, not knowing where he was going.

By **faith** he lived as an alien in the land of promise, as in a foreign land, dwelling in tents with Isaac and Jacob, fellow heirs of the same promise; by **faith** even Sarah herself received ability to conceive, even beyond the proper time of life, since she considered Him faithful who had promised.

Therefore there was born even of one man, and him as good as dead at that, as many descendants as the stars of heaven in number, and innumerable as the sand which is by the seashore.

All these died in **faith**, without receiving the promises, but having seen them and having welcomed them from a distance, and having confessed that they were strangers and exiles on the earth.

Hebrews 10:35 - 11:13

By **faith** Abraham, when he was tested, offered up Isaac, and he who had received the promises was offering up his only begotten son; it was he to whom it was said, "In Isaac your descendants shall be called." He considered that God is able to raise people even from the dead, from which he also received him back as a type.

By **faith** Isaac blessed Jacob and Esau, even regarding things to come.

By **faith** Jacob, as he was dying, blessed each of the sons of Joseph, and worshiped, leaning on the top of his staff.

By **faith** Joseph, when he was dying, made mention of the exodus of the sons of Israel, and gave orders concerning his bones.

By **faith** Moses, when he was born, was hidden for three months by his parents, because they saw he was a beautiful child; and they were not afraid of the king's edict.

By **faith** Moses, when he had grown up, refused to be called the son of Pharaoh's daughter, choosing rather to endure ill-treatment with the people of God than to enjoy the passing pleasures of sin, considering the reproach of Christ greater riches than the treasures of Egypt; for he was looking to the reward.

By **faith** he left Egypt, not fearing the wrath of the king; for he endured, as seeing Him who is unseen. By **faith** he kept the Passover and the sprinkling of the blood, so that he who destroyed the firstborn would not touch them.

By **faith** they passed through the Red Sea as though they were passing through dry land; and the Egyptians, when they attempted it, were drowned.

By **faith** the walls of Jericho fell down after they had been encircled for seven days. By **faith** Rahab the harlot did not perish along with those who were disobedient, after she had welcomed the spies in peace.

And what more shall I say? For time will fail me if I tell of Gideon, Barak, Samson, Jephthah, of David and Samuel and the prophets, who by **faith** conquered kingdoms, performed acts of righteousness, obtained promises, shut the mouths of lions, quenched the power of fire, escaped the edge of the sword, from weakness were made strong, became mighty in war, put foreign armies to flight.

Women received back their dead by resurrection; and others were tortured, not accepting their release, so that they might obtain a better resurrection; and others experienced mockings and scourgings, yes, also chains and imprisonment. They were stoned, they were sawn in two, they were tempted, they were put to death with the sword; they went about in sheepskins, in goatskins, being destitute, afflicted, ill-treated (men of whom the world was not worthy), wandering in deserts and mountains and caves and holes in the ground.

And all these, having gained approval through their **faith**, did not receive what was promised, because God had provided something better for us, so that apart from us they would not be made perfect.

Therefore, since we have so great a cloud of witnesses surrounding us, let us also lay aside every encumbrance and the sin which so easily entangles us, and let us run with endurance the race that is set before us, fixing our eyes on Jesus, the author and perfecter of **faith**, who for the joy set before Him endured the cross, despising the shame, and has sat down at the right hand of the throne of God.

Hebrews 11:34 - 12:2

Make sure that your character is free from the love of money, being content with what you have; for He Himself has said, "I will never desert you, nor will I ever forsake you," so that we confidently say, "The Lord is my helper, I will not be afraid. What will man do to me?"

Remember those who led you, who spoke the word of God to you; and considering the result of their conduct, imitate their **faith**.

Jesus Christ is the same yesterday and today and forever. *Hebrews 13:5-8*

Consider it all joy, my brethren, when you encounter various trials, knowing that the

testing of your **faith** produces endurance. And let endurance have its perfect result, so that you may be perfect and complete, lacking in nothing.

But if any of you lacks wisdom, let him ask of God, who gives to all generously and without reproach, and it will be given to him.

But he must ask in **faith** without any doubting, for the one who doubts is like the surf of the sea, driven and tossed by the wind.

For that man ought not to expect that he will receive anything from the Lord, being a double-minded man, unstable in all his ways. *James 1:2-8*

My brethren, do not hold your **faith** in our glorious Lord Jesus Christ with an attitude of personal favoritism.

For if a man comes into your assembly with a gold ring and dressed in fine clothes, and there also comes in a poor man in dirty clothes, and you pay special attention to the one who is wearing the fine clothes, and say, "You sit here in a good place," and you say to the poor man, "You stand over there, or sit down by my footstool," have you not made distinctions among yourselves, and become judges with evil motives?

Listen, my beloved brethren: Did not God choose the poor of this world to be rich in **faith** and heirs of the kingdom which He promised to those who love Him? *James 2:1-5*

What use is it, my brethren, if someone says he has **faith** but he has no works? Can that **faith** save him?

If a brother or sister is without clothing and in need of daily food, and one of you says to them, "Go in peace, be warmed and be filled," and yet you do not give them what is necessary for their body, what use is that?

Even so **faith**, if it has no works, is dead, being by itself.

But someone may well say, "You have **faith** and I have works; show me your **faith** without the works, and I will show you my **faith** by my works."

You believe that God is one. You do well; the demons also believe, and shudder. But are you willing to recognize, you foolish fellow, that **faith** without works is useless?

Was not Abraham our father justified by works when he offered up Isaac his son on the altar? You see that **faith** was working with his works, and as a result of the works, **faith** was perfected; and the Scripture was fulfilled which says, "And Abraham believed God, and it was reckoned to him as righteousness," and he was called the friend of God.

You see that a man is justified by works and not by **faith** alone.

In the same way, was not Rahab the harlot also justified by works when she received the messengers and sent them out by another way?

For just as the body without the spirit is dead, so also **faith** without works is dead.   *James 2:14-26*

Is anyone among you suffering? Then he must pray.

Is anyone cheerful? He is to sing praises.

Is anyone among you sick? Then he must call for the elders of the church and they are to pray over him, anointing him with oil in the name of the Lord; and the prayer offered in **faith** will restore the one who is sick, and the Lord will raise him up, and if he has committed sins, they will be forgiven him. Therefore, confess your sins to one another, and pray for one another so that you may be healed.

The effective prayer of a righteous man can accomplish much.

Elijah was a man with a nature like ours, and he prayed earnestly that it would not rain, and it did not rain on the earth for three years and six months. Then he prayed again, and the sky poured rain and the earth produced its fruit.   *James 5:13-18*

Blessed be the God and Father of our Lord Jesus Christ, who according to His great mercy has caused us to be born again to a living hope through the resurrection of Jesus Christ from the dead, to obtain an inheritance which is imperishable and undefiled and will not fade away, reserved in heaven for you, who are protected by the power of God through **faith** for a salvation ready to be revealed in the last time.

In this you greatly rejoice, even though now for a little while, if necessary, you have been distressed by various trials, so that the proof of your **faith**, being more precious than gold which is perishable, even though tested by fire, may be found to result in praise and glory and honor at the revelation of Jesus Christ; and though you have not seen Him, you love Him, and though you do not see Him now, but believe in Him, you greatly rejoice with joy inexpressible and full of glory, obtaining as the outcome of your **faith** the salvation of your souls.

1 Peter 1:3-9

If you address as Father the One who impartially judges according to each one's work, conduct yourselves in fear during the time of your stay on earth; knowing that you were not redeemed with perishable things like silver or gold from your futile way of life inherited from your forefathers, but with precious blood, as of a lamb unblemished and spotless, the blood of Christ.

For He was foreknown before the foundation of the world, but has appeared in these last times for the sake of you who through Him are believers in God, who raised Him from the dead and gave Him glory, so that your **faith** and hope are in God.   *1 Peter 1:17-21*

Be of sober spirit, be on the alert. Your adversary, the devil, prowls around like a roaring lion, seeking someone to devour.

But resist him, firm in your **faith**, knowing that the same experiences of suffering are being accomplished by your brethren who are in the world.

After you have suffered for a little while, the God of all grace, who called you to His eternal glory in Christ, will Himself perfect, confirm, strengthen and establish you.

To Him be dominion forever and ever. Amen. *1 Peter 5:8-11*

Simon Peter, a bond-servant and apostle of Jesus Christ, to those who have received a **faith** of the same kind as ours, by the righteousness of our God and Savior, Jesus Christ: Grace and peace be multiplied to you in the knowledge of God and of Jesus our Lord; seeing that His divine power has granted to us everything pertaining to life and godliness, through the true knowledge of Him who called us by His own glory and excellence.

For by these He has granted to us His precious and magnificent promises, so that by them you may become partakers of the divine nature, having escaped the corruption that is in the world by lust.

Now for this very reason also, applying all diligence, in your **faith** supply moral excellence, and in your moral excellence, knowledge, and in your knowledge, self-control, and in your self-control, perseverance, and in your perseverance, godliness, and in your godliness, brotherly kindness, and in your brotherly kindness, love.

For if these qualities are yours and are increasing, they render you neither useless nor unfruitful in the true knowledge of our Lord Jesus Christ.

2 Peter 1:1-8

Whoever believes that Jesus is the Christ is born of God, and whoever loves the Father loves the child born of Him.

By this we know that we love the children of God, when we love God and observe His commandments.

For this is the love of God, that we keep His commandments; and His commandments are not burdensome.

For whatever is born of God overcomes the world; and this is the victory that has overcome the world - our **faith**.

Who is the one who overcomes the world, but he who believes that Jesus is the Son of God? *1 John 5:1-5*

Beloved, while I was making every effort to write you about our common salvation, I felt the necessity to write to you appealing that you contend earnestly for the **faith** which was once for all handed down to the saints.

For certain persons have crept in unnoticed, those who were long beforehand marked out for this condemnation, ungodly persons who turn the grace of our God into licentiousness and deny our only Master and Lord, Jesus Christ.

Now I desire to remind you, though you know all things once for all, that the Lord, after saving a people out of the land of Egypt, subsequently destroyed those who did not believe. *Jude 3-5*

You, beloved, ought to remember the words that were spoken beforehand by the apostles of our Lord Jesus Christ, that they were saying to you, "In the last time there will be mockers, following after their own ungodly lusts." These are the ones who cause divisions, worldly-minded, devoid of the Spirit.

But you, beloved, building yourselves up on your most holy **faith**, praying in the Holy Spirit, keep yourselves in the love of God, waiting anxiously for the mercy of our Lord Jesus Christ to eternal life.

And have mercy on some, who are doubting; save others, snatching them out of the fire; and on some have mercy with fear, hating even the garment polluted by the flesh. *Jude 17-23*

To the angel of the church in Pergamum write: The One who has the sharp two-edged sword says this: "I know where you dwell, where Satan's throne is; and you hold fast My name, and did not deny My **faith** even in the days of Antipas, My witness, My faithful one, who was killed among you, where Satan dwells."

Revelation 2:12-13

To the angel of the church in Thyatira write: The Son of God, who has eyes like a flame of fire, and His feet are like burnished bronze, says this: "I know your deeds, and your love and **faith** and service and perseverance, and that your deeds of late are greater than at first."

Revelation 2:18-19

If anyone has an ear, let him hear. If anyone is destined for captivity, to captivity he goes; if anyone kills with the sword, with the sword he must be killed.

Here is the perseverance and the **faith** of the saints.   *Revelation 13:9-10*

Another angel, a third one, followed them, saying with a loud voice, "If anyone worships the beast and his image, and receives a mark on his forehead or on his hand, he also will drink of the wine of the wrath of God, which is mixed in full strength in the cup of His anger; and he will be tormented with fire and brimstone in the presence of the holy angels and in the presence of the Lamb.

"And the smoke of their torment goes up forever and ever; they have no rest day and night, those who worship the beast and his image, and whoever receives the mark of his name."

Here is the perseverance of the saints who keep the commandments of God and their **faith** in Jesus.

Revelation 14:9-12

HOLY SPIRIT
/ SPIRIT OF GOD^ / SPIRIT OF THE LORD^ / SPIRIT*

Definitions

Holy Spirit   1. The Spirit of God.

               2. God as present and active in the universe.

               3. For most Christians, the third member of the Trinity; the "Holy Ghost".

OLD TESTAMENT

In the beginning God created the heavens and the earth.

The earth was formless and void, and darkness was over the surface of the deep, and the **Spirit of God** was moving over the surface of the waters.

Then God said, "Let there be light"; and there was light. God saw that the light was good; and God separated the light from the darkness.

God called the light day, and the darkness He called night. And there was evening and there was morning, one day.

Genesis 1:1-5

It came about, when men began to multiply on the face of the land, and daughters were born to them, that the sons of God saw that the daughters of men were beautiful; and they took wives for themselves, whomever they chose.

Then the Lord said, "My **Spirit** shall not strive with man forever, because he also is flesh; nevertheless his days shall be one hundred and twenty years."

Genesis 6:1-3

The Lord spoke to Moses, saying, "See, I have called by name Bezalel, the son of Uri, the son of Hur, of the tribe of Judah.

"I have filled him with the **Spirit of God** in wisdom, in understanding, in knowledge, and in all kinds of craftsmanship, to make artistic designs for work in gold, in silver, and in bronze, and in the cutting of stones for settings, and in the

carving of wood, that he may work in all kinds of craftsmanship.

"And behold, I Myself have appointed with him Oholiab, the son of Ahisamach, of the tribe of Dan; and in the hearts of all who are skillful I have put skill, that they may make all that I have commanded you: the tent of meeting, and the ark of testimony, and the mercy seat upon it, and all the furniture of the tent," ~

Exodus 31:1-7

Moses said to the sons of Israel, "See, the Lord has called by name Bezalel the son of Uri, the son of Hur, of the tribe of Judah.

"And He has filled him with the **Spirit of God**, in wisdom, in understanding and in knowledge and in all craftsmanship; to make designs for working in gold and in silver and in bronze, and in the cutting of stones for settings and in the carving of wood, so as to perform in every inventive work.

"He also has put in his heart to teach, both he and Oholiab, the son of Ahisamach, of the tribe of Daniel. He has filled them with skill to perform every work of an engraver and of a designer and of an embroiderer, in blue and in purple and in scarlet material, and in fine linen, and of a weaver, as performers of every work and makers of designs.

"Now Bezalel and Oholiab, and every skillful person in whom the Lord has put skill and understanding to know how to perform all the work in the construction of the sanctuary, shall perform in accordance with all that the Lord has commanded."

Then Moses called Bezalel and Oholiab and every skillful person in whom the Lord had put skill, everyone whose heart stirred him, to come to the work to perform it. *Exodus 35:30 - 36:2*

The Lord said to Moses, "Gather for Me seventy men from the elders of Israel, whom you know to be the elders of the people and their officers and bring them to the tent of meeting, and let them take their stand there with you.

"Then I will come down and speak with you there, and I will take of the **Spirit** who is upon you, and will put Him upon them; and they shall bear the burden of the people with you, so that you will not bear it all alone." *Numbers 11:16-17*

Moses went out and told the people the words of the Lord. Also, he gathered seventy men of the elders of the people, and stationed them around the tent.

Then the Lord came down in the cloud and spoke to him; and He took of the **Spirit** who was upon him and placed Him upon the seventy elders.

And when the **Spirit** rested upon them, they prophesied. But they did not do it again.

But two men had remained in the camp; the name of one was Eldad and the name of the other Medad. And the **Spirit** rested upon them (now they were among those who had been registered, but had not gone out to the tent), and they prophesied in the camp.

So a young man ran and told Moses and said, "Eldad and Medad are prophesying in the camp."

Then Joshua the son of Nun, the attendant of Moses from his youth, said, "Moses, my lord, restrain them."

But Moses said to him, "Are you jealous for my sake? Would that all the Lord's people were prophets, that the Lord would put His **Spirit** upon them!"

Then Moses returned to the camp, both he and the elders of Israel. *Numbers 11:24-30*

When Balaam saw that it pleased the Lord to bless Israel, he did not go as at other times to seek omens but he set his face toward the wilderness.

And Balaam lifted up his eyes and saw Israel camping tribe by tribe; and the **Spirit of God** came upon him.

He took up his discourse and said, "The oracle of Balaam the son of Beor, and the oracle of the man whose eye is opened; the oracle of him who hears the words of God, who sees the vision of the Almighty, falling down, yet having his eyes uncovered, how fair are your tents, O Jacob, your dwellings, O Israel!" *Numbers 24:1-5*

Moses spoke to the Lord, saying, "May the Lord, the God of the spirits of all flesh, appoint a man over the congregation, who will go out and come in before them, and who will lead them out and bring them in, so that the congregation of the Lord will not be like sheep which have no shepherd."

So the Lord said to Moses, "Take Joshua the son of Nun, a man in whom is the **Spirit**, and lay your hand on him; and have him stand before Eleazar the priest and before all the congregation, and commission him in their sight. You shall put some of your authority on him, in order that all the congregation of the sons of Israel may obey him.

"Moreover, he shall stand before Eleazar the priest, who shall inquire for him by the judgment of the Urim before the Lord. At his command they shall go out and at his command they shall come in, both he and the sons of Israel with him, even all the congregation."

Moses did just as the Lord commanded him; and he took Joshua and set him before Eleazar the priest and before all the congregation.

Then he laid his hands on him and commissioned him, just as the Lord had spoken through Moses. *Numbers 27:15-23*

The sons of Israel lived among the Canaanites, the Hittites, the Amorites, the Perizzites, the Hivites, and the Jebusites;

and they took their daughters for themselves as wives, and gave their own daughters to their sons, and served their gods.

The sons of Israel did what was evil in the sight of the Lord, and forgot the Lord their God and served the Baals and the Asheroth.

Then the anger of the Lord was kindled against Israel, so that He sold them into the hands of Cushan-rishathaim king of Mesopotamia; and the sons of Israel served Cushan-rishathaim eight years.

When the sons of Israel cried to the Lord, the Lord raised up a deliverer for the sons of Israel to deliver them, Othniel the son of Kenaz, Caleb's younger brother. The **Spirit of the Lord** came upon him, and he judged Israel.

When he went out to war, the Lord gave Cushan-rishathaim king of Mesopotamia into his hand, so that he prevailed over Cushan-rishathaim.

Then the land had rest forty years. And Othniel the son of Kenaz died. *Judges 3:5-11*

All the Midianites and the Amalekites and the sons of the east assembled themselves; and they crossed over and camped in the valley of Jezreel.

So the **Spirit of the Lord** came upon Gideon; and he blew a trumpet, and the Abiezrites were called together to follow him.

He sent messengers throughout Manasseh, and they also were called together to follow him; and he sent messengers to Asher, Zebulun, and Naphtali, and they came up to meet them. *Judges 6:33-35*

The **Spirit of the Lord** came upon Jephthah, so that he passed through Gilead and Manasseh; then he passed through Mizpah of Gilead, and from Mizpah of Gilead he went on to the sons of Ammon.

Jephthah made a vow to the Lord and said, "If You will indeed give the sons of Ammon into my hand, then it shall be that whatever comes out of the doors of my house to meet me when I return in peace from the sons of Ammon, it shall

be the Lord's, and I will offer it up as a burnt offering."

So Jephthah crossed over to the sons of Ammon to fight against them; and the Lord gave them into his hand. He struck them with a very great slaughter from Aroer to the entrance of Minnith, twenty cities, and as far as Abel-keramim.

So the sons of Ammon were subdued before the sons of Israel. *Judges 11:29-33*

The woman gave birth to a son and named him Samson; and the child grew up and the Lord blessed him.

And the **Spirit of the Lord** began to stir him in Mahaneh-dan, between Zorah and Eshtaol. *Judges 13:24-25*

Samson went down to Timnah with his father and mother, and came as far as the vineyards of Timnah; and behold, a young lion came roaring toward him.

The **Spirit of the Lord** came upon him mightily, so that he tore him as one tears a young goat though he had nothing in his hand; but he did not tell his father or mother what he had done. *Judges 14:5-6*

The men of the city said to him on the seventh day before the sun went down, "What is sweeter than honey? And what is stronger than a lion?"

And he said to them, "If you had not plowed with my heifer, you would not have found out my riddle."

Then the **Spirit of the Lord** came upon him mightily, and he went down to Ashkelon and killed thirty of them and took their spoil and gave the changes of clothes to those who told the riddle.

And his anger burned, and he went up to his father's house. *Judges 14:18-19*

The Philistines went up and camped in Judah, and spread out in Lehi.

The men of Judah said, "Why have you come up against us?"

And they said, "We have come up to bind Samson in order to do to him as he did to us."

Then 3,000 men of Judah went down to the cleft of the rock of Etam and said to

Samson, "Do you not know that the Philistines are rulers over us? What then is this that you have done to us?"

And he said to them, "As they did to me, so I have done to them."

They said to him, "We have come down to bind you so that we may give you into the hands of the Philistines."

And Samson said to them, "Swear to me that you will not kill me."

So they said to him, "No, but we will bind you fast and give you into their hands; yet surely we will not kill you."

Then they bound him with two new ropes and brought him up from the rock.

When he came to Lehi, the Philistines shouted as they met him. And the **Spirit of the Lord** came upon him mightily so that the ropes that were on his arms were as flax that is burned with fire, and his bonds dropped from his hands.

He found a fresh jawbone of a donkey, so he reached out and took it and killed a thousand men with it.

Then Samson said, "With the jawbone of a donkey, heaps upon heaps, with the jawbone of a donkey I have killed a thousand men."   *Judges 15:9-16*

"Afterward you will come to the hill of God where the Philistine garrison is; and it shall be as soon as you have come there to the city, that you will meet a group of prophets coming down from the high place with harp, tambourine, flute, and a lyre before them, and they will be prophesying.

"Then the **Spirit of the Lord** will come upon you mightily, and you shall prophesy with them and be changed into another man. It shall be when these signs come to you, do for yourself what the occasion requires, for God is with you.

"And you shall go down before me to Gilgal; and behold, I will come down to you to offer burnt offerings and sacrifice peace offerings. You shall wait seven days until I come to you and show you what you should do."

Then it happened when he turned his back to leave Samuel, God changed his heart; and all those signs came about on that day.

When they came to the hill there, behold, a group of prophets met him; and the **Spirit of God** came upon him mightily, so that he prophesied among them.

It came about, when all who knew him previously saw that he prophesied now with the prophets, that the people said to one another, "What has happened to the son of Kish? Is Saul also among the prophets?"

A man there said, "Now, who is their father?" Therefore it became a proverb: "Is Saul also among the prophets?"

When he had finished prophesying, he came to the high place. *1 Samuel 10:5-13*

Behold, Saul was coming from the field behind the oxen, and he said, "What is the matter with the people that they weep?" So they related to him the words of the men of Jabesh.

Then the **Spirit of God** came upon Saul mightily when he heard these words, and he became very angry.

He took a yoke of oxen and cut them in pieces, and sent them throughout the territory of Israel by the hand of messengers, saying, "Whoever does not come out after Saul and after Samuel, so shall it be done to his oxen."

Then the dread of the Lord fell on the people, and they came out as one man.
1 Samuel 11:5-7

Jesse made seven of his sons pass before Samuel. But Samuel said to Jesse, "The Lord has not chosen these."

And Samuel said to Jesse, "Are these all the children?"

And he said, "There remains yet the youngest, and behold, he is tending the sheep."

Then Samuel said to Jesse, "Send and bring him; for we will not sit down until he comes here." So he sent and brought him in.

Now he was ruddy, with beautiful eyes and a handsome appearance.

And the Lord said, "Arise, anoint him; for this is he."

Then Samuel took the horn of oil and anointed him in the midst of his brothers; and the **Spirit of the Lord** came mightily upon David from that day forward. And Samuel arose and went to Ramah.

Now the **Spirit of the Lord** departed from Saul, and an evil spirit from the Lord terrorized him. Saul's servants then said to him, "Behold now, an evil spirit from God is terrorizing you. Let our lord now command your servants who are before you.

"Let them seek a man who is a skillful player on the harp; and it shall come about when the evil spirit from God is on you, that he shall play the harp with his hand, and you will be well."

So Saul said to his servants, "Provide for me now a man who can play well and bring him to me."

Then one of the young men said, "Behold, I have seen a son of Jesse the Bethlehemite who is a skillful musician, a mighty man of valor, a warrior, one prudent in speech, and a handsome man; and the Lord is with him."

So Saul sent messengers to Jesse and said, "Send me your son David who is with the flock."

Jesse took a donkey loaded with bread and a jug of wine and a young goat, and sent them to Saul by David his son.   *1 Samuel 16:10-20*

David fled and escaped and came to Samuel at Ramah, and told him all that Saul had done to him. And he and Samuel went and stayed in Naioth.

It was told Saul, saying, "Behold, David is at Naioth in Ramah."

Then Saul sent messengers to take David, but when they saw the company of the prophets prophesying, with Samuel standing and presiding over them, the **Spirit of God** came upon the messengers of Saul; and they also prophesied.

When it was told Saul, he sent other messengers, and they also prophesied. So Saul sent messengers again the third time, and they also prophesied. Then he himself went to Ramah and came as far as the large well that is in

Secu; and he asked and said, "Where are Samuel and David?"

And someone said, "Behold, they are at Naioth in Ramah."

He proceeded there to Naioth in Ramah; and the **Spirit of God** came upon him also, so that he went along prophesying continually until he came to Naioth in Ramah. He also stripped off his clothes, and he too prophesied before Samuel and lay down naked all that day and all that night.

Therefore they say, "Is Saul also among the prophets?"   *1 Samuel 19:18-24*

These are the last words of David.

David the son of Jesse declares, the man who was raised on high declares, the anointed of the God of Jacob, and the sweet psalmist of Israel, "The **Spirit of the Lord** spoke by me, and His word was on my tongue.

The God of Israel said, the Rock of Israel spoke to me, 'He who rules over men righteously, who rules in the fear of God, is as the light of the morning when the sun rises, a morning without clouds, when the tender grass springs out of the earth, through sunshine after rain.'

"Truly is not my house so with God? For He has made an everlasting covenant with me, ordered in all things, and secured; for all my salvation and all my desire, will He not indeed make it grow?"
                              2 Samuel 23:1-5

As Obadiah was on the way, behold, Elijah met him, and he recognized him and fell on his face and said, "Is this you, Elijah my master?"

He said to him, "It is I. Go, say to your master, 'Behold, Elijah is here.' "

He said, "What sin have I committed, that you are giving your servant into the hand of Ahab to put me to death?

"As the Lord your God lives, there is no nation or kingdom where my master has not sent to search for you; and when they said, 'He is not here,' he made the kingdom or nation swear that they could not find you. And now you are saying, 'Go, say to your master, "Behold, Elijah is here." '

"It will come about when I leave you that the **Spirit of the Lord** will carry you where I do not know; so when I come and tell Ahab and he cannot find you, he will kill me, although I your servant have feared the Lord from my youth."

1 Kings 18:7-12

Micaiah said, "Therefore, hear the word of the Lord.

"I saw the Lord sitting on His throne, and all the host of heaven standing by Him on His right and on His left.

The Lord said, 'Who will entice Ahab to go up and fall at Ramoth-gilead?' And one said this while another said that.

"Then a spirit came forward and stood before the Lord and said, 'I will entice him.'

"The Lord said to him, 'How?'

"And he said, 'I will go out and be a deceiving spirit in the mouth of all his prophets.' Then He said, 'You are to entice him and also prevail. Go and do so.'

"Now therefore, behold, the Lord has put a deceiving spirit in the mouth of all these your prophets; and the Lord has proclaimed disaster against you."

Then Zedekiah the son of Chenaanah came near and struck Micaiah on the cheek and said, "How did the **Spirit of the Lord** pass from me to speak to you?"

Micaiah said, "Behold, you shall see on that day when you enter an inner room to hide yourself." *1 Kings 22:19-25*

When the sons of the prophets who were at Jericho opposite him saw him, they said, "The spirit of Elijah rests on Elisha."

And they came to meet him and bowed themselves to the ground before him.

They said to him, "Behold now, there are with your servants fifty strong men, please let them go and search for your master; perhaps the **Spirit of the Lord** has taken him up and cast him on some mountain or into some valley."

And he said, "You shall not send." But when they urged him until he was

ashamed, he said, "Send."

They sent therefore fifty men; and they searched three days but did not find him.

They returned to him while he was staying at Jericho; and he said to them, "Did I not say to you, 'Do not go'?"

2 Kings 2:15-18

The **Spirit** came upon Amasai, who was the chief of the thirty, and he said, "We are yours, O David, and with you, O son of Jesse! Peace, peace to you, and peace to him who helps you; indeed, your God helps you!"

Then David received them and made them captains of the band.

1 Chronicles 12:18

The **Spirit of God** came on Azariah the son of Oded, and he went out to meet Asa and said to him, "Listen to me, Asa, and all Judah and Benjamin: The Lord is with you when you are with Him.

"And if you seek Him, He will let you find Him; but if you forsake Him, He will forsake you."

For many days Israel was without the true God and without a teaching priest and without law. But in their distress they turned to the Lord God of Israel, and they sought Him, and He let them find Him.

2 Chronicles 15:1-4

The king of Israel said to Jehoshaphat, Micaiah said, "Therefore, hear the word of the Lord. I saw the Lord sitting on His throne, and all the host of heaven standing on His right and on His left.

The Lord said, 'Who will entice Ahab king of Israel to go up and fall at Ramoth-gilead?' And one said this while another said that.

"Then a spirit came forward and stood before the Lord and said, 'I will entice him.'

And the Lord said to him, 'How?'

He said, 'I will go and be a deceiving spirit in the mouth of all his prophets.'

Then He said, 'You are to entice him and prevail also. Go and do so.'

"Now therefore, behold, the Lord has put a deceiving spirit in the mouth of these your prophets, for the Lord has proclaimed disaster against you."

Then Zedekiah the son of Chenaanah came near and struck Micaiah on the cheek and said, "How did the **Spirit of the Lord** pass from me to speak to you?"

Micaiah said, "Behold, you will see on that day when you enter an inner room to hide yourself."   *2 Chronicles 18:18-24*

All Judah was standing before the Lord, with their infants, their wives and their children.

Then in the midst of the assembly the **Spirit of the Lord** came upon Jahaziel the son of Zechariah, the son of Benaiah, the son of Jeiel, the son of Mattaniah, the Levite of the sons of Asaph; and he said, "Listen, all Judah and the inhabitants of Jerusalem and King Jehoshaphat: Thus says the Lord to you, 'Do not fear or be dismayed because of this great multitude, for the battle is not yours but God's.

"Tomorrow go down against them. Behold, they will come up by the ascent of Ziz, and you will find them at the end of the valley in front of the wilderness of Jeruel.

'You need not fight in this battle; station yourselves, stand and see the salvation of the Lord on your behalf, O Judah and Jerusalem. Do not fear or be dismayed; tomorrow go out to face them, for the Lord is with you.' "

Jehoshaphat bowed his head with his face to the ground, and all Judah and the inhabitants of Jerusalem fell down before the Lord, worshiping the Lord.
     2 Chronicles 20:13-18

When Jehoiada reached a ripe old age he died; he was one hundred and thirty years old at his death. They buried him in the city of David among the kings, because he had done well in Israel and to God and His house.

But after the death of Jehoiada the officials of Judah came and bowed down to the king, and the king listened to them.

They abandoned the house of the Lord, the God of their fathers, and served the Asherim and the idols; so wrath came upon Judah and Jerusalem for this their guilt.

Yet He sent prophets to them to bring them back to the Lord; though they testified against them, they would not listen.

Then the **Spirit of God** came on Zechariah the son of Jehoiada the priest; and he stood above the people and said to them, "Thus God has said, 'Why do you transgress the commandments of the Lord and do not prosper? Because you have forsaken the Lord, He has also forsaken you.' "

So they conspired against him and at the command of the king they stoned him to death in the court of the house of the Lord.   *2 Chronicles 24:15-21*

When they made for themselves a calf of molten metal and said, "This is your God who brought you up from Egypt," and committed great blasphemies, You, in Your great compassion, did not forsake them in the wilderness; the pillar of cloud did not leave them by day, to guide them on their way, nor the pillar of fire by night, to light for them the way in which they were to go.

You gave Your good **Spirit** to instruct them, Your manna You did not withhold from their mouth, and You gave them water for their thirst.

Indeed, forty years You provided for them in the wilderness and they were not in want; their clothes did not wear out, nor did their feet swell.   *Nehemiah 9:18-21*

They became disobedient and rebelled against You, and cast Your law behind their backs and killed Your prophets who had admonished them so that they might return to You, and they committed great blasphemies.

Therefore You delivered them into the hand of their oppressors who oppressed them, but when they cried to You in the time of their distress, You heard from heaven, and according to Your great compassion You gave them deliverers who delivered them from the hand of their oppressors.

But as soon as they had rest, they did evil again before You; therefore You abandoned them to the hand of their enemies, so that they ruled over them.

When they cried again to You, You heard from heaven, and many times You rescued them according to Your compassion, and admonished them in order to turn them back to Your law.

Yet they acted arrogantly and did not listen to Your commandments but sinned against Your ordinances, by which if a man observes them he shall live. And they turned a stubborn shoulder and stiffened their neck, and would not listen.

However, You bore with them for many years, and admonished them by Your **Spirit** through Your prophets, yet they would not give ear. Therefore You gave them into the hand of the peoples of the lands.

Nevertheless, in Your great compassion You did not make an end of them or forsake them, for You are a gracious and compassionate God.   *Nehemiah 9:26-31*

The **Spirit of God** has made me, and the breath of the Almighty gives me life.
    Job 33:4

Hide Your face from my sins and blot out all my iniquities. Create in me a clean heart, O God, and renew a steadfast spirit within me.

Do not cast me away from Your presence and do not take Your **Holy Spirit** from me.

Restore to me the joy of Your salvation and sustain me with a willing spirit. Then I will teach transgressors Your ways, and sinners will be converted to You.   *Psalm 51:9-13*

They all wait for You to give them their food in due season. You give to them, they gather it up; You open Your hand, they are satisfied with good.

You hide Your face, they are dismayed; You take away their spirit, they expire and return to their dust.

You send forth Your **Spirit**, they are created; and You renew the face of the ground.   *Psalm 104:27-30*

They also provoked Him to wrath at the waters of Meribah, so that it went hard with Moses on their account; because they were rebellious against His **Spirit**, he spoke rashly with his lips.   *Psalm 106:32-33*

Where can I go from Your **Spirit**? Or where can I flee from Your presence?

If I ascend to heaven, You are there; if I make my bed in Sheol, behold, You are there. If I take the wings of the dawn, if I dwell in the remotest part of the sea, even there Your hand will lead me, and Your right hand will lay hold of me.
    Psalm 139:7-10

Teach me to do Your will, for You are my God; let Your good **Spirit** lead me on level ground.

For the sake of Your name, O Lord, revive me. In Your righteousness bring my soul out of trouble.   *Psalm 143:10-11*

Behold, the Lord, the God of hosts, will lop off the boughs with a terrible crash; those also who are tall in stature will be cut down and those who are lofty will be abased. He will cut down the thickets of the forest with an iron axe, and Lebanon will fall by the Mighty One.

Then a shoot will spring from the stem of Jesse, and a branch from his roots will bear fruit.

The **Spirit of the Lord** will rest on Him, the spirit of wisdom and understanding, the spirit of counsel and strength, the spirit of knowledge and the fear of the Lord.

And He will delight in the fear of the Lord, and He will not judge by what His eyes see, nor make a decision by what His ears hear; but with righteousness He will judge the poor, and decide with fairness for the afflicted of the earth; and He will strike the earth with the rod of His mouth, and with the breath of His lips He will slay the wicked.   *Isaiah 10:33 - 11:4*

"Woe to the rebellious children," declares the Lord, "who execute a plan, but not

Mine, and make an alliance, but not of My **Spirit**, in order to add sin to sin; who proceed down to Egypt without consulting Me, to take refuge in the safety of Pharaoh and to seek shelter in the shadow of Egypt!

"Therefore the safety of Pharaoh will be your shame and the shelter in the shadow of Egypt, your humiliation."

Isaiah 30:1-3

Tremble, you women who are at ease; be troubled, you complacent daughters; strip, undress and put sackcloth on your waist, beat your breasts for the pleasant fields, for the fruitful vine, for the land of my people in which thorns and briars shall come up; yea, for all the joyful houses and for the jubilant city. Because the palace has been abandoned, the populated city forsaken.

Hill and watch-tower have become caves forever, a delight for wild donkeys, a pasture for flocks; until the **Spirit** is poured out upon us from on high, and the wilderness becomes a fertile field, and the fertile field is considered as a forest.

Then justice will dwell in the wilderness and righteousness will abide in the fertile field. And the work of righteousness will be peace, and the service of righteousness, quietness and confidence forever.

Then my people will live in a peaceful habitation, and in secure dwellings and in undisturbed resting places; ~

Isaiah 32:11-18

Seek from the book of the Lord, and read: Not one of these will be missing; none will lack its mate. For His mouth has commanded, and His **Spirit** has gathered them.

He has cast the lot for them, and His hand has divided it to them by line. They shall possess it forever; from generation to generation they will dwell in it.

Isaiah 34:16-17

Who has directed the **Spirit of the Lord**, or as His counselor has informed Him? With whom did He consult and who gave Him understanding?

And who taught Him in the path of justice and taught Him knowledge and informed Him of the way of understanding?

Behold, the nations are like a drop from a bucket, and are regarded as a speck of dust on the scales; behold, He lifts up the islands like fine dust. Even Lebanon is not enough to burn, nor its beasts enough for a burnt offering.

All the nations are as nothing before Him, they are regarded by Him as less than nothing and meaningless.

To whom then will you liken God? Or what likeness will you compare with Him?

Isaiah 40:13-18

Behold, My Servant, whom I uphold; My chosen one in whom My soul delights. I have put My **Spirit** upon Him; He will bring forth justice to the nations.

He will not cry out or raise His voice, nor make His voice heard in the street. A bruised reed He will not break and a dimly burning wick He will not extinguish; He will faithfully bring forth justice.

He will not be disheartened or crushed until He has established justice in the earth; and the coastlands will wait expectantly for His law. *Isaiah 42:1-4*

Listen, O Jacob, My servant, and Israel, whom I have chosen: thus says the Lord who made you and formed you from the womb, who will help you, "Do not fear, O Jacob My servant; and you Jeshurun whom I have chosen.

"For I will pour out water on the thirsty land and streams on the dry ground; I will pour out My **Spirit** on your offspring and My blessing on your descendants; and they will spring up among the grass like poplars by streams of water.

"This one will say, 'I am the Lord's'; and that one will call on the name of Jacob; and another will write on his hand, 'Belonging to the Lord,' and will name Israel's name with honor." *Isaiah 44:1-5*

Come near to Me, listen to this: from the first I have not spoken in secret, from the time it took place, I was there. And now the Lord God has sent Me, and His **Spirit**.

Thus says the Lord, your Redeemer, the Holy One of Israel, "I am the Lord your God, who teaches you to profit, who leads you in the way you should go."

Isaiah 48:16-17

"A Redeemer will come to Zion, and to those who turn from transgression in Jacob," declares the Lord.

"As for Me, this is My covenant with them," says the Lord: "My **Spirit** which is upon you, and My words which I have put in your mouth shall not depart from your mouth, nor from the mouth of your offspring, nor from the mouth of your offspring's offspring," says the Lord, "from now and forever.

"Arise, shine; for your light has come, and the glory of the Lord has risen upon you. For behold, darkness will cover the earth and deep darkness the peoples; but the Lord will rise upon you and His glory will appear upon you.

Nations will come to your light, and kings to the brightness of your rising."

Isaiah 59:20 - 60:3

The **Spirit of the Lord God** is upon me, because the Lord has anointed me to bring good news to the afflicted; He has sent me to bind up the brokenhearted, to proclaim liberty to captives and freedom to prisoners; to proclaim the favorable year of the Lord and the day of vengeance of our God; to comfort all who mourn, to grant those who mourn in Zion, giving them a garland instead of ashes, the oil of gladness instead of mourning, the mantle of praise instead of a spirit of fainting.

So they will be called oaks of righteousness, the planting of the Lord, that He may be glorified. *Isaiah 61:1-3*

I shall make mention of the lovingkindnesses of the Lord, the praises of the Lord, according to all that the Lord has granted us, and the great goodness toward the house of Israel, which He has granted them according to His compassion and according to the abundance of His lovingkindnesses.

For He said, "Surely, they are My people, sons who will not deal falsely."

So He became their Savior. In all their affliction He was afflicted, and the angel of His presence saved them; in His love and in His mercy He redeemed them, and He lifted them and carried them all the days of old.

But they rebelled and grieved His **Holy Spirit**; therefore He turned Himself to become their enemy, He fought against them.

Then His people remembered the days of old, of Moses. Where is He who brought them up out of the sea with the shepherds of His flock?

Where is He who put His **Holy Spirit** in the midst of them, who caused His glorious arm to go at the right hand of Moses, who divided the waters before them to make for Himself an everlasting name, who led them through the depths?

Like the horse in the wilderness, they did not stumble; as the cattle which go down into the valley, the **Spirit of the Lord** gave them rest. So You led Your people, to make for Yourself a glorious name. *Isaiah 63:7-14*

He said to me, "Son of man, stand on your feet that I may speak with you!"

As He spoke to me the **Spirit** entered me and set me on my feet; and I heard Him speaking to me.

Then He said to me, "Son of man, I am sending you to the sons of Israel, to a rebellious people who have rebelled against Me; they and their fathers have transgressed against Me to this very day. I am sending you to them who are stubborn and obstinate children, and you shall say to them, 'Thus says the Lord God.'

"As for them, whether they listen or not - for they are a rebellious house - they will know that a prophet has been among them." *Ezekiel 2:1-5*

He said to me, "Son of man, take into your heart all My words which I will speak to you and listen closely. Go to the exiles, to the sons of your people, and speak to them and tell them, whether they listen or not, 'Thus says the Lord God.' "

Then the **Spirit** lifted me up, and I heard a great rumbling sound behind me, "Blessed be the glory of the Lord in His place."

And I heard the sound of the wings of the living beings touching one another and the sound of the wheels beside them, even a great rumbling sound.

So the **Spirit** lifted me up and took me away; and I went embittered in the rage of my spirit, and the hand of the Lord was strong on me.

Then I came to the exiles who lived beside the river Chebar at Tel-abib, and I sat there seven days where they were living, causing consternation among them.

At the end of seven days the word of the Lord came to me, saying, "Son of man, I have appointed you a watchman to the house of Israel; whenever you hear a word from My mouth, warn them from Me." *Ezekiel 3:10-17*

The hand of the Lord was on me there, and He said to me, "Get up, go out to the plain, and there I will speak to you."

So I got up and went out to the plain; and behold, the glory of the Lord was standing there, like the glory which I saw by the river Chebar, and I fell on my face.

The **Spirit** then entered me and made me stand on my feet, and He spoke with me and said to me, "Go, shut yourself up in your house.

"As for you, son of man, they will put ropes on you and bind you with them so that you cannot go out among them.

"Moreover, I will make your tongue stick to the roof of your mouth so that you will be mute and cannot be a man who rebukes them, for they are a rebellious house.

"But when I speak to you, I will open your mouth and you will say to them, 'Thus says the Lord God.'

"He who hears, let him hear; and he who refuses, let him refuse; for they are a rebellious house." *Ezekiel 3:22-27*

It came about in the sixth year, on the fifth day of the sixth month, as I was sitting in my house with the elders of Judah sitting before me, that the hand of the Lord God fell on me there.

Then I looked, and behold, a likeness as the appearance of a man; from His loins and downward there was the appearance of fire, and from His loins and upward the appearance of brightness, like the appearance of glowing metal.

He stretched out the form of a hand and caught me by a lock of my head; and the **Spirit** lifted me up between earth and heaven and brought me in the visions of God to Jerusalem, to the entrance of the north gate of the inner court, where the seat of the idol of jealousy, which provokes to jealousy, was located.

And behold, the glory of the God of Israel was there, like the appearance which I saw in the plain. *Ezekiel 8:1-4*

The **Spirit** lifted me up and brought me to the east gate of the Lord's house which faced eastward.

And behold, there were twenty-five men at the entrance of the gate, and among them I saw Jaazaniah son of Azzur and Pelatiah son of Benaiah, leaders of the people.

He said to me, "Son of man, these are the men who devise iniquity and give evil advice in this city, who say, 'The time is not near to build houses. This city is the pot and we are the flesh.' Therefore, prophesy against them, son of man, prophesy!"

Then the **Spirit of the Lord** fell upon me, and He said to me, "Say, 'Thus says the Lord, "So you think, house of Israel, for I know your thoughts. You have multiplied your slain in this city, filling its streets with them."

Therefore, thus says the Lord God, "Your slain whom you have laid in the midst of the city are the flesh and this city is the pot; but I will bring you out of it.

"You have feared a sword; so I will bring a sword upon you,"'" the Lord God declares. *Ezekiel 11:1-8*

The **Spirit** lifted me up and brought me in a vision by the **Spirit of God** to the exiles in Chaldea. So the vision that I had seen left me.

Then I told the exiles all the things that the Lord had shown me.

Ezekiel 11:24-25

Say to the house of Israel, "Thus says the Lord God, 'It is not for your sake, O house of Israel, that I am about to act, but for My holy name, which you have profaned among the nations where you went.

'I will vindicate the holiness of My great name which has been profaned among the nations, which you have profaned in their midst.

'Then the nations will know that I am the Lord,' declares the Lord God, 'when I prove Myself holy among you in their sight. For I will take you from the nations, gather you from all the lands and bring you into your own land.

'Then I will sprinkle clean water on you, and you will be clean; I will cleanse you from all your filthiness and from all your idols.

'Moreover, I will give you a new heart and put a new spirit within you; and I will remove the heart of stone from your flesh and give you a heart of flesh.

'I will put My **Spirit** within you and cause you to walk in My statutes, and you will be careful to observe My ordinances. You will live in the land that I gave to your forefathers; so you will be My people, and I will be your God.' "   *Ezekiel 36:22-28*

The hand of the Lord was upon me, and He brought me out by the **Spirit of the Lord** and set me down in the middle of the valley; and it was full of bones. He caused me to pass among them round about, and behold, there were very many on the surface of the valley; and lo, they were very dry.

He said to me, "Son of man, can these bones live?"

And I answered, "O Lord God, You know."

Again He said to me, "Prophesy over these bones and say to them, 'O dry bones, hear the word of the Lord.'

Thus says the Lord God to these bones, 'Behold, I will cause breath to enter you that you may come to life.

"I will put sinews on you, make flesh grow back on you, cover you with skin and put breath in you that you may come alive; and you will know that I am the Lord.' "

So I prophesied as I was commanded; and as I prophesied, there was a noise, and behold, a rattling; and the bones came together, bone to its bone.

And I looked, and behold, sinews were on them, and flesh grew and skin covered them; but there was no breath in them.

Then He said to me, "Prophesy to the breath, prophesy, son of man, and say to the breath, 'Thus says the Lord God, "Come from the four winds, O breath, and breathe on these slain, that they come to life."'"

So I prophesied as He commanded me, and the breath came into them, and they came to life and stood on their feet, an exceedingly great army.

Then He said to me, "Son of man, these bones are the whole house of Israel; behold, they say, 'Our bones are dried up and our hope has perished. We are completely cut off.'

"Therefore prophesy and say to them, 'Thus says the Lord God, "Behold, I will open your graves and cause you to come up out of your graves, My people; and I will bring you into the land of Israel.

"Then you will know that I am the Lord, when I have opened your graves and caused you to come up out of your graves, My people.

"I will put My **Spirit** within you and you will come to life, and I will place you on your own land.

"Then you will know that I, the Lord, have spoken and done it,"'" declares the Lord.   *Ezekiel 37:1-14*

Thus says the Lord God, "Now I will restore the fortunes of Jacob and have mercy on the whole house of Israel; and I will be jealous for My holy name.

"They will forget their disgrace and all their treachery which they perpetrated against Me, when they live securely on their own land with no one to make them afraid.

"When I bring them back from the peoples and gather them from the lands of their enemies, then I shall be sanctified through them in the sight of the many nations.

"Then they will know that I am the Lord their God because I made them go into exile among the nations, and then gathered them again to their own land; and I will leave none of them there any longer.

"I will not hide My face from them any longer, for I will have poured out My **Spirit** on the house of Israel," declares the Lord God. *Ezekiel 39:25-29*

He led me to the gate, the gate facing toward the east; and behold, the glory of the God of Israel was coming from the way of the east. And His voice was like the sound of many waters; and the earth shone with His glory.

And it was like the appearance of the vision which I saw, like the vision which I saw when He came to destroy the city. And the visions were like the vision which I saw by the river Chebar; and I fell on my face.

And the glory of the Lord came into the house by the way of the gate facing toward the east.

And the **Spirit** lifted me up and brought me into the inner court; and behold, the glory of the Lord filled the house. *Ezekiel 43:1-5*

It will come about after this that I will pour out My **Spirit** on all mankind; and your sons and daughters will prophesy, your old men will dream dreams, your young men will see visions.

Even on the male and female servants I will pour out My **Spirit** in those days.

I will display wonders in the sky and on the earth, blood, fire and columns of smoke. The sun will be turned into dark-ness and the moon into blood before the great and awesome day of the Lord comes. *Joel 2:28-31*

Is it being said, O house of Jacob: "Is the **Spirit of the Lord** impatient? Are these His doings?" Do not My words do good to the one walking uprightly?

Recently My people have arisen as an enemy - you strip the robe off the garment from unsuspecting passers-by, from those returned from war. *Micah 2:7-8*

The seers will be ashamed and the diviners will be embarrassed. Indeed, they will all cover their mouths because there is no answer from God.

On the other hand I am filled with power - with the **Spirit of the Lord** - and with justice and courage to make known to Jacob his rebellious act, even to Israel his sin. *Micah 3:7-8*

"Take courage, Zerubbabel," declares the Lord, "take courage also, Joshua son of Jehozadak, the high priest, and all you people of the land take courage," declares the Lord, "and work; for I am with you," declares the Lord of hosts.

"As for the promise which I made you when you came out of Egypt, My **Spirit** is abiding in your midst; do not fear!" *Haggai 2:4-5*

The angel who was speaking with me returned and roused me, as a man who is awakened from his sleep. He said to me, "What do you see?"

And I said, "I see, and behold, a lampstand all of gold with its bowl on the top of it, and its seven lamps on it with seven spouts belonging to each of the lamps which are on the top of it; also two olive trees by it, one on the right side of the bowl and the other on its left side."

Then I said to the angel who was speaking with me saying, "What are these, my lord?"

So the angel who was speaking with me answered and said to me, "Do you not know what these are?"

And I said, "No, my lord."

Then he said to me, "This is the word of the Lord to Zerubbabel saying, 'Not by might nor by power, but by My **Spirit**,' says the Lord of hosts." *Zechariah 4:1-6*

The word of the Lord came to Zechariah saying, "Thus has the Lord of hosts said, 'Dispense true justice and practice kindness and compassion each to his brother; and do not oppress the widow or the orphan, the stranger or the poor; and do not devise evil in your hearts against one another.'

"But they refused to pay attention and turned a stubborn shoulder and stopped their ears from hearing. They made their hearts like flint so that they could not hear the law and the words which the Lord of hosts had sent by His **Spirit** through the former prophets; therefore great wrath came from the Lord of hosts.

"And just as He called and they would not listen, so they called and I would not listen," says the Lord of hosts; "but I scattered them with a storm wind among all the nations whom they have not known.

"Thus the land is desolated behind them so that no one went back and forth, for they made the pleasant land desolate." *Zechariah 7:8-14*

In that day I will set about to destroy all the nations that come against Jerusalem.

I will pour out on the house of David and on the inhabitants of Jerusalem, the **Spirit** of grace and of supplication, so that they will look on Me whom they have pierced; and they will mourn for Him, as one mourns for an only son, and they will weep bitterly over Him like the bitter weeping over a firstborn.

In that day there will be great mourning in Jerusalem, like the mourning of Hadadrimmon in the plain of Megiddo. *Zechariah 12:9-11*

"This is another thing you do: you cover the altar of the Lord with tears, with weeping and with groaning, because He no longer regards the offering or accepts it with favor from your hand.

"Yet you say, 'For what reason?' Because the Lord has been a witness between you and the wife of your youth, against whom you have dealt treacherously, though she is your companion and your wife by covenant.

"But not one has done so who has a remnant of the **Spirit**. And what did that one do while he was seeking a godly offspring?

"Take heed then to your spirit, and let no one deal treacherously against the wife of your youth. For I hate divorce," says the Lord, the God of Israel, "and him who covers his garment with wrong," says the Lord of hosts.

"So take heed to your spirit, that you do not deal treacherously." *Malachi 2:13-16*

NEW TESTAMENT

The birth of Jesus Christ was as follows: When His mother Mary had been betrothed to Joseph, before they came together she was found to be with child by the **Holy Spirit**.

And Joseph her husband, being a righteous man and not wanting to disgrace her, planned to send her away secretly.

But when he had considered this, behold, an angel of the Lord appeared to him in a dream, saying, "Joseph, son of David, do not be afraid to take Mary as your wife; for the Child who has been conceived in her is of the **Holy Spirit**.

"She will bear a Son; and you shall call His name Jesus, for He will save His people from their sins."

Now all this took place to fulfill what was spoken by the Lord through the prophet: "Behold, the virgin shall be with child and shall bear a Son, and they shall call His name Immanuel," which translated means, "God with us." *Matthew 1:18-23*

As for me, I baptize you with water for repentance, but He who is coming after me is mightier than I, and I am not fit to remove His sandals; He will baptize you with the **Holy Spirit** and fire.

His winnowing fork is in His hand, and He will thoroughly clear His threshing floor; and He will gather His wheat into the barn, but He will burn up the chaff with unquenchable fire.

Then Jesus arrived from Galilee at the Jordan coming to John, to be baptized by him. But John tried to prevent Him, saying, "I have need to be baptized by You, and do You come to me?"

But Jesus answering said to him, "Permit it at this time; for in this way it is fitting for us to fulfill all righteousness." Then he permitted Him.

After being baptized, Jesus came up immediately from the water; and behold, the heavens were opened, and he saw the **Spirit of God** descending as a dove and lighting on Him, and behold, a voice out of the heavens said, "This is My beloved Son, in whom I am well-pleased."

Then Jesus was led up by the **Spirit** into the wilderness to be tempted by the devil. *Matthew 3:11 - 4:1*

Behold, I send you out as sheep in the midst of wolves; so be shrewd as serpents and innocent as doves.

But beware of men, for they will hand you over to the courts and scourge you in their synagogues; and you will even be brought before governors and kings for My sake, as a testimony to them and to the Gentiles.

But when they hand you over, do not worry about how or what you are to say; for it will be given you in that hour what you are to say. For it is not you who speak, but it is the **Spirit** of your Father who speaks in you. *Matthew 10:16-20*

This was to fulfill what was spoken through Isaiah the prophet: "Behold, My Servant whom I have chosen; My Beloved in whom My soul is well-pleased; I will put My **Spirit** upon Him, and He shall proclaim justice to the Gentiles.

"He will not quarrel, nor cry out; nor will anyone hear His voice in the streets. A battered reed He will not break off, and a smoldering wick He will not put out, until He leads justice to victory.

"And in His name the Gentiles will hope."

Then a demon-possessed man who was blind and mute was brought to Jesus, and He healed him, so that the mute man spoke and saw.

All the crowds were amazed, and were saying, "This man cannot be the Son of David, can he?"

But when the Pharisees heard this, they said, "This man casts out demons only by Beelzebul the ruler of the demons."

And knowing their thoughts Jesus said to them, "Any kingdom divided against itself is laid waste; and any city or house divided against itself will not stand. If Satan casts out Satan, he is divided against himself; how then will his kingdom stand?

"If I by Beelzebul cast out demons, by whom do your sons cast them out? For this reason they will be your judges.

"But if I cast out demons by the **Spirit of God**, then the kingdom of God has come upon you. Or how can anyone enter the strong man's house and carry off his property, unless he first binds the strong man? And then he will plunder his house.

"He who is not with Me is against Me; and he who does not gather with Me scatters.

"Therefore I say to you, any sin and blasphemy shall be forgiven people, but blasphemy against the **Spirit** shall not be forgiven.

"Whoever speaks a word against the Son of Man, it shall be forgiven him; but whoever speaks against the **Holy Spirit**, it shall not be forgiven him, either in this age or in the age to come."

Matthew 12:17-32

While the Pharisees were gathered together, Jesus asked them a question: "What do you think about the Christ, whose son is He?"

They said to Him, "The son of David."

He said to them, "Then how does David in the **Spirit** call Him 'Lord,' saying, 'The Lord said to my Lord, "Sit at My right hand, until I put Your enemies beneath Your feet" '? If David then calls Him 'Lord,' how is He his son?"

No one was able to answer Him a word, nor did anyone dare from that day on to ask Him another question.

Matthew 22:41-46

The eleven disciples proceeded to Galilee, to the mountain which Jesus had designated. When they saw Him, they worshiped Him; but some were doubtful.

And Jesus came up and spoke to them, saying, "All authority has been given to Me in heaven and on earth.

"Go therefore and make disciples of all the nations, baptizing them in the name of the Father and the Son and the **Holy Spirit**, teaching them to observe all that I commanded you; and lo, I am with you always, even to the end of the age."

Matthew 28:16-20

John the Baptist appeared in the wilderness preaching a baptism of repentance for the forgiveness of sins. And all the country of Judea was going out to him, and all the people of Jerusalem; and they were being baptized by him in the Jordan River, confessing their sins.

John was clothed with camel's hair and wore a leather belt around his waist, and his diet was locusts and wild honey.

And he was preaching, and saying, "After me One is coming who is mightier than I, and I am not fit to stoop down and untie the thong of His sandals. I baptized you with water; but He will baptize you with the **Holy Spirit**."

In those days Jesus came from Nazareth in Galilee and was baptized by John in the Jordan.

Immediately coming up out of the water, He saw the heavens opening, and the **Spirit** like a dove descending upon Him; and a voice came out of the heavens: "You are My beloved Son, in You I am well-pleased."

Immediately the **Spirit** impelled Him to go out into the wilderness. And He was in the wilderness forty days being tempted by Satan; and He was with the wild beasts, and the angels were ministering to Him.   *Mark 1:4-13*

Truly I say to you, all sins shall be forgiven the sons of men, and whatever blasphemies they utter; but whoever blasphemes against the **Holy Spirit** never has forgiveness, but is guilty of an eternal sin because they were saying, "He has an unclean spirit."   *Mark 3:28-30*

Jesus began to say, as He taught in the temple, "How is it that the scribes say that the Christ is the son of David? David himself said in the **Holy Spirit**, 'The Lord said to my Lord, "Sit at My right hand, until I put Your enemies beneath Your feet." '

"David himself calls Him 'Lord'; so in what sense is He his son?"

And the large crowd enjoyed listening to Him. *Mark 12:35-37*

Be on your guard; for they will deliver you to the courts, and you will be flogged in the synagogues, and you will stand before governors and kings for My sake, as a testimony to them. The gospel must first be preached to all the nations.

When they arrest you and hand you over, do not worry beforehand about what you are to say, but say whatever is given you in that hour; for it is not you who speak, but it is the **Holy Spirit**. *Mark 13:9-11*

An angel of the Lord appeared to him, standing to the right of the altar of incense. Zacharias was troubled when he saw the angel, and fear gripped him.

But the angel said to him, "Do not be afraid, Zacharias, for your petition has been heard, and your wife Elizabeth will bear you a son, and you will give him the name John.

"You will have joy and gladness, and many will rejoice at his birth. For he will be great in the sight of the Lord; and he will drink no wine or liquor, and he will be filled with the **Holy Spirit** while yet in his mother's womb.

"And he will turn many of the sons of Israel back to the Lord their God.

"It is he who will go as a forerunner before Him in the **Spirit** and power of Elijah, to turn the hearts of the fathers back to the children, and the disobedient to the attitude of the righteous, so as to make ready a people prepared for the Lord."

Zacharias said to the angel, "How will I know this for certain? For I am an old man and my wife is advanced in years."

The angel answered and said to him, "I am Gabriel, who stands in the presence of God, and I have been sent to speak to you and to bring you this good news." *Luke 1:11-19*

In the sixth month the angel Gabriel was sent from God to a city in Galilee called Nazareth, to a virgin engaged to a man whose name was Joseph, of the descendants of David; and the virgin's name was Mary.

And coming in, he said to her, "Greetings, favored one! The Lord is with you."

But she was very perplexed at this statement, and kept pondering what kind of salutation this was.

The angel said to her, "Do not be afraid, Mary; for you have found favor with God.

"And behold, you will conceive in your womb and bear a son, and you shall name Him Jesus. He will be great and will be called the Son of the Most High; and the Lord God will give Him the throne of His father David; and He will reign over the house of Jacob forever, and His kingdom will have no end."

Mary said to the angel, "How can this be, since I am a virgin?"

The angel answered and said to her, "The **Holy Spirit** will come upon you, and the power of the Most High will overshadow you; and for that reason the Holy Child shall be called the Son of God.

"And behold, even your relative Elizabeth has also conceived a son in her old age; and she who was called barren is now in her sixth month. For nothing will be impossible with God."

And Mary said, "Behold, the bondslave of the Lord; may it be done to me according to your word." And the angel departed from her.

Now at this time Mary arose and went in a hurry to the hill country, to a city of Judah, and entered the house of Zacharias and greeted Elizabeth.

When Elizabeth heard Mary's greeting, the baby leaped in her womb; and Elizabeth was filled with the **Holy Spirit**.

And she cried out with a loud voice and said, "Blessed are you among women, and blessed is the fruit of your womb!

"And how has it happened to me, that the mother of my Lord would come to me? For behold, when the sound of your greeting reached my ears, the baby leaped in my womb for joy.

"And blessed is she who believed that there would be a fulfillment of what had been spoken to her by the Lord."

And Mary said: "My soul exalts the Lord, and my spirit has rejoiced in God my Savior. For He has had regard for the humble state of His bondslave; for behold, from this time on all generations will count me blessed.

"For the Mighty One has done great things for me; and holy is His name."

Luke 1:26-49

His father Zacharias was filled with the **Holy Spirit**, and prophesied, saying: "Blessed be the Lord God of Israel, for He has visited us and accomplished redemption for His people, and has raised up a horn of salvation for us In the house of David His servant - as He spoke by the mouth of His Holy prophets from of old - salvation from our enemies, and from the hand of all who hate us; to show mercy toward our fathers, and to remember His Holy covenant, the oath which He swore to Abraham our father, to grant us that we, being rescued from the hand of our enemies, might serve Him without fear, in holiness and righteousness before Him all our days.

"And you, child, will be called the prophet of the Most High; for you will go on before the Lord to prepare His ways; to give to His people the knowledge of salvation by the forgiveness of their sins, because of the tender mercy of our God, with which the Sunrise from on high will visit us, to shine upon those who sit in darkness and the shadow of death, to guide our feet into the way of peace."

And the child continued to grow and to become strong in **Spirit**, and he lived in the deserts until the day of his public appearance to Israel. *Luke 1:67-80*

There was a man in Jerusalem whose name was Simeon; and this man was righteous and devout, looking for the consolation of Israel; and the **Holy Spirit** was upon him. And it had been revealed to him by the **Holy Spirit** that he would not

see death before he had seen the Lord's Christ.

And he came in the **Spirit** into the temple; and when the parents brought in the child Jesus, to carry out for Him the custom of the Law, then he took Him into his arms, and blessed God, and said, "Now Lord, You are releasing Your bondservant to depart in peace, according to Your word; for my eyes have seen Your salvation, which You have prepared in the presence of all peoples, a Light of revelation to the Gentiles, and the glory of Your people Israel."

And His father and mother were amazed at the things which were being said about Him. *Luke 2:25-33*

While the people were in a state of expectation and all were wondering in their hearts about John, as to whether he was the Christ, John answered and said to them all, "As for me, I baptize you with water; but One is coming who is mightier than I, and I am not fit to untie the thong of His sandals; He will baptize you with the **Holy Spirit** and fire.

"His winnowing fork is in His hand to thoroughly clear His threshing floor, and to gather the wheat into His barn; but He will burn up the chaff with unquenchable fire."

So with many other exhortations he preached the gospel to the people.

Luke 3:15-18

When all the people were baptized, Jesus was also baptized, and while He was praying, heaven was opened, and the **Holy Spirit** descended upon Him in bodily form like a dove, and a voice came out of heaven, "You are My beloved Son, in You I am well-pleased." *Luke 3:21-22*

Jesus, full of the **Holy Spirit**, returned from the Jordan and was led around by the **Spirit** in the wilderness for forty days, being tempted by the devil. And He ate nothing during those days, and when they had ended, He became hungry.

And the devil said to Him, "If You are the Son of God, tell this stone to become bread."

And Jesus answered him, "It is written, 'Man shall not live on bread alone.' "

Luke 4:1-4

When the devil had finished every temptation, he left Him until an opportune time.

And Jesus returned to Galilee in the power of the **Spirit**, and news about Him spread through all the surrounding district. And He began teaching in their synagogues and was praised by all.

And He came to Nazareth, where He had been brought up; and as was His custom, He entered the synagogue on the Sabbath, and stood up to read.

And the book of the prophet Isaiah was handed to Him. And He opened the book and found the place where it was written, "The **Spirit of the Lord** is upon Me, because He anointed Me to preach the gospel to the poor.

"He has sent Me to proclaim release to the captives, and recovery of sight to the blind, to set free those who are oppressed, to proclaim the favorable year of the Lord."

And He closed the book, gave it back to the attendant and sat down; and the eyes of all in the synagogue were fixed on Him.

And He began to say to them, "Today this Scripture has been fulfilled in your hearing."

And all were speaking well of Him, and wondering at the gracious words which were falling from His lips; and they were saying, "Is this not Joseph's son?"

Luke 4:13-22

The seventy returned with joy, saying, "Lord, even the demons are subject to us in Your name."

And He said to them, "I was watching Satan fall from heaven like lightning.

"Behold, I have given you authority to tread on serpents and scorpions, and over all the power of the enemy, and nothing will injure you.

"Nevertheless do not rejoice in this, that the spirits are subject to you, but rejoice that your names are recorded in heaven."

At that very time He rejoiced greatly in the **Holy Spirit**, and said, "I praise You, O Father, Lord of heaven and earth, that You have hidden these things from the wise and intelligent and have revealed them to infants. Yes, Father, for this way was well-pleasing in Your sight."

Luke 10:17-21

He said to them, "Suppose one of you has a friend, and goes to him at midnight and says to him, 'Friend, lend me three loaves; for a friend of mine has come to me from a journey, and I have nothing to set before him'; and from inside he answers and says, 'Do not bother me; the door has already been shut and my children and I are in bed; I cannot get up and give you anything.'

"I tell you, even though he will not get up and give him anything because he is his friend, yet because of his persistence he will get up and give him as much as he needs.

"So I say to you, ask, and it will be given to you; seek, and you will find; knock, and it will be opened to you.

"For everyone who asks, receives; and he who seeks, finds; and to him who knocks, it will be opened.

"Now suppose one of you fathers is asked by his son for a fish; he will not give him a snake instead of a fish, will he? Or if he is asked for an egg, he will not give him a scorpion, will he?

"If you then, being evil, know how to give good gifts to your children, how much more will your heavenly Father give the **Holy Spirit** to those who ask Him?"

Luke 11:5-13

I say to you, everyone who confesses Me before men, the Son of Man will confess him also before the angels of God; but he who denies Me before men will be denied before the angels of God.

And everyone who speaks a word against the Son of Man, it will be forgiven him; but he who blasphemes against the **Holy Spirit**, it will not be forgiven him.

When they bring you before the syna-

gogues and the rulers and the authorities, do not worry about how or what you are to speak in your defense, or what you are to say; for the **Holy Spirit** will teach you in that very hour what you ought to say.
Luke 12:8-12

"You are witnesses of these things. And behold, I am sending forth the promise of My Father upon you; but you are to stay in the city until you are clothed with power from on high."

And He led them out as far as Bethany, and He lifted up His hands and blessed them.
While He was blessing them, He parted from them and was carried up into heaven.

And they, after worshiping Him, returned to Jerusalem with great joy, and were continually in the temple praising God.
Luke 12:48-53

The next day he saw Jesus coming to him and said, "Behold, the Lamb of God who takes away the sin of the world!

"This is He on behalf of whom I said, 'After me comes a Man who has a higher rank than I, for He existed before me.' I did not recognize Him, but so that He might be manifested to Israel, I came baptizing in water."

John testified saying, "I have seen the **Spirit** descending as a dove out of heaven, and He remained upon Him. I did not recognize Him, but He who sent me to baptize in water said to me, 'He upon whom you see the **Spirit** descending and remaining upon Him, this is the One who baptizes in the **Holy Spirit**.'

"I myself have seen, and have testified that this is the Son of God."
John 1:29-34

There was a man of the Pharisees, named Nicodemus, a ruler of the Jews; this man came to Jesus by night and said to Him, "Rabbi, we know that You have come from God as a teacher; for no one can do these signs that You do unless God is with him."

Jesus answered and said to him, "Truly, truly, I say to you, unless one is born again he cannot see the kingdom of God."

Nicodemus said to Him, "How can a man be born when he is old? He cannot enter a second time into his mother's womb and be born, can he?"

Jesus answered, "Truly, truly, I say to you, unless one is born of water and the **Spirit** he cannot enter into the kingdom of God. That which is born of the flesh is flesh, and that which is born of the **Spirit** is spirit.

"Do not be amazed that I said to you, 'You must be born again.' The wind blows where it wishes and you hear the sound of it, but do not know where it comes from and where it is going; so is everyone who is born of the **Spirit**."

Nicodemus said to Him, "How can these things be?"

Jesus answered and said to him, "Are you the teacher of Israel and do not understand these things?

"Truly, truly, I say to you, we speak of what we know and testify of what we have seen, and you do not accept our testimony.

"If I told you earthly things and you do not believe, how will you believe if I tell you heavenly things?"
John 3:1-12

He who comes from above is above all, he who is of the earth is from the earth and speaks of the earth. He who comes from heaven is above all.

What He has seen and heard, of that He testifies; and no one receives His testimony.

He who has received His testimony has set his seal to this, that God is true. For He whom God has sent speaks the words of God; for He gives the **Spirit** without measure.

The Father loves the Son and has given all things into His hand. He who believes in the Son has eternal life; but he who does not obey the Son will not see life, but the wrath of God abides on him.
John 3:31-36

The woman said to Him, "Sir, I perceive that You are a prophet. Our fathers worshiped in this mountain, and you people say that in Jerusalem is the place where men ought to worship."

Jesus said to her, "Woman, believe Me, an hour is coming when neither in this mountain nor in Jerusalem will you worship the Father.

"You worship what you do not know; we worship what we know, for salvation is from the Jews.

"But an hour is coming, and now is, when the true worshipers will worship the Father in spirit and truth; for such people the Father seeks to be His worshipers. God is **spirit**, and those who worship Him must worship in spirit and truth."

The woman said to Him, "I know that Messiah is coming (He who is called Christ); when that One comes, He will declare all things to us."

Jesus said to her, "I who speak to you am He." *John 4:19-26*

"It is the **Spirit** who gives life; the flesh profits nothing; the words that I have spoken to you are spirit and are life. But there are some of you who do not believe."

For Jesus knew from the beginning who they were who did not believe, and who it was that would betray Him. *John 6:63-64*

On the last day, the great day of the feast, Jesus stood and cried out, saying, "If anyone is thirsty, let him come to Me and drink. He who believes in Me, as the Scripture said, 'From his innermost being will flow rivers of living water.' "

But this He spoke of the **Spirit**, whom those who believed in Him were to receive; for the **Spirit** was not yet given, because Jesus was not yet glorified.

Some of the people therefore, when they heard these words, were saying, "This certainly is the Prophet." Others were saying, "This is the Christ."

Still others were saying, "Surely the Christ is not going to come from Galilee, is He?" *John 7:37-41*

Philip said to Him, "Lord, show us the Father, and it is enough for us."

Jesus said to him, "Have I been so long with you, and yet you have not come to know Me, Philip?

"He who has seen Me has seen the Father; how can you say, 'Show us the Father'? Do you not believe that I am in the Father, and the Father is in Me?

"The words that I say to you I do not speak on My own initiative, but the Father abiding in Me does His works.

"Believe Me that I am in the Father and the Father is in Me; otherwise believe because of the works themselves.

"Truly, truly, I say to you, he who believes in Me, the works that I do, he will do also; and greater works than these he will do; because I go to the Father.

"Whatever you ask in My name, that will I do, so that the Father may be glorified in the Son. If you ask Me anything in My name, I will do it.

"If you love Me, you will keep My commandments. I will ask the Father, and He will give you another Helper, that He may be with you forever; that is the **Spirit** of truth, whom the world cannot receive, because it does not see Him or know Him, but you know Him because He abides with you and will be in you.

"I will not leave you as orphans; I will come to you. After a little while the world will no longer see Me, but you will see Me; because I live, you will live also. In that day you will know that I am in My Father, and you in Me, and I in you.

"He who has My commandments and keeps them is the one who loves Me; and he who loves Me will be loved by My Father, and I will love him and will disclose Myself to him."

Judas (not Iscariot) said to Him, "Lord, what then has happened that You are going to disclose Yourself to us and not to the world?"

Jesus answered and said to him, "If anyone loves Me, he will keep My word; and My Father will love him, and We will come to him and make Our abode with him.

"He who does not love Me does not

keep My words; and the word which you hear is not Mine, but the Father's who sent Me.

"These things I have spoken to you while abiding with you. But the Helper, the **Holy Spirit**, whom the Father will send in My name, He will teach you all things, and bring to your remembrance all that I said to you.

"Peace I leave with you; My peace I give to you; not as the world gives do I give to you.

"Do not let your heart be troubled, nor let it be fearful." *John 14:8-27*

When the Helper comes, whom I will send to you from the Father, that is the **Spirit** of truth who proceeds from the Father, He will testify about Me, and you will testify also, because you have been with Me from the beginning.

These things I have spoken to you so that you may be kept from stumbling.

They will make you outcasts from the synagogue, but an hour is coming for everyone who kills you to think that he is offering service to God.

These things they will do because they have not known the Father or Me. But these things I have spoken to you, so that when their hour comes, you may remember that I told you of them.

These things I did not say to you at the beginning, because I was with you. But now I am going to Him who sent Me; and none of you asks Me, "Where are You going?"

But because I have said these things to you, sorrow has filled your heart.

But I tell you the truth, it is to your advantage that I go away; for if I do not go away, the Helper will not come to you; but if I go, I will send Him to you.

And He, when He comes, will convict the world concerning sin and righteousness and judgment; concerning sin, because they do not believe in Me; and concerning righteousness, because I go to the Father and you no longer see Me; and concerning judgment, because the ruler of this world has been judged.

I have many more things to say to you, but you cannot bear them now. But when He, the **Spirit** of truth, comes, He will guide you into all the truth; for He will not speak on His own initiative, but whatever He hears, He will speak; and He will disclose to you what is to come.

He will glorify Me, for He will take of Mine and will disclose it to you. All things that the Father has are Mine; therefore I said that He takes of Mine and will disclose it to you.

A little while, and you will no longer see Me; and again a little while, and you will see Me. *John 15:26 - 16:16*

Mary Magdalene came, announcing to the disciples, "I have seen the Lord," and that He had said these things to her.

So when it was evening on that day, the first day of the week, and when the doors were shut where the disciples were, for fear of the Jews, Jesus came and stood in their midst and said to them, "Peace be with you."

And when He had said this, He showed them both His hands and His side.

The disciples then rejoiced when they saw the Lord.

So Jesus said to them again, "Peace be with you; as the Father has sent Me, I also send you."

And when He had said this, He breathed on them and said to them, "Receive the **Holy Spirit**.

"If you forgive the sins of any, their sins have been forgiven them; if you retain the sins of any, they have been retained." *John 20:18-23*

The first account I composed, Theophilus, about all that Jesus began to do and teach, until the day when He was taken up to heaven, after He had by the **Holy Spirit** given orders to the apostles whom He had chosen.

To these He also presented Himself alive after His suffering, by many convincing proofs, appearing to them over a period of forty days and speaking of the things concerning the kingdom of God.

Gathering them together, He commanded them not to leave Jerusalem, but to wait for what the Father had promised, "Which," He said, "you heard of from Me; for John baptized with water, but you will be baptized with the **Holy Spirit** not many days from now."

So when they had come together, they were asking Him, saying, "Lord, is it at this time You are restoring the kingdom to Israel?"

He said to them, "It is not for you to know times or epochs which the Father has fixed by His own authority; but you will receive power when the **Holy Spirit** has come upon you; and you shall be My witnesses both in Jerusalem, and in all Judea and Samaria, and even to the remotest part of the earth."

And after He had said these things, He was lifted up while they were looking on, and a cloud received Him out of their sight.   *Acts 1:1-9*

At this time Peter stood up in the midst of the brethren (a gathering of about one hundred and twenty persons was there together), and said, "Brethren, the Scripture had to be fulfilled, which the **Holy Spirit** foretold by the mouth of David concerning Judas, who became a guide to those who arrested Jesus. For he was counted among us and received his share in this ministry."   *Acts 1:15-17*

When the day of Pentecost had come, they were all together in one place.

And suddenly there came from heaven a noise like a violent rushing wind, and it filled the whole house where they were sitting.

And there appeared to them tongues as of fire distributing themselves, and they rested on each one of them.

And they were all filled with the **Holy Spirit** and began to speak with other tongues, as the **Spirit** was giving them utterance.

Now there were Jews living in Jerusalem, devout men from every nation under heaven. And when this sound occurred, the crowd came together, and were bewildered because each one of them was hearing them speak in his own language.

They were amazed and astonished, saying, "Why, are not all these who are speaking Galileans?

"And how is it that we each hear them in our own language to which we were born? Parthians and Medes and Elamites, and residents of Mesopotamia, Judea and Cappadocia, Pontus and Asia, Phrygia and Pamphylia, Egypt and the districts of Libya around Cyrene, and visitors from Rome, both Jews and proselytes, Cretans and Arabs - we hear them in our own tongues speaking of the mighty deeds of God."

And they all continued in amazement and great perplexity, saying to one another, "What does this mean?"

But others were mocking and saying, "They are full of sweet wine."

But Peter, taking his stand with the eleven, raised his voice and declared to them: "Men of Judea and all you who live in Jerusalem, let this be known to you and give heed to my words. For these men are not drunk, as you suppose, for it is only the third hour of the day; but this is what was spoken of through the prophet Joel: 'And it shall be in the last days,' God says, 'that I will pour forth of My **Spirit** on all mankind; and your sons and your daughters shall prophesy, and your young men shall see visions, and your old men shall dream dreams; even on My bond-slaves, both men and women, I will in those days pour forth of My **Spirit** and they shall prophesy.

'And I will grant wonders in the sky above and signs on the earth below, blood, and fire, and vapor of smoke. The sun will be turned into darkness and the moon into blood, before the great and glorious day of the Lord shall come.

"And it shall be that everyone who calls on the name of the Lord will be saved.' "   *Acts 2:1-21*

"This Jesus God raised up again, to which we are all witnesses. Therefore having been exalted to the right hand of God, and having received from the Father the promise of the **Holy Spirit**, He has poured forth this which you both see and hear.

"For it was not David who ascended into heaven, but he himself says: 'The Lord said to my Lord, "Sit at My right hand, until I make Your enemies a footstool for Your feet." '

"Therefore let all the house of Israel know for certain that God has made Him both Lord and Christ - this Jesus whom you crucified."

Now when they heard this, they were pierced to the heart, and said to Peter and the rest of the apostles, "Brethren, what shall we do?"

Peter said to them, "Repent, and each of you be baptized in the name of Jesus Christ for the forgiveness of your sins; and you will receive the gift of the **Holy Spirit**. For the promise is for you and your children and for all who are far off, as many as the Lord our God will call to Himself."

And with many other words he solemnly testified and kept on exhorting them, saying, "Be saved from this perverse generation!"   *Acts 2:32-40*

When they had placed them in the center, they began to inquire, "By what power, or in what name, have you done this?"

Then Peter, filled with the **Holy Spirit**, said to them, "Rulers and elders of the people, if we are on trial today for a benefit done to a sick man, as to how this man has been made well, it be known to all of you and to all the people of Israel, that by the name of Jesus Christ the Nazarene, whom you crucified, whom God raised from the dead - by this name this man stands here before you in good health.

"He is the stone which was rejected by you, the builders, but which became the chief corner stone.

"And there is salvation in no one else; for there is no other name under heaven that has been given among men by which we must be saved."   *Acts 4:7-12*

When they had been released, they went to their own companions and reported all that the chief priests and the elders had said to them.

And when they heard this, they lifted their voices to God with one accord and said, "O Lord, it is You who made the heaven and the earth and the sea, and all that is in them, who by the **Holy Spirit**, through the mouth of our father David Your servant, said, 'Why did the Gentiles rage, and the peoples devise futile things? The kings of the earth took their stand, and the rulers were gathered together against the Lord and against His Christ.'

"For truly in this city there were gathered together against Your Holy servant Jesus, whom You anointed, both Herod and Pontius Pilate, along with the Gentiles and the peoples of Israel, to do whatever Your hand and Your purpose predestined to occur.

"And now, Lord, take note of their threats, and grant that Your bond-servants may speak Your word with all confidence, while You extend Your hand to heal, and signs and wonders take place through the name of Your Holy servant Jesus."

And when they had prayed, the place where they had gathered together was shaken, and they were all filled with the **Holy Spirit** and began to speak the word of God with boldness.   *Acts 4:23-31*

Joseph, a Levite of Cyprian birth, who was also called Barnabas by the apostles (which translated means Son of Encouragement), and who owned a tract of land, sold it and brought the money and laid it at the apostles' feet.

But a man named Ananias, with his wife Sapphira, sold a piece of property, and kept back some of the price for himself, with his wife's full knowledge, and bringing a portion of it, he laid it at the apostles' feet.

But Peter said, "Ananias, why has Satan filled your heart to lie to the **Holy Spirit** and to keep back some of the price of the land? While it remained unsold, did it not remain your own? And after it was sold, was it not under your control? Why is it that you have conceived this deed in your heart? You have not lied to men but to God."

And as he heard these words, Ananias fell down and breathed his last; and great fear came over all who heard of it.

The young men got up and covered him up, and after carrying him out, they buried him.

Now there elapsed an interval of about three hours, and his wife came in, not knowing what had happened.

And Peter responded to her, "Tell me whether you sold the land for such and such a price?"

And she said, "Yes, that was the price."

Then Peter said to her, "Why is it that you have agreed together to put the **Spirit of the Lord** to the test?

"Behold, the feet of those who have buried your husband are at the door, and they will carry you out as well."

And immediately she fell at his feet and breathed her last, and the young men came in and found her dead, and they carried her out and buried her beside her husband.

And great fear came over the whole church, and over all who heard of these things.

At the hands of the apostles many signs and wonders were taking place among the people; and they were all with one accord in Solomon's portico.

Acts 4:36 - 5:12

When they had brought them, they stood them before the Council.

The high priest questioned them, saying, "We gave you strict orders not to continue teaching in this name, and yet, you have filled Jerusalem with your teaching and intend to bring this man's blood upon us."

But Peter and the apostles answered, "We must obey God rather than men.

"The God of our fathers raised up Jesus, whom you had put to death by hanging Him on a cross.

"He is the one whom God exalted to His right hand as a Prince and a Savior, to grant repentance to Israel, and for-giveness of sins.

"And we are witnesses of these things; and so is the **Holy Spirit**, whom God has given to those who obey Him."

But when they heard this, they were cut to the quick and intended to kill them.

Acts 5:27-33

While the disciples were increasing in number, a complaint arose on the part of the Hellenistic Jews against the native Hebrews, because their widows were being overlooked in the daily serving of food.

So the twelve summoned the congregation of the disciples and said, "It is not desirable for us to neglect the word of God in order to serve tables.

"Therefore, brethren, select from among you seven men of good reputation, full of the **Spirit** and of wisdom, whom we may put in charge of this task.

"But we will devote ourselves to prayer and to the ministry of the word."

The statement found approval with the whole congregation; and they chose Stephen, a man full of faith and of the **Holy Spirit**, and Philip, Prochorus, Nicanor, Timon, Parmenas and Nicolas, a proselyte from Antioch. And these they brought before the apostles; and after praying, they laid their hands on them.

The word of God kept on spreading; and the number of the disciples continued to increase greatly in Jerusalem, and a great many of the priests were becoming obedient to the faith.

And Stephen, full of grace and power, was performing great wonders and signs among the people.

But some men from what was called the Synagogue of the Freedmen, including both Cyrenians and Alexandrians, and some from Cilicia and Asia, rose up and argued with Stephen.

But they were unable to cope with the wisdom and the **Spirit** with which he was speaking.

Acts 6:1-10

"You men who are stiff-necked and uncircumcised in heart and ears are always resisting the **Holy Spirit**; you are doing just as your fathers did. Which one of the prophets did your fathers not persecute?

"They killed those who had previously announced the coming of the Righteous One, whose betrayers and murderers you have now become; you who received the law as ordained by angels, and yet did not keep it."

Now when they heard this, they were cut to the quick, and they began gnashing their teeth at him.

But being full of the **Holy Spirit**, he gazed intently into heaven and saw the glory of God, and Jesus standing at the right hand of God; and he said, "Behold, I see the heavens opened up and the Son of Man standing at the right hand of God."

But they cried out with a loud voice, and covered their ears and rushed at him with one impulse.

When they had driven him out of the city, they began stoning him; and the witnesses laid aside their robes at the feet of a young man named Saul.

They went on stoning Stephen as he called on the Lord and said, "Lord Jesus, receive my spirit!"

Then falling on his knees, he cried out with a loud voice, "Lord, do not hold this sin against them!"

Having said this, he fell asleep.

Acts 7:51-60

When the apostles in Jerusalem heard that Samaria had received the word of God, they sent them Peter and John, who came down and prayed for them that they might receive the **Holy Spirit**. For He had not yet fallen upon any of them; they had simply been baptized in the name of the Lord Jesus.

Then they began laying their hands on them, and they were receiving the **Holy Spirit**.

Now when Simon saw that the **Spirit** was bestowed through the laying on of the apostles' hands, he offered them money, saying, "Give this authority to me as well, so that everyone on whom I lay my hands may receive the **Holy Spirit**."

But Peter said to him, "May your silver perish with you, because you thought you could obtain the gift of God with money!

"You have no part or portion in this matter, for your heart is not right before God. Therefore repent of this wickedness of yours, and pray the Lord that, if possible, the intention of your heart may be forgiven you. For I see that you are in the gall of bitterness and in the bondage of iniquity."

But Simon answered and said, "Pray to the Lord for me yourselves, so that nothing of what you have said may come upon me."

So, when they had solemnly testified and spoken the word of the Lord, they started back to Jerusalem, and were preaching the gospel to many villages of the Samaritans.

But an angel of the Lord spoke to Philip saying, "Get up and go south to the road that descends from Jerusalem to Gaza." (This is a desert road.)

So he got up and went; and there was an Ethiopian eunuch, a court official of Candace, queen of the Ethiopians, who was in charge of all her treasure; and he had come to Jerusalem to worship, and he was returning and sitting in his chariot, and was reading the prophet Isaiah.

Then the **Spirit** said to Philip, "Go up and join this chariot."

Philip ran up and heard him reading Isaiah the prophet, and said, "Do you understand what you are reading?"

And he said, "Well, how could I, unless someone guides me?" And he invited Philip to come up and sit with him.

Now the passage of Scripture which he was reading was this: "He was led as a sheep to slaughter; and as a lamb before its shearer is silent, so He does not open His mouth. In humiliation His judgment was taken away; who will relate His generation? For His life is removed from the earth."

The eunuch answered Philip and said, "Please tell me, of whom does the prophet say this? Of himself or of someone else?"

Then Philip opened his mouth, and beginning from this Scripture he preached Jesus to him.

As they went along the road they came to some water; and the eunuch said, "Look! Water! What prevents me from being baptized?"

[And Philip said, "If you believe with all your heart, you may."

And he answered and said, "I believe that Jesus Christ is the Son of God."]

And he ordered the chariot to stop; and they both went down into the water, Philip as well as the eunuch, and he baptized him.

When they came up out of the water, the **Spirit of the Lord** snatched Philip away; and the eunuch no longer saw him, but went on his way rejoicing.

But Philip found himself at Azotus, and as he passed through he kept preaching the gospel to all the cities until he came to Caesarea.   *Acts 8:14-40*

There was a disciple at Damascus named Ananias; and the Lord said to him in a vision, "Ananias."

And he said, "Here I am, Lord."

And the Lord said to him, "Get up and go to the street called Straight, and inquire at the house of Judas for a man from Tarsus named Saul, for he is praying, and he has seen in a vision a man named Ananias come in and lay his hands on him, so that he might regain his sight."

But Ananias answered, "Lord, I have heard from many about this man, how much harm he did to Your saints at Jerusalem; and here he has authority from the chief priests to bind all who call on Your name."

But the Lord said to him, "Go, for he is a chosen instrument of Mine, to bear My name before the Gentiles and kings and the sons of Israel; for I will show him how much he must suffer for My name's sake."

So Ananias departed and entered the house, and after laying his hands on him said, "Brother Saul, the Lord Jesus, who appeared to you on the road by which you were coming, has sent me so that you may regain your sight and be filled with the **Holy Spirit**."

And immediately there fell from his eyes something like scales, and he regained his sight, and he got up and was baptized; and he took food and was strengthened.

Now for several days he was with the disciples who were at Damascus, and immediately he began to proclaim Jesus in the synagogues, saying, "He is the Son of God."   *Acts 9:10-20*

The church throughout all Judea and Galilee and Samaria enjoyed peace, being built up; and going on in the fear of the Lord and in the comfort of the **Holy Spirit**, it continued to increase.   *Acts 9:31*

While Peter was greatly perplexed in mind as to what the vision which he had seen might be, behold, the men who had been sent by Cornelius, having asked directions for Simon's house, appeared at the gate; and calling out, they were asking whether Simon, who was also called Peter, was staying there.

While Peter was reflecting on the vision, the **Spirit** said to him, "Behold, three men are looking for you. But get up, go downstairs and accompany them without misgivings, for I have sent them Myself."

Peter went down to the men and said, "Behold, I am the one you are looking for; what is the reason for which you have come?"

They said, "Cornelius, a centurion, a righteous and God-fearing man well spoken of by the entire nation of the Jews, was divinely directed by a holy angel to send for you to come to his house and hear a message from you."   *Acts 10:17-22*

Opening his mouth, Peter said: "I most certainly understand now that God is not one to show partiality, but in every nation the man who fears Him and does what is right is welcome to Him.

"The word which He sent to the sons of Israel, preaching peace through Jesus Christ (He is Lord of all) - you yourselves know the thing which took place throughout all Judea, starting from Galilee, after the baptism which John proclaimed.

"You know of Jesus of Nazareth, how God anointed Him with the **Holy Spirit** and with power, and how He went about doing good and healing all who were oppressed by the devil, for God was with Him.

"We are witnesses of all the things He did both in the land of the Jews and in Jerusalem. They also put Him to death by hanging Him on a cross. " *Acts 10:34-39*

While Peter was still speaking these words, the **Holy Spirit** fell upon all those who were listening to the message.

All the circumcised believers who came with Peter were amazed, because the gift of the **Holy Spirit** had been poured out on the Gentiles also. For they were hearing them speaking with tongues and exalting God.

Then Peter answered, "Surely no one can refuse the water for these to be baptized who have received the **Holy Spirit** just as we did, can he?"

And he ordered them to be baptized in the name of Jesus Christ. Then they asked him to stay on for a few days. *Acts 10:44-48*

"At that moment three men appeared at the house in which we were staying, having been sent to me from Caesarea. The **Spirit** told me to go with them without misgivings. These six brethren also went with me and we entered the man's house.

"And he reported to us how he had seen the angel standing in his house, and saying, 'Send to Joppa and have Simon, who is also called Peter, brought here; and he will speak words to you by which you will be saved, you and all your household.'

"And as I began to speak, the **Holy Spirit** fell upon them just as He did upon us at the beginning.

"And I remembered the word of the Lord, how He used to say, 'John baptized with water, but you will be baptized with the **Holy Spirit**.'

"Therefore if God gave to them the same gift as He gave to us also after believing in the Lord Jesus Christ, who was I that I could stand in God's way?"

When they heard this, they quieted down and glorified God, saying, "Well then, God has granted to the Gentiles also the repentance that leads to life." *Acts 11:11-18:5*

The hand of the Lord was with them, and a large number who believed turned to the Lord. The news about them reached the ears of the church at Jerusalem, and they sent Barnabas off to Antioch.

Then when he arrived and witnessed the grace of God, he rejoiced and began to encourage them all with resolute heart to remain true to the Lord; for he was a good man, and full of the **Holy Spirit** and of faith. And considerable numbers were brought to the Lord.

And he left for Tarsus to look for Saul; and when he had found him, he brought him to Antioch. And for an entire year they met with the church and taught considerable numbers; and the disciples were first called Christians in Antioch.

Now at this time some prophets came down from Jerusalem to Antioch. One of them named Agabus stood up and began to indicate by the **Spirit** that there would certainly be a great famine all over the world. And this took place in the reign of Claudius.

And in the proportion that any of the disciples had means, each of them determined to send a contribution for the relief of the brethren living in Judea.

And this they did, sending it in charge of Barnabas and Saul to the elders. *Acts 11:21-30*

There were at Antioch, in the church that was there, prophets and teachers: Barnabas, and Simeon who was called Niger, and Lucius of Cyrene, and Manaen who had been brought up with Herod the tetrarch, and Saul.

While they were ministering to the Lord and fasting, the **Holy Spirit** said, "Set apart for Me Barnabas and Saul for the work to which I have called them."

Then, when they had fasted and prayed and laid their hands on them, they sent them away.

So, being sent out by the **Holy Spirit**, they went down to Seleucia and from there they sailed to Cyprus.

When they reached Salamis, they began to proclaim the word of God in the synagogues of the Jews; and they also had John as their helper.

When they had gone through the whole island as far as Paphos, they found a magician, a Jewish false prophet whose name was Bar-Jesus, who was with the proconsul, Sergius Paulus, a man of intelligence.

This man summoned Barnabas and Saul and sought to hear the word of God. But Elymas the magician (for so his name is translated) was opposing them, seeking to turn the proconsul away from the faith.

But Saul, who was also known as Paul, filled with the **Holy Spirit**, fixed his gaze on him, and said, "You who are full of all deceit and fraud, you son of the devil, you enemy of all righteousness, will you not cease to make crooked the straight ways of the Lord?

"Now, behold, the hand of the Lord is upon you, and you will be blind and not see the sun for a time."

And immediately a mist and a darkness fell upon him, and he went about seeking those who would lead him by the hand.

Then the proconsul believed when he saw what had happened, being amazed at the teaching of the Lord.   *Acts 13:1-12*

The Jews incited the devout women of prominence and the leading men of the city, and instigated a persecution against Paul and Barnabas, and drove them out of their district. But they shook off the dust of their feet in protest against them and went to Iconium.

And the disciples were continually filled with joy and with the **Holy Spirit**.
   Acts 13:50-52

When they arrived at Jerusalem, they were received by the church and the apostles and the elders, and they reported all that God had done with them.

But some of the sect of the Pharisees who had believed stood up, saying, "It is necessary to circumcise them and to direct them to observe the Law of Moses."

The apostles and the elders came together to look into this matter.

After there had been much debate, Peter stood up and said to them, "Brethren, you know that in the early days God made a choice among you, that by my mouth the Gentiles would hear the word of the gospel and believe.

"And God, who knows the heart, testified to them giving them the **Holy Spirit**, just as He also did to us; and He made no distinction between us and them, cleansing their hearts by faith."   *Acts 15:4-9*

We have sent Judas and Silas, who themselves will also report the same things by word of mouth.

For it seemed good to the **Holy Spirit** and to us to lay upon you no greater burden than these essentials: that you abstain from things sacrificed to idols and from blood and from things strangled and from fornication; if you keep yourselves free from such things, you will do well. ~
   Acts 15:27-29

While they were passing through the cities, they were delivering the decrees which had been decided upon by the apostles and elders who were in Jerusalem, for them to observe. So the churches were being strengthened in the faith, and were increasing in number daily.

They passed through the Phrygian and Galatian region, having been forbidden by the **Holy Spirit** to speak the word in Asia; and after they came to Mysia, they were trying to go into Bithynia, and the **Spirit** of Jesus did not permit them; and passing by Mysia, they came down to Troas.   *Acts 16:4-8*

It happened that while Apollos was at Corinth, Paul passed through the upper country and came to Ephesus, and found some disciples.

He said to them, "Did you receive the **Holy Spirit** when you believed?"

And they said to him, "No, we have not even heard whether there is a **Holy Spirit**."

And he said, "Into what then were you baptized?"

And they said, "Into John's baptism."

Paul said, "John baptized with the baptism of repentance, telling the people to believe in Him who was coming after him, that is, in Jesus."

When they heard this, they were baptized in the name of the Lord Jesus.

And when Paul had laid his hands upon them, the **Holy Spirit** came on them, and they began speaking with tongues and prophesying. There were in all about twelve men.   *Acts 19:1-7*

The word of the Lord was growing mightily and prevailing.

Now after these things were finished, Paul purposed in the **Spirit** to go to Jerusalem after he had passed through Macedonia and Achaia, saying, "After I have been there, I must also see Rome."
Acts 19:20-21

Behold, bound by the **Spirit**, I am on my way to Jerusalem, not knowing what will happen to me there, except that the **Holy Spirit** solemnly testifies to me in every city, saying that bonds and afflictions await me.

But I do not consider my life of any account as dear to myself, so that I may finish my course and the ministry which I received from the Lord Jesus, to testify solemnly of the gospel of the grace of God.   *Acts 20:22-24*

Be on guard for yourselves and for all the flock, among which the **Holy Spirit** has made you overseers, to shepherd the church of God which He purchased with His own blood.   *Acts 20:28*

When we came in sight of Cyprus, leaving it on the left, we kept sailing to Syria and landed at Tyre; for there the ship was to unload its cargo.

After looking up the disciples, we stayed there seven days; and they kept telling Paul through the **Spirit** not to set foot in Jerusalem.

When our days there were ended, we left and started on our journey, while they all, with wives and children, escorted us until we were out of the city.

After kneeling down on the beach and praying, we said farewell to one another. Then we went on board the ship, and they returned home again.

When we had finished the voyage from Tyre, we arrived at Ptolemais, and after greeting the brethren, we stayed with them for a day.

On the next day we left and came to Caesarea, and entering the house of Philip the evangelist, who was one of the seven, we stayed with him. Now this man had four virgin daughters who were prophetesses.

As we were staying there for some days, a prophet named Agabus came down from Judea.

And coming to us, he took Paul's belt and bound his own feet and hands, and said, "This is what the **Holy Spirit** says: 'In this way the Jews at Jerusalem will bind the man who owns this belt and deliver him into the hands of the Gentiles.' "

When we had heard this, we as well as the local residents began begging him not to go up to Jerusalem.

Then Paul answered, "What are you doing, weeping and breaking my heart? For I am ready not only to be bound, but even to die at Jerusalem for the name of the Lord Jesus."

And since he would not be persuaded, we fell silent, remarking, "The will of the Lord be done!"   *Acts 21:3-14*

When they had set a day for Paul, they came to him at his lodging in large numbers; and he was explaining to them by solemnly testifying about the kingdom of God and trying to persuade them concerning Jesus, from both the Law of Moses and from the Prophets, from morning until evening.

Some were being persuaded by the things spoken, but others would not believe.

And when they did not agree with one another, they began leaving after Paul had spoken one parting word, "The **Holy Spirit** rightly spoke through Isaiah the prophet to your fathers, saying, 'Go to this people and say, "You will keep on hearing, but will not understand; and you will keep on seeing, but will not perceive; for the heart of this people has become dull, and with their ears they scarcely hear, and they have closed their eyes; otherwise they might see with their eyes, and hear with their ears, and understand with their heart and return, and I would heal them." '

"Therefore let it be known to you that this salvation of God has been sent to the Gentiles; they will also listen."

[When he had spoken these words, the Jews departed, having a great dispute among themselves.]   *Acts 28:23-29*

Paul, a bond-servant of Christ Jesus, called as an apostle, set apart for the gospel of God, which He promised beforehand through His prophets in the Holy Scriptures, concerning His Son, who was born of a descendant of David according to the flesh, who was declared the Son of God with power by the resurrection from the dead, according to the **Spirit** of holiness, Jesus Christ our Lord, through whom we have received grace and apostleship to bring about the obedience of faith among all the Gentiles for His name's sake, among whom you also are the called of Jesus Christ; to all who are beloved of God in Rome, called as saints: Grace to you and peace from God our Father and the Lord Jesus Christ.
Romans 1:1-7

He is not a Jew who is one outwardly, nor is circumcision that which is outward in the flesh.

But he is a Jew who is one inwardly; and circumcision is that which is of the heart, by the **Spirit**, not by the letter; and his praise is not from men, but from God.
Romans 2:28-29

Having been justified by faith, we have peace with God through our Lord Jesus Christ, through whom also we have obtained our introduction by faith into this grace in which we stand; and we exult in hope of the glory of God.

And not only this, but we also exult in our tribulations, knowing that tribulation brings about perseverance; and perseverance, proven character; and proven character, hope; and hope does not disappoint, because the love of God has been poured out within our hearts through the **Holy Spirit** who was given to us.   For while we were still helpless, at the right time Christ died for the ungodly.
Romans 5:1-6

My brethren, you also were made to die to the Law through the body of Christ, so that you might be joined to another, to Him who was raised from the dead, in order that we might bear fruit for God.

For while we were in the flesh, the sinful passions, which were aroused by the Law, were at work in the members of our body to bear fruit for death.

But now we have been released from the Law, having died to that by which we were bound, so that we serve in newness of the **Spirit** and not in oldness of the letter.   *Romans 7:4-6*

There is now no condemnation for those who are in Christ Jesus. For the law of the **Spirit** of life in Christ Jesus has set you free from the law of sin and of death.

For what the Law could not do, weak as it was through the flesh, God did: sending His own Son in the likeness of sinful flesh and as an offering for sin, He condemned sin in the flesh, so that the requirement of the Law might be fulfilled in us, who do not walk according to the flesh but according to the **Spirit**.

For those who are according to the flesh set their minds on the things of the flesh, but those who are according to the **Spirit**, the things of the **Spirit**.

For the mind set on the flesh is death, but the mind set on the **Spirit** is life and peace, because the mind set on the flesh is hostile toward God; for it does not subject itself to the law of God, for it is not even able to do so, and those who are in the flesh cannot please God.

However, you are not in the flesh but in the **Spirit**, if indeed the **Spirit of God** dwells in you. But if anyone does not have the **Spirit** of Christ, he does not belong to Him.

If Christ is in you, though the body is dead because of sin, yet the **Spirit** is alive because of righteousness.

But if the **Spirit** of Him who raised Jesus from the dead dwells in you, He who raised Christ Jesus from the dead will also give life to your mortal bodies through His **Spirit** who dwells in you.

So then, brethren, we are under obligation, not to the flesh, to live according to the flesh - for if you are living according to the flesh, you must die; but if by the **Spirit** you are putting to death the deeds of the body, you will live.

For all who are being led by the **Spirit of God**, these are sons of God. For you have not received a spirit of slavery leading to fear again, but you have received a spirit of adoption as sons by which we cry out, "Abba! Father!"

The **Spirit** Himself testifies with our spirit that we are children of God, and if children, heirs also, heirs of God and fellow heirs with Christ, if indeed we suffer with Him so that we may also be glorified with Him.   *Romans 8:1-17*

We know that the whole creation groans and suffers the pains of childbirth together until now.

And not only this, but also we ourselves, having the first fruits of the **Spirit**, even we ourselves groan within ourselves, waiting eagerly for our adoption as sons, the redemption of our body.

For in hope we have been saved, but hope that is seen is not hope; for who hopes for what he already sees? But if we hope for what we do not see, with perseverance we wait eagerly for it.

In the same way the **Spirit** also helps our weakness; for we do not know how to pray as we should, but the **Spirit** Himself

intercedes for us with groanings too deep for words; and He who searches the hearts knows what the mind of the **Spirit** is, because He intercedes for the saints according to the will of God.

Romans 8:22-27

I am telling the truth in Christ, I am not lying, my conscience testifies with me in the **Holy Spirit**, that I have great sorrow and unceasing grief in my heart.

For I could wish that I myself were accursed, separated from Christ for the sake of my brethren, my kinsmen according to the flesh, who are Israelites, to whom belongs the adoption as sons, and the glory and the covenants and the giving of the Law and the temple service and the promises, whose are the fathers, and from whom is the Christ according to the flesh, who is over all, God blessed forever. Amen.   *Romans 9:1-5*

I know and am convinced in the Lord Jesus that nothing is unclean in itself; but to him who thinks anything to be unclean, to him it is unclean.

For if because of food your brother is hurt, you are no longer walking according to love. Do not destroy with your food him for whom Christ died.

Therefore do not let what is for you a good thing be spoken of as evil; for the kingdom of God is not eating and drinking, but righteousness and peace and joy in the **Holy Spirit**. For he who in this way serves Christ is acceptable to God and approved by men.   *Romans 14:14-18*

May the God of hope fill you with all joy and peace in believing, so that you will abound in hope by the power of the **Holy Spirit**.

And concerning you, my brethren, I myself also am convinced that you yourselves are full of goodness, filled with all knowledge and able also to admonish one another.

But I have written very boldly to you on some points so as to remind you again, because of the grace that was given me from God, to be a minister of

Christ Jesus to the Gentiles, ministering as a priest the gospel of God, so that my offering of the Gentiles may become acceptable, sanctified by the **Holy Spirit**. Therefore in Christ Jesus I have found reason for boasting in things pertaining to God.

For I will not presume to speak of anything except what Christ has accomplished through me, resulting in the obedience of the Gentiles by word and deed, in the power of signs and wonders, in the power of the **Spirit**; so that from Jerusalem and round about as far as Illyricum I have fully preached the gospel of Christ.

And thus I aspired to preach the gospel, not where Christ was already named, so that I would not build on another man's foundation; but as it is written, "They who had no news of Him shall see, and they who have not heard shall understand."

Romans 15:13-21

I urge you, brethren, by our Lord Jesus Christ and by the love of the **Spirit**, to strive together with me in your prayers to God for me, that I may be rescued from those who are disobedient in Judea, and that my service for Jerusalem may prove acceptable to the saints; so that I may come to you in joy by the will of God and find refreshing rest in your company.

Now the God of peace be with you all. Amen. *Romans 15:30-33*

When I came to you, brethren, I did not come with superiority of speech or of wisdom, proclaiming to you the testimony of God. For I determined to know nothing among you except Jesus Christ, and Him crucified.

I was with you in weakness and in fear and in much trembling, and my message and my preaching were not in persuasive words of wisdom, but in demonstration of the **Spirit** and of power, so that your faith would not rest on the wisdom of men, but on the power of God.

Yet we do speak wisdom among those who are mature; a wisdom, however, not of this age nor of the rulers of this age, who are passing away; but we speak

God's wisdom in a mystery, the hidden wisdom which God predestined before the ages to our glory; the wisdom which none of the rulers of this age has understood; for if they had understood it they would not have crucified the Lord of glory; but just as it is written, "Things which eye has not seen and ear has not heard, and which have not entered the heart of man, all that God has prepared for those who love Him."

For to us God revealed them through the **Spirit**; for the **Spirit** searches all things, even the depths of God. For who among men knows the thoughts of a man except the spirit of the man which is in him?

Even so the thoughts of God no one knows except the **Spirit of God**.

Now we have received, not the spirit of the world, but the **Spirit** who is from God, so that we may know the things freely given to us by God, which things we also speak, not in words taught by human wisdom, but in those taught by the **Spirit**, combining spiritual thoughts with spiritual words.

But a natural man does not accept the things of the **Spirit of God**, for they are foolishness to him; and he cannot understand them, because they are spiritually appraised.

But he who is spiritual appraises all things, yet he himself is appraised by no one. For who has known the mind of the Lord, that he will instruct Him? But we have the mind of Christ. *1 Corinthians 2:1-16*

Do you not know that you are a temple of God and that the **Spirit of God** dwells in you?

If any man destroys the temple of God, God will destroy him, for the temple of God is holy, and that is what you are.

1 Corinthians 3:16-17

Do you not know that the unrighteous will not inherit the kingdom of God?

Do not be deceived; neither fornicators, nor idolaters, nor adulterers, nor effeminate, nor homosexuals, nor thieves, nor the covetous, nor drunkards, nor revilers, nor swindlers, will inherit the kingdom of God.

Such were some of you; but you were washed, but you were sanctified, but you were justified in the name of the Lord Jesus Christ and in the **Spirit of** our **God**.

1 Corinthians 6:9-11

Do you not know that your bodies are members of Christ? Shall I then take away the members of Christ and make them members of a prostitute? May it never be!

Or do you not know that the one who joins himself to a prostitute is one body with her? For He says, "The two shall become one flesh."

But the one who joins himself to the Lord is one spirit with Him.

Flee immorality. Every other sin that a man commits is outside the body, but the immoral man sins against his own body.

Or do you not know that your body is a temple of the **Holy Spirit** who is in you, whom you have from God, and that you are not your own?

For you have been bought with a price: Therefore glorify God in your body.

1 Corinthians 6:15-20

A wife is bound as long as her husband lives; but if her husband is dead, she is free to be married to whom she wishes, only in the Lord.

But in my opinion she is happier if she remains as she is; and I think that I also have the **Spirit of God**.

1 Corinthians 7:39-40

Concerning Spiritual gifts, brethren, I do not want you to be unaware.

You know that when you were pagans, you were led astray to the mute idols, however you were led. Therefore I make known to you that no one speaking by the **Spirit of God** says, "Jesus is accursed"; and no one can say, "Jesus is Lord," except by the **Holy Spirit**.

Now there are varieties of gifts, but the same **Spirit**. And there are varieties of ministries, and the same Lord.

There are varieties of effects, but the same God who works all things in all persons.

But to each one is given the manifestation of the **Spirit** for the common good.

For to one is given the word of wisdom through the **Spirit**, and to another the word of knowledge according to the same **Spirit**; to another faith by the same **Spirit**, and to another gifts of healing by the one **Spirit**, and to another the effecting of miracles, and to another prophecy, and to another the distinguishing of **spirits**, to another various kinds of tongues, and to another the interpretation of tongues.

But one and the same **Spirit** works all these things, distributing to each one individually just as He wills. For even as the body is one and yet has many members, and all the members of the body, though they are many, are one body, so also is Christ.

For by one **Spirit** we were all baptized into one body, whether Jews or Greeks, whether slaves or free, and we were all made to drink of one **Spirit**. For the body is not one member, but many.

1 Corinthians 12:1-14

He who establishes us with you in Christ and anointed us is God, who also sealed us and gave us the **Spirit** in our hearts as a pledge. *2 Corinthians 1:21-22*

Are we beginning to commend ourselves again? Or do we need, as some, letters of commendation to you or from you?

You are our letter, written in our hearts, known and read by all men; being manifested that you are a letter of Christ, cared for by us, written not with ink but with the **Spirit** of the living God, not on tablets of stone but on tablets of human hearts.

Such confidence we have through Christ toward God. Not that we are adequate in ourselves to consider anything as coming from ourselves, but our adequacy is from God, who also made us adequate as servants of a new covenant, not of the letter but of the **Spirit**; for the letter kills, but the **Spirit** gives life.

But if the ministry of death, in letters engraved on stones, came with glory, so that the sons of Israel could not look intently at the face of Moses because of the glory of his face, fading as it was, how will the ministry of the **Spirit** fail to be even more with glory?

For if the ministry of condemnation has glory, much more does the ministry of righteousness abound in glory.

2 Corinthians 3:1-9

The Lord is the **Spirit**, and where the **Spirit** of the Lord is, there is liberty.

But we all, with unveiled face, beholding as in a mirror the glory of the Lord, are being transformed into the same image from glory to glory, just as from the Lord, the **Spirit**. *2 Corinthians 3:17-18*

Indeed while we are in this tent, we groan, being burdened, because we do not want to be unclothed but to be clothed, so that what is mortal will be swallowed up by life.

Now He who prepared us for this very purpose is God, who gave to us the **Spirit** as a pledge.

Therefore, being always of good courage, and knowing that while we are at home in the body we are absent from the Lord - for we walk by faith, not by sight - we are of good courage, I say, and prefer rather to be absent from the body and to be at home with the Lord.

Therefore we also have as our ambition, whether at home or absent, to be pleasing to Him. *2 Corinthians 5:4-9*

He made Him who knew no sin to be sin on our behalf, so that we might become the righteousness of God in Him.

And working together with Him, we also urge you not to receive the grace of God in vain - for He says, "At the acceptable time I listened to you, and on the day of salvation I helped you."

Behold, now is "the acceptable time," behold, now is "the day of salvation" - giving no cause for offense in anything, so that the ministry will not be discredited, but in everything commending ourselves

as servants of God, in much endurance, in afflictions, in hardships, in distresses, in beatings, in imprisonments, in tumults, in labors, in sleeplessness, in hunger, in purity, in knowledge, in patience, in kindness, in the **Holy Spirit**, in genuine love, in the word of truth, in the power of God; by the weapons of righteousness for the right hand and the left, by glory and dishonor, by evil report and good report; regarded as deceivers and yet true; as unknown yet well-known, as dying yet behold, we live; as punished yet not put to death, as sorrowful yet always rejoicing, as poor yet making many rich, as having nothing yet possessing all things.

2 Corinthians 5:21 - 6:10

Greet one another with a holy kiss. All the saints greet you.

The grace of the Lord Jesus Christ, and the love of God, and the fellowship of the **Holy Spirit**, be with you all.

2 Corinthians 13:12-14

You foolish Galatians, who has bewitched you, before whose eyes Jesus Christ was publicly portrayed as crucified?

This is the only thing I want to find out from you: Did you receive the **Spirit** by the works of the Law, or by hearing with faith? Are you so foolish?

Having begun by the **Spirit**, are you now being perfected by the flesh? Did you suffer so many things in vain - if indeed it was in vain?

So then, does He who provides you with the **Spirit** and works miracles among you, do it by the works of the Law, or by hearing with faith?

Even so Abraham believed God, and it was reckoned to him as righteousness.

Galatians 3:1-6

Christ redeemed us from the curse of the Law, having become a curse for us - for it is written, "Cursed is everyone who hangs on a tree" - in order that in Christ Jesus the blessing of Abraham might come to the Gentiles, so that we would receive the promise of the **Spirit** through faith.

Galatians 3:13-14

I say, as long as the heir is a child, he does not differ at all from a slave although he is owner of everything, but he is under guardians and managers until the date set by the father. So also we, while we were children, were held in bondage under the elemental things of the world.

But when the fullness of the time came, God sent forth His Son, born of a woman, born under the Law, so that He might redeem those who were under the Law, that we might receive the adoption as sons.

Because you are sons, God has sent forth the **Spirit** of His Son into our hearts, crying, "Abba! Father!"

Therefore you are no longer a slave, but a son; and if a son, then an heir through God.   *Galatians 4:1-7*

You brethren, like Isaac, are children of promise. But as at that time he who was born according to the flesh persecuted him who was born according to the **Spirit**, so it is now also.   *Galatians 4:28-29*

I, Paul, say to you that if you receive circumcision, Christ will be of no benefit to you.

And I testify again to every man who receives circumcision, that he is under obligation to keep the whole Law. You have been severed from Christ, you who are seeking to be justified by law; you have fallen from grace.

For we through the **Spirit**, by faith, are waiting for the hope of righteousness. For in Christ Jesus neither circumcision nor uncircumcision means anything, but faith working through love.   *Galatians 5:2-6*

Walk by the **Spirit**, and you will not carry out the desire of the flesh. For the flesh sets its desire against the **Spirit**, and the **Spirit** against the flesh; for these are in opposition to one another, so that you may not do the things that you please. But if you are led by the **Spirit**, you are not under the Law.

Now the deeds of the flesh are evident, which are: immorality, impurity, sensuality, idolatry, sorcery, enmities, strife,

jealousy, outbursts of anger, disputes, dissensions, factions, envying, drunkenness, carousing, and things like these, of which I forewarn you, just as I have forewarned you, that those who practice such things will not inherit the kingdom of God.

But the fruit of the **Spirit** is love, joy, peace, patience, kindness, goodness, faithfulness, gentleness, self-control; against such things there is no law.

Now those who belong to Christ Jesus have crucified the flesh with its passions and desires.

If we live by the **Spirit**, let us also walk by the **Spirit**. Let us not become boastful, challenging one another, envying one another.

Brethren, even if anyone is caught in any trespass, you who are spiritual, restore such a one in a spirit of gentleness; each one looking to yourself, so that you too will not be tempted.

Bear one another's burdens, and thereby fulfill the law of Christ.
Galatians 5:16 - 16:2

Do not be deceived, God is not mocked; for whatever a man sows, this he will also reap. For the one who sows to his own flesh will from the flesh reap corruption, but the one who sows to the **Spirit** will from the **Spirit** reap eternal life.

Let us not lose heart in doing good, for in due time we will reap if we do not grow weary.   *Galatians 6:7-9*

In Him, you also, after listening to the message of truth, the gospel of your salvation - having also believed, you were sealed in Him with the **Holy Spirit** of promise, who is given as a pledge of our inheritance, with a view to the redemption of God's own possession, to the praise of His glory.

For this reason I too, having heard of the faith in the Lord Jesus which exists among you and your love for all the saints, do not cease giving thanks for you, while making mention of you in my prayers; that the God of our Lord Jesus Christ, the Father of glory, may give to you a spirit of wisdom and of revelation in the knowledge of Him. *Ephesians 1:13-17*

He came and preached peace to you who were far away, and peace to those who were near; for through Him we both have our access in one **Spirit** to the Father.

So then you are no longer strangers and aliens, but you are fellow citizens with the saints, and are of God's household, having been built on the foundation of the apostles and prophets, Christ Jesus Himself being the corner stone, in whom the whole building, being fitted together, is growing into a Holy temple in the Lord, in whom you also are being built together into a dwelling of God in the **Spirit**.

Ephesians 2:17-22

When you read you can understand my insight into the mystery of Christ, which in other generations was not made known to the sons of men, as it has now been revealed to His Holy apostles and prophets in the **Spirit**; to be specific, that the Gentiles are fellow heirs and fellow members of the body, and fellow partakers of the promise in Christ Jesus through the gospel, of which I was made a minister, according to the gift of God's grace which was given to me according to the working of His power. *Ephesians 3:4-7*

I bow my knees before the Father, from whom every family in heaven and on earth derives its name, that He would grant you, according to the riches of His glory, to be strengthened with power through His **Spirit** in the inner man, so that Christ may dwell in your hearts through faith; and that you, being rooted and grounded in love, may be able to comprehend with all the saints what is the breadth and length and height and depth, and to know the love of Christ which surpasses knowledge, that you may be filled up to all the fullness of God.

Now to Him who is able to do far more abundantly beyond all that we ask or think, according to the power that works within us, to Him be the glory in the church and in Christ Jesus to all generations forever and ever. Amen.

Therefore I, the prisoner of the Lord, implore you to walk in a manner worthy of the calling with which you have been called, with all humility and gentleness, with patience, showing tolerance for one another in love, being diligent to preserve the unity of the **Spirit** in the bond of peace.

There is one body and one **Spirit**, just as also you were called in one hope of your calling; one Lord, one faith, one baptism, one God and Father of all who is over all and through all and in all.

But to each one of us grace was given according to the measure of Christ's gift. Therefore it says, "When He ascended on high, He led captive a host of captives, and He gave gifts to men."

Ephesians 3:14 - 4:8

Let no unwholesome word proceed from your mouth, but only such a word as is good for edification according to the need of the moment, so that it will give grace to those who hear.

Do not grieve the **Holy Spirit of God**, by whom you were sealed for the day of redemption.

Let all bitterness and wrath and anger and clamor and slander be put away from you, along with all malice.

Be kind to one another, tenderhearted, forgiving each other, just as God in Christ also has forgiven you.

Ephesians 4:29-32

Be careful how you walk, not as unwise men but as wise, making the most of your time, because the days are evil. So then do not be foolish, but understand what the will of the Lord is.

And do not get drunk with wine, for that is dissipation, but be filled with the **Spirit**, speaking to one another in Psalm and hymns and spiritual songs, singing and making melody with your heart to the Lord; always giving thanks for all things in the name of our Lord Jesus Christ to God, even the Father; and be subject to one another in the fear of Christ.

Ephesians 5:15-21

Take the helmet of salvation, and the sword of the **Spirit**, which is the word of God. With all prayer and petition pray at all times in the **Spirit**, and with this in view, be on the alert with all perseverance and petition for all the saints, and pray on my behalf, that utterance may be given to me in the opening of my mouth, to make known with boldness the mystery of the gospel, for which I am an ambassador in chains; that in proclaiming it I may speak boldly, as I ought to speak.

Ephesians 6:17-20

In every way, whether in pretense or in truth, Christ is proclaimed; and in this I rejoice.

Yes, and I will rejoice, for I know that this will turn out for my deliverance through your prayers and the provision of the **Spirit** of Jesus Christ, according to my earnest expectation and hope, that I will not be put to shame in anything, but that with all boldness, Christ will even now, as always, be exalted in my body, whether by life or by death. For to me, to live is Christ and to die is gain.

Philippians 1:18-21

If there is any encouragement in Christ, if there is any consolation of love, if there is any fellowship of the **Spirit**, if any affection and compassion, make my joy complete by being of the same mind, maintaining the same love, united in spirit, intent on one purpose.

Do nothing from selfishness or empty conceit, but with humility of mind regard one another as more important than yourselves; do not merely look out for your own personal interests, but also for the interests of others. *Philippians 2:1-4*

Beware of the dogs, beware of the evil workers, beware of the false circumcision; for we are the true circumcision, who worship in the **Spirit of God** and glory in Christ Jesus and put no confidence in the flesh, ~ *Philippians 3:2-3*

Paul, an apostle of Jesus Christ by the will of God, and Timothy our brother, to

the saints and faithful brethren in Christ who are at Colossae: Grace to you and peace from God our Father.

We give thanks to God, the Father of our Lord Jesus Christ, praying always for you, since we heard of your faith in Christ Jesus and the love which you have for all the saints; because of the hope laid up for you in heaven, of which you previously heard in the word of truth, the gospel which has come to you, just as in all the world also it is constantly bearing fruit and increasing, even as it has been doing in you also since the day you heard of it and understood the grace of God in truth; just as you learned it from Epaphras, our beloved fellow bond-servant, who is a faithful servant of Christ on our behalf, and he also informed us of your love in the **Spirit**.

For this reason also, since the day we heard of it, we have not ceased to pray for you and to ask that you may be filled with the knowledge of His will in all spiritual wisdom and understanding, so that you will walk in a manner worthy of the Lord, to please Him in all respects, bearing fruit in every good work and increasing in the knowledge of God; strengthened with all power, according to His glorious might, for the attaining of all steadfastness and patience; joyously giving thanks to the Father, who has qualified us to share in the inheritance of the saints in Light.

Colossians 1:1-12

Paul and Silvanus and Timothy, to the church of the Thessalonians in God the Father and the Lord Jesus Christ: Grace to you and peace.

We give thanks to God always for all of you, making mention of you in our prayers; constantly bearing in mind your work of faith and labor of love and steadfastness of hope in our Lord Jesus Christ in the presence of our God and Father, knowing, brethren beloved by God, His choice of you; for our gospel did not come to you in word only, but also in power and in the **Holy Spirit** and with full conviction; just as you know what kind of men we proved to be among you for your sake.

You also became imitators of us and

of the Lord, having received the word in much tribulation with the joy of the **Holy Spirit**, so that you became an example to all the believers in Macedonia and in Achaia.

For the word of the Lord has sounded forth from you, not only in Macedonia and Achaia, but also in every place your faith toward God has gone forth, so that we have no need to say anything.

1 Thessalonians 1:1-8

Brethren, we request and exhort you in the Lord Jesus, that as you received from us instruction as to how you ought to walk and please God (just as you actually do walk), that you excel still more. For you know what commandments we gave you by the authority of the Lord Jesus.

For this is the will of God, your sanctification; that is, that you abstain from sexual immorality; that each of you know how to possess his own vessel in sanctification and honor, not in lustful passion, like the Gentiles who do not know God; and that no man transgress and defraud his brother in the matter because the Lord is the avenger in all these things, just as we also told you before and solemnly warned you.

For God has not called us for the purpose of impurity, but in sanctification. So, he who rejects this is not rejecting man but the God who gives His **Holy Spirit** to you. *1 Thessalonians 4:1-8*

Do not quench the **Spirit**; do not despise prophetic utterances. But examine everything carefully; hold fast to that which is good; abstain from every form of evil.

Now may the God of peace Himself sanctify you entirely; and may your spirit and soul and body be preserved complete, without blame at the coming of our Lord Jesus Christ. *1 Thessalonians 5:19-23*

We should always give thanks to God for you, brethren beloved by the Lord, because God has chosen you from the beginning for salvation through sanctification by the **Spirit** and faith in the truth.

It was for this He called you through

our gospel, that you may gain the glory of our Lord Jesus Christ.

2 Thessalonians 2:13-14

By common confession, great is the mystery of godliness: He who was revealed in the flesh, was vindicated in the **Spirit**, seen by angels, proclaimed among the nations, believed on in the world, taken up in glory.

But the **Spirit** explicitly says that in later times some will fall away from the faith, paying attention to deceitful spirits and doctrines of demons, by means of the hypocrisy of liars seared in their own conscience as with a branding iron, men who forbid marriage and advocate abstaining from foods which God has created to be gratefully shared in by those who believe and know the truth. *1 Timothy 3:16 - 4:3*

Retain the standard of sound words which you have heard from me, in the faith and love which are in Christ Jesus.

Guard, through the **Holy Spirit** who dwells in us, the treasure which has been entrusted to you. *2 Timothy 1:13-14*

Remind them to be subject to rulers, to authorities, to be obedient, to be ready for every good deed, to malign no one, to be peaceable, gentle, showing every consideration for all men.

For we also once were foolish ourselves, disobedient, deceived, enslaved to various lusts and pleasures, spending our life in malice and envy, hateful, hating one another.

But when the kindness of God our Savior and His love for mankind appeared, He saved us, not on the basis of deeds which we have done in righteousness, but according to His mercy, by the washing of regeneration and renewing by the **Holy Spirit**, whom He poured out upon us richly through Jesus Christ our Savior, so that being justified by His grace we would be made heirs according to the hope of eternal life.

This is a trustworthy statement; and concerning these things I want you to speak confidently, so that those who have believed God will be careful to engage in good deeds. These things are good and profitable for men.   *Titus 3:1-8*

For this reason we must pay much closer attention to what we have heard, so that we do not drift away from it.

For if the word spoken through angels proved unalterable, and every transgression and disobedience received a just penalty, how will we escape if we neglect so great a salvation?

After it was at the first spoken through the Lord, it was confirmed to us by those who heard, God also testifying with them, both by signs and wonders and by various miracles and by gifts of the **Holy Spirit** according to His own will.
                                      Hebrews 2:1-4

Moses was faithful in all His house as a servant, for a testimony of those things which were to be spoken later; but Christ was faithful as a Son over His house - whose house we are, if we hold fast our confidence and the boast of our hope firm until the end.

Therefore, just as the **Holy Spirit** says, "Today if you hear His voice, do not harden your hearts as when they provoked Me, as in the day of trial in the wilderness, where your fathers tried Me by testing Me, and saw My works for forty years.

Therefore I was angry with this generation, and said, 'They always go astray in their heart, and they did not know My ways'; as I swore in My wrath, 'They shall not enter My rest.' "

Take care, brethren, that there not be in any one of you an evil, unbelieving heart that falls away from the living God.
                                      Hebrews 3:5-12

Leaving the elementary teaching about the Christ, let us press on to maturity, not laying again a foundation of repentance from dead works and of faith toward God, of instruction about washings and laying on of hands, and the resurrection of the dead and eternal judgment. And this we will do, if God permits.

For in the case of those who have once been enlightened and have tasted of the heavenly gift and have been made partakers of the **Holy Spirit**, and have tasted the good word of God and the powers of the age to come, then have fallen away, it is impossible to renew them again to repentance, since they again crucify to themselves the Son of God and put Him to open shame.
                                      Hebrews 6:1-6

When these things have been so prepared, the priests are continually entering the outer tabernacle performing the divine worship, but into the second, only the high priest enters once a year, not without taking blood, which he offers for himself and for the sins of the people committed in ignorance.

The **Holy Spirit** is signifying this, that the way into the Holy place has not yet been disclosed while the outer tabernacle is still standing, which is a symbol for the present time.

Accordingly both gifts and sacrifices are offered which cannot make the worshiper perfect in conscience, since they relate only to food and drink and various washings, regulations for the body imposed until a time of reformation.

But when Christ appeared as a high priest of the good things to come, He entered through the greater and more perfect tabernacle, not made with hands, that is to say, not of this creation; and not through the blood of goats and calves, but through His own blood, He entered the holy place once for all, having obtained eternal redemption.

For if the blood of goats and bulls and the ashes of a heifer sprinkling those who have been defiled sanctify for the cleansing of the flesh, how much more will the blood of Christ, who through the eternal **Spirit** offered Himself without blemish to God, cleanse your conscience from dead works to serve the living God?

For this reason He is the mediator of a new covenant, so that, since a death has taken place for the redemption of the transgressions that were committed under the first covenant, those who have been called may receive the promise of the eternal inheritance. *Hebrews 9:6-15*

By one offering He has perfected for all time those who are sanctified.

And the **Holy Spirit** also testifies to us; for after saying, "This is the covenant that I will make with them after those days, says the Lord: I will put My laws upon their heart, and on their mind I will write them,"

He then says, "and their sins and their lawless deeds I will remember no more."

Now where there is forgiveness of these things, there is no longer any offering for sin. *Hebrews 10:14-18*

Anyone who has set aside the Law of Moses dies without mercy on the testimony of two or three witnesses.

How much severer punishment do you think he will deserve who has trampled under foot the Son of God, and has regarded as unclean the blood of the covenant by which he was sanctified, and has insulted the **Spirit** of grace? *Hebrews 10:28-29*

You adulteresses, do you not know that friendship with the world is hostility toward God? Therefore whoever wishes to be a friend of the world makes himself an enemy of God.

Or do you think that the Scripture speaks to no purpose: "He jealously desires the **Spirit** which He has made to dwell in us"? *James 4:4-5*

Peter, an apostle of Jesus Christ, to those who reside as aliens, scattered throughout Pontus, Galatia, Cappadocia, Asia, and Bithynia, who are chosen according to the foreknowledge of God the Father, by the sanctifying work of the **Spirit**, to obey Jesus Christ and be sprinkled with His blood: May grace and peace be yours in the fullest measure. *1 Peter 1:1-2*

As to this salvation, the prophets who prophesied of the grace that would come to you made careful searches and inquiries, seeking to know what person or time the **Spirit** of Christ within them was indicating as He predicted the sufferings of Christ and the glories to follow.

It was revealed to them that they were not serving themselves, but you, in these things which now have been announced to you through those who preached the gospel to you by the **Holy Spirit** sent from heaven - things into which angels long to look.

Therefore, prepare your minds for action, keep sober in spirit, fix your hope completely on the grace to be brought to you at the revelation of Jesus Christ. *1 Peter 1:10-13*

Beloved, do not be surprised at the fiery ordeal among you, which comes upon you for your testing, as though some strange thing were happening to you; but to the degree that you share the sufferings of Christ, keep on rejoicing, so that also at the revelation of His glory you may rejoice with exultation.

If you are reviled for the name of Christ, you are blessed, because the **Spirit** of glory and **of God** rests on you. *1 Peter 4:12-14*

We have the prophetic word made more sure, to which you do well to pay attention as to a lamp shining in a dark place, until the day dawns and the morning star arises in your hearts.

But know this first of all, that no prophecy of Scripture is a matter of one's own interpretation, for no prophecy was ever made by an act of human will, but men moved by the **Holy Spirit** spoke from God. *2 Peter 1:19-21*

Beloved, if our heart does not condemn us, we have confidence before God; and whatever we ask we receive from Him, because we keep His commandments and do the things that are pleasing in His sight.

This is His commandment, that we believe in the name of His Son Jesus Christ, and love one another, just as He commanded us.

The one who keeps His commandments abides in Him, and He in him. We know by this that He abides in us, by the **Spirit** whom He has given us.

Beloved, do not believe every spirit, but test the spirits to see whether they are from God, because many false prophets have gone out into the world.

By this you know the **Spirit of God**: Every spirit that confesses that Jesus Christ has come in the flesh is from God; and every spirit that does not confess Jesus is not from God; this is the spirit of the antichrist, of which you have heard that it is coming, and now it is already in the world.

You are from God, little children, and have overcome them; because greater is He who is in you than he who is in the world.

They are from the world; therefore they speak as from the world, and the world listens to them.

We are from God; he who knows God listens to us; he who is not from God does not listen to us. By this we know the spirit of truth and the spirit of error.

1 John 3:21 - 4:6

No one has seen God at any time; if we love one another, God abides in us, and His love is perfected in us.

By this we know that we abide in Him and He in us, because He has given us of His **Spirit**.   *1 John 4:12-13*

Whoever believes that Jesus is the Christ is born of God, and whoever loves the Father loves the child born of Him.

By this we know that we love the children of God, when we love God and observe His commandments.

For this is the love of God, that we keep His commandments; and His commandments are not burdensome. For whatever is born of God overcomes the world; and this is the victory that has overcome the world - our faith.

Who is the one who overcomes the world, but he who believes that Jesus is the Son of God?

This is the One who came by water and blood, Jesus Christ; not with the water only, but with the water and with the blood. It is the **Spirit** who testifies, because the **Spirit** is the truth.

For there are three that testify: The **Spirit** and the water and the blood; and the three are in agreement.   *1 John 5:1-8*

These are grumblers, finding fault, following after their own lusts; they speak arrogantly, flattering people for the sake of gaining an advantage.

But you, beloved, ought to remember the words that were spoken beforehand by the apostles of our Lord Jesus Christ, that they were saying to you, "In the last time there will be mockers, following after their own ungodly lusts."

These are the ones who cause divisions, worldly-minded, devoid of the **Spirit**.

But you, beloved, building yourselves up on your most Holy faith, praying in the **Holy Spirit**, keep yourselves in the love of God, waiting anxiously for the mercy of our Lord Jesus Christ to eternal life.

Jude 16-21

I, John, your brother and fellow partaker in the tribulation and kingdom and perseverance which are in Jesus, was on the island called Patmos because of the word of God and the testimony of Jesus.

I was in the **Spirit** on the Lord's day, and I heard behind me a loud voice like the sound of a trumpet, saying, "Write in a book what you see, and send it to the seven churches: to Ephesus and to Smyrna and to Pergamum and to Thyatira and to Sardis and to Philadelphia and to Laodicea."   *Revelation 1:9-11*

He who has an ear, let him hear what the **Spirit** says to the churches.

To him who overcomes, I will grant to eat of the tree of life which is in the Paradise of God.   *Revelation 2:7*

He who has an ear, let him hear what the **Spirit** says to the churches.

He who overcomes will not be hurt by the second death.   *Revelation 2:11*

He who has an ear, let him hear what the **Spirit** says to the churches.

To him who overcomes, to him I will give some of the hidden manna, and I will give him a white stone, and a new name written on the stone which no one knows but he who receives it.   *Revelation 2:17*

He who overcomes, and he who keeps My deeds until the end, to him I will give authority over the nations; and he shall rule them with a rod of iron, as the vessels of the potter are broken to pieces, as I also have received authority from My Father; and I will give him the morning star.

He who has an ear, let him hear what the **Spirit** says to the churches.
    Revelation 2:26-29

He who overcomes will thus be clothed in white garments; and I will not erase his name from the book of life, and I will confess his name before My Father and before His angels.

He who has an ear, let him hear what the **Spirit** says to the churches.
    Revelation 3:5-6

He who overcomes, I will make him a pillar in the temple of My God, and he will not go out from it anymore; and I will write on him the name of My God, and the name of the city of My God, the new Jerusalem, which comes down out of heaven from My God, and My new name.

He who has an ear, let him hear what the **Spirit** says to the churches.
    Revelation 3:12-13

He who overcomes, I will grant to him to sit down with Me on My throne, as I also overcame and sat down with My Father on His throne.

He who has an ear, let him hear what the **Spirit** says to the churches.

After these things I looked, and behold, a door standing open in heaven, and the first voice which I had heard, like the sound of a trumpet speaking with me, said, "Come up here, and I will show you what must take place after these things."

Immediately I was in the **Spirit**; and behold, a throne was standing in heaven, and One sitting on the throne.
    Revelation 3:21 - 4:2

I heard a voice from heaven, saying, "Write, 'Blessed are the dead who die in the Lord from now on!' "

"Yes," says the **Spirit**, "so that they may rest from their labors, for their deeds follow with them."   *Revelation 14:13*

One of the seven angels who had the seven bowls came and spoke with me, saying, "Come here, I will show you the judgment of the great harlot who sits on many waters, with whom the kings of the earth committed acts of immorality, and those who dwell on the earth were made drunk with the wine of her immorality."

And he carried me away in the **Spirit** into a wilderness; and I saw a woman sitting on a scarlet beast, full of blasphemous names, having seven heads and ten horns.

The woman was clothed in purple and scarlet, and adorned with gold and precious stones and pearls, having in her hand a gold cup full of abominations and of the unclean things of her immorality, and on her forehead a name was written, a mystery, "BABYLON THE GREAT, THE MOTHER OF HARLOTS AND OF THE ABOMINATIONS OF THE EARTH."

And I saw the woman drunk with the blood of the saints, and with the blood of the witnesses of Jesus. When I saw her, I wondered greatly.   *Revelation 17:1-6*

One of the seven angels who had the seven bowls full of the seven last plagues came and spoke with me, saying, "Come here, I will show you the bride, the wife of the Lamb."

And he carried me away in the **Spirit** to a great and high mountain, and showed me the holy city, Jerusalem, coming down out of heaven from God, having the glory of God. Her brilliance was like a very costly stone, as a stone of crystal-clear jasper.   *Revelation 21:9-11*

"I, Jesus, have sent My angel to testify to you these things for the churches. I am the root and the descendant of David, the bright morning star."

The **Spirit** and the bride say, "Come." And let the one who hears say, "Come."

And let the one who is thirsty come; let the one who wishes take the water of life without cost.   *Revelation 22:16-17*

FASTING
/ FAST* / FASTINGS / FASTED

Definitions

Fast 1. To abstain from food.

2. An abstinence from food, or a limiting of one's food, or to eat only certain kinds of food, especially as a voluntary spiritual discipline or religious observance.

3. A time or period of fasting.

OLD TESTAMENT

The Lord said to Moses, "Write down these words, for in accordance with these words I have made a covenant with you and with Israel."

So he was there with the Lord forty days and forty nights; he did not eat bread or drink water. And he wrote on the tablets the words of the covenant, the Ten Commandments.   *Exodus 34:27-28*

When I went up to the mountain to receive the tablets of stone, the tablets of the covenant which the Lord had made with you, then I remained on the mountain forty days and nights; I neither ate bread nor drank water.

The Lord gave me the two tablets of stone written by the finger of God; and on them were all the words which the Lord had spoken with you at the mountain from the midst of the fire on the day of the assembly.

It came about at the end of forty days and nights that the Lord gave me the two tablets of stone, the tablets of the covenant.

Then the Lord said to me, "Arise, go down from here quickly, for your people whom you brought out of Egypt have acted corruptly. They have quickly turned aside from the way which I commanded them; they have made a molten image for themselves."

The Lord spoke further to me, saying,

"I have seen this people, and indeed, it is a stubborn people. Let Me alone, that I may destroy them and blot out their name from under heaven; and I will make of you a nation mightier and greater than they."

So I turned and came down from the mountain while the mountain was burning with fire, and the two tablets of the covenant were in my two hands. And I saw that you had indeed sinned against the Lord your God. You had made for yourselves a molten calf; you had turned aside quickly from the way which the Lord had commanded you.

I took hold of the two tablets and threw them from my hands and smashed them before your eyes. I fell down before the Lord, as at the first, forty days and nights; I neither ate bread nor drank water, because of all your sin which you had committed in doing what was evil in the sight of the Lord to provoke Him to anger.

For I was afraid of the anger and hot displeasure with which the Lord was wrathful against you in order to destroy you, but the Lord listened to me that time also. The Lord was angry enough with Aaron to destroy him; so I also prayed for Aaron at the same time. *Deuteronomy 9:9-20*

The sons of Israel came against the sons of Benjamin the second day. Benjamin went out against them from Gibeah the second day and felled to the ground again 18,000 men of the sons of Israel; all these drew the sword.

Then all the sons of Israel and all the people went up and came to Bethel and wept; thus they remained there before the Lord and **fasted** that day until evening. And they offered burnt offerings and peace offerings before the Lord.

The sons of Israel inquired of the Lord (for the ark of the covenant of God was there in those days, and Phinehas the son of Eleazar, Aaron's son, stood before it to minister in those days), saying, "Shall I yet again go out to battle against the sons of my brother Benjamin, or shall I cease?"

And the Lord said, "Go up, for tomorrow I will deliver them into your hand."

Judges 20:24-28

When the day came that Elkanah sacrificed, he would give portions to Peninnah his wife and to all her sons and her daughters; but to Hannah he would give a double portion, for he loved Hannah, but the Lord had closed her womb. Her rival, however, would provoke her bitterly to irritate her, because the Lord had closed her womb. It happened year after year, as often as she went up to the house of the Lord, she would provoke her; so she wept and would not eat.

Then Elkanah her husband said to her, "Hannah, why do you weep and why do you not eat and why is your heart sad? Am I not better to you than ten sons?" Then Hannah rose after eating and drinking in Shiloh. ~ *1 Samuel 1:4-9*

Samuel spoke to all the house of Israel, saying, "If you return to the Lord with all your heart, remove the foreign gods and the Ashtaroth from among you and direct your hearts to the Lord and serve Him alone; and He will deliver you from the hand of the Philistines." So the sons of Israel removed the Baals and the Ashtaroth and served the Lord alone.

Then Samuel said, "Gather all Israel to Mizpah and I will pray to the Lord for you."

They gathered to Mizpah, and drew water and poured it out before the Lord, and **fasted** on that day and said there,

"We have sinned against the Lord." And Samuel judged the sons of Israel at Mizpah. *1 Samuel 7:3-6*

Saul's anger burned against Jonathan and he said to him, "You son of a perverse, rebellious woman! Do I not know that you are choosing the son of Jesse to your own shame and to the shame of your mother's nakedness? For as long as the son of Jesse lives on the earth, neither you nor your kingdom will be established. Therefore now, send and bring him to me, for he must surely die."

But Jonathan answered Saul his father and said to him, "Why should he be put to death? What has he done?"

Then Saul hurled his spear at him to strike him down; so Jonathan knew that his father had decided to put David to death.

Then Jonathan arose from the table in fierce anger, and did not eat food on the second day of the new moon, for he was grieved over David because his father had dishonored him.

1 Samuel 20:30-34

Samuel said to Saul, "Why have you disturbed me by bringing me up?" And Saul answered, "I am greatly distressed; for the Philistines are waging war against me, and God has departed from me and no longer answers me, either through prophets or by dreams; therefore I have called you, that you may make known to me what I should do."

Samuel said, "Why then do you ask me, since the Lord has departed from you and has become your adversary? The Lord has done accordingly as He spoke through me; for the Lord has torn the kingdom out of your hand and given it to your neighbor, to David.

"As you did not obey the Lord and did not execute His fierce wrath on Amalek, so the Lord has done this thing to you this day.

"Moreover the Lord will also give over Israel along with you into the hands of the Philistines, therefore tomorrow you and your sons will be with me. Indeed the

Lord will give over the army of Israel into the hands of the Philistines!"

Then Saul immediately fell full length upon the ground and was very afraid because of the words of Samuel; also there was no strength in him, for he had eaten no food all day and all night.

The woman came to Saul and saw that he was terrified, and said to him, "Behold, your maidservant has obeyed you, and I have taken my life in my hand and have listened to your words which you spoke to me. So now also, please listen to the voice of your maidservant, and let me set a piece of bread before you that you may eat and have strength when you go on your way."

But he refused and said, "I will not eat."

However, his servants together with the woman urged him, and he listened to them. So he arose from the ground and sat on the bed.

The woman had a fattened calf in the house, and she quickly slaughtered it; and she took flour, kneaded it and baked unleavened bread from it. She brought it before Saul and his servants, and they ate.

Then they arose and went away that night. *1 Samuel 28:15-25*

When the men of Israel who were on the other side of the valley, with those who were beyond the Jordan, saw that the men of Israel had fled and that Saul and his sons were dead, they abandoned the cities and fled; then the Philistines came and lived in them.

It came about on the next day when the Philistines came to strip the slain, that they found Saul and his three sons fallen on Mount Gilboa. They cut off his head and stripped off his weapons, and sent them throughout the land of the Philistines, to carry the good news to the house of their idols and to the people. They put his weapons in the temple of Ashtaroth, and they fastened his body to the wall of Beth-shan.

Now when the inhabitants of Jabesh-gilead heard what the Philistines had done to Saul, all the valiant men rose and walked all night, and took the body of Saul and the bodies of his sons from the wall of Beth-shan, and they came to Jabesh and burned them there.

They took their bones and buried them under the tamarisk tree at Jabesh, and **fasted** seven days. *1 Samuel 31:7-13*

David took hold of his clothes and tore them, and so also did all the men who were with him.

They mourned and wept and **fasted** until evening for Saul and his son Jonathan and for the people of the Lord and the house of Israel, because they had fallen by the sword. *2 Samuel 1:11-12*

David said to Nathan, "I have sinned against the Lord."

And Nathan said to David, "The Lord also has taken away your sin; you shall not die. However, because by this deed you have given occasion to the enemies of the Lord to blaspheme, the child also that is born to you shall surely die." So Nathan went to his house.

Then the Lord struck the child that Uriah's widow bore to David, so that he was very sick. David therefore inquired of God for the child; and David **fasted** and went and lay all night on the ground.

The elders of his household stood beside him in order to raise him up from the ground, but he was unwilling and would not eat food with them.

Then it happened on the seventh day that the child died. And the servants of David were afraid to tell him that the child was dead, for they said, "Behold, while the child was still alive, we spoke to him and he did not listen to our voice. How then can we tell him that the child is dead, since he might do himself harm!"

But when David saw that his servants were whispering together, David perceived that the child was dead; so David said to his servants, "Is the child dead?" And they said, "He is dead."

So David arose from the ground, washed, anointed himself, and changed his clothes; and he came into the house of the Lord and worshiped. Then he came to his own house, and when he requested, they set food before him and he ate.

Then his servants said to him, "What is this thing that you have done? While the child was alive, you **fasted** and wept; but when the child died, you arose and ate food."

He said, "While the child was still alive, I **fasted** and wept; for I said, 'Who knows, the Lord may be gracious to me, that the child may live.' But now he has died; why should I **fast**? Can I bring him back again? I will go to him, but he will not return to me."   *2 Samuel 12:13-23*

Naboth the Jezreelite had a vineyard which was in Jezreel beside the palace of Ahab king of Samaria. Ahab spoke to Naboth, saying, "Give me your vineyard, that I may have it for a vegetable garden because it is close beside my house, and I will give you a better vineyard than it in its place; if you like, I will give you the price of it in money."

But Naboth said to Ahab, "The Lord forbid me that I should give you the inheritance of my fathers."

So Ahab came into his house sullen and vexed because of the word which Naboth the Jezreelite had spoken to him; for he said, "I will not give you the inheritance of my fathers." And he lay down on his bed and turned away his face and ate no food.

But Jezebel his wife came to him and said to him, "How is it that your spirit is so sullen that you are not eating food?" So he said to her, "Because I spoke to Naboth the Jezreelite and said to him, 'Give me your vineyard for money; or else, if it pleases you, I will give you a vineyard in its place.' But he said, 'I will not give you my vineyard.' "

Jezebel his wife said to him, "Do you now reign over Israel? Arise, eat bread, and let your heart be joyful; I will give you the vineyard of Naboth the Jezreelite." So she wrote letters in Ahab's name and sealed them with his seal, and sent letters to the elders and to the nobles who were living with Naboth in his city.

Now she wrote in the letters, saying, "Proclaim a **fast** and seat Naboth at the head of the people; and seat two worthless men before him, and let them testify against him, saying, 'You cursed God and the king.' Then take him out and stone him to death."

So the men of his city, the elders and the nobles who lived in his city, did as Jezebel had sent word to them, just as it was written in the letters which she had sent them. They proclaimed a **fast** and seated Naboth at the head of the people.

Then the two worthless men came in and sat before him; and the worthless men testified against him, even against Naboth, before the people, saying, "Naboth cursed God and the king." So they took him outside the city and stoned him to death with stones.

Then they sent word to Jezebel, saying, "Naboth has been stoned and is dead." When Jezebel heard that Naboth had been stoned and was dead, Jezebel said to Ahab, "Arise, take possession of the vineyard of Naboth, the Jezreelite, which he refused to give you for money; for Naboth is not alive, but dead."

When Ahab heard that Naboth was dead, Ahab arose to go down to the vineyard of Naboth the Jezreelite, to take possession of it.   *1 Kings 21:1-16*

Surely there was no one like Ahab who sold himself to do evil in the sight of the Lord, because Jezebel his wife incited him. He acted very abominably in following idols, according to all that the Amorites had done, whom the Lord cast out before the sons of Israel.

It came about when Ahab heard these words, that he tore his clothes and put on sackcloth and **fasted**, and he lay in sackcloth and went about despondently.

Then the word of the Lord came to Elijah the Tishbite, saying, "Do you see how Ahab has humbled himself before Me? Because he has humbled himself before Me, I will not bring the evil in his days, but I will bring the evil upon his house in his son's days."

Three years passed without war between Aram and Israel. *1 Kings 21:25 - 22:1*

When all Jabesh-gilead heard all that the Philistines had done to Saul, all the valiant men arose and took away the body of Saul and the bodies of his sons and brought them to Jabesh, and they buried their bones under the oak in Jabesh, and **fasted** seven days.

So Saul died for his trespass which he committed against the Lord, because of the word of the Lord which he did not keep; and also because he asked counsel of a medium, making inquiry of it, and did not inquire of the Lord.

Therefore He killed him and turned the kingdom to David the son of Jesse.
1 Chronicles 10:11-14

The sons of Moab and the sons of Ammon, together with some of the Meunites, came to make war against Jehoshaphat.

Then some came and reported to Jehoshaphat, saying, "A great multitude is coming against you from beyond the sea, out of Aram and behold, they are in Hazazontamar (that is Engedi)."

Jehoshaphat was afraid and turned his attention to seek the Lord, and proclaimed a **fast** throughout all Judah. So Judah gathered together to seek help from the Lord; they even came from all the cities of Judah to seek the Lord.
2 Chronicles 20:2-4

I proclaimed a **fast** there at the river of Ahava, that we might humble ourselves before our God to seek from Him a safe journey for us, our little ones, and all our possessions.

For I was ashamed to request from the king troops and horsemen to protect us from the enemy on the way, because we had said to the king, "The hand of our God is favorably disposed to all those who seek Him, but His power and His anger are against all those who forsake Him." So we **fasted** and sought our God concerning this matter, and He listened to our entreaty. *Ezra 8:21-23*

Shecaniah the son of Jehiel, one of the sons of Elam, said to Ezra, "We have been unfaithful to our God and have married foreign women from the peoples of the land; yet now there is hope for Israel in spite of this. So now let us make a covenant with our God to put away all the wives and their children, according to the counsel of my lord and of those who tremble at the commandment of our God; and let it be done according to the law. Arise! For this matter is your responsibility, but we will be with you; be courageous and act."

Then Ezra rose and made the leading priests, the Levites and all Israel, take oath that they would do according to this proposal; so they took the oath.

Then Ezra rose from before the house of God and went into the chamber of Jehohanan the son of Eliashib. Although he went there, he did not eat bread nor drink water, for he was mourning over the unfaithfulness of the exiles. *Ezra 10:2-6*

The words of Nehemiah the son of Hacaliah. Now it happened in the month Chislev, in the twentieth year, while I was in Susa the capitol, that Hanani, one of my brothers, and some men from Judah came; and I asked them concerning the Jews who had escaped and had survived the captivity, and about Jerusalem.

They said to me, "The remnant there in the province who survived the captivity are in great distress and reproach, and the wall of Jerusalem is broken down and its gates are burned with fire."

When I heard these words, I sat down and wept and mourned for days; and I was **fasting** and praying before the God of heaven. *Nehemiah 1:1-4*

On the twenty-fourth day of this month the sons of Israel assembled with **fasting**, in sackcloth and with dirt upon them. The descendants of Israel separated themselves from all foreigners, and stood and confessed their sins and the iniquities of their fathers.

While they stood in their place, they read from the book of the law of the Lord their God for a fourth of the day; and for another fourth they confessed and worshiped the Lord their God. *Nehemiah 9:1-3*

When Mordecai learned all that had been done, he tore his clothes, put on sackcloth and ashes, and went out into the midst of the city and wailed loudly and bitterly. He went as far as the king's gate, for no one was to enter the king's gate clothed in sackcloth.

In each and every province where the command and decree of the king came, there was great mourning among the Jews, with **fasting**, weeping and wailing; and many lay on sackcloth and ashes. *Esther 4:1-3*

Esther told them to reply to Mordecai, "Go, assemble all the Jews who are found in Susa, and **fast** for me; do not eat or drink for three days, night or day. I and my maidens also will **fast** in the same way. And thus I will go in to the king, which is not according to the law; and if I perish, I perish."

So Mordecai went away and did just as Esther had commanded him. *Esther 4:15-17*

Queen Esther, daughter of Abihail, with Mordecai the Jew, wrote with full authority to confirm this second letter about Purim. He sent letters to all the Jews, to the 127 provinces of the kingdom of Ahasuerus, namely, words of peace and truth, to establish these days of Purim at their appointed times, just as Mordecai the Jew and Queen Esther had established for them, and just as they had established for themselves and for their descendants with instructions for their times of **fasting** and their lamentations.

The command of Esther established these customs for Purim, and it was written in the book. *Esther 9:29-32*

Malicious witnesses rise up; they ask me of things that I do not know. They repay me evil for good, to the bereavement of my soul.

But as for me, when they were sick,

my clothing was sackcloth; I humbled my soul with **fasting**, and my prayer kept returning to my bosom.

I went about as though it were my friend or brother; I bowed down mourning, as one who sorrows for a mother. *Psalm 35:11-14*

I have become estranged from my brothers and an alien to my mother's sons. For zeal for Your house has consumed me, and the reproaches of those who reproach You have fallen on me.

When I wept in my soul with **fasting**, it became my reproach. When I made sackcloth my clothing, I became a byword to them. Those who sit in the gate talk about me, and I am the song of the drunkards. *Psalm 69:8-12*

Let this be the reward of my accusers from the Lord, and of those who speak evil against my soul. But You, O God, the Lord, deal kindly with me for Your name's sake; because Your lovingkindness is good, deliver me; for I am afflicted and needy, and my heart is wounded within me.

I am passing like a shadow when it lengthens; I am shaken off like the locust. My knees are weak from **fasting**, and my flesh has grown lean, without fatness. Help me, O Lord my God; save me according to Your lovingkindness. *Psalm 109:20-26*

Cry loudly, do not hold back; raise your voice like a trumpet, and declare to My people their transgression and to the house of Jacob their sins. Yet they seek Me day by day and delight to know My ways, as a nation that has done righteousness and has not forsaken the ordinance of their God. They ask Me for just decisions, they delight in the nearness of God.

"Why have we **fasted** and You do not see? Why have we humbled ourselves and You do not notice?" Behold, on the day of your **fast** you find your desire, and drive hard all your workers.

Behold, you **fast** for contention and

strife and to strike with a wicked fist. You do not **fast** like you do today to make your voice heard on high.

Is it a **fast** like this which I choose, a day for a man to humble himself? Is it for bowing one's head like a reed and for spreading out sackcloth and ashes as a bed? Will you call this a **fast**, even an acceptable day to the Lord?

Is this not the **fast** which I choose, to loosen the bonds of wickedness, to undo the bands of the yoke, and to let the oppressed go free and break every yoke? Is it not to divide your bread with the hungry and bring the homeless poor into the house; when you see the naked, to cover him; and not to hide yourself from your own flesh?

Then your light will break out like the dawn, and your recovery will speedily spring forth; and your righteousness will go before you; the glory of the Lord will be your rear guard.

Then you will call, and the Lord will answer; you will cry, and He will say, "Here I am." If you remove the yoke from your midst, the pointing of the finger and speaking wickedness, and if you give yourself to the hungry and satisfy the desire of the afflicted, then your light will rise in darkness and your gloom will become like midday.

And the Lord will continually guide you, and satisfy your desire in scorched places, and give strength to your bones; and you will be like a watered garden, and like a spring of water whose waters do not fail. *Isaiah 58:1-11*

Thus says the Lord to this people, "Even so they have loved to wander; they have not kept their feet in check. Therefore the Lord does not accept them; now He will remember their iniquity and call their sins to account."

So the Lord said to me, "Do not pray for the welfare of this people. When they **fast**, I am not going to listen to their cry; and when they offer burnt offering and grain offering, I am not going to accept them. Rather I am going to make an end of them by the sword, famine and pestilence." *Jeremiah 14:10-12*

In the fourth year of Jehoiakim the son of Josiah, king of Judah, this word came to Jeremiah from the Lord, saying, "Take a scroll and write on it all the words which I have spoken to you concerning Israel and concerning Judah, and concerning all the nations, from the day I first spoke to you, from the days of Josiah, even to this day. Perhaps the house of Judah will hear all the calamity which I plan to bring on them, in order that every man will turn from his evil way; then I will forgive their iniquity and their sin."

Then Jeremiah called Baruch the son of Neriah, and Baruch wrote on a scroll at the dictation of Jeremiah all the words of the Lord which He had spoken to him. Jeremiah commanded Baruch, saying, "I am restricted; I cannot go into the house of the Lord. So you go and read from the scroll which you have written at my dictation the words of the Lord to the people in the Lord's house on a **fast** day.

"And also you shall read them to all the people of Judah who come from their cities. Perhaps their supplication will come before the Lord, and everyone will turn from his evil way, for great is the anger and the wrath that the Lord has pronounced against this people."

Baruch the son of Neriah did according to all that Jeremiah the prophet commanded him, reading from the book the words of the Lord in the Lord's house.

Now in the fifth year of Jehoiakim the son of Josiah, king of Judah, in the ninth month, all the people in Jerusalem and all the people who came from the cities of Judah to Jerusalem proclaimed a **fast** before the Lord.

Then Baruch read from the book the words of Jeremiah in the house of the Lord in the chamber of Gemariah the son of Shaphan the scribe, in the upper court, at the entry of the New Gate of the Lord's house, to all the people. *Jeremiah 36:1-10*

The king gave orders, and Daniel was brought in and cast into the lions' den. The king spoke and said to Daniel, "Your

God whom you constantly serve will Himself deliver you."

A stone was brought and laid over the mouth of the den; and the king sealed it with his own signet ring and with the signet rings of his nobles, so that nothing would be changed in regard to Daniel.

Then the king went off to his palace and spent the night **fasting**, and no entertainment was brought before him; and his sleep fled from him. Then the king arose at dawn, at the break of day, and went in haste to the lions' den.   *Daniel 6:16-19*

In the first year of Darius the son of Ahasuerus, of Median descent, who was made king over the kingdom of the Chaldeans - in the first year of his reign, I, Daniel, observed in the books the number of the years which was revealed as the word of the Lord to Jeremiah the prophet for the completion of the desolations of Jerusalem, namely, seventy years. So I gave my attention to the Lord God to seek Him by prayer and supplications, with **fasting**, sackcloth and ashes.

I prayed to the Lord my God and confessed and said, "Alas, O Lord, the great and awesome God, who keeps His covenant and lovingkindness for those who love Him and keep His commandments, we have sinned, committed iniquity, acted wickedly and rebelled, even turning aside from Your commandments and ordinances. Moreover, we have not listened to Your servants the prophets, who spoke in Your name to our kings, our princes, our fathers and all the people of the land."
                                        Daniel 9:1-6

Gird yourselves with sackcloth and lament, O priests; wail, O ministers of the altar! Come, spend the night in sackcloth O ministers of my God, for the grain offering and the drink offering are withheld from the house of your God.

Consecrate a **fast**, proclaim a solemn assembly; gather the elders and all the inhabitants of the land to the house of the Lord your God, and cry out to the Lord. Alas for the day! For the day of the Lord is near, and it will come as destruction from the Almighty.   *Joel 1:13-15*

The Lord utters His voice before His army; surely His camp is very great, for strong is he who carries out His word. The day of the Lord is indeed great and very awesome, and who can endure it?

"Yet even now," declares the Lord, "return to Me with all your heart, and with **fasting**, weeping and mourning; and rend your heart and not your garments."

Now return to the Lord your God, for He is gracious and compassionate, slow to anger, abounding in lovingkindness and relenting of evil. Who knows whether He will not turn and relent and leave a blessing behind Him, even a grain offering and a drink offering for the Lord your God?

Blow a trumpet in Zion, consecrate a **fast**, proclaim a solemn assembly, gather the people, sanctify the congregation, assemble the elders, gather the children and the nursing infants. Let the bridegroom come out of his room and the bride out of her bridal chamber.   *Joel 2:11-16*

The word of the Lord came to Jonah the second time, saying, "Arise, go to Nineveh the great city and proclaim to it the proclamation which I am going to tell you." So Jonah arose and went to Nineveh according to the word of the Lord.

Now Nineveh was an exceedingly great city, a three days' walk. Then Jonah began to go through the city one day's walk; and he cried out and said, "Yet forty days and Nineveh will be overthrown."

Then the people of Nineveh believed in God; and they called a **fast** and put on sackcloth from the greatest to the least of them. When the word reached the king of Nineveh, he arose from his throne, laid aside his robe from him, covered himself with sackcloth and sat on the ashes.

He issued a proclamation and it said, "In Nineveh by the decree of the king and his nobles: Do not let man, beast, herd, or flock taste a thing. Do not let them eat or drink water. But both man and beast must be covered with sackcloth; and let men call on God earnestly that each may turn from his wicked way and from the violence which is in his hands. Who knows, God may turn and relent and withdraw His burning anger so that we will not perish."

When God saw their deeds, that they turned from their wicked way, then God relented concerning the calamity which He had declared He would bring upon them. And He did not do it.   *Jonah 3:1-10*

In the fourth year of King Darius, the word of the Lord came to Zechariah on the fourth day of the ninth month, which is Chislev. Now the town of Bethel had sent Sharezer and Regemmelech and their men to seek the favor of the Lord, speaking to the priests who belong to the house of the Lord of hosts, and to the prophets, saying, "Shall I weep in the fifth month and abstain, as I have done these many years?"

Then the word of the Lord of hosts came to me, saying, "Say to all the people of the land and to the priests, 'When you **fasted** and mourned in the fifth and seventh months these seventy years, was it actually for Me that you **fasted**? When you eat and drink, do you not eat for yourselves and do you not drink for yourselves?' "   *Zechariah 7:1-6*

The word of the Lord of hosts came to me, saying, "Thus says the Lord of hosts, 'The **fast** of the fourth, the **fast** of the fifth, the **fast** of the seventh and the **fast** of the tenth months will become joy, gladness, and cheerful feasts for the house of Judah; so love truth and peace.'

"Thus says the Lord of hosts, 'It will yet be that peoples will come, even the inhabitants of many cities. The inhabitants of one will go to another, saying, "Let us go at once to entreat the favor of the Lord, and to seek the Lord of hosts; I will also go."

So many peoples and mighty nations will come to seek the Lord of hosts in Jerusalem and to entreat the favor of the Lord.' "   *Zechariah 8:18-22*

NEW TESTAMENT

After being baptized, Jesus came up immediately from the water; and behold, the heavens were opened, and he saw the Spirit of God descending as a dove and lighting on Him, and behold, a voice out of the heavens said, "This is My beloved Son, in whom I am well-pleased."

Then Jesus was led up by the Spirit into the wilderness to be tempted by the devil. And after He had **fasted** forty days and forty nights, He then became hungry. And the tempter came and said to Him, "If You are the Son of God, command that these stones become bread."

But He answered and said, "It is written, 'Man shall not live on bread alone, but on every word that proceeds out of the mouth of God.' "   *Matthew 3:16 - 4:4*

Whenever you **fast**, do not put on a gloomy face as the hypocrites do, for they neglect their appearance so that they will be noticed by men when they are **fasting**. Truly I say to you, they have their reward in full.

But you, when you **fast**, anoint your head and wash your face so that your **fasting** will not be noticed by men, but by your Father who is in secret; and your Father who sees what is done in secret will reward you.   *Matthew 6:16-18*

The disciples of John came to Him, asking, "Why do we and the Pharisees **fast**, but Your disciples do not **fast**?" And Jesus said to them, "The attendants of the bridegroom cannot mourn as long as the bridegroom is with them, can they? But the days will come when the bridegroom is taken away from them, and then they will **fast**."   *Matthew 9:14-15*

When they came to the crowd, a man came up to Jesus, falling on his knees before Him and saying, "Lord, have mercy on my son, for he is a lunatic and is very ill; for he often falls into the fire and often into the water. I brought him to Your disciples, and they could not cure him."

And Jesus answered and said, "You unbelieving and perverted generation, how long shall I be with you? How long shall I put up with you? Bring him here to Me."

And Jesus rebuked him, and the demon came out of him, and the boy was cured at once.

Then the disciples came to Jesus privately and said, "Why could we not drive it out?"

And He said to them, "Because of the littleness of your faith; for truly I say to you, if you have faith the size of a mustard seed, you will say to this mountain, 'Move from here to there,' and it will move; and nothing will be impossible to you. [But this kind does not go out except by prayer and **fasting**.]"   *Matthew 17:14-21*

John's disciples and the Pharisees were **fasting**; and they came and said to Him, "Why do John's disciples and the disciples of the Pharisees **fast**, but Your disciples do not **fast**?"

And Jesus said to them, "While the bridegroom is with them, the attendants of the bridegroom cannot **fast**, can they? So long as they have the bridegroom with them, they cannot **fast**. But the days will come when the bridegroom is taken away from them, and then they will **fast** in that day."   *Mark 2:18-20*

There was a prophetess, Anna the daughter of Phanuel, of the tribe of Asher. She was advanced in years and had lived with her husband seven years after her marriage, and then as a widow to the age of eighty-four. She never left the temple, serving night and day with **fastings** and prayers.

At that very moment she came up and began giving thanks to God, and continued to speak of Him to all those who were looking for the redemption of Jerusalem.   *Luke 2:36-38*

Jesus, full of the Holy Spirit, returned from the Jordan and was led around by the Spirit in the wilderness for forty days,

being tempted by the devil. And He ate nothing during those days, and when they had ended, He became hungry.

And the devil said to Him, "If You are the Son of God, tell this stone to become bread."

And Jesus answered him, "It is written, 'Man shall not live on bread alone.' "   *Luke 4:1-2*

They said to Him, "The disciples of John often **fast** and offer prayers, the disciples of the Pharisees also do the same, but Yours eat and drink."

And Jesus said to them, "You cannot make the attendants of the bridegroom **fast** while the bridegroom is with them, can you? But the days will come; and when the bridegroom is taken away from them, then they will **fast** in those days."   *Luke 5:33-35*

He also told this parable to some people who trusted in themselves that they were righteous, and viewed others with contempt: "Two men went up into the temple to pray, one a Pharisee and the other a tax collector. The Pharisee stood and was praying this to himself: 'God, I thank You that I am not like other people: swindlers, unjust, adulterers, or even like this tax collector. I **fast** twice a week; I pay tithes of all that I get.'

"But the tax collector, standing some distance away, was even unwilling to lift up his eyes to heaven, but was beating his breast, saying, 'God, be merciful to me, the sinner!'

"I tell you, this man went to his house justified rather than the other; for everyone who exalts himself will be humbled, but he who humbles himself will be exalted."   *Luke 18:9-14*

There were at Antioch, in the church that was there, prophets and teachers: Barnabas, and Simeon who was called Niger, and Lucius of Cyrene, and Manaen who had been brought up with Herod the tetrarch, and Saul.

While they were ministering to the Lord and **fasting**, the Holy Spirit said,

"Set apart for Me Barnabas and Saul for the work to which I have called them."

Then, when they had **fasted** and prayed and laid their hands on them, they sent them away. *Acts 13:1-3*

After they had preached the gospel to that city and had made many disciples, they returned to Lystra and to Iconium and to Antioch, strengthening the souls of the disciples, encouraging them to continue in the faith, and saying, "Through many tribulations we must enter the kingdom of God."

When they had appointed elders for them in every church, having prayed with **fasting**, they commended them to the Lord in whom they had believed.
Acts 14:21-23

When considerable time had passed and the voyage was now dangerous, since even the **fast** was already over, Paul began to admonish them, and said to them, "Men, I perceive that the voyage will certainly be with damage and great loss, not only of the cargo and the ship, but also of our lives." *Acts 27:9-10*

~ End of Scriptures ~

IMPROVING THE SOLA SCRIPTURA TOPICAL BIBLE
SEVEN SYMBOLS SERIES

This edition of the **Sola Scriptura Topical Bible**: *Seven Symbols of Healing* is as complete and accurate as possible at the time of its publication, but there is always room for improvement.

Sola Scriptura, and the works that are based upon its text, is open to comment, review and criticism. As the many eyes and minds of the group are better than a few, it is hoped that people from around the world would share their input to help further refine future editions this work. As such, everyone is encouraged to submit their comments, corrections and suggestions, using the form at: solascriptura.ca/outreach/

All input to help improve this topical Bible is greatly appreciated, and may enhance future editions of this work! Thank You!

If you enjoyed reading this book, please help spread The Word, by leaving an honest and positive review at:

amazon.com/dp/198827186X

goodreads.com/book/show/69241395-sola-scriptura-topical-bible

Other editions of this publication,
Sola Scriptura Topical Bible: *Seven Symbols of Healing*

Kindle: ISBN 978-1-77885-035-6   ePub: ISBN 978-1-77885-031-8
PDF: ISBN 978-1-77885-032-5   Hard Cover: ISBN 978-1-77885-034-9

Available at: solascriptura.ca   *See more* **Seven Symbols** *on the following page.*

Editions of: **Sola Scriptura Topical Bible**: *Top 20 Spiritual Symbols*

1. Angel	8. Demon	15. Pray
2. Baptism	9. Devil / Satan	16. Resurrection
3. Believe	10. Faith	17. Salvation
4. Christ + Messiah	11. Gospel	18. Son of God
5. Church	12. Hell	19. Son of Man
6. Commandments	13. Holy Spirit / Spirit	20. Tithe
7. Covenant	14. Kingdom	

Kindle: ISBN 978-1-988271-14-9   ePub: ISBN 978-1-988271-13-2
PDF: ISBN 978-1-988271-12-5
Hard Cover: ISBN 978-1-988271-87-3   Paperback: ISBN 978-1-988271-86-6

Available at: solascriptura.ca

Look for these other Titles in the SEVEN SYMBOLS Series:

JESUS	The CHURCH	SALVATION
Christ + *Messiah*	Church	Salvation
Son of God	Kingdom	Redemption
Son of Man	Baptism	Atonement
Holy Spirit	Gospel	Repentance
Shepherd	Salvation	Forgive
Crucify	Apostle	Believe
Resurrection	Saint	Faith

GOD	EVIL	MARRIAGE
Eternal	The Devil	Marriage
Highest Heaven	Demons	Wedding
Holy Spirit	The Anti-Christ	Bride + Groom
Glory	Hell	Husband
Father	Hades / Sheol	Harlot
Angels	Idolatry	Adultery
Wisdom	Blasphemy	Divorce

THE LAW	JUDAISM	NATURE
Covenant	Commandment	Mountain
Commandment	Circumcise	Drought
Justice	Sabbath	Earthquake
Discipline	Tithe	Storm
Prison	Jubilee	Flood
Confess	High Priest	Cloud
Test	Feast	Rainbow

Available at: solascriptura.ca

Other publications by Daniel John:

Five Column: *Four Gospel Harmony & Word-For-Word Merger* ISBN 978-1-9882710-1-9

The Synoptic Gospel: *The Story of The Life of Jesus* ISBN 978-1-988271-44-6

The Red Letter Gospel: *All The Words of Jesus Christ in Red* ISBN 978-1-988271-08-8

are available at: synopticgospel.com